Conflict Resolution Through Communication

FRED E. JANDT
State University of New York
State University College at Brockport

HARPER & ROW, Publishers
New York, Evanston, San Francisco, London

To my family:
mother, father, brother,
sister-in-law, and nephew

 For information address
Harper & Row, Publishers, Inc.,
10 East 53rd Street, New York, N.Y. 10022

Standard Book Number: 06–043278–0
Library of Congress Catalog Card Number: 72–12007

Conflict Resolution Through Communication

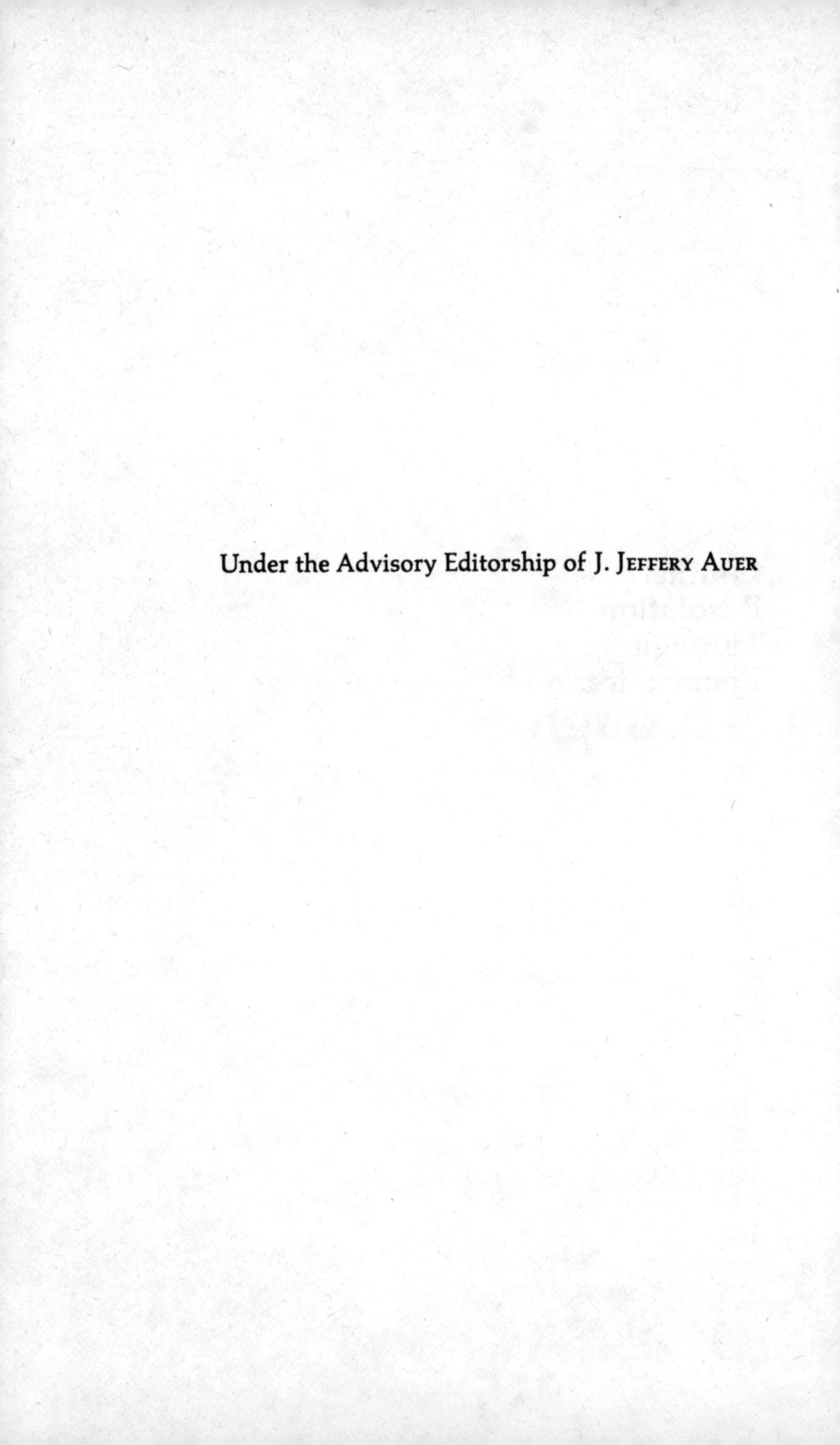

Under the Advisory Editorship of J. Jeffery Auer

Contents

Preface

In situations of social conflict, man has reached to his highest heights and stooped to his lowest depths. Through conflict man has killed millions of his brothers and sisters and has created the United Nations. Though conflict may be expressed in campus and ghetto riots, conflict may also be expressed in action groups. Though conflict may result in divorce, it may also result in a loving reconciliation. Saul D. Alinsky, an organizer of community-action groups, has explained the nature of social conflict: "Life is conflict and in conflict you're alive; action does not admit age into the arena. Sudden death, yes; but gradual age, no."[1]

Social conflict, as defined by Lewis A. Coser, is "a struggle over values or claims to status, power, and scarce resources, in which the aims of the conflicting parties are not only to gain the desired values but also to neutralize, injure, or eliminate their rivals."[2] The study of social conflict is rooted in the works of Karl Marx and the German sociologist Georg Simmel. American sociology

[1] Saul D. Alinsky, "Introduction to the Vintage Edition," *Reveille for Radicals*, New York, Vintage Books, 1969, p. vii.

[2] Lewis A. Coser, "Conflict: Social Aspect," in *International Encyclopedia of the Social Sciences*, ed. David L. Sills, New York: Free Press, 1968, vol. 3, p. 232.

had neglected the study of conflict until the appearance in the late 1950s of the works by Jessie Bernard, Lewis A. Coser, and the translations of Ralf Dahrendorf. These works deal primarily with social conflict on the societal level. It is a purpose of this book to provide a broader basis for the study of conflict—to apply theories of conflict and conflict resolution to testing on levels from dyadic conflict through societal conflict and to provide an understanding of conflict that cannot be obtained from the primary sources exclusively.

By definition, conflict involves two or more people, and only through communication can we engage in social conflict and the resolution of that conflict. Social conflict is not possible without verbal or nonverbal communication. Conflict is an important part of the totality of human communicative behavior. It is a purpose of this book to focus on communication as an important variable in conflict and conflict resolution.

The focus in this book is conflict among humans arising from and resolved through social interaction. Such topics as impersonal conflict (man versus his environment), intrapersonal conflict (cognitive dissonance), role conflict, conflict of interest, religious conflict, and conflict of laws as commonly defined are excluded by this defining focus unless the behavior of interest described by these terms is social interaction. Additionally, games (such as Prisoner's Dilemma) are excluded because that extensive body of literature is readily available, and frequently games do not permit unrestricted or realistic interaction between the players, thus making generalization difficult.

The participation in unrestricted and realistic conflict for research and study is difficult in the classroom. Role playing and games are inadequate solutions. A final purpose of this book is to present simulation as a viable mechanism for research and classroom study of conflict, because simulations permit less restricted and more realistic interaction than games. The simulation *Interactive Synecology* is designed for that purpose.

In total, this book is designed for three groups. It may be used as a supplementary text for basic speech or communication courses as a unit in conflict. The simulation would be a profitable classroom activity at this level. Used with Simmel and Coser as primary sources, this book may be used as a text for advanced courses in conflict. Further, because the study of communication is interdisciplinary, this book is suitable as a supplementary text in social psychology, sociology, education, business, and political science courses.

It is difficult to trace the genesis of an idea—particularly all the various experiences which go into the creation of a simulation such as Interactive Synecology. I gratefully acknowledge, however, my exposure to *Hypothetica,* a simulation devised by Richard Budd, as it was used by Delmer M. Hilyard, James C. McCroskey, and R. Samuel Mehrley at Michigan State University Department of Communication—Agency for International Development Communication Seminar No. 303, November 24–30, 1968. The specific situation upon which the simulation is based is described in the January 30, 1970, issue of *Life.*[3] The actual title of the simulation was suggested in conversation with Alex DiPuccio. Various developmental forms of the simulation were first used at Bowling Green State University in a sophomore-level discussion course, spring quarter, 1970, and later used at State University College at Brockport in a freshman-level public speaking course, fall and spring semesters, 1970–1971; in 36 sections of a freshman-level interpersonal communication course taught by graduate assistants, fall and spring semesters, 1971–1972; and in a senior-level course "Conflict Resolution Through Communication," fall semester, 1971. In one form the simulation was presented as a teaching demonstration at the convention of the Speech Association of the Eastern States, March 25, 1971, at the Hotel Commodore, New York City. The experiences of the students and instructors involved, particularly Donald C. Friday, Elizabeth E. Hein, Russell Kivatisky, James P. Maher, and Max Suskind, have been helpful in the development of the final form of the simulation as it is presented in this book. The bibliography for the book was developed with the assistance of Stephen

[3]Unknown at the time of development, an amazingly parallel situation to the simulation was reported in the July 30, 1971, issue of *Life.*

McGuckin and my students in the fall, 1971, "Conflict Resolution Through Communication" class at State University College at Brockport. Dennis Jasinski provided production assistance. I find it impossible to name or adequately express my thanks to the many students, friends, and enemies who have helped me.

FRED E. JANDT

Foreword

"This book constitutes a welcome addition to the literature of . . ." undoubtedly qualifies as the most wearisome commonplace found at the beginning of forewords and prefaces. Still, since in this instance the stylistic shoe fits, I have chosen to wear it yet again: Professor Jandt's book does, indeed, constitute a welcome addition to the communication literature, not only because of its sound conception but also because of its concern with a problem area that has received too little attention from students of communication. Works such as Jandt's enable us to commence our homework in earnest.

For centuries, communication scholars have devoted the lion's share of their energies to the study of persuasion. To be sure, persuasion provides one means for resolving conflict; disputes can be avoided or reconciled if one party can induce the other to accept its viewpoint. But despite its many triumphs, the failures of persuasion as an instrument of conflict resolution are amply documented in the chronicle of history. That these failures puzzle some staunch supporters of the persuasive process is illustrated by a disarmingly naive statement to which I was once privy. "You know," said a respected professor of rhetoric and public address, "with all the persuasive speaking that was going on at the time, I'll never understand why we had the Civil War."

One might ask whether any approach to conflict resolution rooted in words could have averted this national tragedy. Possibly not. But the point to be emphasized here is that persuasion often implies acquiescence: Conflicts are averted or resolved (at least temporarily) because one of the disputants submits to the will of the other. Arguments are the rhetorical staple of persuasion, and one *wins* or *loses* an argument. If parties are not prepared to submit to verbal defeat, and if they possess other resources for pursuing resolution of the conflict, the breakdown of persuasion is inevitable. Thus, persuasion's utility in the realm of conflict is limited. Other communication-centered paradigms of conflict resolution must be pondered, paradigms that do not rely on a zero sum game assumption. In this regard, several selections in this book should start the cognitive wheels spinning.

My preceding remarks are not meant to negate the value of studying persuasion as *one* means of conflict management. Even here, however, most persuasion research has been conducted in situations far afield from the real-world arena of conflict and competing interest. How persuasive discourse works in a university classroom or a laboratory is one thing; how it functions in a heated family quarrel or a bitter dispute over the division of man's economic returns may be quite another. Obviously, to understand the uses and limitations of persuasion as a tool for managing controversy, one needs to scrutinize its operations in a controversial situation, a point that the Sherifs, among others, have made forcefully. In order to achieve this objective, appreciation and awareness of the conceptual complexity of conflict are essential; the student of persuasion cannot assess the relative impact of a persuasive communication without understanding the dynamics of the social, political, and economic context in which the message is embedded. Among others, the selections found in Part II of this book, entitled *Conflict Theory*, provide valuable insights into the complex nature of conflict situations.

Thus far, given my own interests in persuasion, my remarks admittedly smack of ethnocentrism. Still, there is good reason to remind communication scholars of their tendency toward intellectual provincialism. Hopefully, such a reminder will stir them to action; it will encourage them to examine other communication approaches to conflict management, as well as to gear their research efforts toward the study of actual conflict situations. Nor are my words relevant only to the communication researcher. All of us spend considerable time at the task of conflict management: in our homes, our jobs, our social, educational, and political institutions. In fact, in almost all our daily commerce with others, much of our communication aims at averting or resolving conflict. The seeds of conflict are eternally present; and in many cases, failure to deal successfully with conflict results in drastic personal or collective consequences. Because of the centrality of conflict to the human condition, the search for fuller understanding of its origins, functional dynamics, and consequences is essential.

This is not to say that the quest is a simple one. Many obstacles and problems confront the individual seeking heightened sensitivity to the nature of conflict. The selections in Jandt's volume underscore some of the complexity of human conflict: to define and to explicate conceptually the *conflict* construct is itself no mean task. Articles such as those of Mack and Snyder, Blake and Mouton, and Deutsch provide valuable insights into the process of construct explication. No doubt these authors would readily admit that they have not spoken the last word on the subject; their papers are meant to provoke conceptual thought, not to stifle it. Still, their ideas, along with others in the book, provide a framework for thinking about conflict and suggest potential fruitful research avenues for students of communication to travel.

But before one can embark on such a journey, he must choose a conveyance. The laboratory and the field represent two vehicles available to our traveler. To carry the analogy a step further, the laboratory can be likened to a private limousine and the field to public transportation. In the cloistered confines of the former, the researcher can partially create an environment to study and to manipulate; if he wants a rear seat-bar or a private telephone, he may install them; if he tires of them, he may have them removed. The disadvantage, of course, is that he may lose touch with what is going on outside the curtained windows. In the din and clamor of the latter, the researcher's fellow travelers often jostle him with such bewildering confusion and rapidity that he becomes uncertain whether he is approaching his stop, or whether he has, in fact, passed it. Still, if he can keep his wits together, he can derive satisfaction from the knowledge that his ride has exposed him to a glimpse of reality not readily accessible to the limousine passenger.

Probably, one can never hope to understand a society's transportation system until he has partaken of both experiences. By the same token, our understanding of the role of communication in conflict can best be enhanced by the cooperative ventures of laboratory and field researchers. Selections such as those of Druckman and of Sereno and Mortensen illustrate the application of laboratory methods to the study of conflict management. By contrast the studies of Goldberg and of McGinn, Harburg, and Ginsburg, among others, demonstrate how valuable insights about communication and conflict can be gleaned from field research. I view the relationship between these two approaches to inquiry as symbiotic, not parasitic or dependent: Findings from field studies suggest further problems for laboratory exploration; results obtained in the laboratory assist in modifying and amplifying generalizations derived in field settings. That this volume strikes a nice balance between the two research postures is another point in its favor.

Since I have always held that comprehensive theories of communication must take account of individual difference variables, I applaud the selections in Part III, *Individual Differences*. Obviously, it is a truism to assert that all persons will not react to conflict situations in the same way; or for that matter, to state that different communication strokes are needed for different conflictful folks. Cultural influences, dogmatism, ego-involvement: These and a host of other individual difference variables undoubtedly mediate attempts to resolve conflict through communication. While researchers have hardly penetrated the surface of this mediational murk, the three articles chosen by Jandt indicate how some of the conceptual and procedural snarls can be untangled.

Noting a tone of lavish praise of Jandt's volume, the interested reader would be justified in asking if some critical remarks are not also in order. Let me, then, confess to one disappointment that I harbor, a disappointment that says much more about the current status of communication research than it does about the book itself. Discounting the original contributions of Jandt and Hilyard, few of the selections were written by persons who would label themselves *communication researchers.* That we have been such intellectual Johnny-come-latelys is a source of concern for me; as I have already stated, our research visions have suffered from acute myopia. Still, there are straws in the wind that forecast the communication researcher's heightened interest in the role of communication in conflict management. The recent conference on communication and conflict, sponsored by the Speech Communication Association, is one such omen; this book itself is another. Hopefully a future revised edition of *Conflict Resolution Through Communication* will lean more heavily on the theoretical, empirical, and methodological contributions of communication researchers. Moreover, I have a hunch that this first edition itself will be a relevant variable in ensuring that such a desirable intellectual state of affairs will actually come to pass.

East Lansing, Michigan GERALD R. MILLER

Introduction: Conflict Resolution Through Communication

Pointing to population increase as man's greatest problem in the years to come to the turn of the century, Carl R. Rogers contends that there must be and there can be better ways of resolving social conflict through the more open communication characteristic of encounter groups.[1] That professional organizations recognize the need to understand social conflict is evidenced by a series of specialized reports: The World Academy of Art and Science,[2] the American Society for Cybernetics,[3] and the Speech Communication Association sponsored conference dealing with future research directions on the role of communication in the process of conflict.[4] That diverse researchers are studying social conflict is evidenced by new editions of readings by Elton Mc-

[1]Carl R. Rogers, "Interpersonal Relationships: U.S.A. 2000," *Journal of Applied Behavioral Science* 4, 1968, 265–280.

[2]Stuart Mudd, ed., *Conflict Resolution and World Education* (The Hague: Dr. W. Junk Publishers, 1966).

[3]Douglas E. Knight, Huntington W. Curtis, and Lawrence J. Fogel, *Cybernetics, Simulation, and Conflict Resolution* (New York: Spartan Books, 1971).

[4]Speech Communication Association (Statler Hilton Hotel, New York City, 10001) sponsored conference held March 2–4, 1972, at Sugar Loaf, Temple University, Philadelphia; Gerald R. Miller, chairman, Speech Communication Research Board, and Conference Coordinator.

Neil,[5] Janusz Zawodney,[6] Lewis Coser,[7] Paul Swingle,[8] and Clagett Smith.[9]

Social conflict is a term we assign to particular human communicative behaviors. Two assumptions are implicit in this statement. First, social conflict is communicative behavior. There can be no conflict without verbal and nonverbal communication. Humans define their relationships by communication, and a relationship characterized by conflict is a relationship—hence, a form of communicative behavior. Second, social conflict is *not* a "thing" in the language of General Semantics. Conflict exists when the parties involved agree in some way that the behaviors associated with their relationship are labeled as "conflict" behaviors. Thus, conflict is not an external reality, but conflict is associated with an attitude determining perceptions and behaviors held by members of a relationship.

It is a popular idea that social conflict represents failure, that conflict is bad or evil and should be avoided at all costs. We appear to be so frightened of uncontrolled conflict that we have established elaborate systems where conflict is legitimate. For example, open conflict between employees and management is not socially approved and is punishable by law. Collective bargaining and certain grievance procedures, however, are socially approved means of regulating conflict between employees and management. A similar system has even been proposed for the "control" of conflict initiated by minorities.[10]

Perhaps this attitude is culturally learned. The possible alter-

[5]Elton Burbank McNeil, ed., *The Nature of Human Conflict* (Englewood Cliffs, N.J.: Prentice-Hall, 1965).

[6]Janusz Kazimierz Zawodney, comp., *Man and International Relations: Contributions of the Social Sciences to the Study of Conflict and Integration* (San Francisco: Chandler, 1966).

[7]Lewis A. Coser, *Continuities in the Study of Social Conflict* (New York: Free Press, 1967).

[8]Paul G. Swingle, ed., *The Structure of Conflict* (New York: Academic, 1970).

[9]Clagett G. Smith, ed., *Conflict Resolution: Contributions of the Behavioral Sciences* (Notre Dame, Ind.: University of Notre Dame Press, 1971).

[10]Bernard P. Indik and Georgina M. Smith, "Resolution of Social Conflict Through Collective Bargaining: An Alternative to Violence," *The George Washington Law Review 37*, 1969, 848–861.

natives to conflict are in general: (1) separation of the parties, (2) one party winning all, the other party losing all, and (3) a new creative relationship—sometimes labeled as compromise. Separation of the parties, however, does not resolve conflict; it only postpones conflict resolution. The second alternative is perhaps the most commonly accepted in our society. It is not a universally accepted truth that one party must win at the expense of another party losing, but this attitude is prevalent in our society dominated by competitive football, baseball, basketball, and monopoly.

To some extent, then, conflict may well be desirable in that it fosters the third, creative alternative of new relationships. Man has been most creative through conflict. The list of accomplishments arising out of conflict includes an impressive number of organizations, ranging from the formation of the United States of America in 1776, to labor unions, the NAACP, La Raza Unida, the United Nations, and the student activist movement of the late 1960s.

Rather than being undesirable, conflict is desirable from at least two standpoints. It has been demonstrated that through conflict man is creative. Further, a relationship in conflict *is* a relationship—not the absence of one. Such a relationship may result in creativity because of its intensity.

Verbal abuse, fights, strikes, riots, and other such intense behaviors characterize conflict relationships. Intensity of a relationship should not necessarily be avoided. As Alinsky observed, it is only through that degree of intensity that we are fully alive.

Given the intensity of a conflict situation, two consequences are deducible that are potentially fruitful areas for research; given the intensity of social conflict, we react as a whole person, that is, there are physiological correlates of social conflict. No one can deny that he "feels differently" in situations of social conflict. The study by Jacobs et al.[11] of visits to a college infirmary by male students suggests this relationship. Second, we

[11]Martin A. Jacobs, Aron Spilken, and Martin Norman, "Relationship of Life Change, Maladaptive Aggression, and Upper Respiratory Infection in Male College Students," *Psychosomatic Medicine 31*, 1969, 31–44.

are less able to maintain our defenses. The relationship between our self-concept and our behavior is more direct and less mediated by our defenses. In situations of social conflict, therefore, we may reveal our "true" selves. The Geis study may be taken as evidence that a measurable personality variable can influence the outcome of group interaction in a relevant conflict situation.[12] The high correlation between paper-and-pencil measures of an agreement with a Machiavellian outlook and success in interpersonal bargaining in a game situation lend credence to this proposition.

The process of conflict and conflict resolution might best be studied by examining conflict in different settings, from the small group, to the organization, or to society. The common aspects in these different settings may clarify the conflict process. The most commonly occurring small group is the *dyad* and the most commonly occurring dyad in our present social framework is monogamous marriage. Conflict and conflict resolution within this dyad have also been institutionalized by society through divorce. Thus, conflict in this family unit is one setting for the study of the process of conflict and conflict resolution.

A small group created and institutionalized by society for its self-preservation is the classroom. Yet conflict in the classroom is avoided by teachers who are untrained to deal with interpersonal conflict. That the student "learns" to avoid dealing openly with conflict in the classroom certainly carries forward into his adult life.

The encounter group, on the other hand, as a special form of small-group behavior is designed to deal with conflict in open communication. Yet this activity, viewed primarily as therapeutic, has produced little quantitative evidence as to the process of conflict and conflict resolution. Organizations in any society require much small-group activity. The success of that activity is a concern to the organization; however, most writers in the

[12]Florence Geis, "The Con Game," in *Studies in Machiavellianism*, eds. Richard Christie and Florence L. Geis (New York: Academic, 1970, pp. 106–129).

area of organizational conflict have failed to grasp the potential of the situation.

Conflict in the larger context of a society is an important setting for the study of the process of conflict and conflict resolution. In North American society, whether it be the conflict generated by the peace movement on college campuses or by minority groups in American cities, there are commonalities to all of the previously discussed settings for conflict. While massive, violent uprising may be a thing of the past, there will continue to be issues in society which generate conflict. In 1973, it may be busing school children; in 1975, it may be housing; in 1984 or 2000, it may be pervasive overcrowding.

The study of conflict and conflict resolution in whatever setting may be the most significant and rewarding study of the decade. Increasing population and rapid change can only mean more frequent interpersonal encounters, and more frequent interpersonal encounters can only mean more conflict. It is hoped that through the study of conflict and conflict resolution, its more creative aspects will be explored and realized.

PART I
Simulation and Conflict

Just as NASA astronauts simulate space-dockings and moon walks, we can simulate interpersonal encounters. Through simulation, NASA astronauts repeatedly practice and learn skills in a relatively safe environment without deadly risks. Similarly, by simulation we can learn the interpersonal skills of conflict resolution in the relatively safe classroom without the risks of deadly fights and wars. Additionally, as a simulation is a "game" which is "played," we can increase our satisfactions by having fun and enjoyment—which certainly does involve one much more in the learning process. While a simulation involves "fun," it is also an excellent learning laboratory for the observation of our own behaviors and those of others, and for experiencing new behaviors in a situation that reproduces or highlights selected portions of the real world.

Interactive Synecology is an attempt to provide a simulation that focuses on communication and conflict, which can be used by adults from high school through graduate levels.[1, 2]

[1]Tucker and Gorden have described a few of the simulation games available and have discussed their possible use in speech courses. See Raymond K. Tucker, "Computer Simulations and Simulation Games: Their Place in the Speech Curriculum," *The Speech Teacher 17*, 1968, 128–133; and Wil-

Interactive Synecology is a simulation designed for the study of interpersonal communicative behaviors in a conflict situation. The simulation attempts to structure a situation in which intense conflict is likely to occur and in which the participants may learn to control, use, and resolve conflict through interpersonal communication. In the simulation, the conflict can be quite realistic, thus providing a learning laboratory for the participants to observe certain behaviors and to learn certain skills.

For maximum benefits, the participants should analyze the interpersonal behaviors and relationships revealed during the simulation. Readings, such as those included in this book, help to prepare participants for the analysis phase of the simulation. The simulation is designed for what can be learned through either individual or group analysis of behaviors exhibited during the simulation.

The important defining characteristic of simulations is that the game represents a model of external reality through which the players interact in much the same way as they would in reality. As a

---

liam I. Gorden, "Recent Educational Games," *The Southern Speech Journal 34*, 1969, 235–236; "Academic Games in the Speech Curriculum," *Central States Speech Journal 20*, 1969, 269–279, and "Rhetoric-Communication Concepts Illustrated by Several Academic Games: Metaphor and Mystique at Play," *Today's Speech* 19, 1971, 27–33. In *Nine Men Plus*, Gorden has also prepared an academic game-simulation of Supreme Court decisions on free speech and free press (Dubuque, Ia.: Brown, 1971).

[2]Useful bibliographic sources for those interested in simulation techniques are Roland Werner and Joan T. Werner, *Bibliography of Simulations: Social Systems and Education* (La Jolla, Calif.: Western Behavioral Sciences Institute, 1969), and Steven J. Kidder, "Simulation Games: Practical References, Potential Use, Selected Bibliography," Report No. 112 (Baltimore, Md.: Center for Social Organization of Schools, Johns Hopkins University, August, 1971). General references include R. P. Abelson, "Simulation of Social Behavior," *Handbook of Social Psychology* (Cambridge, Mass.: Addison-Wesley, 1969); S. S. Boocock and E. O. Schild, eds., *Simulation Games in Learning* (Beverly Hills, Calif.: Sage, 1968); James S. Coleman, Sarane Boocock, and E. O. Schild, eds., "Simulation Games and Learning Behavior, Parts I and II," special issues of *American Behavioral Scientist 10*, October–November, 1966; J. R. Raser, *Simulation and Society* (Boston: Allyn & Bacon, 1969); Clarice S. Stoll and Michael Inbar, eds., "Social Simulations," special issue of *American Behavioral Scientist 12*, July–August, 1969; Michael Inbar and Clarice S. Stoll, *Social Science Simulations* (New York: Free Press, 1971); and issues of *Simulation and Games: An International Journal of Theory, Design, and Research.*

simulation, Interactive Synecology does not perfectly reproduce the world; it highlights certain behaviors and, by so doing, distorts the world. The simulation structures a situation in which conflict is likely to occur. Participants may object to this distortion if they and the instructor are not ready to learn through simulation. A simulation is only a technique and not an end in and of itself.

One requirement must be met before any simulation–NASA moonwalks or Interactive Synecology—can be successful. Each participant must willingly suspend disbelief; each participant must be able to "pretend." If this requirement is satisfied, then a well-designed simulation can be a worthwhile learning experience. Interactive Synecology requires assigned role playing—that is, specific roles are assigned but the personality characteristics of that role are not specified, and the players may then react as they themselves would in that role.

That conflict can be simulated has been demonstrated by the well-known "Robber's Cave" experiment conducted by Muzafer Sherif and his colleagues at the University of Oklahoma.[3] As an experiment it combined observation in a natural setting with manipulation of variables. Sherif structured conflict between two groups of 11-year-old boys at a camp called "Robbers Cave." Conflict was induced between the two groups by giving them different and conflicting goals. Overt hostilities eventually broke out. Through the infusion of *superordinate* goals (goals that could not be achieved without both groups cooperating), the tension between the two groups was reduced and eliminated.

Any simulation focusing on conflict should demonstrate that conflict is potentially desirable as well as potentially destructive. Conflict can both increase group cohesion (a desirable quality) and can result in fights and wars (a certainly less desirable quality). Further, a simulation focusing on conflict should demonstrate that the development and control of conflict is determined through communication. Since most of that communication is interpersonal communication, a logical perspective for the study of conflict is the communication process. Interactive Synecology provides a laboratory for the observation and exercise of these behaviors through face-to-face small-group experi-

[3]Muzafer Sherif et al. *Intergroup Conflict and Cooperation: The Robber's Cave Experiment* (Norman: University of Oklahoma, 1961).

ences. Information transmission, manipulation, perception, leadership styles, problem solving, and other communication behaviors may be studied by means of this simulation. Interactive Synecology seems to demonstrate quite well, for example, defensive-supportive communication climates.[4]

Interactive Synecology is an extremely loosely structured or highly *entropic* simulation. Participants continually express the desire for more structure. Participants should perhaps be briefed as to this their opportunity in Interactive Synecology to create almost any type of society they wish to or institute any norms, rules, or behaviors they desire so long as they are consistent with the existing structure and with the previous occurrences in the simulation. Recent research has produced some evidence that participants in a simulation even under conditions of complete ignorance as to the nature and rules of business games were able to decipher the most important characteristics of the games, along with the variables and the ranges of minimum and maximum performance.[5]

Interactive Synecology may be played in two sessions (the first, a shorter session to go over the concepts involved in a simulation and to collect the choice sheets; the second, a longer session to run the simulation) or in several one-hour classes. The instructor has three major jobs: to conduct the preparatory lecture-discussions; to establish the groups; and to conclude the simulation after it is completed. It is recommended that 20 percent of the participants be assigned to The Chemical Company (TCC) group, 20 percent to the summer-residents group, 45 percent to the permanent-residents group, and 15 percent to the Small State College (SSC) students group. After the instructor has conducted preparatory discussions and established the groups, he should then act as an observer only. The instructor should not attempt to help the participants in any way; thus allowing the participants maximum freedom to learn.

The instructor does have the crucial role of concluding the simula-

[4]Jack R. Gibb, Defensive Communication," *Journal of Communication 11*, 1961, 141–148.

[5]G. C. Philippatos and D. R. Moscato, "Experimental Learning Aspects of Business Game Playing with Incomplete Information About the Rules," *Psychological Reports 25*, 1969, 479–486.

tion when, in his judgment, the opportunity for learning is peaking. There is no quantitive outcome that determines a specific time for stopping the simulation. Rather, the outcome should be thought of as qualitative and, hence, non-zero-sum. All participants may benefit from the experience. It is probably better that no participant knows when the situation is concluding, as some will object no matter when the simulation terminates.

While research on learning from games is still in its infancy, some educators believe that a simulation is a self-contained learning experience. For others who desire additional activities, suggestions for student papers are included. Some participants do not need the stimulus of debriefing discussions and written analyses to learn from a simulation; perhaps it is an aid to others. Those who do learn without debriefing may assist others to understand the experience.

Many simulations work well for their designers, but other users have difficulty. Interactive Synecology has been used successfully in its present form by graduate-assistant instructors; however, adaptation by other users is encouraged.

Probably no two simulations are alike entirely, or for that matter should they be. As a general guide, however, the following phases are representative of the past uses of Interactive Synecology.

Lecture-discussions of communication and conflict

Lecture-discussions on simulations

Collection of Choice Sheets

Distribution of Assignment Sheets

Distribution of General Information Sheets, Map of Resort Island, and each group's Information Sheet

Individual group meetings

Mayor's called town meeting (which may include formal presentation by some or all of the groups)

. . .

Conclusion of simulation

Discussion of simulation

Written papers based on simulation

Student evaluations of simulation

It is necessary to study student evaluation of any simulation.[6] There is some suggestion in the evaluations of previous uses of Interactive Synecology to support the instructors' feeling that during and immediately after the experience, participants feel highly uncomfortable. Weeks later, however, the instructors perceive the students expressing the feelings that the simulation was the "highlight" of the course. As an "uncomfortable" experience, perhaps the simulation takes on added value over time.

Research on learning from simulations and research using simulations in experimental designs are in their infancy. Simulations offer a unique opportunity to measure behavior in lifelike settings that often cannot be tested by other means. It would seem that the more closely the test situation approximates the real-life situation, the more powerful the predictions that can be made.[7] Examples of experimental studies using simulations are those of Harold Guetzkow,[8] Ian Morley and Geoffrey Stephenson,[9] and Clarice Stoll and Paul

[6]The Center for Social Organization of Schools (Johns Hopkins University, Baltimore, Md.) has produced several evaluations of simulations. For examples see Samuel A. Livingston, "Two Types of Learning in a Business Simulation," Report No. 104, and "Effects of a Legislative Simulation Game on the Political Attitudes of Junior High School Students," Report No. 114; Keith J. Edwards and John T. Guthrie, "The Training Effects of a Behavior Modification Game," Report No. 116; Samuel A. Livingston, "Simulation Games and Attitudes Toward the Poor: Three Questionnaire Studies," Report No. 118; and Keith J. Edwards, "Students' Evaluations of a Business Simulation Game as a Learning Experience," Report No. 121.

[7]Useful sources for using simulations for measurement are Norman Frederiksen, "Proficiency Tests for Training Evaluation," in *Training Research and Education*, ed. Robert Glaser (New York: Science Editions, Wiley, 1965), pp. 323–346, Christine H. McGuire and David Babbott, "Simulation Technique in the Measurement of Problem-Solving Skills," *Journal of Educational Measurement* 4, 1967, 1–10, and H. Del Schalock, "Situational Response Testing: An Application of Simulation Principles to Measurement," in *Instructional Simulation: A Research Development and Dissemination Activity*, ed. Paul A. Twelker (Monmouth, Oreg.: Teaching Research Division, Oregon State System of Higher Education, February, 1969).

[8]Harold Guetzkow, "A Use of Simulation in the Study of Inter-Nation Relations," *Behavioral Science* 4, 1959, 183–191.

[9]Ian E. Morley and Geoffrey M. Stephenson, "Interpersonal and Interparty Exchange: A Laboratory Simulation of an Industrial Negotiation at the Plant Level," *British Journal of Psychology 60*, 1969, 543–545.

McFarlane.[10] Interactive Synecology provides a setting for the study of communication and conflict.

The proof of any simulation is in its use. The use of Interactive Synecology for classroom and research purposes is encouraged. There is no fee for its use. It is only requested that users share their experiences and results with the author.

[10]Clarice S. Stoll and Paul T. McFarlane, "Player Characteristics and Interaction in a Parent-Child Simulation Game," *Sociometry 32*, 1969, 259–272.

NAME ____________________

CHOICE SHEET

The simulation *Interactive Synecology* may be described as a closed society composed of five discrete groups. Four of these groups are described below. The fifth group is the elected government officials (including a mayor and a state representative) and Chamber of Commerce representatives from the permanent residents group.

Each person in the class is a member of one of these five groups. Please express your preference for being a member of a particular group by ranking. Rank as "1" the group you most want to be a member, and so on until you have ranked all four groups. (Remember, the fifth group will be elected by the permanent residents group from their members to represent them.)

There is no guarantee you will be assigned to your first choice, but all attempts will be made to follow your expressed preference.

RANK	GROUP DESCRIPTION
________	A major chemical company planning the construction of a new plant
________	Highly skilled and professional people who share a common vacation area
________	Activist students attending a state college
________	The permanent residents of an offshore island

I, ____________________, who have ranked the permanent residents group as my first choice, also desire to place my name in nomination for:

________ Mayor

________ State representative

________ Chamber of commerce representative

________ ____________________

____
Signature

GROUP ASSIGNMENTS FOR INTERACTIVE SYNECOLOGY

The group assignments for the simulation Interactive Synecology are as follows:

THE CHEMICAL COMPANY (TCC):

THE SUMMER RESIDENTS:

STUDENTS FROM THE SMALL STATE COLLEGE (SSC):

THE PERMANENT RESIDENTS:

The nominations for Mayor are:

The nominations for state representative are:

The nominations for chamber of commerce representative(s) are:

The nominations for ________________ are:

GENERAL INFORMATION SHEET FOR INTERACTIVE SYNECOLOGY

Through its New York City office, The Chemical Company (TCC) has announced plans to construct a $100-million chemical plant on Resort Island. Construction of such a plant insures substantial tax monies, additional jobs, and indirect benefits, such as improved communication and transportation facilities.

Resort Island, which is located off the Louisiana coastline, has miles of some of the most beautiful unspoiled shores on the Gulf of Mexico. Its permanent population of some 3000 residents is concentrated in the island's one town located on the southwestern portion of the island. Public schools and a small state college (SSC) are conveniently located on the mainland.

Many of the island's permanent residents commute by ferryboat to their mainland jobs. The remainder of the population is dependent upon the island's tourist industry, which during peak periods more than doubles the island's population. The tourists are attracted to the island's beaches and to the excellent fishing.

In addition to permanent residents and tourists, Resort Island has a substantial number of summer residents who have built resort homes and cottages for their annual stay on the island. Most of the summer residents had initially visited the island as tourists and had been attracted by its unspoiled beauty and isolation.

The Chemical Company (TCC) has already acquired the entire northeastern portion of the island for the proposed chemical plant. The area was purchased from a bankrupt, small electrical equipment manufacturing company for whom the permanent residents of Resort Island had had that portion of the island properly zoned for industrial use. TCC was attracted to Resort Island because of the area's climate and rich oil deposits. Anticipating objections from the island's residents, TCC is attempting to line up local and state officials for support. The company has even hired the island's state representative as its legal counsel in the state.

The situation has virtually polarized all who are concerned into five distinct groups:

(1) The Chemical Company (TCC),
(2) the summer residents of Resort Island,
(3) the permanent residents of Resort Island,
(4) students from the Small State College (SSC), and
(5) elected representatives (government officials, including the mayor and the state representative, and chamber of commerce members) from the permanent residents group.

The mayor of the island's town has called a town meeting during which each group will have an opportunity to present its position. Before the meeting, each group is to organize and prepare for that meeting.

INFORMATION SHEET FOR THE CHEMICAL COMPANY (TCC) GROUP

The Chemical Company (TCC) is one of the country's 25 largest corporations. It has assets of over $3 billion. Its net profit for the last fiscal year was over $400 million. Over 100,000 people are directly employed by TCC.

Construction of its plant on Resort Island will bring many benefits to the area. For example, TCC may need to build a permanent highway bridge connecting the island to the mainland. It could offer to employ many of the permanent residents at the plant.

Anticipating objections to the construction of its plant on Resort Island, TCC has hired the island's state representative as its legal counsel in the state. The representative is a member of the elected government officials and chamber of commerce representatives group. TCC may communicate with their legal counsel at any time.

INFORMATION SHEET FOR THE SUMMER RESIDENTS GROUP

The summer residents own resort homes and cottages on the island. The summer residents spend only a few weeks a year on the island on vacation from their permanent homes and jobs across the United States.

The summer residents are generally better educated and have highly skilled or professional jobs.

Some see the construction of a chemical plant on the island in economic terms—the value of their property might increase; others feel its construction will spoil Resort Island's vacation desirability.

The summer residents may communicate with the permanent residents at any time.

Figure 1. Map of Resort Island

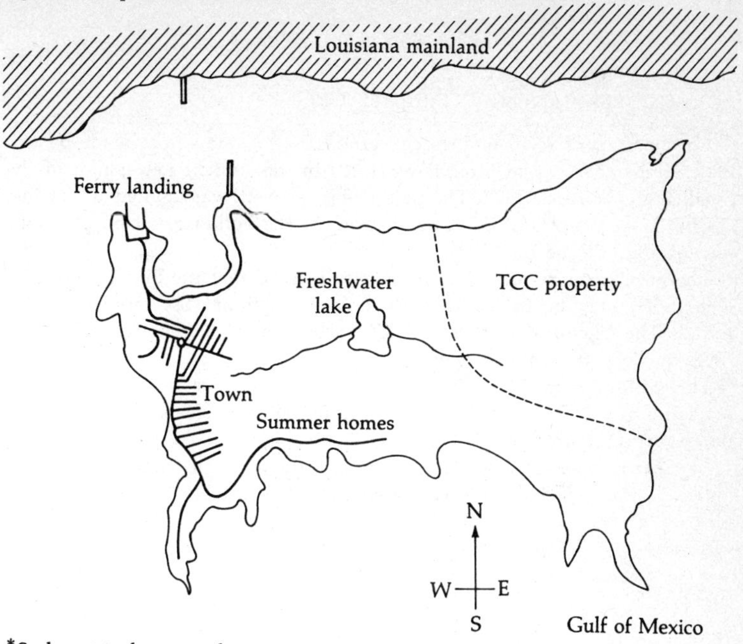

Louisiana mainland
Ferry landing
Freshwater
lake
TCC property
Town
Summer homes
N
W
E
S
Gulf of Mexico

*Scale: 1 inch = 2 miles.

Figure 2. Model of Private Communication Channels in *Interactive Synecology*

Summer
residents
Permanent
residents
Students
attending Small
State College
(SSC)
Elected
representatives
Via the state
representative
The Chemical
Company
(TCC)

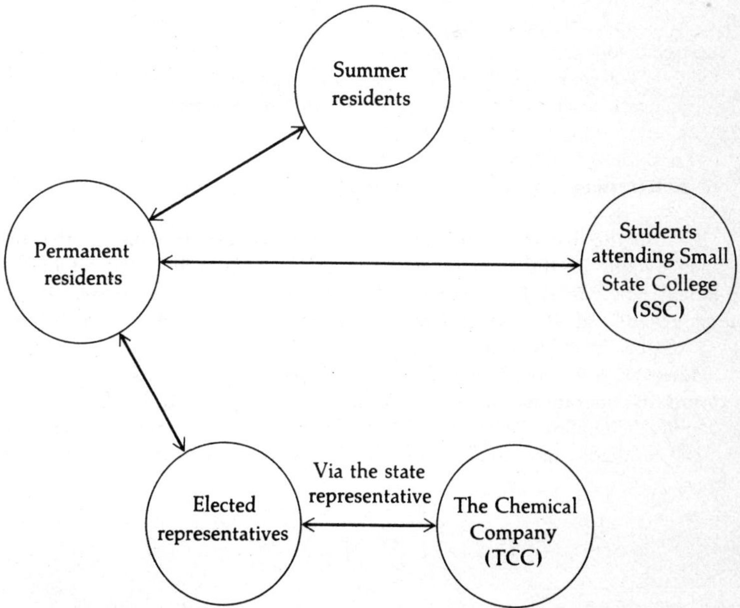

INFORMATION SHEET FOR THE PERMANENT RESIDENTS GROUP

The permanent residents are concerned about a statement made by one of their members in an interview printed in the student newspaper of the Small State College (SSC). The permanent resident was quoted as saying, "If the kids go out and lie down in front of the bulldozers, I hope no one is hurt, but I'll be on their side."

The permanent residents have recently learned that the Small State College (SSC) may be forced to close unless additional tax monies can be found. The Chemical Company (TCC) would bring in enough additional taxes to keep the college open.

The editor of the island's newspaper is a member of the permanent residents group. The editor prints an issue when he feels he has enough news for one.

The permanent residents may communicate with the summer residents and with their elected representatives at any time.

INFORMATION SHEET FOR THE STUDENTS FROM THE SMALL STATE COLLEGE (SSC) GROUP

The Small College (SSC) is located on the mainland, convenient to Resort Island. Of the permanent residents and their children who are able to attend college, most attend SSC.

SSC is a 4-year liberal arts institution with some professional and graduate education. The school is fully accredited and has a regional reputation as an educationally strong college.

The student body is politically active; the campus fully participated in the Moratorium Day activities in 1969 and in the Kent State strike in 1970.

Most of the discussion on campus at present is centered on a statement made by one of the permanent residents in an interview printed in the student newspaper. The permanent resident was quoted as saying, "If the kids go out and lie down in front of the bulldozers, I hope no one is hurt, but I'll be on their side."

However, it is also known that the school may be forced to radically curtail its operations unless additional tax monies can be found. The Chemical Company (TCC) would bring in enough additional revenue.

The students may communicate with the permanent residents at any time.

INFORMATION SHEET FOR ELECTED GOVERNMENT OFFICIALS AND CHAMBER OF COMMERCE REPRESENTATIVES GROUP

The elected government officials and chamber of commerce representatives are an alliance between government and business.

The island's state representative, a member of this group, has been hired as The Chemical Company's legal counsel in the state. He may communicate with the TCC group at any time.

The mayor of the island's one town, who is also a member of this group, has taken the initiative to call a town meeting which will bring all who are concerned together for the first time. The mayor and the other members of the elected government officials and chamber of commerce representatives group need to plan and conduct that town meeting.

The elected government officials and chamber of commerce representatives may communicate with the permanent residents at any time.

SUGGESTIONS FOR STUDENT PAPERS BASED ON INTERACTIVE SYNECOLOGY

1. Describe the relationship between frustration and aggression based upon your observations in Interactive Synecology.
2. Describe and evaluate the transmission of information you observed in the simulation.
3. Describe and evaluate the attempts at manipulation you observed in the simulation.
4. Evaluate the decision-making process as you observed it in the simulation.
5. Describe the different styles of leadership you observed in the simulation.
6. Describe group pressures on deviants as you observed it in the simulation.
7. Describe and evaluate the constructive use of conflict as you observed it in the simulation.
8. Describe and evaluate the barriers created as conflict developed. What attempts, if any, were made to remove those barriers?
9. Discuss the observations you can now make about your own and others' communicative behaviors as a result of this simulation.
10. If you were to repeat Interactive Synecology, how would you modify your behavior?
11. As participants in the simulation you could have created any form of society you desired. Why did you "play the game" as you did?

STUDENT EVALUATION OF INTERACTIVE SYNECOLOGY

In order to aid your instructor in evaluating the simulation Interactive Synecology, would you please complete this questionnaire as carefully and as objectively as you can? No attempt will be made to determine who completed the questionnaire.

Below are five statements about the simulation. Please indicate the *one* response for *each* statement which best corresponds to your impression by circling one of the *numbers*. Write any comment you might have after any question.

1. I found the suggested readings for this simulation to be:
   excellent 1 2 3 4 5 poor
   Comments:

2. I believe the assigned paper(s) based on this simulation was helpful:
   strongly agree 1 2 3 4 5 strongly disagree
   Comments:

3. I am more conscious of my own behavior in groups now than I was before I participated in this simulation.
   strongly agree 1 2 3 4 5 strongly disagree
   Comments:

4. I would recommend this simulation to a friend.
   strongly agree 1 2 3 4 5 strongly disagree
   Comments:

5. If circumstances permitted it, I would elect to participate in another simulation.
   strongly agree 1 2 3 4 5 strongly disagree
   Comments:

PART II
Conflict Theory

Theories of social conflict were developed earlier than Socratic times. Hanson has traced conflict theories up through the works of Marx.[1] The social conflict theories of Marx led to the sociology of Simmel and to the social conflict theories of Lewis A. Coser, Jessie Bernard, and Ralf Dahrendorf. Recent theoretical monographs include those by Galtung who discusses the mechanisms of conflict resolution,[2] by Fink who analyzes the conceptual and terminological complexities of conflict theory,[3] and by Converse who reviews the first 12 volumes of *The Journal of Conflict Resolution.*[4]

Raymond W. Mack and Richard C. Snyder, in "The Analysis of Social Conflict—Toward an Overview and Synthesis," have integrated the bulk of the literature on social conflict to 1957 into a listing and assessment of 50 propositions providing a framework for the analysis

[1]David Jay Hanson, "The Idea of Conflict in Western Thought," *International Review of History and Political Science 5,* 1968, 90–105.

[2]Johan Galtung, "Institutionalized Conflict Resolution: A Theoretical Paradigm," *Journal of Peace Research 4,* 1965, 348–397.

[3]Clinton F. Fink, "Some Conceptual Difficulties in the Theory of Social Conflict," *Journal of Conflict Resolution 12,* 1968, 412–460.

[4]Elizabeth Converse, "The War of All Against All: A Review of *The Journal of Conflict Resolution,* 1957–1968," *Journal of Conflict Resolution 12,* 1968, 471–532.

of conflict. This analytical framework is useful for organizing existing knowledge and for generating testable hypotheses.

Robert R. Blake and Jane Srygley Mouton, in "The Fifth Achievement," describe the *conflict grid* in a broader perspective than the organizational setting. The title of their essay refers to a fifth way of resolving conflict (after science, politics, law, and hierarchy)—a climate in which men work out their differences face to face. The conflict grid identifies two basic considerations: the degree of concern with the people with whom we are in conflict and the degree of concern with the results or the resolution of the disagreement.

RAYMOND W. MACK
RICHARD C. SNYDER

The Analysis of Social Conflict-- Toward an Overview and Synthesis

I. INTRODUCTION

It is clearly evident from the citations and bibliography presented elsewhere in this issue that a vast literature on social conflict has accumulated. Even allowing for a high degree of selectivity, the list of relevant writings is imposing. Over the years research suggestions and problem- or policy-oriented proposals have grown in number and sophistication. Action programs designed to reduce or eliminate conflict have been subjected to critical appraisal. Attention has been focused on a wide variety of conflict and conflict situations: intrapersonal, interpersonal, interorganizational, and intergroup. In particular, war and peace, labor and management, personality, interest groups, race, ethnology, and ideology have been central topics of conflict analysis. There is, of course, a differential distribution of research and writing among the major categories of social conflict, but none has been totally neglected.

From Raymond W. Mack and Richard C. Snyder, "The Analysis of Social Conflict—Toward an Overview and Synthesis," *Journal of Conflict Resolution 1*, 1957, 212–248. The stimulation and facilities provided in such generous measure by the Center (for Advanced Study in the Behavioral Sciences) helped in the preparation of this symposium and are gratefully acknowledged.

As preceding pages amply reveal, such a broad area of research and analysis is marked by diverse approaches and purposes and by the usual methodological problems and disagreements. To a certain extent this is both natural and in some sense welcome. On the other hand, it has been remarked (11, 12, chap. i) that a priori postures toward social conflict have delayed, if not prevented, the acquisition of systematic, socially applicable knowledge. The view of conflict as completely and always "bad" and the attribution of war to "herd instincts" are cases in point. Given the pervasiveness of conflict phenomena and the diversity of approaches to inquiry, it is legitimate to ask whether the apparent intellectual disorder reflects an inherently incoherent focus of social analysis—a focus artificially created by a label—or whether the disparateness of data and interpretations is due in part to interdisciplinary compartmentalization, to academic individualism, or to rapid growth, with its consequent inattention to direction.

Obviously, "conflict" is for the most part a rubber concept, being stretched and molded for the purposes at hand. In its broadest sense it seems to cover everything from war to choices between ice-cream sodas or sundaes. At any rate, the distinctions between conflict and non-conflict are fuzzy at best and at worst are not made at all. There is also a persistent tendency to regard *all* conflict as bad, as susceptible to *complete elimination,* given "good will," "understanding," and so on, and as basically different from "co-operation." The conflict–co-operation dichotomy has been pushed to the point where one is defined in terms of the absence of the other. Relatively little effort has been made to specify analytically different properties of conflict as a generic phenomenon and to differentiate explicitly between conflict and closely related concepts. Systematic and fruitful classification of conflict and conflict situations has only just begun. Variables cited to account for conflict tend to be many in number and to be unrelated or unrelatable in many instances. With several notable exceptions to be noted later, the identification and evaluation of basic propositions have been neglected. For criticism of the present state of the "sociology of conflict" and of theoretical and other inadequacies see Bernard (3), Hager (22), Coser (12, chap. i), Sheppard (35), and Sorensen (38). Inadequate conceptualization and theorizing have had important consequences. First, generalization across disciplinary or subject-matter lines has been slow to develop and, where it does appear, is often implicit. Second, it has been difficult to link propositions systematically. Third, research has not always been guided by hypotheses of acceptable power and significance. Fourth, no well-rounded body of case materials based on comparative types, unifying concepts, and general hypotheses has developed.

In the absence of some sort of framework of conflict analysis —related concepts, definitions, models, questions, hypotheses, etc.—it becomes difficult to choose rationally between alternative approaches: the sociological versus the social-psychological, the "conflict is functional" versus "conflict is dysfunctional," the causes of conflict (e.g., war) versus the conditions of nonconflict (e.g., peace), "peoples" versus "governments" research, the "human-relations" approach versus the "power-relations" approach, and so on. So, too, it becomes difficult to transfer relevant knowledge from one arena of social conflict to another.

Despite the accumulation of experience and writing, certain basic queries remain unanswered. Only a few need be set forth here. Why do serious situations sometimes *not* develop into violent conflict while not so serious ones do? Why do some conflicts rather quickly run a natural course while others do not? What kinds of group attachments to which men are susceptible (in particular situations) are closely related to well-delineated lines of cleavage in society? What is the effect of size of groups on intergroup conflict? Does increased social mobility increase or decrease social conflict? Is desire to convert others to a set of beliefs more conducive to intense conflict than desire for scarce resources? Do differing value commitments have greater conflict potential when the corresponding behavior patterns are not brought into face-to-face confrontation than when they are? Under what conditions are psychological mechanisms crucial to the emergence of conflict? Why do some forms of group identification accompany intergroup conflict while others do not? Under what conditions do differing needs, demands, and aspirations, combined with appraisals of interaction situations, produce conflict behavior? Such questions suggest either gaps in knowledge and/or the ineffective organization of existing knowledge (8).

For the foregoing reasons, we wish to argue the need for further intellectual stocktaking—for a propositional survey and assessment and for more precise conceptualization. We shall only attempt to suggest in simplified form the general lines along which this might be carried out. The essays which comprise the heart of this symposium exemplify a significant trend in this direction. We shall push some of the implications a step further. Needless to say, the acquisition of new knowledge will depend primarily on empirical research. For a recent critical evaluation of conflict research, the reader should consult the very useful UNESCO volume, *The Nature of Conflict: Studies on the Sociological Aspects of International Tensions* ("Tensions and Technology Series" [1957]). This volume represents a different kind of intellectual stocktaking and stands in complementary relationship to the present essay.

II. BASIC PROPOSITIONS

A reasonably thorough scanning of the literature reveals that the materials for an orderly and general index of propositions on social conflict are available. Coser has reformulated and analyzed sixteen of Simmel's propositions concerning intergroup conflict (12, chaps. ii–ix). Williams has presented one hundred and two propositions dealing with racial, ethnic, and religious conflict (39). Indeed, the latter has provided a model which might well be copied for other areas of conflict. Cooper has reviewed the psychological literature on war (11). Jackson has discussed eight major propositions regarding international mediation (23, pp. 126–70). Chase summarizes the findings and principles from several branches of social science which bear on sixteen levels of conflict—from two persons to the East-West crisis (7). Rose offers twenty-one hypotheses on effective industrial mediation devices (33). Dubin (17) has built his analysis of industrial conflict around five central propositions, together with twenty-five corollaries.

Listing propositions could easily be an empty exercise. Why is a propositional survey useful, and what are the necessary rules for constructing it? To begin with, it is universally recognized that a body of knowledge about anything consists primarily of a set of existential propositions which are in varying degrees verified. A necessary step in stocktaking is, therefore, the pinpointing of major generalizations. Once they are made explicit and rendered in propositional form, critical assessment is possible. A series of questions can and should be put to any set of propositions: What evidence can be mobilized in support or disproof? Which are educated guesses? Which are generally agreed to or disagreed from by qualified experts? Which need further testing and/or reformulation? Which represent cumulative, consistent observations?

In order to avoid an almost infinite list of propositions based on indiscriminate choice, criteria are required. Williams (39, p. 50) suggests three: (1) those of potential importance for understanding social conflict and for application to policy problems; (2) those which offer the most promise of fruitfully guiding empirical research; and (3) those of most probable validity. These criteria direct initial attention to propositions which are of sufficient generality to provide a framework for more particular propositions (lower order of generality), which highlight the necessary and sufficient causes of social conflict, which provide a basis for linking different kinds of social conflict (e.g., industrial and international), and which can be ordered into a theory having explanatory and predictive power.

Some examples (paraphrased) drawn from the literature will illustrate, omitting for the moment the question of verification and qualification:

PROPOSITION 1: Intragroup harmony tends to reduce intergroup friction (industrial relations) (24, p. 201).

PROPOSITION 2: Certain personality characteristics germane to particular national groups are conflict-instigating (international relations) (27).

PROPOSITION 3: The more totalitarian a group, organization, or society, the greater the likelihood that its leaders will be aggressive (general) (18, p. 33).

PROPOSITION 4: The more compartmentalized and restricted are the claims of a particular faith to define and regulate religious values, the less likely is religious group membership to be divisive (religious conflict) (40, p. 15).

PROPOSITION 5: The more fixed the size of the "pie" to be divided, the more intense the conflict (industrial relations) (26, p. 230).

PROPOSITION 6: Violence is more likely when a minority group is not content to accept the designation of low rank by majority groups and when it attempts to redefine the situation to permit its assimilation or equal ranking (racial conflict) (14, p. 420).

PROPOSITION 7: The main source of persistence of intergroup hostility is the interlocking and mutual reinforcement of realistic and unrealistic conflict elements (general) (39, p. 41).

PROPOSITION 8: As unions gain power, the duration of strikes decreases (industrial relations) (35, p. 337).

PROPOSITION 9: Conflict with outgroups increases internal cohesion (general) (12, p. 88).

PROPOSITION 10: Warlike attitudes may be expressions of deep-lying personality factors laid down in child-rearing (international relations) (18, p. 34).

PROPOSITION 11: If the power of two parties is not grossly unequal, agreement is more likely when both are least rigid in their positions (industrial and international relations) (23, p. 137).

PROPOSITION 12: The major source of international tension resides between, rather than within, nations (international relations) (9, p. 17).

PROPOSITION 13: Far from being necessarily dysfunctional, a certain degree of conflict is an essential element in group formation and the persistence of group life (general) (12, p. 31).

PROPOSITION 14: Religious conflict persists because of the need to preserve or protect one's power position (religious conflict) (21, p. 40).

PROPOSITION 15: Conflict between groups becomes institutionalized (general) (17, p. 187).

These fifteen propositions, drawn more or less randomly from a larger sample, differ markedly from one another. Nevertheless, they are all focused on social conflict, and, to the extent that they are sustained by adequate evidence, they are not trivial. On the other hand, if the list were increased tenfold, the resulting revelation would be counterbalanced by an impression of confusion and incompleteness. For as soon as the process of ordering and evaluating the propositions began, it would be noticed that no explicit scheme of classification is present beyond the mere reference to the social conflict arena to which each was originally applied, that essential terms are undefined, and that the conditions under which the various propositions are alleged to hold true are not specified. Also the crucial question of relevant, acceptable, and sufficient evidence of proof or disproof is ignored. It is our contention that these problems, together with the application of Williams' criteria, are not susceptible of self-evident solutions. Propositions stated as they are above are literally imbedded in an invisible context.

There are, of course, a number of classification devices which might be employed, among them the one mentioned in our earlier introduction (intrapersonal, intergroup, interorganizational, international, etc.) and the one implied by the identifications in parentheses following each proposition above (industrial, racial, religious, etc.). Williams classifies his propositions roughly according to conflict types, sources, and responses. The UNESCO study referred to earlier in effect discusses research findings in terms of two broad classes of approaches—the sociological and the psychological. However, there may be advantages in considering a somewhat different kind of classificatory scheme. One advantage is that of juxtaposing propositions drawn from observations in different areas of social conflict. If certain propositions on, say, industrial relations and international relations remain in completely separate categories, possible connections (logical and empirical) may be overlooked. Or if aspects of conflict analysis are not distinguished, propositions cannot be ordered and examined effectively.

Classification is one problem. Another is definition. Proposition 7, for example, hinges significantly on the respective definitions of realistic and unrealistic conflict. In Proposition 11, what does "power of two parties" actually mean? What is involved in the institutionalization of conflict as stated in Proposition 15? Does conflict itself have a common meaning throughout? Still another problem is the condition under which the propositions hold true. One implication of Proposition 4 is that persons of certain faiths may have a minimal involvement in their religion and that they may share non-religious values with others whose religious values conflict with their own, offsetting religious-value conflict. Proposition 2 seems to imply either that citizens exert a great deal of influence on war decisions or that policy-makers all share certain general personality characteristics.

Propositions must also be compared and related to one another. Often propositions are flatly contradictory—or so it seems. Two pairs of examples drawn from international and religious conflict will illustrate:

PROPOSITION 16: Ideational and symbological conflicts are more important than economic or political conflicts in straining international relations (5, p. 107).

PROPOSITION 17: Change in the relative power position of nations is the source of tension leading to conflict (9, p. 20).

PROPOSITION 18: Religious intergroup conflict is most likely to develop when there are no cross-pressures at work within the individual (10, p. 45).

PROPOSITION 19: Intensity of positions taken in religious conflict is a function of guilt and insecurity feelings over having taken such positions (8, p. 64).

Obviously, sufficient pertinent data would be needed to judge the relative validity of these competing propositions or to reconcile them. But, more than that, it would be necessary to probe the fundamental nature of conflict as well as types of conflict and conflict situations.

Knowledge is advanced by linking propositions. Here are three propositions which may be integrated into a more inclusive one:

PROPOSITION 20: Social conflicts are primarily realistic conflicts of power (12, p. 52).

PROPOSITION 14: Religious conflict persists because of the need to preserve or protect one's power position (21, p. 40).

PROPOSITION 17: Change in the relative power position of nations is the source of tension leading to conflict (9, p. 20).

PROPOSITION 21 (combining 20, 14, 17): Social conflict is normally accompanied by a felt or actual discrepancy in the power relations of the parties.

Many of the propositions which are current in the literature of a particular field ought to be analyzed to discover whether, in fact, they have greater generality. Jackson (23), as already indicated, has explored the possibility of applying principles drawn from industrial mediation to the problem of mediation between nations. As Williams (40, p. 12) points out in the case of ethnic and racial conflict, the propositions applicable to these kinds of intergroup conflict have not been shown to be equally applicable to religious conflict. However, it is more than idle speculation to inquire whether the "cross-pressures" proposition (No. 18) is, in fact, generalizable to international conflict. Is international conflict lessened when nationals are subject to conflicting loyalties either within their nation or across national frontiers? Similarly, take these propositions:

PROPOSITION 22: If an adversary's strength could be measured prior to engagement in conflict, antagonistic interests might be adjusted without conflict.

Does this apply to *all* kinds of social conflict?

PROPOSITION 23: Misunderstandings and misuse of words often contribute to lessening conflict between labor and management (26, p. 233).

If this is true, and, to the extent that it is true, would it hold for international conflict? Again it should be emphasized that more than empirical data is needed to answer these questions. Some way of putting industrial and international conflict on a comparable basis for the purposes at hand is also required.

III. THE PROBLEM OF CONCEPTUALIZATION AND CHOICES OF MAJOR VARIABLES

Having argued that the classification, ordering, and evaluation of basic propositions require prior intellectual operations, we shall now explore a tentative framework of analysis which might aid in these pursuits.

Definitions and Distinctions

Unless the phenomena denoted by the term "conflict" are limited and differentiated, the concept becomes too inclusive. On the whole, it is easier to begin by specifying what is not considered to be conflict. A review of the literature reveals certain distinctions which are apparently agreed upon or at least commonly made. *Competition* is not regarded as conflict or a form of conflict, though it may be an important source of the latter (12, p. 134; 26, p. 230; 38, p. 263; 44, p. 198). Competition involves striving for scarce objects (a prize or a resource usually "awarded" by a third party) according to established rules which strictly limit what the competitors can do to each other in the course of striving; the chief objective is the scarce object, not the injury or destruction of an opponent per se. A football game played normally according to the rules is competition *until* one or more players begin to assault one another in a manner forbidden by the rules; then it becomes a conflict.

Though closely related to conflict, the following are also considered differentiable: *antagonistic interests* (12, p. 135); *misunderstandings* (2, p. 118); *aggressiveness* (2; 12, p. 58); *hostility or hostile sentiments* (39, pp. 42–43; 12 , p. 37); *desire or intention to oppose* (26, p. 233); *social cleavages* (e.g., along class lines) (8, p. 64); *logical irreconcilability of goals or interests* (44, pp. 193–94); *tensions* (44); and *rivalry* (44). The attitudes, behaviors, and states of affairs signified by these terms *may* be among the underlying sources of conflict. Or such factors *may* accompany or intensify conflict. But it seems generally agreed that none of the terms is a proper synonym for conflict, nor are the factors denoted singly or in combination sufficient preconditions of social conflict. However, there is no general agreement as to whether any one or more is a necessary precondition for conflict to arise or continue. On the other hand, the potential relevance of the factors is clear. These problems can be clarified by confronting the nature, sources, and conditions of conflict.

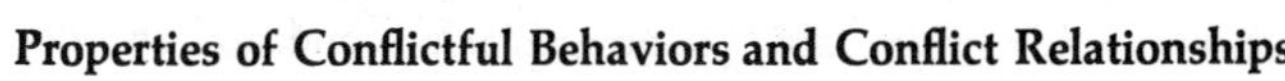

Properties of Conflictful Behaviors and Conflict Relationships

We shall not attempt a formal definition of conflict. Rather, a set of properties will be suggested which *in toto* will constitute a model for identifying and characterizing conflict phenomena and situations. Without claiming to be exhaustive, we shall insist that the essential elements are included and that conflict does not exist if the empirical conditions implied by properties 1–5 are not present. For the moment we shall avoid the awkward problem of the relationship between subjective (i.e., from the standpoint of the actor or actors) and objective (i.e., from the standpoint of an observer) perspectives. The following formulation is not original; we have attempted to synthesize and somewhat formalize the contributions of the papers in this volume and other sources:

1. *Conflict requires at least two parties or two analytically distinct units or entities* (i.e., actor, organism, group, individual, collectivity, etc.).

a) Social conflict is, by definition, an interaction relationship between two or more parties.

b) One-party conflict (intrapersonal or individual conflict) may be viewed as *either* individual-environment or actor-nature conflict (in which case the parties may be human and non-human entities), *or* the individual in conflict with himself (conflict of two or more needs and values).

c) "Games against nature" as provided in some formulations of game theory can be regarded as social conflict, but other forms of one-party conflict can be regarded as socially significant non-social conflict.

d) A minimum "contact" (not necessarily face-to-face) and "visibility" are implied (39, pp. 42–43).

2. *Conflict arises from "position scarcity" and "resource scarcity"* (2, p. 112).

a) Position scarcity is a condition in which an object cannot occupy two places at the same time, an object cannot simultaneously serve two different functions, a role cannot be simultaneously occupied or performed by two or more actors, and different prescribed behaviors cannot be carried out simultaneously.

b) Resource scarcity is a condition in which the supply of desired objects (or states of affairs) is limited so that parties cannot have *all* they want of anything.

c) Different underlying value judgments may condition the demand or need for scarce resources and positions.

d) Hence mutually exclusive and/or mutually incompatible values and opposed values are inevitable characteristics of conflict.

3. *Conflictful behaviors are those designed to destroy, injure, thwart, or otherwise control another party or other parties, and a conflict relationship is one in which the parties can gain (relatively) only at each other's expense* (26, p. 230).

a) The key is the intent of action and the object of action.

b) Gains for one party result either from a net loss to the other party or from one party's having less of what he wants than he would have had in the absence of opposition.

c) Many tactics and techniques may be manifest in conflictful behaviors which are not necessarily always identified with conflict per se.

d) Expressive behaviors, such as anger, hostility, shouting, aggressiveness, may or may not accompany conflictful behavior.

4. *Conflict requires interaction among parties in which actions and counteractions are mutually opposed* (26, 44).

a) Conflict cannot exist without action.

b) The action-reaction-action sequence must embody the pursuit of exclusive or incompatible values.

c) Threats are actions.

5. *Conflict relations always involve attempts to gain control of scarce resources and positions or to influence behavior in certain directions; hence a conflict relationship always involves the attempt to acquire or exercise power or the actual acquisition or exercise of power* (35).

a) Power is defined as control over decisions (i.e., disposition of scarce resources and positions) and as the basis of reciprocal influence between or among parties (i.e., control over behaviors).

b) Conflict reflects power strains (i.e., the need or desire to achieve or change control), and opposed actions are directed to changing or preserving existing power relations (i.e., control over objects and behaviors).

6. *Conflict relations constitute a fundamental social-interaction process having important consequences* (17, p. 183).

a) Conflict is not a breakdown or cessation of social interaction.

b) The conflict process has important functions for the parties and for the larger social system of which it is a part.

c) Conflict has a cost dimension.

7. *A conflict process or relation represents a temporary tendency toward disjunction in the interaction flow between parties* (37, p. 230).

a) Disjunction results from the presence of mutually incompatible tendencies which disrupt the normal or persistent patterns of behavior, norms, and expectations of the parties and their responses to each other.

8. *Conflict relations do not represent a breakdown in regulated conduct but rather a shift in the governing norms and expectations.*

a) Disjunctive tendencies do not continue to the point where the interaction is completely disrupted because the conflict process is subject to its own rules and limits.

If the foregoing provides a basis for at least a crude distinction between conflict and non-conflict, it does not go far enough. Thus far we have indicated that there must be *parties* and *a particular kind of interactional relationship between parties.* But there are kinds and forms of conflict relations; there are sources of conflict; various conditions affect the nature and duration of conflict; conflict has certain functions or consequences; and, finally, conflict always occurs in an environmental context which transcends the conflict relationship itself.

Types of Conflict

We shall mention some major distinctions only briefly. One obvious distinction is implied in property 1: conflict *within* persons (intraparty) and conflict *between* persons or groups. Both meet the criteria set forth, and respective analogies can be pursued usefully. For example, persons undergoing psychotic conflict can quite literally destroy themselves. However, the primary emphasis in this volume is on social conflict, which, by definition, is interactional. Perhaps the most significant question is the impact of intrapersonal conflict on social conflict—a problem to which we shall return later.

An important and familiar distinction is between *realistic* and *non-realistic* conflict (12, p. 49; 39, p. 40). Realistic conflict is characterized by opposed means and ends, by incompatibility of values and interests. Non-realistic conflict arises from the need for tension release, from deflected hostility, from historical tradition, and from ignorance or error. The two types differ in origin and in the ultimate motivation behind opposed action. In realistic conflict, wants and needs seem to be, or become, incompatible because of other factors, that is, resource and position scarcity. But non-realistic conflict, for example, would be continued opposed action between nations whose actual conflicting interests had long since been reconciled. Propositions 2 and 16, listed above, clearly are based on the alleged existence of much non-realistic conflict among nations. Proposition 7 states a relation between the two types—an important generalization which might be lost in the absence of the distinction. Along similar lines Kerr (26, p. 234) draws a distinction between *real* and *induced* conflict, the latter being cases where representatives of conflicting groups have ends to be gained (e.g., their own prestige) apart from the ends in dispute between groups. This would be the situation if labor-union leaders precipitated a conflict with management in order to strengthen their hold over the union membership. Coser differentiates *basic cleavages*—conflict over the very nature of a consensual framework within which individuals and groups have hitherto operated—and conflicts over means and subordinate ends within a consensual framework (12, p. 73). This parallels Simpson's distinction between *non-communal* and *communal* conflicts, respectively (36, p. 17). An illustration of a basic cleavage–non-communal type of conflict would be the American Civil War. The opposite type would be exemplified by a conflict between an income tax and a sales tax, assuming general agreement to levy taxes of some kind.

An implicit distinction is usually drawn between *institutionalized* and *non-institutionalized* conflict. The former is characterized by explicit rules, predictable behavior, and continuity, as in the case of collective bargaining. Most racial conflict is, on the other hand, non-institutionalized. *Disorganized* conflict, as in the case of a riot (regardless of organized effort to initiate it), may take place within an institutional framework or not, the former being illustrated by an unauthorized, partially supported strike. Organized conflict, such as a war between armies, is obviously different from a spontaneous border clash between irregular armed units. *Extreme* (35, p. 324), *aggressive* (26, p. 232), and *violent* (12, p. 88) conflict are also differentiated from *non-violent, "diplomatic"* conflict—chiefly on the basis of coercive means versus persuasive means and on the assumption that, in the former, destruction or crippling of one of the parties is highly possible.

It appears useful to separate *primary, face-to-face conflicts* from *secondary, mediated conflicts*. Generally speaking, the rank and file of labor and the rank and file of management do not face each other in a conflict relation. Rather, chosen representatives speak for well-organized collectivities. On the other hand, in a town meeting or a legislature or in racial or ethnic contacts, conflict relations are, for the most part, direct. Closely related is another set of opposite types: *personal subjective conflict* and *impersonal objective conflict*. A conflict between husband and wife would fit the first category, and a conflict between two lawyers, each representing a client, would fit the second. A difference between *conflicts of right* and *conflicts of interest* may be noted. A conflict of right concerns the application of agreed standards to specified actions; a conflict of interest concerns the changing of old standards or the introduction of new standards—roughly, the distinction is between judicial and legislative conflict. This distinction applies to industrial, international, racial, and ethnic conflict.

Opposed values have been specified as inevitable concomitants of conflict, but any preliminary typology should include mention of types of conflict which are predominantly value conflicts per se. *Ideological conflict* is characterized by a clash of "conceptions of the desirable" (28, p. 391) and prescriptive norms and beliefs which do or should govern particular behaviors. For purposes of this analysis, ideologies can be classified as relatively open and relatively closed in terms of the extent to which alien or opposed values and belief can or will be accommodated or absorbed. Ideological conflict can be further classified according to the significance of the clash of absolute values, i.e., no "higher values" exist to mediate "lower values," and thus one set must triumph, or there must be benevolent neutrality. Conflict of religious dogmas exemplifies this, as well as certain conflicting political ideologies. Religious conflict is likely to be intense where conversion from one faith to another is required or where one faith regards another as "infidel"; but the same would hold true of non-religious ideologies.

Cultural conflict is a term used so broadly that it often includes all other types and even subsumes "social." Presumably, of course, conflicts between cultures, depending on the nature of the contacts, might well include conflicting ideologies, religions, interests, rights, and all the other types suggested above. A breakdown of cultural conflict into component elements, then, would be facilitated by a typology and by the basic conceptualization of conflict. Frazier has pointed out that initial contacts between races and cultures are essentially biological (19, p. 46). At this stage, conflict is biological in the sense that the two parties do not regard each other as human; no common moral order prevails to restrain conduct or otherwise regulate behavior. It seems likely in view of wide differences in the circumstances under which racial and cultural contacts lead to intermarriage and general acculturation that there is a primitive psychological factor at work too. At any rate, the analysis of contemporary conflict between races and cultures ought to recognize the fundamental importance of initial psychobiological contacts and the persistent attitudes which they generate (19, chaps. i, ii, xvii).

The foregoing is obviously only the beginning of a typology. For the moment we shall allow the bases of the classification to remain implicit. As we develop the analysis, new types will be added, and classificatory bases will be made explicit.

UNDERLYING SOURCES OF CONFLICT. Properties 1–5 set forth above may be viewed as a set of analytic preconditions of conflict, but, as formulated, they say nothing about the empirical content in particular cases. For example, position and resource scarcity is one of the necessary preconditions of conflict; yet we have to look elsewhere for the factors which produce, or account for, a specific pattern of scarcity. Underlying sources are those empirical phenomena which may result in the existence of the five preconditions of conflict. Perhaps the line between sources and preconditions will seem arbitrary and difficult to draw. The distinction seems required, nonetheless, because the presence or persistence of underlying source factors does not necessarily mean that conflict, as defined, will arise. An observer is often embarrassed to discover that conflict does not arise despite the apparent indication of important source factors effectively at work in the social situation. Or conflict may arise in the absence of certain source factors. If the parties cannot "reach" each other by opposed action or if initiative is not assumed by at least one of the parties, a conflict interaction is impossible. Conversely, the decisions of one or more parties may, in effect, define a position or resource scarcity which an observer would find did not exist by his objective standards.

Most social scientists now accept the principle of multiple causality; hence there is no one basic source of conflict. In view of the preoccupation with the evil consequences of conflict, it is not surprising that the literature on causation overbalances the rest (7, chaps. i, iv; 11; 24; 42). Indeed, so far as particular areas of conflict are concerned, underlying sources have been rather thoroughly catalogued. It is fairly easy merely to list the most significant sources of, say, war (42). The central problem is, of course, to determine the particular combination of underlying source factors in a given situation which does result in the analytic preconditions. In general, the catalogues of conflict sources which are available do not, for the most part, provide the observer with more than a list of alternative possibilities which he would want to explore in any single instance. Above all, there is little guidance as to patterns of combination which produce conflict and to the conditions under which they are formed. The latter point suggests that difficulties are further compounded because the combination of sources and the translation of these into the preconditions may be influenced by nonsource factors, which is one reason why we shall discuss conditions of conflict in the next section.

Emphasis on the sources of conflict has not been due solely to the scientist's attempt to answer the question of why conflict arises. Because of preoccupation with conflict as a costly social problem, sources are natural foci for reforms and changes which will supposedly reduce or eliminate conflict. If the source of conflict is a psychological state called "tension," tension reduction is an indicated strategy. If the source is ignorance, as in the case of some non-realistic conflict, education will eliminate or minimize the "cause" of such conflict. And so on. Now there is impressive evidence that a direct approach to the removal or adaptation of sources per se is not necessarily an effective way to curb conflict. Freeman (20, p. 86) argues that race itself may not be the "proper first object" of concern in controlling racial conflict and goes on to suggest that the key may be in the behavioral patterns exhibited in the *generic* phenomena of conflict —which means putting racial conflict in a broader framework of the sort being outlined here. One of Simmel's basic propositions, as reformulated by Coser (12, p. 55) is that hostile or aggressive impulses do not account for social conflict. Williams (39, p. 40) insists that factors producing conflict are not necessarily those most important for control purposes. It is interesting to compare Wright's analysis of theories of causes of wars (42) with Cottrell's five models of a peaceful world (13). In the former, conditions of peace turn out to be the inverse of sources of war (in the theories he reviews); in the latter, the requisites of peace (non-violent conflict relations) are derived from quite different bases.

While it is true that the specific sources of, say, industrial conflict and international conflict are quite different, it is also true that generalized sources and types of sources may be identified. A generalized source is one which is not peculiar to any one arena or kind of conflict. Insofar as "tensions" are, in fact, a source of conflict, they may be either general personality conditions which can be focused on a range of particular situations, or they can be closely connected with only certain interaction relationships. Tensions between unions and managements may arise from the shrinking pie to be divided between them, or tensions from other sources may induce the demands which are made upon the existing pie. Presumably, the latter might also be expressed in ethnic or religious or other intergroup conflict. The search for underlying sources in the first case carries one only as far as the size of the pie; in the second, it requires a much wider range of inquiry. Two questions arise. First, how deep should the search for underlying factors (this usually involves personality dynamics) be pushed? Second, are there certain basic motive patterns or facts of social life which might serve to account partially for a variety of conflict relations? Some explanations of conflict are based on the alleged consequences of what might be called "psychoanalytic mechanisms," such as Proposition 1 cited earlier (18, p. 34; 27). Some are somewhat closer to the surface, as it were, being rooted in psychological variables, such as inferiority feelings or hostility and the like (39, chap. i). Still others are more sociological in nature, i.e., discontents over income, job conditions (26, p. 230). More or less in accord with these three levels of sources, two writers (34, p. 25) have asserted that three primary motives underlie intergroup conflict: (*a*) desire for acquisition of scarce values (political or power conflict); (*b*) desire to convert others (ideological conflict); and (*c*) desire to prevent contact with inferiors (racist conflict). On the surface at least, there is no common agreement on the first question, namely, Should the search for source factors be pushed to the psychoanalytic level? But the lack of agreement is due partly to the failure to make consistent distinctions among types of and parties to conflict, and to link sources explicitly with conditions and contexts. Furthermore, the problem of psychological and sociological levels of explanation should not obscure an integrative question: Under what social conditions do psychological mechanisms operate as sources of conflict?

On the second question, it seems generally agreed that scarcity of desired objects, states of affairs, and resources in nature and culture, the division of labor in organized society, and social differentiation lead inevitably to potentially conflictful cleavages and antagonistic interests. It is (or seems to be) further agreed that these factors, as well as more deeply psychological ones, contribute to a reservoir of "free-floating" aggression, hostility, and tension which, in turn, *may* lead to conflictful behaviors.

This is illustrated by the mechanisms of projection and displacement which may be focused on any object or group (industrial, international, ethnic, etc.) in a conflict situation. Hence two general categories of sources emerge: those centering on interactional relationships, e.g., a conflict over land between cattle grazers, and those centering on certain internal characteristics of parties or intrapersonal (personality dynamics) factors, e.g., the frustration-aggression hypothesis. Propositions embodying explanations for the rise of conflict, which can be grouped according to these two categories, will be discussed in the next two sections. One utility of the distinction between realistic and non-realistic conflict now becomes clear. Realistic conflicts are presumed to have their origin primarily in interactional factors; non-realistic conflicts are presumed to be accountable for primarily in terms of non-interactional factors. Thus industrial conflict is inherent in the institutional situation in which labor and management interact: both cannot make the same decisions separately, their roles give rise to different values, total income from a given business is limited and cannot satisfy maximum demands by each side, and so on (26, p. 230). Religious conflict, in contrast, is inherent in the private nature of religious experience, in the nature of religious values as substitutes for other social values, and in the manner of transmission of religious beliefs (10, p. 49).

Concern over the origins of conflict draws attention to potential responses to conflict situations and to the decisions which result in moving from a desire to oppose to acts of opposition. In ascertaining why some situations lead to actual conflict interaction while others do not, it is necessary to identify certain crucial foci of analysis. Responses or decisions may result in the origination of conflict interaction, in withdrawal from a potential conflict situation, in a change from non-violent to violent or extreme conflict, or in accommodation to a stable conflict relationship. These outcomes, more often than not, depend on choices. Therefore, the conditions which affect such choices must be probed, and similar cases which have different outcomes must be compared. Two possible foci will be mentioned here. First, in the case of secondary, mediated intergroup conflict, Deutsch's decision-making and communications approach would seem particularly useful. His approach suggests, for example, that a central question concerning the outbreak of war is: Under what conditions do foreign policy-makers decide, in effect, that all viable alternatives have been reduced to one? Is it possible to identify a "point of no return" in a conflict relation progressing toward war? What effect do the nature, flow, and interpretation of information have on the foreclosure of alternatives? Analyzing war decisions along these lines represents a much more fundamental approach than the listing of causes of war or the attribution of single, overpowering motives to nations. A second focus of analysis is more appropriate for individual responses to primary, immediated intergroup conflict. One lead is supplied by the cross-pressures hypothesis (Proposition 18), which indicates that conflict potential is dampened if individuals are pulled in opposite directions by their group affiliations or incompatible values. On the other hand, one of two contradictory pulls may triumph over the other. Thus Brown's approach-avoidance analysis may yield some hypotheses regarding the circumstances under which conflicting stimuli will produce either of two responses. Though it is an obvious example, we can cite cases where individuals are not necessarily prevented from discriminatory acts against minorities by their religious values which prescribe the Golden Rule. Clearly, in this situation the minority member does not represent an ambiguous stimulus—as would be true if the discriminatory individual saw him as both an undesirable inferior and a human being deserving of equal treatment. The converse of the cross-pressures hypothesis is that group conflicts are more likely to develop and to be intense when there is no conflict within the individual. Basically, in this situation the stimulus is unambiguous, and the "approach" response tendency is the stronger.

It is noteworthy that these two general approaches—and there are others which focus on decisions and responses—require simultaneous attention to psychological and sociological variables. The behavior of decision-makers is to be viewed as a resultant of such factors as individual perceptions and institutionalized information flows. The behavior of individuals responding to conflict or possible conflict is to be viewed as a resultant of competitory response tendencies and the nature of stimuli in the social environment.

Conditions of Conflict

The main reason for analyzing the accompanying conditions of conflict separately is that particular sources which result in the analytic preconditions do not account for the origin, form, intensity, duration, reduction, or resolution of conflict. This can be demonstrated by Dahlke's (14, pp. 421–24) analysis of race riots, which, he argues, are highly probable when (*a*) the period is one of change and mobility; (*b*) the minority group has an outstanding trait or characteristic which can become a basis for negative assessments; (*c*) lawful authorities assign the minority group a subordinate status; (*d*) one or more major associations or organizations direct the attack against the minority; (*e*) the press and other media have been minority-baiting; and (*f*) suitable personnel (students and marginal workers) are available for initiating action.

Clearly, the notion of conditions opens up a wide range of relevant factors. In calling attention to the analytic separation of these factors, we mean only to say that certain elements inherent in the nature of parties to conflict, in the interaction relationships between parties, and in the social context will often account for the origin, form, intensity, duration, limits, and resolution of conflict. Conditions are not, then, a special category of factors but a way of viewing the impact of the elements to be discussed in succeeding sections.

To illustrate in a preliminary fashion, we list sample propositions:

PROPOSITION 24: Mediation increases the possibility of resolving conflict when parties are small (33, p. 194).

PROPOSITION 25: Realistic conflict need not be accompanied by hostility and aggressiveness (12, p. 58).

PROPOSITION 26: It is more difficult to mediate controversy where costs of aggressive conflict are high (26, p. 239).

PROPOSITION 27: Social conflict cannot be integrative and functional in the absence of community (36, p. 42).

PROPOSITION 28: Ideological conflict is more intense and the parties thereto are more intransigent because of objectification of issues and lack of inhibitions on personal attacks (12, p. 115).

PROPOSITION 29: A high degree of intimacy between the parties, as contrasted with a high degree of functional interdependence, will intensify conflict (12, p. 67).

In addition, two other conditioning factors are of importance. Our specification of the essential properties of conflict relations stressed the power component. To the extent that conflict is over the nature of the respective roles of the parties in decision-making with respect to mutual interests, the form, intensity, and duration of the conflict will depend on the length of time it takes to test the power relationship conclusively and the means available to each party for exerting control. Intensity will also be affected by the cruciality of the decision-making functions at issue. A long war, a long strike, or a long bargaining period may indicate roughly an equal power equation or the failure to find adequate indexes of power. Another condition of great importance is the amount of information available to, and interpreted correctly by, the parties to conflict. Bernard (2, p. 111) has graphically portrayed the potential impact of this factor.

The Social Context of Conflict

The conditions discussed above were those primarily confined to the parties and to their relationship. However, it is axiomatic that conflict occurs in, affects, and in turn is affected by, a surrounding environment. Conflict must be researched and analyzed against the background of the total social system in which it occurs (39, p. 47). Once again, all we can hope to do here is outline the crucial considerations by means of illustrative propositions.

Social change affects conflict in a number of ways. Changes are constantly shifting the bases of potentially antagonistic interests and the relative power positions of individuals and groups. As the value potentiality of the social environment shifts, new demands, new frustrations, and new incompatibilities arise. Population growth, invention, urbanization, mobility—indeed, all the changes which result in and are resultants of greater social complexity—affect the sources of conflict, the nature and number of parties to conflict, the instrumentalities of conflict, the issues of conflict, modes of settlement, and so on (10; 14; 17, p. 179; 22; 26; 29, pp. 3–22; 30; 35; 39, pp. 43 ff.). The same general point applies to international conflict, which has its own social context:

PROPOSITION 30: Important alternations in the balance of forces as between societies occurs as a result of profound changes internal to one or more societies (9, p. 19).

Social organization will determine the number and kinds of parties to conflict within any society. In a complex industrial urban society realistic conflict will tend to be carried on by highly organized groups having diverse memberships and specialized representatives and negotiators. In a less complex communal society, there will tend to be more direct, face-to-face interpersonal conflict. Social differentiation (status, occupational roles, power positions, etc.) will tend to define lines of consensus and cleavage, to lead to the formation of groups and groupings which are foci of consensus and cleavage. In a recent book, *Race and Culture Contacts in the Modern World,* Frazier organizes his analysis around the ecological, economic, political, and social organization. The impact of the social context on racial conflict is clearly shown. For example, economic racial conflict does not arise where the division of labor is based on objective standards of competitive success (p. 331). Whyte's study, *Pattern for Industrial Peace,* is concerned with a more immediate context of conflict: the relation between company structure and labor-management relations. Changes in organization are correlated with three stages of development: from disorganized conflict to organized conflict to organized co-operation.

Interinstitutional strain, as in the case of religious and political institutions in the United States, may create intrapersonal conflict (religious versus secular values) and/or intergroup conflict over such issues as public aid to parochial schools (40, pp. 12–20). Coser (12, p. 77) and Williams (40, p. 12) have argued that a "loosely organized society" with many crisscrossing pressures and influences on individuals and groups reduces the possibility of single, rigid, and intense conflicts which divide the whole society or a large segment of it and also provides stability despite extensive conflict. Thus a multiplicity of potential or actual conflict situations, combined with shared values which cut across lines of cleavage, prevents any one conflict situation or kind of conflict (e.g., religious) from dominating the relations of sizable groups and large numbers of individuals. Closely related to this is Simmel's notion of safety-valve institutions which channel hostility and drain off residual conflict responses (12, pp. 41–44).

This suggests another significant aspect of the social context of conflict. Normally, no matter how serious a conflict exists between particular groups and individuals, there will always be *disinterested* or neutral, but nonetheless affected, outsiders (or, indirectly, "third" parties). If conflict completely divides a local, national, or international community, which means in effect that there are no outsiders, solutions become very difficult indeed. This is partly because there are no available neutral conciliators or mediators and partly because no one has a vested interest in the cessation of conflict (25, p. 297). The pressure for liquidation or control of social conflict from disinterested but affected bystanders is one of the primary limits on its duration, extension, and intensity. Both labor and management in the United States have been compelled to recognize a "public interest," and one of the functions of the United Nations is to mobilize worldwide public pressure on disputants.

The availability and permissibility of the instrumentalities of conflict are obviously dependent on the social environment. Firearms are strictly controlled in most societies as a means for settling interpersonal conflict. In many Latin American countries military rebellion is a recognized mode of carrying on political conflict. It took many years for the strike to be sanctioned as a proper instrument in industrial conflict. There has been a long history of attempts to establish legitimate and illegitimate uses of war as an instrument of national policy.

One of the major problems of the social order at all levels of society is the control of violent conflict. Hence one of the tasks of public policy, social engineering, and scientific study of human behavior is to determine what kinds of social arrangements are conducive to non-violent conflict (31).

PROPOSITION 31: The more integrated into the society are the parties to conflict, the less likely will conflict be violent (26, p. 243).

But, as important as violent conflict is as a basic form or type, the problem is, in fact, much broader. Order and conflict (all types) are persistent states of any social system. While to an extent they are, or appear to be, opposites, both can and must exist side by side. Furthermore, the relationship between them will determine the degree of social stability. Basically, the stability-instability balance will be a resultant of the success or failure of the normative order in regulating conflicts of interest (30, pp. 139–40). Conflict induces a constant pressure of factual situations on the normative order. In turn, conflict is in some manner controlled by social norms. As already remarked, social change—its rate and direction—is an ultimate source of conflict because, as the factual social order undergoes transition, new incompatibilities and antagonistic interests arise. The relevant regulatory norms either will accommodate (permit) acceptable "solutions" or will be modified (or perhaps consistently violated) to take account of the actual power relations between the parties.

If we are interested in generalizing propositions about social conflict from one area of behavior to another, it is obviously necessary to compare relevant social contexts (23, chap. i; 26, p. 235). To the extent that the social environments of industrial and international conflict differ, *some* propositions will not hold for both. For example, it is unclear whether the international social environment has yet produced a reservoir of mediators and conciliators such as exist in most complex industrial societies. Perhaps one of the reasons that the propositions from racial and ethnic intergroup conflict do not apply to religious conflict is that the social context even in a single society is different. Thus far in the United States, for example, there has been clear separation between religious and political institutions (church and state), while racial and ethnic factors permeate family, educational, economic, and political institutions.

The Functions of Conflict

Since preoccupation with conflict often centers on its most violent, abhorrent, and socially costly forms, it is likely that the average reader will regard *all* conflict as universally bad. Proposition 13, listed above, boldly states the contrary view. There is no way of evaluating this proposition unless the functions and consequences of conflict are systematically examined. It is noteworthy that most contemporary social scientists lay stress on the constructive consequences of conflict relations (7, 12, 22, 24, 26, 29, 36, 38). Coser (12, chaps. ii, viii) has summarized sociological thinking on this point with particular reference to social groups. Dubin's five central propositions (17, p. 179) constitute a broader thesis: Intergroup conflict is a fundamental institutionalized social process which determines the direction of social change and, in effect, defines social welfare. Though most of his analysis is drawn from experience in industrial relations, the propositions have wider applicability.

It is unnecessary to review the whole range of functions served by social conflict. Several major propositions will suffice:

PROPOSITION 32: Conflict sets group boundaries by strengthening group cohesiveness and separateness (12).

PROPOSITION 33: Conflict reduces tension and permits maintenance of social interaction under stress (26, p. 232; 12, chap. iii).

PROPOSITION 34: Conflict clarifies objectives (29, p. 16).

PROPOSITION 35: Conflict results in the establishment of group norms (24, pp. 196–97).

PROPOSITION 36: Without conflict, accommodative relations would result in subordination rather than agreement (38, p. 263).

The foregoing is a brief reminder that there are important positive social functions served by conflict. Evidence discussed by writers in support of Propositions 32–36 would tend to support the more general Proposition 13 presented earlier. This perspective does not, of course, imply that conflict is not often dysfunctional and very costly. One of the most difficult problems in conflict analysis is to arrive at a method for determining the dividing line between constructive functions and dysfunctions. Clearly, the question of the cost of social conflict involves different relevant criteria. It may seem a macabre joke to emphasize the constructive consequences of conflict in an age of nuclear weapons or in the face of the three-year Kohler strike in Kohler, Wisconsin. On the other hand, no scholar, reformer, critic, or politician has ever denied that conflict is an all-pervasive fact of human life, nor does anyone deny that society persists in spite of violent and costly conflict. As a matter of fact, the functional and dysfunctional aspects of conflict are opposite sides of the same coin.

As a crude first approximation to a meaningful distinction, it might be suggested that conflict is, *on balance*, dysfunctional to the extent that its positive functions are impaired or neutralized under certain conditions. For example, the normal course of a realistic conflict may under some circumstances generate, instead of relieve, hostility or tension. Indeed, a realistic conflict may be transformed into a non-realistic conflict, which may, in turn, undermine institutionalized modes of resolving realistic conflict and also raise costs far beyond what is proportionate to any advantages accruing to the parties or affected bystanders. A long strike which results in obscuring objectives, in an almost total breakdown of interaction and mutual dependence, in hostility which becomes unrelated to the goals of the parties, and in confusion of actual power relations is dysfunctional and wasteful. Functional conflict encourages collaboration and a more efficient division of labor between parties because of heightened consciousness of purpose and strengthening of positions taken. It is one of the characteristics of dysfunctional conflict that it is difficult to say, as time goes on, what the conflict is about.

Violence at the international level is often accompanied by a tragic lack of reliable knowledge about the objectives and power potentials of the respective contenders and by inadequacy of machinery through which the positive functions of conflict can be realized. In terms of the whole thesis being developed here, the most abhorrent and costly social conflicts should be viewed not as abrupt breaks in "order" and "co-operation" but as transitions or abrupt shifts from one kind of conflict relationship to another. However, it is quite likely that predominantly dysfunctional conflict will lead to a cessation of interaction at some point.

While socially useful and socially undesirable consequences of conflict can and should be kept separate, it is probably true that they go together. From some vantage points at least, it is difficult to imagine any conflict having only one kind of consequence. Therefore, part of the problem of differentiation of the functional and dysfunctional aspects of conflict is the identification of conditions under which dysfunctional consequences can be minimized. A fundamental research question is, then, How and why do the dysfunctional consequences come to predominate?

Summary

Though the framework for conflict analysis outlined so far has centered on the concept, types, sources, conditions, context, and functions of conflict, it is clear from the brief comment and propositions that such aspects cannot be discussed without mentioning the connection between relevant party characteristics and the conflict relationship, the nature of conflict interaction itself, and the problem of conflict resolution and control. We shall therefore develop the framework one step further in the next two sections by considering two major foci of conflict analysis—party characteristics and interaction. Since the problem of conflict resolution and control has already been touched upon, we shall continue to refer to it where it naturally fits our scheme instead of treating it separately.

IV. THE PARTIES TO CONFLICT: IMPLICATIONS OF NATURE, NUMBER, AND INTERNAL CHARACTERISTICS

The term *party* here will be taken to include individual actors, culture, coalition, social class, personality, nation, organization, organism, system, or group. Party refers to analytic units, regardless of level of generality, *between* which, or in some cases *within* which, conflict takes place. It is assumed that each of these unit types may be viewed operationally as an abstraction of certain observable tendencies and actions of persons and of certain relationships.

Identification and Establishment

This raises the question of identification, which often is not self-evident or given in the particular situation. At the same time, we have proposed that one of the preconditions of a conflict relationship is visibility of parties to each other. Logically, this implies that if the parties are *not subjectively* identifiable, conflict, as defined, cannot exist, though potentially it may be likely if and when identification does take place. It is one of the notable caprices of social conflict that parties may be misidentified, i.e., an individual or group may be *assumed* to be the opponent in a clash of mutually incompatible goals or values when objectively such is not the case at all. As a matter of fact, one of the major features of a sequence of preconflict-conflict-postconflict actions and reactions may be a process of establishing visibility and/or changing identifications of parties. Matters are further complicated by the social context, which may include, as noted, bystander or neutral elements which are affected but not technically involved. The line between party and non-party may be a fine one indeed. Sympathy strikes, for example, would seem to be instances of where unions not parties to a particular conflict become, in effect, by their correlated action, parties to another (and new) conflict. And, if the sympathy strike occurs in a highly integrated industry, the sympathy strike may actually add a party to the original conflict.

The problem of the identity of parties to conflict is not just a methodological exercise. An observer's identification and the participants' identification may or may not coincide. What may appear to be a realistic conflict between labor and management may, in fact, be what has been called an "induced" conflict, i.e., one between officials on both sides. Thus another of our earlier distinctions is useful and points to phenomena which may not be self-evident. For example, political party conflict is often the induced kind. Once the distinction is made, its base seems obvious, but the implications are perhaps not so obvious. Not only is diagnosis of the *sources* of such conflicts likely to be in error (or at least incomplete), but the conditions and effective modes of resolution may be quite different. One general hypothesis might be: *Induced conflict is likely to be more intense than realistic conflict because of the coincidence of group and personal values.* A second general hypothesis might be: *Induced conflicts arise more from imbalance or ambiguity of power relations, whereas realistic conflicts arise more from incompatibility of objectives.* A third general hypothesis might be: *Induced conflicts are not readily susceptible to normal mediation procedures.*

In the sphere of international affairs, an observer might argue that, in a given case, governments are the real parties, whereas, subjectively, whole nations may be perceived as parties. Apart from the fact that in the social world it is the latter which really counts, actors in conflict situations attempt to manipulate the nature and number of parties. Diplomats and foreign policymakers may attempt to *delimit* severely the parties to international conflict by separating the government from the people of a foreign nation: "Our quarrel is not with you but with your leaders." Conversely, governmental leaders may attempt deliberately to *extend* either the number or size of opposing parties by saying to a whole population: "This conflict directly involves your welfare, and you had better restrain your leaders or else." The practice of equating group interests and general welfare represents (among other things) an attempt to enlarge the size or change the constituency of one party. It might be supposed that the enlargement-through-changed-identification tendency, where manifest in a monolithic or highly stratified social context, would cause conflict to spread. The establishment of visible and recognized parties is thus part of the conflict process. The following proposition will illustrate:

PROPOSITION 37: The early stages of conflict are often carried on with the object of establishing the intergroup nature of conflict (24, p. 195).

A proportionately large number of strikes at the beginning of the organized labor movement supports the conclusion that one of the primary objectives was recognition of the union as a party in industrial conflict. As one writer has pointed out, conflicts do not necessarily presuppose *established* and *coherent groups* (24). On the other hand, a party to conflict may be created by the search for an "enemy" and by another party—provided, of course, that there is conflictful interaction, once the latter has been found.

Number of Parties

We have been concentrating on conflict involving two or more parties, and we have already drawn a distinction between conflict involving a single entity [Judson S. Brown, "Principles of Intrapersonal Conflict," *Journal of Conflict Resolution 1*, 1957, 135–154] and conflict between parties or entities of whatever number. Comments here would not, of course, apply to the former.

Actually, little seems to be known about the effect on social conflict of the sheer number of parties. On a common-sense basis it would seem that the larger the number of parties to a conflict, the more complex the power relations and the more ambiguous the incompatibility of values. Several tentative hypotheses may be suggested:

1. The larger the number of parties, the more difficult it will be to discover a common solution, in which all parties can achieve at least some gain over previous power positions.
2. The larger the number of parties, the less intense will be the non-realistic components of the conflict relationship.
3. There is a persistent tendency to reduce multiple-party conflict to two-party conflict via coalitions and blocs.

If one of the functions of conflict is the clarification of goals and the exploration of common aims, this will depend on the distribution of reliable information among parties and the potential existence of an area of value compatibility. An increase in the number of parties enhances the chance of communications failure and reduces the range of alternative solutions acceptable to all parties. On the other hand, a large number of parties will tend to diffuse hostility and antagonism because more outlets or objects are provided. The tendency to reduce the number of parties to conflict is obviously due to the need to make power more effective and to arrive at a clear-cut definition of power relations which is somewhat stable. Diffuse power relations are notoriously unstable. The general hypothesis would be: *Social conflict tends toward bipolarization of power relations and to centralize the bases of effective power.* This tendency is clearly reflected in the formation of coalitions.

Internal Characteristics of Parties

The problem here is a dual one: the determination of relevant characteristics and the linking of these to clearly differentiated units of analysis. If we keep in mind what has been said previously, it is possible to suggest a crude check list of characteristics. Naturally, since it is not at all clear a priori what range of internal characteristics is relevant to particular types of conflict situations, any list must be derived in part from the postulated properties of conflict, in part from hypothesized relationships between characteristics of parties and aspects of conflict, and in part from further empirical investigation. The following dimensions might serve as a point of departure: *motives, values, and attitudes; beliefs, perceptual frameworks, and information; degree of internal organization and intraparty relationships; size; strength; and extraparty factors having internal implications.* Each of these kinds of characteristics deserves considerable exposition, but only brief illustration is possible here.

1. It has already been indicated that some observers (for example, Propositions 1, 2, and 10 above) attribute the source of conflict to motivational, value, and attitudinal factors and that other observers have linked these same party characteristics to the conditions of conflict (for example, Proposition 16 above).

To take one arena, there are numerous psychoanalytic hypotheses bearing on international conflict and war (18), of which the following are additional examples:

PROPOSITION 38: Persons with character disorders have a predilection for public positions, and the public has a predilection for electing such persons (11, p. 9).

PROPOSITION 39: Intrapersonal conflict between aggressive impulses and socially sanctioned moral norms of behavior leads to projection of aggression on external groups (31).

In general, these hypotheses involve a causal connection between personality dynamics or psychological mechanisms operating at the individual actor level and some aspect of intergroup conflict. Individual attitudes or general personality characteristics are cited to account for, say, national policies leading to conflict or a war decision. More specifically, the implications of Brown's analysis of intrapersonal conflict for intergroup conflict are at issue.

We have noted earlier that the broad issue of the desirability of pushing intergroup conflict analysis to this depth of motivation is unsettled. There is agreement, implicitly or explicitly, that conflict should be viewed in the context of the needs, beliefs, perceptions, values, and attitudes of individuals and groups. However, there also seems to be agreement (*a*) that hostility, aggression, or particular personality disorders are not necessarily concomitants of conflict, and (*b*) that realistic or objective conflict may itself induce prejudice, unfavorable stereotypes, and hostility. The latter point implies that the relationship between party characteristics and conflict interaction is reciprocal, not unilateral. More than this, not all individual responses are destructive; constructive responses can be conflict-inducing. Thus ethnocentricity may be functional in the sense of being a factor in group survival and co-operation, while at the same time it is a potential source or condition of conflict. Even were such not the case, counterhypotheses to the ones cited are present in the literature:

PROPOSITION 40: The source of international tension resides between, rather than within, nations (9, p. 20).

PROPOSITION 41: Belligerents in recent wars have not enjoyed greater sexual, economic, or prestige frustrations, . . . nor have they been more viciously manipulated by their leaders than have non-belligerents (9).

There are two important points to be considered in evaluating or verifying propositions of this kind. First, the nature of the analytic unit which is to be denoted as the party to conflict becomes crucial. Is a nation, as a group, to be thought of in terms of its whole population or only in terms of the officials who act in its behalf? Proposition 2 seems to include all members of a nation, including policy-makers, and hence flies in the face of much evidence that official decisions are the result of rational processes. Proposition 38, on the other hand, hypothesizes a link between personality factors affecting masses of individuals in society and the selection of officials who have "character disorders" which presumably influence national policies. Propositions 2 and 38 both typically assume complete identity or homogeneity of motives, values, attitudes, and perceptions among citizens and between citizens and policy-makers and also ignore the organizational setting in which governmental decisions are made. Now it is perfectly conceivable that rational policy-makers may feel bound to act on the basis of a public opinion, which, in turn, is formed by underlying non-rational or irrational personality factors. Thus the aggressive tendencies of the people as a whole *could* lead to a conflict policy formulated by policy-makers who were not themselves subject to these tendencies. However, this is quite a different proposition.

Similarly, is a labor union, as a party to conflict, to be designated as the entire membership or as the union leaders? Kerr's distinction between real and induced conflict implies that the latter is related to characteristics of union and management officials and not to characteristics of union membership and a company viewed as collectivities. Nor would we expect to apply a psychoanalytic hypothesis concerning individual behavior to a complex organization or a system in Boulding's terminology without the significant qualification that in each case we referred to certain individuals whose behavior was the focus of analysis.

It is perfectly permissible to speak of organizational or system goals, ideology, information, and so on, as long as the properties of such entities are not confused with those of individual actors considered as total personalities.

Second, motivation, values, and attitudes as party characteristics must be related to a specific situation, to a particular conflict interaction context. As one writer has put it (1, chap. i), we must do more than specify a psychological mechanism which is unrelated to an objective state of affairs; rather, we must seek emotional predispositions which cause individuals to perceive and react to real conflict situations.

A somewhat different perspective on the relationships between individual characteristics and intergroup relations is offered by Guetzkow in his *Multiple Loyalties: Theoretical Approach to a Problem in International Organization* (6). One of the basic propositions which emerges from this study is:

> PROPOSITION 42: Citizen loyalty to the nation and citizen loyalty to some kind of supranational organization are not incompatible, provided that the latter is perceived to meet new or independent needs (6, pp. 39–40).

Behind this proposition is a more general one to the effect that multiple loyalties may or may not produce conflict within the individual, thus leading him to withdraw one set of loyalties in favor of another or to be caught in indecisiveness. In a preliminary test of the proposition, Guetzkow used UNESCO survey data and compared multiplists (those citizens with both national and supranational loyalties), patriots (those citizens with exclusive loyalty to the nation), and the alienated (those whose loyalties were primarily supranational). Results were then correlated with such indexes as education, economic status, age, and attitude toward the future. The larger problem being explored here is, of course, the impact of loyalty to one group or set of values on the relations of groups or sets of values. Does loyalty to one preclude loyalty to others? Does loyalty to one group necessarily enhance the possibility of group conflict because multiple loyalties cannot be held by the individual? Guetzkow's thesis appears to represent the positive side to the cross-pressures thesis noted above: cross-pressures mitigate against exclusive loyalties and hence reduce conflict potential; but, to the extent that multiple loyalties can be accommodated, mutually exclusive loyalties to different groups or values need not induce conflict within the individual and may foster intergroup collaboration.

The role of values in conflict analysis can be highlighted by a reminder that value incompatibility is, by definition, an element in conflict. Hence the examination of the respective values (preferred state of affairs, standards of conduct, criteria of choice among goals and actions, etc.) of opposing parties is inescapable. More specifically, ideological and religious conflict should be mentioned in this connection. Very often opposed values can be compromised or partially accommodated, but often they cannot. Ideological conflict may be marked by the fact that a basic value of one party (e.g., freedom of speech in a free society) requires the absolute denial of a basic value of another party (e.g., an official ideology in a totalitarian society). Religious conflict may be marked not only by a clash of ultimate values but by a commitment to conversion of those of different faith. Proposition 4 calls attention to the general problem of the relation between the claims of a faith or an ideology to define and regulate religious and political values and the intensity and resolution of conflict. In general, the more inclusive or broader the claim, the less susceptible is the conflict to some form of resolution. The conditions under which religious and other values tend to become inclusive or the conditions under which incompatible value commitments can be held without inducing conflictful behavior are thus extremely important.

2. Propositions 2, 4, 10, and 19 refer to traits shared by so many individual members of a group that the behavior of the group as a whole is alleged to reflect them. But none of them states anything about intraparty relations or the nature and degree of organization among individual members or components. Another dimension of party characteristics concerns these factors. These propositions, two of which have been cited previously, will illustrate:

PROPOSITION 43: Conflict between the Soviet Union and the United States is to be understood partly in terms of institutional rivalry (15, p. 31).

PROPOSITION 1: Intragroup harmony and solidarity reduce intergroup friction (24, p. 201).

PROPOSITION 9: Conflict with outgroups increases internal cohesion (12, p. 73).

PROPOSITION 44: Conflict between loosely organized groups (i.e., members are only peripherally involved in group activities or loyalty) is less intense (12, pp. 68–69).

PROPOSITION 45: As organizations become more bureaucratic, nonrealistic conflict decreases, induced conflict increases (26, p. 235).

PROPOSITION 46: Internal political structures which effectively channel and accommodate discontent are less likely to exhibit external aggressiveness (32, pp. 196–97).

The range of factors suggested is, of course, extensive, even in this small selected set of propositions. Perhaps the most critical point is obvious enough: There is a basic reciprocal functional relationship between the structure and internal dynamics of any group and intergroup conflict interaction. In analyzing these functional relationships, it is once again necessary to bear in mind that propositions will differ, depending on whether we are discussing unorganized individuals as comprising a group, leader-follower, or citizen–policy-maker relations; a heterogeneous political organization; a complex bureaucracy; a total political or social system; or a particular set of institutions. In the absence of additional research, it is difficult to tell whether there is a limited number of strategic aspects of intraparty organization which yield hypotheses of broad generality. At first glance, the existing literature seems to suggest at least three related aspects: (1) degree of internal cohesion and intimacy; (2) degree of centralization of internal control, including group representatives or a bureaucracy; and (3) degree and exclusiveness of commitment to group or organizational values.

Intraparty organization and relations may or may not contribute to either the inducement of conflict or its resolution and control. Familiar propositions fall roughly into two categories—positive and negative. Positive ones are associated with the general view of conflict as a fundamental interaction process which serves needed social functions. Negative ones stress the role of intraparty characteristics in the origin, intensification, and enlargement of conflict. Obviously, this reflects the fact that internal cohesion, centralization of control, and exclusiveness of commitment to group values may be empirically either functional or dysfunctional. On the one hand, for example, all three aspects are functional in the sense that clarification of opposed goals and mobilization of power are facilitated. On the other hand, dysfunctional consequences may follow—needless intensification, enhancement of non-realistic factors, and enlargement of conflict beyond the parties whose interests are really at stake.

What is more important, perhaps, is that the three aspects point to the "management of forces" which conflict requires. The quality of leadership and morale become significant in the instigation and maintenance of conflict relations. No analysis of social conflict would be adequate without due attention to leadership as a party characteristic. This is implied at several points in the foregoing scheme, particularly in connection with motivational elements and induced conflict. It is easier to grant the importance of leadership than to specify what an orderly and bounded inquiry would entail. Leadership is too ambiguous a concept. At a minimum, it would be desirable to formulate a set of leadership roles and role functions and to relate these to types, sources, context, conditions, and consequences of conflict.

One kind of leadership role might be that of the intellectual. Among other things, the intellectual leader is one who uses and creates ideas, and one consequence is to objectify conflict. Earlier we hypothesized that depersonalization or objectification tended to intensify conflict, to neutralize certain limits on modes of resolution. Joining these propositions and assuming each to be true to some extent, we emerge with a general hypothesis: *Effective intellectual leadership tends to intensify social conflict.* Empirical investigation would be required to confirm or refute this statement and to ascertain the conditions under which it holds. Provided that data are available, it would be interesting to compare conflict situations in which intellectual leadership was present with those in which it was either negligible or absent.

Another relevant internal characteristic of parties to conflict follows naturally from the discussion of management of conflict. Dubin has suggested the need for a typology of organizations and groups in terms of the centrality of conflict in their activities. Clearly, a conspiratorial group (e.g., the Communist party) or an organized interest group (e.g., the National Association of Manufacturers) is much more conflict-oriented than is a company like General Motors. One would expect that the former types would pay much more attention to the "management of forces" and to the relationship between internal organization and conflict interaction. In general, it might be expected that the more central conflict is to the operations of a group or organization, the more highly developed will be the techniques of conflict waging. For groups and organizations whose missions are not primarily conflict-directed, conflict avoidance or quicker resolution might be expected.

3. The size and strength of parties are two further dimensions. Implications of these gross variables may be in some sense obvious, but propositions embodying them are much less numerous. A well-known relationship between party size and conflict has been observed in the case of interethnic and interracial opposition. In general, it is said that, as a minority group increases in size, conflict is intensified or arises in the first instance. Where the Negro population is small relative to whites in southern communities, conflict over segregation is less intense. High intensity seems to be correlated with a 60–40 or near 50–50 ratio, though the exact numerical proportion has not been ascertained. Religious conflict appears less serious or nonexistent where, say, Protestants are almost completely surrounded by Catholics and vice versa. Rose argues that mediation increases the possibility of resolving conflict when the parties are small (33, p. 194). Coser observes that small parties tend to make themselves rigid and inelastic, to withstand pressure toward dissolution, and also tend to absorb the whole individual person in group commitment (12, p. 98). Hence smaller groups may en-

gage in more intense conflict relations and may be much more intransigent regarding resolution. The content or issues of conflict may be affected by group size: the larger the group, the lower the common denominator of group goals.

Party strength has several ramifications and is related to a fundamental property of conflict interaction already discussed, namely, the power relation. Paradoxically, the need for and accomplishment of a readjustment of power relations is both a source of conflict (21) and a function of conflict (17, p. 191). A further paradox is that in some cases the readjustment of power relations requires, or aims at, the complete destruction or crippling of an opposing party, and, in other cases, the weakening of one of the parties beyond a certain point is a distinct disadvantage to the other. Power is an object of conflict and a conditioner of conflict: Relative weaknesses may lead to conflict, and the comparative strength of parties will partially determine the new power relation which emerges from conflict. Previous distinctions will be helpful here, among them the differentiation of institutionalized and non-institutionalized conflict.

In the case of institutionalized conflict where continuity of interaction and regularized rules or expectations are essential, the conflicting parties have a vested interest in each other's strength (24, p. 201). There is considerable evidence that industrial conflict has become much more stabilized as unions have grown stronger. Proposition 8 (35, p. 337) above suggests that, as unions gain power, the duration of strikes is decreased. Furthermore, the enforcement of rules of conduct and mutual obligations which result from conflict interaction depend heavily on a minimum self-control (i.e., power to control internal decisions) by the two parties involved. In the case of non-institutionalized conflict, these considerations probably do not apply. Indeed, it may well be that it is precisely the lack of vested interest in continuity and stability which accounts for the instability and inconclusiveness of much non-institutionalized conflict.

Another facet of the party-strength factor relates to sources of conflict. This is epitomized in the following proposition already mentioned:

PROPOSITION 17: Changes in the relative power positions of nations are the source of tension leading to international conflict (9, p. 20).

Although applied to phenomena of international conflict, the proposition would appear to apply to most intergroup conflict, except perhaps where groups are unorganized individuals or where conflict is religious in nature. We should also draw a distinction between the recognized and the unrecognized power of groups, that is, a factual change in the power status of one party which is not accepted as a condition of interaction by an opposing party. As noted earlier, the establishment of recognized parties may be the key factor in the initial phase of conflict. Group weakness, on the other hand, may induce conflict where the capacity for enduring frustration of group wants or needs is low (4, pp. 215–16).

Obviously, one of the primary conditions of conflict interaction is the respective influence that two parties can bring to bear on each other in the attempt to control outcomes or otherwise direct behavior along intended lines. Factors range from the capacity to endure threatened deprivation to the capacity to inflict damage, from bargaining skill to flexibility of requirements. The central underlying problem is the identification and measurement of the bases of effective reciprocal influence in conflict interaction. More scholarly effort has been expended on the analysis of potential power and on the calculation of gross power factors available to conflicting parties than on the determination of why under particular conditions a bargain is closer to the desired optimum result of one party than the other, or why one party yields more control over joint decision-making to the other. Conflict analysis clearly joins another strategic focus of analysis—social power. Conceivably, the overemphasis on the more dramatic forms of conflict resolution, such as force or financial superiority, has tended to obscure this broader connection. This is an added reason for the explicit postulation of the significance of the power relation in social conflict.

4. Finally, we come to extraparty factors which affect the links between intraparty characteristics and conflict interaction. The concept of context is once again relevant. Three proposi-

tions, drawn from different areas of social conflict, will indicate the general point:

PROPOSITION 18: Religious intergroup conflict is most likely to develop and to be intense when there are no cross-pressures at work within the individual (10, p. 46).

PROPOSITION 47: To the extent that workers and unions are integrated into the general society, the propensity to strike is decreased (35, p. 337).

PROPOSITION 48: The higher the level of prosperity, the less intense the conflict between ethnic and racial majorities and minorities.

Proposition 18 implies that when individuals are affected by shared values which offset or run counter to religious values which put them into opposition with others, religious conflict will be less likely to develop. For example, the Catholic and Protestant businessmen who share certain goals and prescribed behaviors are less susceptible to conflict on religious grounds than are Catholics and Protestants who do not share these goals and behaviors. Proposition 47 states, in effect, that when parties to industrial conflict are accorded roughly equal status, privileges, and opportunities, there is a tendency to avoid violent conflict. Proposition 48, a very familiar thesis, calls attention to the fact that psychological mechanisms and opposed interests are unlikely under conditions where the majority group does not regard improvement in the status of a minority group as a direct threat to its access to material goods which are becoming scarcer because of a decline in economic activity.

One basic question concerning conflict at the group, society, and international levels is: What social arrangements conduce to non-violent or non-aggressive conflict? On the basis of present evidence, the answer is not at all clear. Another basic question concerns the relations of major social conflicts to one another. Williams (41, p. 531) has remarked on the canceling out or non-cumulative incidence of conflict in American society. Coser (12, pp. 68–69) has alerted us to the significance of the degree of individual involvement in a single conflict group. A hypothesis worth examining might be formulated as follows: *The larger the number of conflicts in any particular context, the less likely that any one will become all-inclusive with respect to persons, groups, energies, and resources.* Wright (44, pp. 202, 203) suggests, on the other hand, that there is a tendency for all international conflict to become total and absolute. Under what conditions is either or both true?

Summary

In the preceding section we have attempted to outline some of the major aspects of the problem of exploring connections between a set of typical characteristics of parties to conflict and the pattern of conflict interaction. It is essential to emphasize again that propositions which properly fall under this heading must be evaluated in the light of the conceptual elements set forth in Section III. Thus certain propositions are relevant for one type of conflict but not for others. Propositions bearing on the sources or functions of conflict will not necessarily apply to the conditions of conflict. Again, the unit of analysis may introduce significant qualifications for the range of empirical phenomena covered by a particular proposition. As discussed immediately above, the context of conflict gives rise to propositions. Therefore, there is good reason initially to take any proposition involving a party characteristic and conflict interaction and relate it systematically to types, units, contexts, functions, sources, or conditions of conflict. Finally, the breakdown of this section into number, establishment and identification, and characteristics of parties to conflict also offers another basis for classifying conflicts.

V. CONFLICT AS AN INTERACTION SYSTEM

Conflict has been characterized as a basic social-interaction process, and the tendency toward some degree of institutionalization has been noted. The conflict relation has been postulated as existing in a social context and as embodying a power component. Hence it is not a long step to viewing conflict as a system in the general sense employed by Boulding. Two elements of any conflict system—parties and issues—have been discussed, and a third—the power relation—has been touched upon at several points. In view of this background, we shall confine ourselves to a limited number of additional elements and to a short commentary on each. Various elements of conflict systems are, of course, related to one another and to factors mentioned earlier.

Modes of Resolution

There is a variety of methods for resolving or controlling conflict—many more than can be mentioned here. Arbitration, mediation (more often than not used synonymously with conciliation), negotiation, inquiry, legislation, judicial settlement, informal consensus (meeting of minds through discussion), the market, violence or force, authoritative command, and varieties of voting procedures are familiar ones. A range of techniques is implied in the phrase "intergroup therapy": interracial housing, co-operative living experiments, education for tolerance, interfaith movements, and so on. When "bargaining" and "negotiation" are not used in a specific technical sense, as in the case of collective bargaining in industry or diplomatic negotiation, these terms apply to many conflict situations. For each mode there are particular types—compulsory versus voluntary arbitration, conciliation recommendations which are not binding versus those which are, majority vote versus unanimity, and so on. Essentially, modes may be regarded as a set of rules for handling the need for resolution or accommodation. Different rules produce different results in different situations, and the rules themselves are a frequent conflict issue. Furthermore, some modes are appropriate for some conflict systems and not others. Voting between an equal number of representatives of labor and management would nearly always be indecisive, while arbitration is hardly a suitable mode of settlement for conflict among political parties. These trivial examples illustrate an important point, namely, that modes of resolution are fundamentally related to the nature of conflict. Evidence indicates that proposed modes of resolution are often inappropriate. Thus no amount of "better understanding through better communication" by itself is going to resolve a genuine power conflict. Mediation cannot function effectively if conflict is between unorganized groups, because mediation requires representatives who can speak authoritatively enough for each group that agreements become binding. At any rate, conflict systems can and should be characterized according to their predominant mode (or combination of modes) of resolution. Basically, Dahl and Lindblom have analyzed the handling of political and economic conflict in terms of basic social processes in their *Politics, Economics, and Welfare.*

Given the growing significance of interorganizational conflict or conflict between highly organized groups, mediation deserves special attention. This mode probably now dominates or is coming to dominate the area of collective bargaining and is becoming more frequent in the area of international relations. Experience has accumulated to the point where observers are beginning to generalize about it and to hypothesize the conditions under which it is or is not successful. The works of Rose (33) and Jackson (23), cited previously, exemplify this. Jackson has analyzed eight propositions which, he argues, hold for both industrial and international relations; two are repeated here:

PROPOISTION 49: Public debate is occasionally an aid in the mobilization of public interest, but extended public debate by the parties tends to harden their views.

PROPOSITION 50: Techniques for getting parties together on agreement, once mediation has started, are very similar in international and labor fields.

Such propositions must be evaluated in the light of similarities and differences between the two areas of conflict (23, pp. 119 ff.; 26, p. 235). However, it appears true that data have not been systematically related to the specified conditions under which mediation is successful, nor do we have a sufficient number of detailed case studies of the process. Nonetheless, there is substantial agreement among experts on the conditions of successful mediation. It is agreed on all sides that the personal qualifications and professional skills of the mediator are essential to mediation success. Something might be gained from a comparison of the model qualities of an industrial mediator, which can be found in the literature, with the attributes and skills of Dr. Ralph Bunche and Secretary-General Hammarskjöld, who have functioned effectively as mediators for the United Nations. The progress of mediation at the international level would seem to be heavily dependent on an available group of knowledgeable and trusted mediators. Experience with this problem within societies might be revealing for future developments in international organization. Moreover, Kerr's (26, p. 236) distinction between tactical and strategic mediation may be useful. Rather than being aimed at basic solutions to major issues, Kerr sees tactical mediation as resulting in reduced irrationality, removal of non-rational conflict elements, creation of possible new solutions, and assistance in the graceful retreat of parties from overly rigid positions. Various agencies and processes within the United Nations, many hidden from public view, should be examined as manifestations of tactical mediation. Observations based on industrial mediation (16, pp. 72 ff.) indicate definite phases to the conflict resolution process. The initial phase is likely to be one of strong language and positions of apparent inflexibility—a phase the layman is probably most familiar with and which he either mistakes for the general tenor of the whole process or assumes to be irrelevant. This spectacular phase, unless seen in the light of a sequential set of phases, may be very misleading. In more general terms, the ceremonial aspect of conflict resolution through mediation turns out to be functional, and its abolition, which many equate with the "solution" to conflict, would have serious consequences for the likelihood of eventual agreement. However, if conflict becomes entirely or predominantly ceremonial, complexity and rigidity of rules may be the reason (26, p. 236).

In considering conflict resolution, the distinction between violent (or aggressive) and non-violent modes provides another way of classifying systems. Wars, strikes, riots, armed rebellions, and physical assaults are all violent or aggressive modes. From many points of view the chief problem is to channel conflict resolution into non-violent, non-aggressive modes. Some writers blame the seriousness of human conflict on ultimate weapons available (1), and violent modes have been in some respects overemphasized as the essence of conflict systems. The overemphasis on violent modes has, of course, been a reflection of their cost, overtness, and dramatic impact, but it has had the effect of obscuring the relation between non-violent and violent modes, of inspiring superficial solutions, and of divorcing modes of resolution from the underlying nature of conflict interaction. A general hypothesis can be stated as follows: *The possibility of aggressive conflict or employment of violence tends to set a terminal point to controversy.* A related general hypothesis is: *The more destructive the means available to both parties to a conflict, the less likely is it that the ends for which conflict is waged can be served if such means are used.* At first glance, these tentative propositions may be an affront to the reader who is thinking of frequent wars and strikes and who reads and hears threats among superpowers possessing nuclear weapons. Obviously, these hypotheses imply important conditions and qualifications. The first implies a common interest in joint survival and some degree of functional interrelatedness between the parties. The second implies a rough equality of capacity to administer destruction and the absence of values which decree total elimination of one or both parties. Serious though these qualifications are, they help to sharpen the questions to be asked of empirical evidence.

Several familiar reminders are appropriate here. In the evolution from individual or group self-help to the monopoly of the instrumentalities of force in the hands of government, it is essential to note that violent modes of conflict settlement did not disappear but were *institutionalized,* i.e., their employment was subject to restrictive conditions and other modes of resolution were made available. The same thing can be said of strikes: as mediation and other modes of resolution of industrial conflict have grown in significance, the strike was *not* abolished but was related to the other modes in the collective-bargaining system in such a way as to curb its use without removing it as an incentive to agreement. It hardly seems likely that mediation could have developed if strikes had been abolished. Similarly, it may be seriously questioned whether international mediation would develop merely because nuclear weapons were abolished. Many disarmament solutions neglect the central function of violent modes: to make bargaining more conclusive and more effective. Attempts by conflicting parties to control violent modes can be interpreted as a recognition that the utility of aggressive conflict has become severely limited.

The necessity to relate the nature of conflict situations to modes of resolution can be seen in another connection. There is, of course, a substantial literature on bargaining generally and on effective strategies in "social games."[1] For the most part, attention is focused on descriptions of bargaining and games of strategy and on prescriptions for rational behavior where opposing parties are making choices under conditions of uncertainty. We should say in passing that, although this type of analysis employs formal mathematical or economic models which, as yet, have had relatively little empirical application to a wide range of social conflicts, very useful insights into the nature of conflict have been forthcoming. The title of H. Duncan Luce and Howard Raiffa's book is *Conflict, Collusion, and Conciliation*—a thorough discussion of what in our language we have called "modes of resolution" (i.e., solutions) for certain kinds of social conflicts or "games."[2] Propositions derived from game theoretical analysis can be used as guides to empirical research. However, the main point here is that, along with other key assumptions, it is assumed that bargaining can and should lead to an intersection of demands by parties to conflict such that both "win" (see Braithwaite, *Theory of Games as a Tool for the Moral Philosopher*), and there are strategies in social

[1]See, e.g., M. Shubik (ed.), *Readings in Game Theory and Political Behavior* (New York: Doubleday, 1954); J. D. Williams, *The Compleat Strategyst* (New York: McGraw-Hill Book Co., 1954); O. Morgenstern, "The Theory of Games," *Scientific American*, 180 (1949), 22 ff.; J. Bernard, "The Theory of Games as a Modern Sociology of Conflict," *American Journal of Sociology*, 59 (1954), 411–24; N. W. Chamberlain, *A General Theory of Economic Process* (New York: Harper & Row, 1955), chaps. 6–9.

[2]R. Duncan Luce and Howard Raiffa, *Games and Decisions: An Introduction to the Behavioral Models Project* (New York: Wiley, 1957)—Editor's note.

games which will yield optimum results (this may involve minimizing losses) to the opponents under given conditions. Psychologists, on the other hand, have been concerned with situations in which there is ambivalence toward alternative states of affairs or outcomes and in which conflict is intensified precisely because plus and minus values either do not cancel out or cannot be "resolved" by the choice of a particular value or combination of values. This suggests that value conflict, in the sense of ideological conflicts mentioned above, requires a different type of mode of resolution from those prescribed in bargaining strategies or game theory. For the latter kind of conflict, some sort of value integration seems required, that is, conflicting goal values are converted into instrumental values serving a superordinate goal value. For example, two independent nations may not be able to reach a mutually satisfactory trade bargain because any alternative point of mutually beneficial agreement may have other negatively valued (including non-economic adverse consequences) aspects. But, by organizing themselves into a single trade unit (economic union), trade relations may subserve a higher value, such as a more advantageous all-round division of labor between them or closer political ties.

We have only sketched some of the implications of modes of resolution for conflict systems. What is needed is a systematic comparison of the consequences of various modes with respect to types, sources, conditions, and functions of conflict. The next step is to test the applicability of resulting propositions across the major areas of social conflict.

Power Relations

In a previous section we discussed party strength as a factor in the general relationship between party characteristics and conflict interaction. Clearly, however, power is a relational concept, and it is the nature and distribution of power among the parties *and* relative to the issues of conflict which are significant. Accommodation to preconflict changes in comparative party strength and clarification of mutual control over decisions have also been established as functions of the conflict relation. Thus the power-relations component of any conflict system consists of the respective bases of effective influence on which the parties can operate *and* the allocation of control over decisions which occur during the interaction. There seems to be no inherent reason why, empirically, the bases of influence and distribution of control over behavioral choices cannot be identified and measured with some degree of precision whether the parties are unorganized groups or individuals or bureaucracies. As remarked previously, this task is not easy, and such knowledge as we have has not been codified in these terms.

If we can assume for a moment that power relations have been at least crudely defined, two characteristic patterns might serve to differentiate conflict systems: (1) *diffuseness* and *specificity* and (2) *stability* and *instability*. In most situations it is likely that these concepts represent a continuum rather than mutually exclusive polar opposites. Diffuseness-specificity implies a distinction between a system characterized by a broad range of effective bases of influence and ambiguity of control over decisions, as against a system embodying a narrow range of effective bases of influence and definite prescriptions for control over decisions. This dimension appears to be related to other variables—the number of parties and internal organization. Interracial or interethnic conflict would appear, in general, to manifest multiple parties and lack of centralized relations within parties. Face-to-face relations among parties are likely to cover a number of life-situations and hence to offer several possible influence relationships. In contrast, labor-management conflict is predominantly characterized by centralized interaction and formal allocation of decision-making power.

An unstable power relation is one in which no durable resolution of power conflicts or establishment of regular joint decision-making patterns is possible (or has been achieved) and/or in which there is no accepted means of measuring the power balance. The perishable nature of coalitions is probably related to the difficulty of stabilizing power relations under certain conditions. Instability accompanies shifting agenda of issues, i.e., the relationship must accommodate a large number of issues generally unpredictable in advance and rapid changes in internal characteristics of parties. When the bases of effective influence are primarily of a subtle psychological kind rather than force or economic bargaining, indexes of power are difficult to determine. This seems to be true of, say, party conflict in the French Chamber of Deputies and of contemporary international politics.

What are the implications of the power factor for the problem of resolution and control of conflict? For one thing, to the extent that the function of conflict is the clarification and stabilization of power relations, modes of resolution which omit or cannot basically affect these relations are likely to be ineffective (35). It is not only that opposed goals are at stake in conflict situations but that control over the choices governing alternative goals and means is also at stake. "Human-relations" approaches which attempt exclusively to create a sense of common goals while bypassing the joint decision-making phase may therefore be wide of the mark in many situations.

The difficulty of estimating power in advance of a concrete test is undoubtedly a major obstacle in preventing conflict or in reducing the likelihood of extreme conflict (12, p. 35). Hence the problem of social conflict resolution may be viewed in a dual aspect: The necessity to devise advance measurements of power outcomes and the substitution of small-scale (i.e., discussion or vote) methods for large-scale (i.e., a strike or war) methods in trials of power. In effect, the parties to conflict need to know beforehand whether a better decision can be reached via one mode of resolution than by another. A straw vote, an advisory court opinion, and a mediation process are all examples of ways of avoiding premature or mistaken trials whose possibly adverse consequences cannot be avoided, once they occur. Misinformation or guesses concerning conflict outcomes tend to result in situations in which all parties lose or in which interaction is completely disrupted and therefore must be painfully re-established. No one knows how often parties to conflict have allowed themselves to be boxed in and driven to actions they themselves acknowledged to be undesirable.

Despite the universal common-sense recognition of the need

for face-saving and graceful retreats when ultimate tests of power are bound to be adverse or inconclusive, we know little about the effective detection and accommodation of this stage in a conflict interaction. In areas of disorganized social conflict typified by diffuse and unstable power relations, the possibility of dysfunctional interaction is much greater, especially in the case of unrealistic conflict.

Nature and Degree of Institutionalization

The foregoing comments lead to another dimension of conflict systems. Institutionalization of conflict generally means continuity of interaction; regularized procedures for handling changes in conditions, goals, and power; interdependence of parties; and the creation of new norms (24). Out of institutionalized conflict come new social policies. As conflict is partially resolved at various stages through time, certain issues disappear, and a common law governing formerly disputed matters is built up. Ways of measuring power relations and correcting imbalances without aggressive conflict or violence are developed. Institutionalization requires the combination of conflict and co-operation, since rules and procedures cannot function in the absence of voluntary obedience or enforcement through sanctions (29, p. 17). Even war, the ultimate in conflict, is co-operative to the extent necessary to permit communication between enemies and administration of mutually advantageous rules. Thus the frequent rigid dichotomy between harmony and opposition, co-operation and conflict, is very misleading. As Sumner pointed out, co-operation can be antagonistic and can result from bribed interdependence. In any event, institutionalized conflict and co-operation go together. Co-operation does not imply an absence of conflict or vice versa.

Non-institutionalized conflict or conflict interaction having a low degree of institutionalization is marked by chronic recurrence of unsettled issues, by an absence of agreed procedures for review of relations, and by discontinuity of interaction or drastic shifts in the mode of resolution. This type of system is correlated, if not causally linked, with diffuse and unstable power relations. Hypothetically, a higher degree of institutionalization is similarly linked to more specific and stable power relations. A general hypothesis, which could be tested empirically, is: *The higher the degree of institutionalization, the greater the consistency and balance of strength of the parties to conflict.* The pressures of functional interdependence between parties and the need to preserve predictable conflict relations result in modes of resolution which stop short of the complete destruction or crippling of one of the parties. Indeed, it is no accident that wars, for example, seem to be terminated while there is still an entity for the victor to deal with, some minimal organization to make possible a new formulation of the now altered power relation.

There are noteworthy differences in the nature of institutionalization of conflict. The conflict relation may be autonomous in the sense that the parties voluntarily establish an informal social control of their interactions. Or a conflict relation may be regulated by legal norms enforced from outside the conflict system. Industrial collective bargaining in Great Britain is an expression of the former and collective bargaining in the United States is an expression of the latter. International conflict is for the most part a mixture, with predominant emphasis on autonomy. The growth and success of industrial bargaining suggest that the appropriate social context of conflict can permit autonomous conflict resolution as exemplified by experience in Great Britain.

Another pattern of institutionalization relates to centralization and decentralization of conflict systems. In general, political institutionalization is centralized with respect to some area of jurisdiction (or political unit), while the institutionalization of economic conflict, in free societies at least, is more decentralized. Centralized institutionalization of conflict is exemplified by national legislation, a local ordinance binding on all members of the community, or by an authoritative Supreme Court decision. Decentralized institutionalization is exemplified by the market. Hence social policies which accommodate conflicting goals, demands, and needs may evolve from a central decision-making agency which lays down rules and determines power relations or from the cumulative impact of a number of separate bargains whether between individuals or firms or between consumers and producers. One of the most familiar and persistent problems of political economy is, of course, the relative merits of these two general patterns of conflict systems. Progressive income taxation and redistribution of purchasing power through sliding-scale wage or income provisions represent two different approaches to one aspect of social welfare.

There is good reason to assume, in the absence of strong evidence to the contrary, a persistent tendency toward institutionalization of social conflict. From the foregoing, three directions of this tendency can be inferred. First, particular institutionalization for particular kinds of conflict may evolve. Second, institutionalization may be based on the support of existing machinery in the social context outside a given conflict system. Third, these two patterns may be combined. Conflict which is essentially disorganized, unrealistic, characterized by diverse modes of resolution, diffuse and unstable power relations, and, on balance, more dysfunctional than functional, tends to lead to institutionalization through mechanisms operating in the social context—usually a centralized institution. Conflict which manifests the opposite properties tends to lead to autonomous, decentralized, and more particularistic institutionalization. Racial conflict would probably fall into the first category and industrial conflict clearly into the second. The conditions leading to a combination are not immediately clear. Presumably, the general character of the culture and social organization would be controlling, but such a statement is not very specific. A major subject for inquiry is the set of factors which affect the degree and form of institutionalization.

It is difficult to escape the conviction that the resolution and control of social conflict are intimately related to the nature and degree of institutionalization. Superficially, it would appear that conflict relations are functional and stable (i.e., predictable and subject to semiautomatic adjustment to new conditions) to the extent that *appropriate* institutionalization exists. The fact that wars and strikes are institutionalized in an important sense in no way undercuts the argument that it is the institutionalization of other modes and the relationship of various modes within an institutional framework which are crucial.

Direct, Unmediated Systems Versus Mediated Representational Systems

Another aspect of conflict systems which can be analytically differentiated is closely bound up with the previous dimension. Again, intuitive observation suggests a sizable difference between much interpersonal and unorganized group conflict, on the one hand, and organized intergroup or interorganizational conflict, on the other. The model for the latter, which would cover a large sector of social conflict, can be indicated briefly:

1. The relationships among two sets of representatives or bargainers and the relationships among each set of bargainers or representatives
   a) The values and perceptions of the representatives or bargainers
2. The nature of the membership or constituency represented
   a) The values and perceptions of the memberships
   b) Degree of unity and kinds of relations among members
3. The relationship between representatives or bargainers and the membership or constituency
   a) Nature and consequences of authority relationship
   b) Nature and function of leadership
4. The role of the mediator or mediating agencies (if present)
   a) Qualities and effectiveness of mediation
   b) Relationship of mediating function to the social context
5. Interrelation of bargaining or representational system to social context
   a) Institutional links (e.g., sanctions)
   b) Non-institutional links (e.g., interested publics)

This model, though highly general and though it includes no basis for deriving links among the five sets of variables, does offer a possibly fruitful method of organizing and classifying propositions which then could be connected in the description and explanation of a conflict system which conformed to the underlying assumptions. Furthermore, direct unmediated systems could be analyzed in terms of the presence or absence of the five components. Nor is there any reason why the other characteristics of conflict systems discussed above could not be incorporated in the model as well as the party characteristics, also discussed above. It should be noted that the model is not restricted to formal mediation as a mode of resolution. If non-institutionalization and institutionalization imply a continuum, then the closer to the non-institutionalization end a particular system is, the less likely is the system to conform to the specifications of the model.

System Limitations and Boundaries

Finally, we come to the limitations on conflict, a subject best left to this point because so much of what has been said bears on it. Since conflict has been so often associated with social instability, waste, destruction, random outbursts of violence, and long-drawn-out struggles, it is easy to equate conflict with a breakdown of control or to underestimate its limits. But social conflict behavior is rarely, if ever, random and without limitations.

One of the properties of any system is that it is boundary-maintaining. That is, for the purposes at hand, an observer can usually discover empirical distinctions between the related parts which comprise the system and other phenomena which are either unrelated or, from the observer's standpoint, unimportant. Thus the parties to conflict and the conflict interaction (including its components) can be empirically separated from what was earlier called the "social context." The social context consists of non-system factors which the observer *does* think are important. Apart from system boundaries (or limits) in this sense, the other meaning of limitation on conflict concerns those factors (inside or outside the system) which tend to affect the intensity, duration, enlargement, and mode of resolution of the conflict interaction process. As presented by Boulding, the proper way to connect system and non-system boundaries and limitations is by a concept of an "open system," i.e., one which is characterized by internal changes in relationships among constituent parts *and* one which is susceptible to influences from outside its boundaries. Implicitly, at least, many propositions on conflict are based on a closed system or on an ever expanding system or on a system which manifests only disequilibrium as its essential property. There is ground for distrusting all three as approaches to the study of conflict.

Major limitations on conflict can be listed briefly. Intrasystem limits are (1) functional interdependence between parties, (2) regulation through institutionalized norms and procedures, (3) the need for continued communication between parties, (4) conflict cost, (5) availability and feasibility of certain modes of resolution, (6) inertia and organizational inefficiency of parties, (7) ignorance or misunderstanding, and (8) avoidance taboos. Most of these are self-evident on the basis of the preceding discussion. Thus the implications of conflict cost as a limitation on conflict are rather obvious. It may be that some conflict systems have as their outstanding feature the desire of one or both parties to inflict maximum disorder on the conflict relationship —subversion or a rebellion would be examples. Nonetheless, in conflict systems having predominantly highly institutionalized non-violent modes of resolution, there is a limit on tolerable disorder. The restoration of order following a disruption of normal interaction places a burden on each party. The contractual spacing of conflict resolution, e.g., a one-year or more union-management agreement, confirms this natural limitation. Even during a steel strike, a union will assign some of its members to keeping open-hearth furnaces banked.

The last three limitations have not been mentioned before. Party weakness has been mentioned as a source of conflict under some conditions, but inertia and organizational inefficiency may also limit conflict. Many social conflicts become less intense or die out altogether because one or both parties simply run out of sustained drive. Conflict relations may be emotionally satisfying and substantively rewarding, but they are also burdensome. Sustained conflict, if vigorously waged, puts a great premium on energy and resources, neither of which is unlimited in supply. Ignorance and misunderstanding are normally cited as sources and conditioners of conflict. However, it is not always recognized that these same factors may also prevent or minimize conflict. How much more conflict would there be if individuals and groups really thoroughly and correctly understood each other's motives, words, and deeds? Kerr argues (26, p. 233): "In fact, misunderstanding and the misuse of words have probably made a substantial contribution to industrial peace." Diplomatic language, often dismissed as double talk, makes possible "planned misunderstandings" which keep tensions down and provide opportunity for clarification prior to ultimate or aggressive measures. Avoidance taboos, a term mostly employed by social anthropologists, denote behavioral restraints which have not been broadly examined as a limiting factor in conflict. Everyone is aware of "things which are just not said or done," regardless of provocation. Such restraints, if operative at enough key junctures of interpersonal and intergroup relations, may be a much more powerful limitation on conflict than is realized. Religious conflict in the contemporary United States is undoubtedly restrained by avoidance taboos.

Limitations arising outside any conflict system can be classified as follows: (1) shared cultural and social values which neutralize or dominate conflicting values; (2) institutional sanctions against certain kinds of power relations and modes of resolution; (3) third parties interested in control or resolution; (4) crisscrossing of other conflict systems which prevents enlargement or bipolarization around any single system; and (5) "cross-pressures" which create ambivalences within parties.

To the extent that there are "natural limits" to conflict, the lesson for the problem of resolution and control would seem to be this: *Social strategies designed to keep conflict functional and to prevent violent or aggressive conflict ought to be based in part on deliberate attempts to capitalize on natural limits.* This may involve giving up notions of "abolishing" conflict, of "final" resolutions, and may direct attention to less obvious control devices. Avoidance taboos, for example, may be easier to inculcate and enforce than centralized political controls.

Clarification and invigoration of existing common values may be more feasible than finding formulae for reconciling some conflicting values.

Summary

Counting parties and issues, seven properties of conflict systems have been outlined. Aside from providing categories to locate and relate descriptive and causal propositions, this part of the analytic framework has other potential uses. Given a particular conflict system and given X empirical content of categories 1 through 7, an observer might be able to hypothesize about the sources, conditions, functions, context, and type of conflict. Or, for example, if there are multiple parties (category 1), if the issue is one of political power (category 2), if power relations are diffuse and unstable (category 3), if the conflict is relatively non-institutionalized (category 5), if the conflict is direct and immediate (category 6), and if limitations (internal and external) are either absent or minimal, then an observer might predict a violent mode of resolution (category 4).

VI. CONCLUSION

When all is said and done, there is no substitute for more reliable and systematic knowledge produced by soundly conceived and executed research. The kind of analysis attempted here can aid in posing significant questions, in exposing areas of ignorance, and in generating testable hypotheses. Furthermore, an explicit framework provides a way of codifying existing unfunded common-sense knowledge and research findings. We also feel that detailed studies will be more cumulative if it is possible to compare meaningfully cases and situations from a wide range of social conflicts. Meanwhile, the search for a limited number of major variables, the formulation of bold hypotheses, cross-field generalizations, and typification have their place in conflict analysis.

REFERENCES

1. Andrzejewski, S. *Military Organization and Society.* London: Routledge, 1954.
2. Bernard, Jessie. *Journal of Conflict Resolution,* 1 (1957), 111.
3. Bernard, Jessie. "Where Is the Modern Sociology of Conflict?" *American Journal of Sociology,* 56 (1950), 11–16.
4. Boasson, C. "The Relevance of Research to the Problems of Peace." In *Research for Peace,* pp. 215–216. Oslo: Institute for Social Research, 1954.
5. Boulding, K. "Economic Issues in International Conflict," *Kyklos,* 6 (1953), 99–115.
6. Center for Research on World Political Institutions. Publication No. 4. Princeton: Princeton University, 1955.
7. Chase, S. *Roads to Agreement.* New York: Harper & Row, 1951.
8. Chein, I. "Research Needs," *Journal of Social Issues,* 12 (1956), 57–66 (for an appraisal of the lack of knowledge concerning religious conflict).
9. Chertok, E. "Sources of International Tension," *Bulletin of the Research Exchange on the Prevention of War,* 3 (1955), No. 17.
10. Coleman, J. "Social Cleavage and Religious Conflict," *Journal of Social Issues,* 12 (1956), 45.
11. Cooper, J. B. "Psychological Literature on the Prevention of War," *Bulletin of the Research Exchange on the Prevention of War,* 3 (1955), 2–15.
12. Coser, L. *The Functions of Social Conflict.* Glencoe, Ill.: Free Press, 1956.
13. Cottrell, W. F. "Research To Establish Conditions for Peace," *Journal of Social Issues,* 11 (1955), 13–20.
14. Dahlke, O. "Race and Minority Riots: A Study in the Typology of Violence," *Social Forces,* 30 (1952), 420.
15. Davis, A. K. "Conflict between Major Social Systems," *Social Forces,* 30 (1951), 31.
16. Douglas, A. "The Peaceful Settlement of Industrial and Intergroup Conflict," *Journal of Conflict Resolution,* 1 (1957), 72 ff.
17. Dubin, R. "Industrial Conflict and Social Welfare," *Journal of Conflict Resolution,* 1 (1957), 179–199.
18. Farber, M. "Psychoanalytic Hypotheses in the Study of War," *Journal of Social Issues,* 11 (1955), 33.
19. Frazier, E. F. *Race and Culture Contacts in the Modern World.* New York: Knopf, 1957.
20. Freeman, F. D. "Theory and Strategy of Action in Race Relations," *Social Forces,* 30 (1951), 86.

21. Glock, C. Y. "Issues That Divide: A Postscript," *Journal of Social Issues*, 12 (1956), 40.
22. Hager, D. J. "Introduction: Religious Conflict," *Journal of Social Issues*, 12 (1956), 3–11.
23. Jackson, E. *Meeting of Minds*. New York: McGraw-Hill, 1952.
24. Kahn-Freund, D. "Intergroup Conflicts and Their Settlement," *British Journal of Sociology*, 5 (1954), 201.
25. Kecskemeti, P. *Meaning, Communication, and Value*. Chicago: University of Chicago Press, 1952.
26. Kerr, C. "Industrial Conflict and Its Mediation," *American Journal of Sociology*, 60 (1954), 230.
27. Klineberg, O. *Tensions Affecting International Understanding*. New York: Social Science Research Council, 1950.
28. Kluckhohn, C. "Values and Value-Orientations in the Theory of Action: An Exploration in Definition and Classification." In Parsons, Talcott, and Shils, E. A. (eds.), *Toward a General Theory of Action*. 1951.
29. Kornhauser, A., Dubin, R., and Ross, A. M. *Industrial Conflict*. New York: McGraw-Hill, 1954.
30. Lockwood, D. "Some Remarks on 'the Social System,'" *British Journal of Sociology*, 7 (1956), 134–145.
31. Parsons, T. "Certain Primary Sources and Patterns of Agression in the Social Structure of the Western World." In Bryson, L., *et al.*, *Conflicts of Power in Modern Culture*. 1947.
32. Rickman, J. "Psychodynamic Notes," In Cantril, H. (ed.), *Tensions That Cause Wars*. 1950.
33. Rose, A. "Needed Research on the Mediation of Labor Disputes," *Personnel Psychology*, 5 (1952), 196–199.
34. Rose, A. M., and Rose, C. B. "Intergroup Conflict and Its Mediation," *International Social Science Bulletin*, 6 (1954), 25.
35. Sheppard, H. "Approaches to Conflict in American Sociology," *British Journal of Sociology*, 5 (1954), 324–342.
36. Simpson, G. *Conflict and Community: A Study in Social Theory*. New York: T. S. Simpson, 1937.
37. Singer, K. "Resolution of Conflict," *Social Research*, 6 (1949), 230.
38. Sorensen, R. C. "The Concept of Conflict in Industrial Sociology," *Social Forces*, 29 (1951), 263–67.
39. Williams, R. M., Jr. *The Reduction of Intergroup Tensions*. New York: Social Science Research Council, 1947.
40. Williams, R. M., Jr. "Religion, Value-Orientations, and Intergroup Conflict," *Journal of Social Issues*, 12 (1956), 15.
41. Williams, R. M., Jr. *American Society*. New York: Knopf, 1950.
42. Wright, Q. *A Study of War*. 2 vols. Chicago: University of Chicago Press, 1942.

43. Wright, Q. "Criteria for Judging the Relevance of Researches on the Problems of Peace." In *Research for Peace*, pp. 68–82. Olso: Institute for Social Research, 1954.
44. Wright, Q. "The Nature of Conflict," *Western Political Quarterly*, 4 (1951), 198.

ROBERT R. BLAKE
JANE SRYGLEY MOUTON

The Fifth Achievement

A great new challenge to the American way of conducting its national life is taking shape. Conformity with older patterns is breaking down. Yet creative definitions of new patterns are not forthcoming, or at best are coming at a snail's pace. Unless the challenge of finding new patterns that can serve to strengthen society is successfully met, some of the nation's most cherished human values may very well be sacrificed. If we can meet it, however, our deeply embedded beliefs as to the role of men in society may not only be reinforced but may find even richer and more extensive applications in the society of tomorrow.

What is this challenge?

We widely acknowledge the objective of an open and free society based on individual responsibility and self-regulated participation by all in the conduct of national life. That men will differ in the ways they think and act is accepted as both inevitable and desirable. Indeed, this is one hallmark of an open society. Differences are intrinsically valuable. They provide the rich possibility that alternatives and options will be discovered

Reproduced by special permission from *The Journal of Applied Behavioral Science*, "The Fifth Achievement," Robert R. Blake and Jane Srygley Mouton 6, 1970, 413–426, copyright 1970 by NTL Institute for Applied Behavioral Science.

for better and poorer ways of responding to any particular situation. Preserving the privilege of having and expressing differences increases our chances of finding "best" solutions to the many dilemmas that arise in living. They also add the spice of variety and give zest to human pursuits.

When it is possible for a man to make a choice from among several solutions, and when he can make this choice without infringing upon another man's freedom or requiring his cooperation, there is genuine autonomy. This is real freedom.

But in many situations not every man can have his own personal solution. When cooperation and coordination are required in conducting national life—in government, business, the university, agencies of the community, the home, and so on—differences that arise must find reconciliation. A solution must be agreed upon and embraced which can provide a pattern to which those involved are prepared to conform their behavior. Yet efforts to reconcile differences in order to achieve consensus-based patterns of conduct often only serve to promote difficulties. When disagreements as to sound bases for action can be successfully resolved, freedom can be retained and necessary solutions implemented. Dealing with the many and varied misunderstandings that are inevitable in a society dedicated to preserving the privilege of having and expressing differences is the challenge. As individuals, we find this hard to do. As members of organized groups, we appear to find it even more difficult.

FOUR CLASSICAL SOLUTIONS FOR RESOLVING CONFLICTS

In the conduct of society there are at least four major and different kinds of formal, structural arrangements which we rely on for resolving differences. They are the scientific method; politics; law, with its associated police powers; and organizational hierarchy.

Of undisputed value in finding the objective solution to which agreement can readily be given are the methods of science. A well-designed experiment confirms which of several alternatives is the most valid basis of explanation while simultaneously demonstrating the unacceptability of the remaining explanations.

Our political mechanisms are based on the one-man-one-vote approach to problem solving. This provides for the resolution of differences according to a weighting approach, and the basis is usually that the majority prevail. By this means, decisions can be made and actions taken even though differences may remain. Simply being outvoted, however, does not aid those on the losing side in changing their intellectual and emotional attitudes. While it ensures that a solution is chosen, the fact that it is often on a win-lose or a compromise basis may pose further problems when those who are outvoted resolve to be the winners of the future. Often the underlying disagreements are deepened.

Legal mechanisms apply only in resolving differences when questions of law are involved and other means of reaching agreement usually have met with failure. With application of associated police powers, the use of force is available to back up legal mechanisms when law is violated. But this constitutes a far more severe solution to the problem. The ultimate failure of law which invites the use of military power is in effect a court of last resort.

Within society's formal institutions such as business, government, education, and the family, organizational hierarchy, or rank, can and does permit the resolution of differences. The premise is that when a disagreement arises between any two persons of differing rank, the one of higher rank can impose a solution unilaterally based on his position. In the exercise of authority, suppression may also sacrifice the validity of a solution, since there is no intrinsic basis of truth in the idea that simply because a man is the boss of other men he is ordained with an inherent wisdom. While this arrangement provides a basis for avoiding indecision and impasse, it may and often does have the undesirable consequence of sacrificing the support of those to whom it is applied for the solution of the problem, to say nothing of its adverse effects on future creativity.

These classical solutions to dealing with differences—science, politics, law, and hierarchy—represent real progress in learning to conduct the national life. Where it can be applied, scientific method provides a close to ideal basis for resolving differences. That politics, courts of justice, and organizational hierarchy, though more limited, are necessary is indisputable. But that they are being questioned and increasingly rejected is also indisputable. Even if they were not, none of these alone nor all of them together provide a sound and sufficient basis for the development of a truly problem-solving society.

WHAT IS THE FIFTH ACHIEVEMENT?

There is another essential ingredient. It is a sharply increased understanding by every man of the roots of conflict and the human skills of gaining the resolution of differences. The acquisition of such insight and skill by every man could provide a social foundation for reaching firm and sound understandings on a direct man-to-man basis of the inevitable disagreements that arise in conducting the national life. This kind of deepened skill in the direct resolution of differences could do much to provide a realistic prospect that the antagonisms, cleavages, or injustices real and imagined in society today can be reduced if not eliminated. It offers the promise that the sicknesses of alienation and apathy, the destructive aggressions, and the organization-man mentality can be healed.

The *fifth achievement,* then, is in the establishment of a problem-solving society where differences among men are subject to resolution through insights that permit protagonists themselves to identify and implement solutions to their differences upon the basis of committed agreement. That men ultimately will be able to work out, face to face, their differences is a hoped-for achievement of the future. Extending their capacity to do so could reduce the number of problems brought before the bench or dealt with through hierarchy. At the same time, scientific and political processes could be strengthened if progress were made in this direction. Even more important, it could perhaps lead to the resolution of many conflicts on a local level that block the development of a creative and committed problem-solving community. Success in meeting this challenge in the period ahead is perhaps the surest way to preserve and strengthen the values of a free society while protecting and even strengthening the privilege of having and expressing differences.

HOW TO INCREASE SKILL IN MANAGING CONFLICT

Why do men rely on these other four approaches to conflict settlement while placing lower value on the resolution of differences in a direct, man-to-man way? One explanation for this might be that they do not hold in concert a conceptual basis for analyzing situations of disagreement and their causes. It should be said that conceptual understanding, while necessary for strengthening behavior, is clearly not in itself a sufficient basis for learning the skills of sound resolution of conflict. Personal entrapment from self-deception about one's motivations is too great. Insensitivity about one's behavior and the reactions of others to it is too extensive. To connect a conceptual analysis to one's own behavior and conduct in ways that permit insight and change seems to require something more in the way of personal learning.

Classroom learning methodologies that could enable men to gain insights regarding conflict and acquire skills for resolving it seem to be impoverished. To aid men in acquiring both the conceptual understanding for managing conflict and the skills to see their own reactions in situations of conflict, man-to-man feedback seems to be an essential condition. A variety of situations involving laboratory learning that permit this have been designed (Bach & Wyden, 1969; Blake & Mouton, 1968; Bradford, Gibb, & Benne, 1964; Schein & Bennis, 1965). They set the stage for men to learn to face their differences and find creative and valid solutions to their problems.

Success in mastering this fifth achievement will undoubtedly require reconception of the classroom in ways that permit the study of conflict as a set of concepts and the giving and receiving of feedback in ways that enable men to see how to strengthen their own capacities and skills for coping with it directly.

Conceptual Analysis of Conflict

This paper concentrates upon a first step toward this Fifth Achievement by presenting a conceptual basis for analyzing situations of conflict. The *conflict grid* in Figure 1 is a way of identifying basic assumptions when men act in situations where differences are present, whether disagreement is openly expressed or silently present (Blake & Mouton, 1964; Blake, Shepard, & Mouton, 1964).

Whenever a man meets a situation of conflict, he has at least two basic considerations in mind. One of these is the *people* with whom he is in disagreement. Another is *production of results*, or getting a resolution to the disagreement. It is the amount and kind of emphasis he places on various combinations of each of these elements that determine his thinking in dealing with conflict.

Basic attitudes toward people and toward results are visualized on nine-point scales. These form the grid in Figure 1. The nine-point scale representing concern for producing a result provides the horizontal axis for the grid. The phrase "concern for" does not show results produced but rather denotes the degree of emphasis in his thinking that the man places on getting results. The 1 end represents low concern, and the 9 represents the highest possible concern. The same applies on the vertical or concern-for-people axis. Considering the interactions of these two scales, there are 81 possible positions. Each describes an intersection between the two dimensions.

The following pages discuss strategies of managing conflict according to the five basic theories—those appearing at the four corners and the center of the figure. When these basic styles are understood, one can predict for each how a man operating under that style is likely to handle conflict. There are eight additional important theories composed from various mixtures of these five, but basic issues of conflict resolution can be seen in dealing with these "pure" theories.

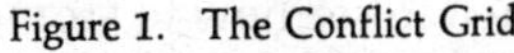
Figure 1. The Conflict Grid

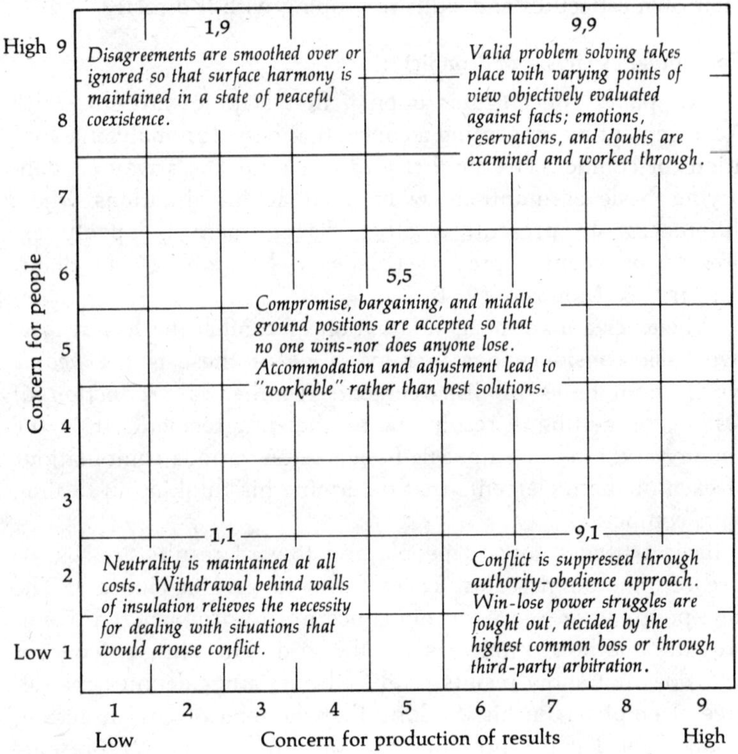

No one style is exclusively characteristic of one man in comparison with another, although one style may be dominant in a man's actions. Furthermore, even though one may be dominant for a time, it may be abandoned and replaced by another when the first has been ineffective in achieving resolution.

What are some of the ways of dealing with conflict?

Conflict can be controlled by overpowering it and suppressing one's adversary (9,1 in the lower right corner of the grid). An ultimate expression of this is in the extremes of police power and military action. Extracting compliance by authority-obedience is possible when rank is present. The conflict can be cut off and suppressed in this way, "Yours not to question why!" When rank is not available, a win–lose basis expresses the same set of assumptions. Winning for one's own position predominates over seeking a valid solution.

Another strategy is to smooth conflict by cajolery, by letting a man know that with a little patience he will find that all is right (1,9 in the upper left corner). The assumption of sweetness and light often leads to resolution by people's retracting from previously held positions, preferring personal acceptance to solution validity. This can promote accord and harmony, but it sacrifices conviction and insight into differences, while decreasing the likelihood of achieving valid solutions. Staying out of situations that provoke controversy or turning away from topics that promote disagreement represents a set of assumptions about how to live in a conflict-free way (1,1 in the lower left corner). Then one need not be stirred up even though the issue may need resolution. A man can remain composed if he does not let himself be drawn into controversy; he avoids it by remaining neutral. This kind of "see no disagreement, hear no disagreement, and speak no disagreement" represents a withdrawal from social responsibility in a world where the resolution of differences is key to finding sound solutions. It is the ultimate in alienation.

A third set of assumptions leads to a middle-of-the-road solution to differences through accommodation and adjustment. Disagreement is settled through bargaining a compromise solution (5,5). The assumptions underlying compromising of one's convictions are at the root of this approach. It means agreeing so as to be agreeable, even to sacrificing sound action; settling for what you can get rather than working to get what is sound in the light of the best available facts and data.

The mental attitude behind the one-man-one-vote approach often leads to the endorsement of positions calculated to get majority support even though this means giving up a solution of deeper validity. The same assumptions often prevail behind the scenes in out-of-court settlements.

Outside the sphere of industrial management, solutions to

major political and international problems of recent years provide classic examples of 5,5 splitting. One is the "separate but equal" approach to solving what is seen as the race problem. The cessation of hostilities in Korea by the establishment of the thirty-eighth parallel as a line of demarcation between North and South in the early Fifties is another. This set a precedent for setting up the "Demilitarized Zone" between North and South Vietnam. The Berlin Wall is probably the most significant symbol of the East-West split. The 5,5 attitude is reflected daily by news reporters and commentators who quote "unidentified but high-level sources" or hide their sources by attributing their facts merely to "usually reliable sources."

Under a 9,9 approach, disagreement is valued as an inevitable result of the fact that strong-minded people have convictions about what is right. A man says, "Nothing is sacrosanct. What are the facts? What are the causes? What are the conclusions?" Reservations and emotions that interrupt agreement based on logic and data are confronted through candid discussion of them directly with the person involved in the disagreement. Insight and resolution are possible but involve maturity and real human skill. This approach may be time-consuming in the short run but time-conserving over the long term. It permits men to disagree, to work out their disagreements in the light of facts, and ultimately to understand one another. Such problem-solving constructiveness in conflict situations is the fundamental basis for realizing the fifth achievement.

Conflict, Conformity, and Creative Problem Solving

How does effective conflict management interrelate with other social processes of seemingly equal or greater significance in strengthening society? Indeed, it might be maintained that the challenge to society seen today is in nonconformity with its norms, rather than in faulty management of conflict.

In what ways are conflict and conformity interdependent (Blake & Mouton, 1961)? Men in everyday life do conform to the expectations of others and the patterns of their institutions. This readiness to conform reduces conflict and is what permits regularity, order, and predictability. To adhere to common norms provides a basis for organized effort. From conformity with conventionalized social and organizational practices can come a sense of identification, belonging, and *esprit de corps.* On the other hand, failure to conform may stir conflict with one's colleagues and associates so that the nonconformist is rejected. Indeed, anxiety about rejection can be so overwhelming that, for many, conformity becomes an end in itself rather than a means to cooperation through interdependence. Under these circumstances, the capacity to challenge outmoded traditions, precedents, and past practices is lost. With sound ways of approaching and resolving conflict, outmoded patterns can successfully be challenged and upgraded by replacement of them with agreements which themselves can promote problem solving and creativity. In this way, finding new and better ways to accomplish personal, organizational, national, and perhaps even international objectives becomes possible.

Just stimulating people to challenge and contest status quo conformities, however, is likely to do little more than provoke disagreement and controversy, increase polarization, and ultimately end in win–lose, impasse, compromise, or chaos. Yet the status quo requirements must continuously be challenged in a problem-solving and creative way, not in a manner that pits man against man to see who can win or, even worse, in a way that ends in anarchy.

The conflict grid is useful in seeing the more subtle connections among conflict and conformity and creative problem solving. Conformity to the 9,1 authority–obedience demands that are involved in hierarchical rank is exemplified by the boss, teacher, or parent who gives the orders to subordinates, students, or children who are expected to obey. The exercise of initiative which produces differences is equivalent to insubordination. Conformity under 9,1 may produce the protocol of surface compliance, but the frustrations of those who are suppressed are often evident. Ways of striking back against the boss, teacher, or parent appear. Such acts may be open ones of resistance and rebellion or disguised ones of sabotage, cheating, or giving agreement without following through. Each of these in a certain sense involves reverse creativity, where ingenuity is exercised in attacking or "beating" the system. It is creativity in resentment of the system, not in support of it.

In another type of conformity, the rules of relationship are, "Don't say anything if you can't say something nice" (1,9). Togetherness, social intimacy, and warmth engendered by yielding one's convictions in the interests of personal acceptance are certainly objectionable solutions in a society where having and expressing differences is relied on as the basis for finding sound courses of action. It can produce a quorum of agreement but smother creative problem solving in sweetness and love. The kind of disagreement that might provoke resentment is avoided. The opportunity for creative problem solving to emerge is absent.

Another kind of conformity relates to adhering to the form and not to the substance of life. Here people conform by going through the motions expected of them, treadmilling through the days, months, and years (1,1). In this way, survival is accomplished by being visible without being seen.

Organization-man conformity (5,5) entails positively embracing the status quo with minimum regard for the soundness of status quo requirements. Yet, even here, as new problems arise, differences appear and disagreements become evident. There are several kinds of 5,5 actions that on shallow examination may give the appearance of approaching problems from an altered, fresh, and original point of view. Pseudo-creativity may be seen when new approaches, even though they constitute only small departures from the outmoded past, are recommended on the basis of their having been tried elsewhere. Under these circumstances a man is forwarding actions taken by others rather than promoting examination of actions on the basis of his own convictions. In this way, he can suggest, while avoiding the challenge or rejection of his own convictions. Deeper examination of 5,5 behavior leads to the conclusion that imitation rather than innovation is the rule.

In other instances, solutions which are proposed as compromise positions can give the impression of "flexibility" in thought. When adjustment and accommodation, backing and filling, twisting and turning, shifting and adapting take place in the spirit of compromise, the motivation behind them is usually to avoid interpersonal emotions resulting from confrontation. Behaving in this manner is a reaction to disagreement, and it means that personal validity is being eroded.

Flexibility is a highly valued component in mature and effective behavior. But is it not contradictory to advocate flexibility on the one hand and to forewarn against compromise on the other? This question is important to clarify.

Flexibility calls for deliberate examination of options and alternatives. It means having back-up tactics that permit swift resolution of unforeseen circumstances, a climate that permits people to move back and forth and in and out from one situation to another, but based on facts, data, and logic of the situation as it unfolds. These are the characteristics of creative problem solving that permit gains to be made as opportunities arrive; that permit opportunities to be created, threats to be anticipated, and risks that result when people fail to react to be reduced.

Thus there are actions to adjust a difference to keep peace and actions to adjust to altered circumstances for better results. It is most important to distinguish between the two kinds. Flexibility for better results is likely to have a stamp of 9,9 on it; "flexibility" to keep peace by avoiding clash of personalities is in the 5,5 area. One is enlivening and promotes creativity. The other leads to the perpetuation of the organization-man mentality of status quo rigidities.

In the final analysis, conformity is to be valued. The problem is to ensure that the thinking of men conforms with sound purposes and premises. Conformity which means adherence to premises of human logic so that decisions reached are furthering growth capacity in sound and fundamental ways is what every individual might be expected to want. It is what man should want in the underpinnings of his daily interactions. It is conformity at this level that promotes the pursuit of creative and innovative solutions. Only when the values of a nation stimulate experimentation and promote a truly constructive attitude toward discovery and innovation is the full potential from creative efforts available as a source of thrust for replacing outmoded status quo conformities with more problem-solving requirements (9,9).

What Men Want—Transnationally

Though varying widely in their ways of *actually* dealing with conflict, studies show that leaders in the United States, Great Britain, the Middle and Far East all indicate that they would *prefer* the 9,9 approach of *open confrontation* as the soundest way of managing situations of conflict, particularly under circumstances where outmoded conformities are under examination (Mouton & Blake, 1970). Though extremely difficult, it appears to be the soundest of several possible choices. This is not to imply that every decision should be made by a leader through calling a meeting or obtaining team agreement. Nor for a crisis situation does it imply that a leader should withhold exercising direction. But a 9,9 foundation of interdependence can build a strong basis for an open, problem-solving society in which men can have and express differences and yet be interrelated in ways that promote the mutual respect, common goals, and trust and understanding they must have to achieve results in ways that lead to personal gratification and maturity.

POSSIBILITIES OF THE FIFTH ACHIEVEMENT FOR STRENGTHENING SOCIETY

This challenge to America, the need for men to learn to confront outmoded status quo requirements and to manage the resultant conflict in such ways as to promote creative problem solving, promises much for the decades ahead, if we can meet and master it.

Consider for a moment the possibility of success in mastering this fifth achievement. What might it mean?

1. Enriched family life rather than the steady rise in the divorce rate.

2. Sounder child rearing, evidenced in teen-age youngsters capable of expression and action in dealing in a problem-solving rather than a protest way with adults and the institutions of society also capable of interacting in an equally sound way.

3. The conversion of academic environments from subject-oriented learning centers to ones that expand the capacity of individuals for contributing creatively to the evolving character of society.

4. The betterment of communities in ways that more fully serve human wants.

5. The more rapid integration of minorities into a more just society, with the reduction and eventual elimination of disenfranchised, alienated segments.

6. Fuller and more creative use of human energies in conducting the organizations that serve society.

7. A greater readiness to support and utilize science for approaching problems when evidence, facts, and data come to have an ever greater value as the bases for gaining insight.

8. A strengthening of politics by readiness to advocate positions on the basis of statesmanlike convictions rather than to adopt positions for political expediency.

9. Reliance on knowledge rather than rank in the resolution of differences and disagreements in organization situations.

10. A stronger basis for mind-meeting agreements rather than resorting to legal actions to force a resolution of disputes.

If erosion of social institutions has not already become too great, all of these aims can perhaps be forwarded over time by our classical institutions for settling conflicts. But surely men capable of resolving their conflicts directly would forward human progress with a dramatic thrust—and on a far more fundamental and therefore enduring basis.

If this fifth achievement is to be realized, it is likely that greater use of the behavioral sciences will be essential. For in the behavioral sciences may well lie the key to a more rewarding and progressive society in which men can share and evaluate their differences, learn from them, and use conflict as a stepping stone to the greater progress that is possible when differences can be resolved in a direct, face-to-face way.

Will this challenge be met, or will the cherished freedom of having and expressing differences be sacrificed?

REFERENCES

Bach, G. R., and Wyden, P. *The Ultimate Enemy.* New York: Morrow, 1969.

Blake, R. R., and Mouton, Jane S. The experimental investigation of interpersonal influence. In A. D. Biderman and H. Zimmer (Eds.), *The Manipulation of Human Behavior.* New York: Wiley, 1961.

Blake, R. R., and Mouton, Jane S. *The Managerial Grid.* Houston: Gulf, 1964.

Blake, R. R., and Mouton, Jane S. *Corporate excellence through grid organization development: A systems approach.* Houston: Gulf, 1968.

Blake, R. R., Shepard, H. A., and Mouton, Jane S. *Managing intergroup conflict in industry.* Houston: Gulf, 1964.

Bradford, L. P., Gibb, J. R., and Benne, K. D. (Eds.) *T-group theory and laboratory method: Innovation in re-education.* New York: Wiley, 1964.

Mouton, Jane S., and Blake, R. R. Issues in transnational organization development. In B. M. Bass, R. B. Cooper, and J. A. Haas (Eds.), *Managing for task accomplishment.* Lexington, Mass.: D. C. Heath, 1970. Pp. 208–224.

Schein, E. H., and Bennis, W. G. (Eds.) *Personal and organizational change through group methods: The laboratory approach.* New York: Wiley, 1965.

PART III
Individual Differences

While the central focus of Part II centered on general theories of social conflict, the focus of this section is individual behavior in situations of social conflict. There are differences in how individuals behave in conflict situations. Some individuals may avoid conflict situations, while others may seek to encourage conflict. Such differences may be attributed to learning from past experiences, to personality variables, to the effects of group membership, or to a combination of these and other factors. Much of the research concerning individual differences has been with games; not much research concerning individual differences has been done in situations of unrestricted and realistic interaction.

In this and the following sections, it is interesting to note how quickly much of the language has changed. Most of the selections in this book were written in the 1960s, and each reflects the language nuances of the time. Particularly, references to minority groups have changed. It may be true that rapid language change is reflective of conflict situations.

Noel F. McGinn, Ernest Harburg, and Gerald P. Ginsburg in "Responses to Interpersonal Conflict by Middle Class Males in Guadalajara and Michigan," attempt to measure crosscultural differences in the resolution of interpersonal conflict and suggest that learning from our particular cultural experiences may explain some differences in conflict behavior.

Daniel Druckman in "Dogmatism, Prenegotiation Experience, and Simulated Group Representation as Determinants of Dyadic Behavior in a Bargaining Situation" reports on an investigation of both personality and situational variables in the conflict behavior of a simulated labor-management bargaining situation.

Kenneth K. Sereno and C. David Mortensen in "The Effects of Ego-Involved Attitudes on Conflict Negotiation in Dyads" report on an investigation of ego-involvement (or the degree of importance or relevance of a topic to the individual as revealed by his commitment or stand on that issue) and negotiation behavior in dyads.

NOEL F. McGINN
ERNEST HARBURG
GERALD P. GINSBURG

Responses to Interpersonal Conflict by Middle-Class Males in Guadalajara and Michigan

The main purpose of this report is to describe an attempt to measure cross-cultural differences in the resolution of interpersonal conflict. It is believed that the instrument described in this report, and others like it, can be used successfully by anthropologists and other social scientists who want to be able to describe group differences with a minimum of prolonged observation.

The subjects used in the research were middle-class males. While there is little detailed research on middle-class Mexicans (Wagley and Harris 1955), there are perhaps enough general observations to permit an estimation of the validity of the instrument.

There is a consensus that the core of the Mexican male's self-concept is more deeply based on emotional relations than his American counterpart. In part this is expressed through friendship relations. The American concept seems to be more deeply associated with material achievements. Mexicans tend to define

From Noel F. McGinn, Ernest Harburg, and Gerald P. Ginsburg, "Responses to Interpersonal Conflict by Middle-Class Males in Guadalajara and Michigan," reproduced by permission of the American Anthropological Association from *American Anthropologist* 67, no. 6 (1965), 1483–1494. This research was supported in part by a grant from the Horace H. Rackham School of Graduate Studies of the University of Michigan.

reality in terms of interpersonal relationships, while Americans are more prone to define the world in terms of external, objective relationships (Díaz-Guerrero 1959).

In outlining the forms which this emphasis on the emotional and the interpersonal takes in Mexican society Gillin (1961) cites "personalism" as a unifying value in middle-class Mexican life. Drawing on many sources Gillin asserts that the middle-status Mexican requires strong personal intimacy in his social relations; trust is only extended to persons with whom such a relation exists. As Ramírez puts it, ". . . the Mexican can cross himself, humiliate himself . . . but can't 'crack' himself, that is, let the outer world penetrate to his intimacy" (1961: 99). In contrast, the American may enter into a relationship of "impersonal confidence" or trust without intimacy, a relationship unknown among Mexicans according to Gillin. Moreover, for Mexicans, personal worth derives more from intimate relations than from visible achievement.

As a result of a study with 1,000 young adult Texans and 900 Mexican youth Peck and Díaz-Guerrero conclude that (1963: 109):

> The "American" pattern ("Texan" would be a more safely limited term) depicts the respect relationship as one between equals. One can admire and look up to another person, it seems, perhaps for some specific attribute, without feeling generally inferior or subordinate. . . . The Mexican pattern looks equally self-consistent and quite different. It pictures "respect" as an extremely intimate relationship involving a good deal of strong personal feeling. For some, part of this feeling is negative, in opposition to the very positive emotions of love and affection that are expressed . . . there is considerable concern about not interfering in the other person's life, or trespassing on his rights—perhaps a more immediate danger when life is so close, emotion-laden, and so intimately bound up. . . .

According to Gillin (1961) the Mexican would be more upset by denials of his personal qualities (such as manliness) than by criticisms of acquired talents (such as skill in a task). As a close, personal friend is the only person capable of judging these abilities, the Mexican is relatively immune to criticisms by strangers (which he handles with wit and sharp humor) while the North American, who more extensively evaluates himself by his visible achievements, is often disturbed by criticisms from strangers or those he does not consider friends.

Among its many cultural forms, "personalism" may also be viewed in terms of Mexican *friendliness,* which is said to be more emotionally involving among Mexican males than among Americans. Perhaps the best example is contained in the idea of a promise. A Mexican tends to say "yes" to almost any request, but then may not comply with it. The reason, according to such authors as Ramírez (1961) and Reyes Nevárez (1952) is that it would be rude to say "no," and endanger the possibility of making a friend or lead to losing one. As Mexicans know this, they are not upset when the promise is not kept, but such an experience is culturally defined by Americans to produce disturbance. Díaz-Guerrero states that the Mexican "would rather lose an argument than a friend. . . . Mexicans will not only lose arguments but time and money so as not to lose interpersonal fun" (1959: 187). More specifically, Whyte and Holmberg (1956) explain that the Latin American tends to express himself in such a way that personal relations will remain harmonious—at least on the surface. At the same time the Mexican tends to see interpersonal relations as controlled by himself, as manipulable, while Americans tend to regard these relations as a given state of affairs, not subject to control (Díaz-Guerrero 1959).

In summary, if, as assumed, the Mexican tends to base his self-concept on positive interpersonal relations, then a threatened break in friendship would lead to efforts to preserve the friendship. The North American, having other means by which to maintain a positive self-image, would not only be less inclined to attempt to preserve the friendship relation, but might even be willing to sacrifice the friendship in order to maintain self-respect based upon external achievements.

In attempting to measure cross-cultural reactions to conflict with friends, a test was devised by Harburg (1962) using Newcomb's balance theory (1959). This theory states that an "A-

B-X" system exists when the perceiver, A, is emotionally oriented to another person, B, and to an object, X, and perceives that B is similarly "Cooriented" to himself and to X. The situation is balanced when A perceives that his attitude toward X and that of B's are similar. However, when A perceives that his attitude to X is discrepant in sign and/or intensity from that of B's, the system is defined as imbalanced, and A experiences a strain or tension toward balancing the system. The theory can then specify a variety of coping responses which A might make in trying to balance the situation, or reduce strain.

Coping responses refer to cognitive or overt responses in an A-B-X system which are aroused in the perceiver by perception of objective or hypothetical imbalanced situations and which are intended to resolve the discrepancy through changes in sign and/or intensity of attitudes. We can thus begin to describe the "defensive" responses of a person by observing his coping responses to imbalanced social situations in which he is orienting himself to other persons and ideas. Like other techniques of communication, it is believed that these coping responses are common in a culture and transmitted in early socialization. They enter into the makeup of the "social self," and serve to distinguish individuals in their attempts to resolve interpersonal and social conflicts.

Two general types of coping patterns used in resolving such conflict may be termed "associative" (yielding to others) and "dissociative" (withdrawing). In A-B-X terms, associative responses occur in imbalanced situations such that A changes his own attitude to X in order that it become more similar in sign or intensity with B's attitude, and maintains his liking for B. As with other coping responses, this does not mean that permanent attitude change occurs; it refers to an attempt to reduce strain created by the situational imbalance. In A-B-X terms, dissociative responses occur when A tends to neutralize his attraction for B (like B less), or increase his negative orientations (dislike B), or maintain discrepancy (disagree with B).

From our previous discussion of Mexican and North American values and customs, one would expect Mexicans to prefer associative coping responses to imbalanced A-B-X situations and North Americans to respond dissociatively.

METHOD

Populations

In selecting populations to be compared, we selected only middle- or upper-middle-class young males enrolled at college-educational levels. The degree to which one might reasonably infer national character traits is therefore restricted by design. Furthermore, the local regional context of each population compels us to refer more often in the remainder of the article to Guadalajara and Michigan students rather than to Mexicans and North Americans.

There were two Michigan groups and two Guadalajara groups. The first Michigan group consisted of 91 male freshmen and sophomores at the University of Michigan, all taking an introductory psychology course, and thus required to serve as subjects for research. The mean age of this group was 19.5 years. The second group consisted of 83 undergraduate and graduate students at the University of Michigan who agreed to participate in the research after being contacted. The mean age of this group was 19.6 years. The Mexican subjects, also all males, consisted of the entire senior class (95) of a private preparatory school, and the freshman class (79) of a private university, both in Guadalajara. The subjects agreed to participate in the research after having been contacted through the school authorities. The mean ages of the Guadalajara groups were 17.5 and 20.7 years, respectively.

All of the Guadalajara preparatory school subjects planned a university career. They, and the university students, represented an upper-middle class in Guadalajara society and were more homogeneous in origin than the Michigan groups, but average class rankings were similar. All of the Guadalajara subjects were at least nominal Catholics, while the Michigan subjects were, in the main, self-identified as Protestants. Psychological testing was a new experience for the Guadalajara subjects, while those from Michigan could be considered fairly sophisticated.

Responses to Interpersonal Conflict

The technique employed was a modification of the *semantic differential* (Osgood, Suci, and Tannenbaum 1957). Scales for the semantic were carefully chosen to measure a variety of opposing reactions in a two-person situation of conflict, using hypotheses proposed by Newcomb (1959). It was expected that the situations (concepts) and scales used would be familiar and stressing for middle-class subjects, and would demonstrate differences between the two sub-cultures sampled.

After an introduction designed to develop maximum rapport, each subject wrote in the initials of three male students in the same school. Person (1) was a best friend, person (7) a student whom the subject *strongly* disliked, and person (9) a slightly disliked person who was quite good in an activity (X) in which the subject liked to do well. At each place where these numbers appeared in the questionnaire, the subject filled in the initials of the person he had chosen (and the activity), thus refreshing his awareness of the identity of the person in question.

The subjects then read, and were administered orally, instructions for taking the semantic differential. These instructions closely paralleled those recommended by Osgood et al. (1957). The subjects then responded to a set of three concepts intended as a "warm-up." The first concept was different for the Guadalajara and Michigan subjects (Making a Speech to the Class vs. Driving a Car) because the Mexican students might not have had much experience in the first activity. However, identical scales were used. The subjects next responded to the three conflict situations. The concepts and scales used are presented in Tables 2–4. An example follows below:

Now, imagine this situation has just occurred; (fill in initials)

You like __________ (1); you strongly dislike __________ (7).

You *have just learned* that your best friend __________ (1) really likes __________ (7) extremely well.

In this situation I would probably:

feel uneasy ___: ___: ___: ___: ___: ___: ___:feel pleasant

like (1) more ___: ___: ___: ___: ___: ___: ___:like (1) less

Subjects placed one mark on each of the scales in any of the seven positions, the intensity of the judgment represented by each position having been carefully explained in the instructions.

The English form was translated into Spanish by a Colombian graduate student at the University of Michigan. A Mexican graduate student then checked the translation and changed all words that might not be familiar to Mexicans.[1] In the process of administration to the Guadalajara subjects, subjects were strongly urged to report any unfamiliar words. None did so. The Guadalajara subjects were, on the whole, more attentive than those at Michigan and took more time to complete the forms (45 minutes total administration time for Guadalajara compared to 35 minutes for Michigan). As can be seen in Table 1, the subjects from Guadalajara used extreme judgments more often than those from Michigan. Osgood, et al. (1957) report this response tendency to be typical of unsophisticated subjects.

Numbers from 1 to 7 were assigned to each of the seven-scale positions of the semantic differential beginning with 1 at the left of the scale. The Mann-Whitney U Test (Siegel 1956)

[1]We are deeply indebted to Dr. Julián Villarreal for generously giving his time and bilingual skills in the task of translation.

TABLE 1 **Percentage of Subjects Taking Each Scale Position Across All Scales and All Situations**

Subjects	Position on Scale						
	1	2	3	4 (neutral)	5	6	7
Guadalajara, Mexico (N = 174)	19.1	15.9	13.0	14.0	9.9	12.8	15.3
Michigan, United States (N = 174)	12.4	16.9	19.5	9.6	17.4	14.4	9.8

which uses ranks and avoids assumptions of normality of distribution and equal variances was applied to the distributions for each scale. The probabilities presented in Tables 2–4 refer to the test performed on the full, ungrouped distributions, and indicate the probability that such a difference in the Guadalajara and Michigan distributions could be obtained by chance. All probabilities are for a two-tail test.

In Tables 2–4 the *grouped* percentages (1–3, 4, 5–7) are presented for convenience. Because the U test was applied to the *full* distributions, some of the probabilities do not seem to fit with the grouped percentages: this is an artifact of the grouping.

The presentation of results will be concerned only with those differences which could occur by chance less than five times in ten thousand events ($p < .0005$). The differences between the two groups are that significant for 16 of the 34 scales.

RESULTS

Table 2 shows that the Michigan students differed from the Guadalajara subjects on 8 of the 14 scales for the situation "Best friend likes disliked person." The Michigan subjects, more frequently than those from Guadalajara, stated that they would: feel uneasy; like (1) less; think that (1) may be mistaken; disagree with (1); dislike (7) as before; talk with (1) about (7); and, not have expected (1)'s attitude. The Guadalajara students more frequently than those from Michigan stated that they would avoid feeling irritated with (1).

Table 3 reports frequencies of responses to the situation "Best friend won't write letter of reference." There are significant differences for five of the ten scales. Michigan subjects more frequently stated that they would: feel job was important; like (1) less; and, not have expected (1)'s attitude. The Guadalajara subjects more frequently responded with: (1) might think the job was no good for me; and, try to change (1)'s attitude.

The percentages of responses to the situation "Mildly disliked person criticizes ability" are presented in Table 4. There are significant differences for three of the ten scales. The Michigan

TABLE 2 **Responses of Mexican and American Male Students to the Following Situations**

You like_____(1); you strongly dislike_____(7).
You have just learned that your best friend (1) really likes (7) extremely well.

In This Situation I Would Probably: Low Score–High Score		Percentage of Subjects Responding in Each Category 1-3	4	5-7	Probability[a]
feel uneasy–feel pleasant	Michigan	82	12	6	<.0001
	Guadalajara	44	11	45	
like (1) more–like (1) less	Michigan	9	47	44	<.0005
	Guadalajara	33	39	28	
think (1) may be mistaken–think (1) may be right	Michigan	66	8	26	<.0001
	Guadalajara	36	12	52	
want (7) to dislike (1)–want (7) to like (1)	Michigan	37	32	31	.4412
	Guadalajara	40	29	31	
(1) really could like (7)–(1) really could not like (7)	Michigan	47	6	47	.0086
	Guadalajara	54	11	35	
try to change (1)'s attitude toward (7).–avoid trying to change (1)'s attitude toward (7)	Michigan	55	6	39	.1470
	Guadalajara	41	26	33	
avoid feeling irritated at (1)–feel irritated at (1)	Michigan	59	5	36	<.0001
	Guadalajara	76	15	9	
agree with (1)–disagree with (1)	Michigan	10	12	78	<.0001
	Guadalajara	41	18	41	
feel I should know (7) better–feel I knew (7) enough	Michigan	38	5	57	.0016
	Guadalajara	56	11	33	
dislike (7) as before–try to like (7) better	Michigan[b]	65	5	30	<.0001
feel anxious about my relation with (1)–feel sure about my relation with (1)	Michigan	30	10	60	.1686
	Guadalajara	26	11	63	
talk with (1) about (7)–avoid talking with (1) about (7)	Michigan	69	5	26	<.0005
	Guadalajara	47	19	34	
be sure about my judgment of (7)–be doubtful about my judgment of (7)	Michigan	58	5	37	.0990
	Guadalajara	61	7	32	
not have expected (1)'s attitude–have expected (1)'s attitude	Michigan	82	8	10	<.0001
	Guadalajara	49	18	33	

[a]Mann-Whitney U Test.

[b]Editor's note: Guadalajara data for this item not shown in original publication.

TABLE 3 Responses of Mexican and American Male Students to the Following Situation

You are competing with several others for a desirable job.

You need a character reference and you use the name of your best friend ______ (1). (later tells you he would rather not recommend you for the job and asks you to select som one else.

In This Situation I Would Probably:	Percentage of Subjects Responding in Each Category				Probability
Low Score—High Score		1-3	4	5-7	
trust (1) less—trust (1) more	Michigan	72	11	17	.968
	Guadalajara	63	14	23	
feel anxious at (1)'s refusal—feel irritated at (1)'s refusal	Michigan	52	3	45	.031
	Guadalajara	52	11	37	
believe (1) is making a mistake—believe (1) may be right	Michigan	58	5	37	.187
	Guadalajara	52	11	37	
feel angry at (1)—avoid feeling angry at (1)	Michigan	61	3	36	.016
	Guadalajara	42	9	49	
(1) might think I was not able to do the job—(1) might think the job was no good for me	Michigan	52	15	33	<.000
	Guadalajara	31	15	54	
try to change (1)'s attitude—avoid trying to change (1)'s attitude	Michigan	47	5	48	<.000
	Guadalajara	64	10	26	
demand to know why (1) did it—say no more about it to (1)	Michigan	63	3	34	.230
	Guadalajara	60	6	34	
feel job was important—feel job was unimportant	Michigan	84	8	8	<.000
	Guadalajara	59	11	30	
like (1) more—like (1) less	Michigan	12	36	51	<.000
	Guadalajara	36	35	29	
have expected (1)'s attitude—not have expected (1)'s attitude	Michigan	5	3	92	<.000
	Guadalajara	39	13	48	

[a]Mann-Whitney U Test.

subjects more frequently responded in the direction: feel irritated about (9)'s remark; feel like being sarcastic to (9); and, have expected (9)'s remark.

TABLE 4 Responses of Mexican and American Male Students to the Following Situation

While you are doing (X), ________(9) tells you, "You are doing wrong and pretty poorly."

In This Situation I Would Porbably: Low Score—High Score		Percentage of Subjects Responding in Each Category 1-3	4	5-7	Probability[a]
feel (9) is showing off—feel (9) is trying to help me	Michigan	62	5	33	.0614
	Guadalajara	60	8	32	
feel anxious about (9)'s remark—feel irritated about (9)'s remark	Michigan	25	6	69	<.0005
	Guadalajara	49	9	42	
feel hurt by (9)'s remark—feel like being sarcastic to (9)	Michigan	20	12	68	<.0005
	Guadalajara	39	17	44	
doubt (9)'s judgment about the "error"—doubt my judgment about the "error"	Michigan	67	4	29	.8728
	Guadalajara	55	20	25	
(9) may be right; I appreciate it—(9) may be right; still dislike the remark	Michigan	33	5	62	.2412
	Guadalajara	38	10	52	
feel more dislike for (9)—feel less dislike for (9)	Michigan	61	26	13	.0466
	Guadalajara	50	27	23	
seek out "error" by myself—get (9) to explain "error" to me	Michigan	51	4	45	.9124
	Guadalajara	47	5	48	
feel calm about (9)—feel angry at (9)	Michigan	36	12	52	.4654
	Guadalajara	41	15	44	
feel it's none of (9)'s business—feel (9) might be concerned	Michigan	51	6	43	.3270
	Guadalajara	53	11	36	
not have expected (9)'s remark—have expected (9)'s remark	Michigan	24	6	70	<.0005
	Guadalajara	43	12	45	

[a]Mann-Whitney U Test.

DISCUSSION

Table 5 summarizes the results presented above. The results indicate that the Michigan subjects were more upset by the conflict with their friend, and more willing than the Guadalajara students to break the friendship as a result of this conflict. In the first situation the strain felt by the Michigan subjects is represented by their more extreme responses of feeling uneasy,

TABLE 5 Summary of Differences Between Mexicans and Americans in Reactions to Interpersonal Conflict*
(N = 174 in each group)

Situation A. You like *(1)*; you strongly dislike *(7)*; you *have just learned* that your best friend *(1)* really likes *(7)* extremely well.

Mexicans more extreme than Americans in the direction:

avoid feeling irritated at (1)

Americans more extreme than Mexicans:

feel uneasy
like (1) less
think (1) may be mistaken
disagree with (1)
dislike (7) as before
talk with (1) about (7)
not have expected (1)'s attitude

Situation B. You are competing with several others for a desirable job. You need a character reference, and you use the name of your best friend *(1)*.
(1) later tells you he would rather not recommend you for the job and ask you to select someone else.

Mexicans more extreme than Americans in the direction:

try to change (1)'s attitude
(1) might think the job was no good for me

Americans more extreme than Mexicans:

feel job was important
like (1) less
not have expected (1)'s attitude

Situation C. While you are doing *(X)*, *(9)* tells you, "You are doing wrong and pretty poorly."

Americans more extreme than Mexicans in the direction:

feel irritated about (9)'s remark
feel like being sarcastic to (9) (as opposed to *feel hurt*)
have expected (9)'s remark

---

*Adapted from: McGinn, Harburg and Ginsburg, 1963.

feeling surprise, and disagreeing with their friend. At the same time, their solution to the conflict is clearly stated in their more frequent response of liking their friend less and thinking him wrong in his judgment. In terms of the A-B-X model described earlier, the most frequent solution to the situation of imbalance among friends chosen by the Michigan subjects is one that would change the A-B relationship and leave the A-X relationship intact.

The responses of the Guadalajara students indicate their recognition of the reality of their friend liking their "enemy" and the relative lack of irritation or uneasiness because of the disagreement. This suggests that for the Guadalajara subjects the strength of the A-B bond, or friendship, is less a function of agreement on opinions than for the Michigan subjects, or less subject to strain as a result of disagreement.

This hypothesis is supported by the pattern of responses to the second situation. More of the Guadalajara subjects (54% as compared to 33% of the Michigan students) indicated confidence in their friend's intention (best friend might think job not good for me) and at the same time a willingness to try and change his opinion (64% as compared to 47% of the Michigan subjects).

Again, in this situation, the Michigan subjects' responses to the strain in the relationship tended to be to minimize the importance of the friendship, liking their friend less (52% as compared to 29% of the Guadalajara students). The achievement values of the Michigan subjects are indicated in the response of 84% of them (as compared to 59% of the Guadalajara group) that the job was important for them. (Parenthetically it should be noted that words such as achievement, challenge, and others referring to long-term striving for success are not commonly used in Guadalajara. Words such as success have a meaning that implies a thing that happened, rather than a caused event).

The differences with respect to the third situation indicate that the Michigan subjects were more disturbed by the criticism of their ability than were the Guadalajara subjects. This suggests that learned abilities were more relevant in terms of self-evaluation for the Michigan subjects than for those from Guadalajara.

Summing up, Michigan students report more disturbance in their relation with their best friend as a result of disagreement and a subsequent tendency to break the friendship rather than change their position. It is possible that the Guadalajara subjects resolve their disturbance by denying that it actually poses a threat to the friendship. Michigan students are more upset by criticism of their abilities by disliked persons, while Guadalajara students tended toward more temperate responses.

One final observation might aid in the interpretation of the results. Ramírez (1961) has asserted that Mexicans rely much more on the defense mechanism of denial than do North Americans. It might be thus expected that criticism by friends would be denied by Mexicans. North Americans, on the other hand, given the relative lesser importance of friendship and an accompanying greater use of verbal aggression, might be expected to respond in kind to criticisms by friends.

Alternative Explanations

Since the primary purpose of this report is to illustrate the potential of the research instrument, it would be valuable to consider carefully the possibility that the response differences obtained came from other than cultural differences. It might be that the concept of "best friend" has a different meaning in Guadalajara than at the University of Michigan. If there are differences in the subjective meaning of this term in the two cultures, we would not then be comparing responses to the same situation. As a partial check of this possibility, subjects were asked to indicate the degree of liking they had for their best friend, using a scale from 0 to 100 percent. The variability within both groups exceeded any difference between them. Similar results were obtained with estimation of disliking for person (7) and (9). This offers support for a hypothesis that friendship relations have the same meanings in both cultures.

Secondly, it is possible that the test-taking attitudes of the two groups produced differences. For example, as seen in Table 1, the Guadalajara subjects were more extreme in their judgments. However, as more of the significant differences involved Michigan subjects in the extreme position, this can be ruled out. The sophistication of the Michigan students with psychological testing precluded their feeling anxious in the testing situation. The Guadalajara students, on the other hand, might well have had some anxiety about expressing their feelings. If the Guadalajara students did give false responses, it is significant that they chose the particular pattern of responses they did.

The difference in mean ages between the two groups could have produced differences. Accordingly, mean differences between the two Guadalajara samples were compared. There were only three significant differences, all in responses to the third situation, for the scales: feel anxious about (9)'s remark; feel hurt by (9)'s remark; and (9) might be right, I appreciate it. In each case, the *younger* Guadalajara group was closer to the mean of the Michigan subjects. It can be concluded that age was not an important factor, and that with greater age Mexicans should differ even more in their responses as compared to those of Americans.

One might question the adequacy of the translation. None of the responses to the material suggested a lack of understanding, nor did the Guadalajara subjects report any difficulties. Further, the conformance of the results to behavioral observations argues that the translation did succeed in presenting both groups of subjects with the same stimulus.

Finally, it must be stated that any interpretation of "pencil-and-paper" tests can only be adequately made in association with behavior in a social situation. In further work with both of the Michigan groups, it was found that students who gave "dissociative" responses (specifically, hostility toward B) on the written form tended to reveal "associative" behavior (yielding to friend) when placed in face-to-face experimental situation where they were forced to argue with a liked peer about important content areas where discrepancy existed (Harburg 1962). Could it be that if Mexican students were placed in a similar situation where discrepancies concerned highly relevant content, that the "tendency to please" might give way to resistance of an extreme sort and overt dissociation? Gillin (1961) states that this device of pleasing the other is part of the elaborately precautionary patterns of ceremonial politeness which serve as a constant buffer to the heavy emotional bases of friendships in which Mexicans, more so than North Americans, invest.

REFERENCES

Díaz-Guerrero, R.
1959 Mexican assumptions about interpersonal relations. Etcetera 16: 185–188.

Gillin, J. P.
1961 Some signposts for policy. *In* Social change in Latin America. New York, Vintage.

Harburg, E.
1962 Covert hostility: its social origins and relationship with overt compliance. Ph.D. dissertation, University of Michigan, Ann Arbor.

McGinn, N. F., E. Harburg, and G. P. Ginsburg
1963 Perceptions of middle class Mexican and American males about parent-child and interpersonal relations. Delivered before the First International Conference of the Western Regional Chapter of the American Academy of Psychotherapists, Puerto Vallarta, Jalisco, Mexico.

Newcomb, T. M.
1959 Individual systems of orientation. *In* Psychology: the study of a science, ed. S. Koch, Vol. 3. New York, McGraw-Hill.

Osgood, C. E., G. J. Suci, and P. H. Tannenbaum
1957 The measurement of meaning. Urbana, Illinois, University of Illinois Press.

Peck, R. F. and R. Díaz-Guerrero
1963 Two core-culture patterns and the diffusion of values across their border. *In* Memorias del VII Congreso Interamericano de Psicología. México, Sociedad Interamericana de Psicología.

Ramírez, S.
1961 El Mexicano: Psicología de sus motivaciones. México, Pax-México.

Reyes Nevárez, S.
1952 El Amor y la Amistad en el Mexicano. México, Porrua y Obregón.

Siegel, S.
1956 Nonparametric statistics for the behavioral sciences. New York, McGraw-Hill.

Wagley, C. and M. Harris
1955 A typology of Latin American subcultures. American Anthropologist 57:428–451.

Whyte, W. F. and A. R. Holmberg
1956 Human problems of U.S. enterprise in Latin America. Human Organization 15:1–4.

DANIEL DRUCKMAN

Dogmatism, Prenegotiation Experience, and Simulated Group Representation as Determinants of Dyadic Behavior in a Bargaining Situation

Several investigators in the area of conflict resolution have been concerned with the problem of how people approach one another as individuals or group representatives in a situation where they come together to resolve differences and where compromise is possible. Two orientations, characterized by Gladstone (1962), seem especially appropriate to this type of confrontation. An egoistic orientation is defined by a strong motive to win, evidenced in noncompromise behavior, a perception of the other in terms of stereotypical categories, and the judgment of an outgroup product to be of inferior quality. Blake and Mouton (1962) spelled out a similar syndrome which they called "win-lose" motivation. The experimental production of egoistic motivation was demonstrated by Sherif, Harvey, White, Hood, and Sherif (1961) with children in a camp setting, and Blake and

From Daniel Druckman, "Dogmatism, Prenegotiation Experience, and Simulated Group Representation as Determinants of Dyadic Behavior in a Bargaining Situation," *Journal of Personality and Social Psychology 6,* 1967, 279–290. This paper is based on a dissertation submitted to the Graduate School of Northwestern University in partial fulfillment of the requirements for the degree of Doctor of Philosophy. The author gratefully acknowledges Winfred F. Hill and Marjorie Druckman for their helpful comments and aid in preparing this manuscript.

Mouton (1962) with adults in an industrial setting. An integrative orientation is one in which the importance of collaboration for mutual benefit is realized. Compromise as a means of conflict resolution is predicted to result from this orientation.

Few investigators have attempted to specify the variables responsible for the predominance of one or the other orientation or have separated individual style from situational variables in accounting for the behavior observed. Instead, explanations have relied upon either group relatedness or personality viewed largely as mutually exclusive alternatives.

Group Relatedness

Blake and Mouton (1962) and Sherif and Sherif (1965) observed that there has been a tendency among many investigators to attribute motivation to factors within the individual rather than to properties of the group in which he is a member. They called this the *psychodynamic fallacy*. Committedness, according to these authors, should account for more variance in intergroup posture than should personality.

Studies on intergroup relations have demonstrated the production of competitive motivation after having teams independently develop a position or group product. Unilateral participation, rather than attachment to the group per se, may have been responsible for such behavior as the inability objectively to assess the value of competing positions and competitive nonyielding. The constraints placed upon a representative due to unilateral position formation have been illuminated by Blake (1959), Mack and Snyder (1957), and Rusk (1955). Pearson (1959) claimed that ambiguity serves as an aid to problem solving. Turk and Lefcowitz (1962), in a recent restatement of a major part of Sumner's (1906) ethnocentrism syndrome, considered acts of assertion on the part of representatives to be more likely under high ingroup solidarity (position consensus).

In the human relations training laboratories created by Blake and Mouton (1961, 1962) members interacted only with their own group on the development of an assigned problem, and representatives were elected to debate the merits of their group's product. Deadlock in agreeing on the best solution was the invariable result. A unilateral definition of the problem was apparent insomuch as, after studying the competitor's position, most participants showed that they knew more about their own solution and saw little that the positions shared in common. Bass and Dunteman (1963), Blake and Mouton (1961), and Ferguson and Kelley (1964) produced evaluative bias under conditions in which laboratory groups worked independently on the creation of one or more products. From the subject's point of view it is probable that group problem-solving effectiveness was at stake.

However, in most of the experimental studies of intergroup relations, unilateral participation in the development of a product was not separated from group membership or group representation (e.g., Bass & Dunteman, 1963; Blake & Mouton, 1962; Sherif et al., 1961). Another example of a possible confounding factor was seen in a study by Campbell (1960). He found that two-person union and management teams had difficulty in finding a compromise acceptable to both teams after having formed independent strategies. Is this rigid behavior a function of prenegotiation experience or group loyalty, or is it due to an interaction between these two variables?

A few investigators were able to examine the effects of one of these variables while holding the other constant. Bass (1963) had individuals negotiate as representatives of abstract organizations rather than laboratory groups. Agreement was reached quickly if negotiators did not form strategies or spell out positions before bargaining. That is, when future negotiators defined the problem from a bilateral perspective, compromise resulted without deadlock. However, when they spelled out their own position before bargaining, a significantly longer time period was necessary before agreement could be reached, and negotiations often ended in deadlock. Vegas, Frye, and Cassens (1964) and Ferguson and Kelley (1964) found group membership to be the important variable. The former study demonstrated no perceptual distortion and early agreement among two individuals on which one produced the best essay when neither represented a group product. The latter investigators found that subjects who were members of laboratory groups but who did not participate in the formation of the group product overvalued both the ingroup and its products as much as members who took part in product formation. The extent of bias was correlated with attraction to the group irrespective of taking part in product formation. However, without an orthogonal design it is not possible to determine the relative amount of variance accounted for by each of these variables. The Bass study yielded no information on the effect of group membership, while the Ferguson and Kelley study was inconclusive with respect to unilateral product formation.

Personality

Whether a representative behaves competitively or in a conciliatory fashion may depend partially on attributes that he brings to the situation, other than those determined by his role. While several investigators argue against psychodynamic explanations, some experimental work points toward personality correlates of bargaining behavior.

Some personality variables which have been shown to be related to cooperative or competitive choices in a Prisoner's Dilemma game include internationalism-isolationism (Lutzker, 1960), cooperative, individualistic, or competitive motivational orientations (Deutsch, 1962), family orientation (Crowne, 1966), and F-scale authoritarianism (Deutsch, 1960). However, Robinson and Wilson[1] failed to replicate the latter finding when two-man teams competed. While they found a significant ingroup-outgroup bias in both competitive choices and personality-trait ratings, this was not related to authoritarian attitudes.

A correspondence between behavior at the interpersonal and intergroup levels was provided in the research of Blake and Mouton (1961). The elected representatives shared certain rated

[1]C. Robinson and W. Wilson, "Intergroup Attitudes and Strategies in Non Zero Sum Dilemma Games: II. Selective Bias in both Authoritarians and Nonauthoritarians," unpublished manuscript, University of Hawaii, 1965.

behavioral characteristics that distinguished them from nonrepresentatives. These subjects were rated by all participants as significantly more nonyielding, independent, and resistant to external influences during the ingroup caucus. This is also an accurate description of how they behaved in the intergroup session. Thus the variables of personality type, unilateral planning, and group commitment could not be separated in accounting for the nonyielding behavior of representatives during the intergroup debate.

Among the characteristics of the dogmatic personality delimited by Rokeach (1960) is blind loyalty to a system. He presented experimental evidence on the tendency of closed-minded subjects not to defect from instructions coming from an external authority. There were significant differences between closed-minded and open-minded subjects on defection from the experimenter's instructions even when they made no sense. Jamias (1964) demonstrated that closed-minded respondents were significantly affected by the values of the social systems within which they lived, while open-minded participants were not. Thus another individual difference variable may have relevance for the behavior of a group representative.

The intention of the present study was to investigate the relative contribution of personality and situational variables as determinants of orientation in a non-zero-sum, simulated, labor-management bargaining game. The investigator sought to determine whether an egoistic orientation or nonyielding behavior is a function of commitment to a planned bargaining posture. The behavior of groups that had formulated a strategy was contrasted with the behavior of groups which had not previously decided upon a strategy. Lack of significant differences in behavior between the conditions indicates that the manipulation made no difference, but does not exclude the possibility that nonyielding behavior is a function of group loyalty. In order to determine if this is the case it was necessary to examine bargaining behavior on the part of representatives not coming from laboratory groups. The personality variable is discussed in the design section.

METHOD

Design

The manipulations were arranged into a 2 x 2 x 2 design with 15 replications (9 male dyads and 6 female dyads) in each cell. The first variable represented an attempt to produce a unilateral versus a bilateral definition of the problem by manipulation of prebargaining environments. The second variable attempted to separate the effects of group commitment per se from the constraints imposed by position taking. Finally, to see whether personality made a difference, representatives were chosen on the basis of extreme scores on a modification of the Dogmatism Scale devised by Rokeach (1960). Each session was homogeneous in attitudinal disposition and sex. Across all eight conditions 120 dyads or 240 subjects were run through the simulation. A brief discussion of the basis for role assignments will be followed by specific details on each manipulation.[2]

Union Versus Company. Participants were assigned to either a union (employee role) or company (employer role) team on the basis of their scores on a 24-item attitude scale. The scale is balanced with an equal number of items worded in the directions of prounion, anticompany, antiunion, and procompany. The split-half reliability, corrected by the Spearman-Brown formula, is .72. This selection criterion was used with the intention of increasing the identification of subjects with the position that they were given. Subjects indicated, on a postnegotiation question, that their assigned role coincided highly with their own general beliefs. The mean across all subjects was 2.16 on a 5-point scale ranging from "completely coincided" to "did not coincide at all." The differences in role identification between males and females, company or employer and union or employee representatives, and high and low dogmatics were nonsignificant.

Typical of the scale are the following items, worded in each of the four directions:

ANTICOMPANY

Most violence found at picket lines is instigated by management itself.

PROCOMPANY

Management should have the sole right to determine fringe benefits.

[2]The instructions for each condition, questionnaires, attitude scales, and additional information concerning the procedure are contained in Druckman (1966) and may be obtained through University Microfilms, 313 North First Street, Ann Arbor, Michigan.

PROUNION

Unions struggle to keep existing work rules in order to ensure the health and safety of the worker, not to make unnecessary work or featherbed.

ANTIUNION

The motives governing the actions of top union officials are prestige and financial gain, and not the welfare of the workers.

Approximately the upper and lower quartiles of the labor-management scale distribution were eligible for participation. However, only those also scoring in the upper or lower quartiles of a modified Dogmatism Scale were used. The scores ranged from 33 to 118, with a mean of 76.09. The mean score of the union and employee representatives was 62.73 ($V = .112$),[3] while the mean for the company and employer representatives was 89.47 ($V = .097$).

UNILATERAL POSITION FORMATION VERSUS BILATERAL DISCUSSION. In the strategy condition the two teams (or individuals) were separated into different rooms for approximately 40 minutes. The instructions for the group condition were as follows:

> The next 40 minutes will be spent with your own team. You are to use this time to plan your bargaining strategy. First gain an understanding of the issues. Then you may formulate a list of points defining the rationale or arguments for your team's position on each issue. You should decide on items that you think each man representing you should remain firm on. This strategy may be prepared so as to guide the negotiators through the bargaining session. It may also include potential concessions, anticipations for trading, setting goals, and the like.

In general, it is felt that these strategy instructions set the stage for the more typical prebargaining environment under which collective bargaining takes place.

Joint study conditions were created with the intent of releasing bargainers from commitment to a rigid position. The instructions for the group condition were as follows:

> The next 40 minutes will be spent in bilateral study. You are to use this time for learning as much as possible about company and

[3]The coefficient of variability $\left(V = \frac{s}{x} \right)$ rather than the standard deviation was used as a measure of dispersion for both scales. Blablock (1960, p. 73) claimed that when the means are large and spread out it might be somewhat misleading to compare the absolute magnitudes of the standard deviations.

union perspectives. Study the issues in order to gain understanding of both points of view as well as areas of greater or lesser agreement between proponents of either. Do not formulate or plan any strategies for bargaining from either position. Do not take a position and argue its merits against someone who might profess to the opposite position. Finally, do not form coalitions with other team members to bargain or debate from a position.

If at any point the discussion seems to break down into an inter-team competition, the experimenter will stop it and remind participants of the goal. You should act bipartisan with respect to the issues during this session. There is no need to use any form of propaganda in order to obtain later gains. Feel free to enter the discussion at any point and openly discuss the issues. The emphasis is on informality and there is no one observing you or recording data. Understanding is the goal![4]

Blake and Mouton (1962) used a similar procedure where members from opposing teams questioned each other to gain understanding of both positions. However, this came after each team formulated a strategy, and biases were found in comprehension of the two positions, even when members admitted to understanding both solutions.

Group Versus No Group. Some subjects debated their position as employers or employees in a simulated nonunionized company, while others were members of laboratory teams and representatives of abstract labor or management organizations. Since three bargaining pairs were run in one group session, there were 20 group runs and 60 individual runs. Each participant in the individual conditions was explicitly told that he was only bargaining for himself, and any decision on a settlement applied only to that particular employee and had no direct relevance for the contracts of other employees. The instructions, including the nature of the hypothetical company and the task, were essentially the same for both conditions except for modifications in wording which took into account the change in structure when individuals rather than teams competed. In fact, just two changes in format were necessitated in order that the task be made more appropriate to employer-employee interaction. Details on these procedures are discussed in the section on the task description.

[4]Apart from the creation of unilateral and bilateral groups, the nature of the instructions concerning appropriate behavior during these sessions may have influenced negotiating behavior. Experiments are in progress in an attempt to clarify the effect of varying the instructions for the prebargaining session both for unilateral and bilateral arrangements.

ATTITUDES. Since two subject variables were used in selection, care had to be taken to avoid confounding them. Due to an apparent ideological bias in the F scale it might have been rather difficult to find high-F prolaborites or low-F antilaborites. Rokeach (1960) successfully developed a scale which is somewhat impervious to ideological content. Correlations between his Dogmatism Scale and scales of political-economic conservatism are low and nonsignificant. The D Scale was further modified by the investigator in order to remove vestiges of apparent ideological content which might have been associated with prolabor or promanagement attitudes. An attempt was also made to choose or construct items which sampled certain conceptual components of the dogmatism variable such as resisting pressures to change one's opinion, rejection of disbelievers, etc. There are 48 items fairly evenly divided over these various categories. Sixteen were borrowed from Rokeach (1960). In order to obviate an acquiescent response set from influencing the results, items are worded in two directions, reflecting both a high- and a low-dogmatic ideology. The split-half reliability, corrected by the Spearman-Brown formula, is .72.

Typical of the scale are the following original items, worded in both directions:

HIGH DOGMATIC

I feel quite justified in sticking to a position that I feel strongly about even in the face of strong opposition.

One must be as critical as possible of the ideas of one's opponents.

LOW DOGMATIC

If progress is ever to be made in this world, we must encourage cooperation between conflicting political and religious groups.

A leader should look to his opponents for good ideas as well as to his supporters.

Approximately the upper and lower quartiles of the modified D-Scale distribution were eligible for participation. However, only those also scoring in the upper and lower quartiles of the labor-management scale were used. That correlated subject variables were avoided is attested to by the interscale correlation of .011. There was no problem in recruiting procompany and prounion subjects at both extremes of the modified D Scale. The scores ranged from 87 to 177, with a mean of 128.30. The mean score for high dogmatics was 143.70 (V=.062), while the mean for low dogmatics was 112.92 (V=.067).

Recruitment of Subjects

Items from the labor-management scale and the modified Dogmatism Scale were administered together. The position of a given item was randomly determined. Respondents were to indicate the extent of their agreement on a 5-point scale ranging from strongly agree to strongly disagree.[5] In order to attain enough subjects at the extremes of both scale distributions, the questionnaire was administered to 850 students from five undergraduate psychology classes at Northwestern University. Respondents were informed that we were interested in recruiting people who had similar attitudes for participation in an interesting experiment.

As soon as both scales were scored, eligible respondents were placed in one of eight categories arranged by sex, dogmatism, and prounion or procompany. Conditions were assigned to sessions each week before subjects were contacted. Both levels of the three variables were interspersed in a randomlike manner in sessions during a given week.

Procedure

The situation facing the subjects was constructed in such a way so as to incorporate a number of parameters of a particular real world conflict. A complex simulation model was chosen over simpler, more popular situations on the presumption that subject behavior might come closer to their behavior in other conflict of interest situations, and the results might have more predictive validity for the situation being simulated. The simulation technique used also lends itself to the study of the effects of group commitment. A non-zero-sum collective bargaining game devised by Campbell (1960) was considerably modified for this experiment.

The following task description is for those subjects who were assigned to be representatives of laboratory teams which simulated an organization. Slight modifications, discussed below, were introduced when individuals bargained for themselves. Upon entering the laboratory the participants were told that they were being given the opportunity to learn about the bargaining process through participation and informed of research evidence indicating that simulations of processes were a more effective learning device than attending lectures or reading case studies.

Participants were then assigned to a three-member union or company team. They were told that assignment was made specifically on the basis of attitudes toward labor unions and management, but simi-

[5]Both scales have been deposited in their entirety with the American Documentation Institute. Order Document No. 9408 from ADI Auxiliary Publications Project, Photoduplication Service, Library of Congress, Washington, D.C. 20540. Remit in advance $1.25 for microfilm or $1.25 for photocopies and make checks payable to: Chief, Photoduplication Service, Library of Congress.

larity on other more general attitudes was also used as a criterion. The hypothetical company was called the Acme Steel Corporation. They were told that negotiations had been going on for awhile, but no contract had been signed. They were the newly chosen representatives. Both teams received four issues, each arranged on a 17-step scale with the position of the union and company, when negotiations broke off, at either extreme. Between these extremes some possible compromises were listed for the convenience of the bargainers. Below each position on the scale the estimated cost to the company in thousands of dollars for the duration of the contract, if the issue were settled at that position, was listed. In the individual sessions the cost was in dollars, but the scale was identical (e.g., $320 rather than $32,000). An example of an issue scale is as follows:

Percentage of company payment[6]

	0	10	20	30	40	50	60	70	80	
Company	(0)	(4)	(8)	(12)	(16)	(20)	(24)	(28)	(32)	Union

An issue was chosen on the basis of relevance to broader problems or a widely publicized grievance and whether it could be quantitatively defined. The scale range for each issue was as follows:

ISSUE	COMPANY POSITION	UNION POSITION
Wages	No raise	$ .16 raise per hour
Off-Job training	No vocational school payment	80% tuition fees paid by company
Hospital plan	20% premium payment	100% premium payment by company
Paid vacation	2 weeks for 1 year of service (no increase for more years)	3 weeks for 10 years of service (scale started at 3 weeks for 25 years)

In terms of cost to the company and union demands, the wage issue was the most expensive, while paid vacation was the least expensive. The other two were equally expensive and fell in between.

In order to give the bargainers some perspective and to provide a common starting point for position formation, a page of background information was provided. A brief statement of company and union

[6]This is a 17-step scale insofar as bargainers were able to use intervals of 5%.

rationale for their demands and "going rates" at four other similar hypothetical companies in the industry were included. The average going rate on each issue was between the starting union and company positions at Acme. Such information as profit and loss statements, company budgets, union funds, and a detailed history of company operations was not provided in an attempt to insure that the results would not be a function of built-in parameters and so that the teams would be given sufficient latitude to be flexible or rigid.

The experiment was divided into two phases. The first phase consisted of either studying the issues on a bilateral basis or planning strategies unilaterally. Participants in both conditions were not told of the exact procedure to be used in the bargaining session. Before the next phase all participants were asked to privately rank the importance of the four issues. The second phase consisted of randomly dividing the six bargainers into three union-company pairs for contract negotiations. In order to reduce the potential influence on any dyad coming from another pair or to insure independence, the pairs were separated into three corners of the room, and screens were placed around each bargaining table. To make sure that team identification was maintained, the representatives were told that the results of their negotiations would be included with the results of the bargaining efforts of their partners, and net gains in terms of a total score for the team would be computed. Thus each subject was bargaining for his team and, perhaps, expected to be measured against how well his two colleagues fared. This competitive set was pitted against the advantages of a quick settlement. The latter pressure was created by informing the bargainers that each 5 minutes of debate time would cost $5,000 (or $50 in the no-group condition) to each side in lost wages or profits.

The intergroup phase lasted for 30 minutes and was divided into 5-minute intervals, each 5 minutes representing a simulated day. Announcement of each 5 minutes of debate time was made by the experimenter. The latter's role was that of "referee," but he did not specifically observe each bargaining pair. In order for a contract to be settled, agreement must have been reached on each of the four issues. Bargainers were provided with contracts. If an issue was settled, they were asked to circle the position of settlement or write it in if it fell between two listed positions and initial their contract opposite the scale. If an issue was not settled at the deadline, the bargainers were asked to indicate, independently, the amount of movement that they were willing to concede in order to obtain an agreement.

Bargaining pairs were instructed to provide some indication of the approximate amount of time needed to discuss each issue. Each bargainer was given a time sheet arranged such that he would only have to record the time on his watch at the start of discussion of an issue and then again when ready to move on to another issue. If two or more issues were being discussed simultaneously, they were to record the same time for each of the issues. Many dyads did discuss issues simultaneously, and "package agreements" were occasionally negotiated. Bargainers did not have to settle an issue to move on to another one. They could go back to unsettled issues.

At the end of the second phase all representatives were brought together to fill out postnegotiation-reaction questionnaires. Some of the questions included the defensibility of one's starting position on each issue, the degree to which one wanted to see his team (or himself) come out favorably, and the extent to which compromise was perceived as defeat. None of the subjects was sophisticated enough about the manipulations to have his data invalidated.

While the participants were filling out the postnegotiation questionnaire, the experimenter combined the results for all dyads in order to give each team an idea of how it fared relative to the other. The resulting figures indicated how far the company and union teams were willing to move from their starting positions. The computational procedure is discussed in Druckman (1966).

RESULTS

It was assumed that the firmness of the two negotiators' commitment to their respective positions would be reflected in four measures of conflict resolution: the speed of resolution, average distance apart, average amount of yielding, and number of unresolved issues. Since the behavior of one representative in a bargaining dyad was not independent of the behavior of his opponent, the unit of analysis was the bargaining dyad rather than the individual bargainer. A special attempt was made to insure the independence of the three dyads in a group session during bargaining. Any given dyad was kept virtually unaware of the progress, situation, or completion of any other pair of bargainers. Since the independence of issues during debate is questionable, the effect of the manipulated conditions was assessed across the four issues.

Due to the imposition of a deadline on bargaining, there were both settled and unsettled contracts. Since it is hypothesized that the outcome of bargaining is a function of the manipulated conditions, both settled and unsettled contracts must be given equal consideration in any statistical analysis. The technique for inclusion of all contracts is specific to the measure used and is discussed below.

Speed of Resolution

A reciprocal transformation was performed on the time measure in order to insure stability in the variances (Edwards, 1960) and so that deadlocks could be taken into consideration. Deadlocks were assumed to be settled in an infinite amount of time. The reciprocal of infinity is zero so that deadlocks could be treated as zero values and included in the distribution with the reciprocals of all the other obtained values. Thus all unsettled contracts received the same score.

The harmonic mean times (the reciprocal of the mean of the reciprocals of the original values) are presented in Table 1. Bass (1963) claimed that the harmonic mean time can be interpreted as the speed with which the conflict is resolved, while the mean time is the length of time required to resolve the conflict. The harmonic means are somewhat inflated due to deadlocks. Table 2 reports the results of an analysis of variance performed on the reciprocals of the time measure. The strategy-study effect is highly significant. While the mean difference between high and low dogmatics is large and in the predicted direction, the effect does not quite reach significance. The group-no group main effect and the interactions account for a negligible portion of the total variance.

Average Distance Apart and Average Yielding

The indication of how far a bargainer was willing to go in order to obtain agreement on unsettled issues made it feasible to include all contracts, resolved and unresolved, in determining the average distance apart across all issues as well as the average yielding per contract.[7] Since each scale had the same num-

[7]Yielding to compromise and the amount of movement that one is willing to concede in order to obtain an agreement were equated in obtaining the measure of average yielding. Both are indicative of a "desire to compromise" rather than "the most desirable position for settlement."

ber of steps, it was possible to equate yielding from one scale to another.

Since the results for these two measures were highly similar, they are reported together. The results of analyses of variance for both measures, as reported in Table 2, show two main effects to be significant. High dogmatics were significantly further apart in their positions at the end of the bargaining session and yielded significantly less than low dogmatics. Strategy experience kept bargainers significantly further apart and resulted in significantly less yielding than study experience. While bargainers who represented groups were further apart and yielded less than bargainers who represented themselves, the mean difference was not large enough to be significant. The means are reported in Table 1. None of the interactions for either measure approached significance. When issues were included as a classification category, for both measures, neither the issue main effect nor any Issue $\times$ Condition interaction was significant. Thus high scores on the modified Dogmatism Scale and strategy prenegotiation experience kept bargainers further apart and produced less yielding irrespective of the issue being bargained for.

Number of Unresolved Issues

Each contract was represented by a score ranging from 0 to 4, depending upon how many issues were not settled. The Mann-Whitney *U* test, with a correction for ties, was used to analyze this data for each variable. A feature of this test is that the effect of tied ranks on p is practically negligible.

Table 3 shows the number of bargaining dyads or contracts with 0, 1, 2, 3, or 4 issues unresolved for each condition. Strategy experience before bargaining led to a higher rate of unresolved issues per contract than bilateral study experience. A Mann-Whitney *U* test yielded a z of 2.53 which is highly significant ($p < .005$). High dogmatics resolved fewer issues, on the average, per contract than low dogmatics. A z of 2.40 is highly significant ($p < .008$). Whether an individual represented himself or a group did not seem to have an effect on how many issues were resolved. A z of .608 is not significant.

TABLE 1 Means for Three Measures of Conflict Resolution

		Unilateral Strategy			Bilateral Study			
		Group Representation	Self Representation		Group Representation	Self Representation	High Dogmatic	Low Dogmatic
Speed of Resolution in Minutes	High Dogmatic	67.35	58.24		28.91	23.76	44.57[a]	
	Low Dogmatic	32.51	37.42		23.92	23.33		29.30[a]
	Unilateral Strategy	48.90[b]		Bilateral Study	24.98[b]			
	Group Representation	38.17[c]		Self Representation		35.69[c]		
Average Distance Apart	High Dogmatic	2.450	1.683		1.500	.667	1.575[a]	
	Low Dogmatic	.733	1.350		.300	.250		.658[a]
	Unilateral Strategy	1.554[b]		Bilateral Study	.679[b]			
	Group Representation	1.246[c]		Self Representation		.988[c]		
Average Yielding	High Dogmatic	6.942	7.208		7.250	7.667	7.267[a]	
	Low Dogmatic	7.642	7.325		7.850	7.875		7.673[a]
	Unilateral Strategy	7.279[b]		Bilateral Study	7.660[b]			
	Group Representation	7.421[c]		Self Representation		7.519[c]		

[a]Means for dogmatic-attitudes' main effect.
[b]Means for Unilateral Strategy-Bilateral Study main effect.
[c]Means for Group Representation-Self Representation main effect.

From the American Institutes for Research Creative Talents Awards Monograph, CTA Series No. 7, July 1969, Table 1, p. 76.

ABLE 2 Analyses of Variance of Three Measures of Conflict Resolution

		Reciprocal of Time to Complete Contracts		Average Distance Apart		Average Yielding	
ource	df	MS	F	MS	F	MS	F
ogmatic Attitudes (A)	1	.00211	2.30	25.208	5.34*	4.951	4.46*
nilateral Strategy–Bilateral Study (B)	1	.00965	10.54**	22.969	4.86*	4.361	3.93*
roup Representation–Self Representation (C)	1	.00009	<1	2.002	<1	.288	<1
X B	1	.00058	<1	.352	<1	.000	<1
X C	1	.00030	<1	8.802	1.86	1.782	1.60
X C	1	.00019	<1	1.008	<1	.453	<1
X B X C	1	.00000	<1	.675	<1	.069	<1
ithin Replicates	112	.00092		4.722		1.111	
tal	119						

$^{*}p < .05$.
$^{**}p < .01$.

From the American Institutes for Research Creative Talents Awards Monograph, CTA ries No. 7, July 1969, Table 2, p. 77.

TABLE 3 Number of Bargaining Dyads with 0, 1, 2, 3, or 4 Unresolved Issues

	Number of Unresolved Issues				
	0	1	2	3	4
Strategy	31	6	9	4	10
Study	43	7	4	3	3
High Dogmatic	31	7	8	5	9
Low Dogmatic	43	6	5	2	4
Group	38	8	5	4	5
No Group	36	5	8	3	8

Role Differences in Yielding Behavior

Dyadic analyses could not take into account differential bargaining behavior as a function of assigned role or the defensibility of the built-in positions. Thus, a five-way analysis of variance was performed with the intention of examining differential yielding as a function of assigned role and issue rather than in the effect of the manipulated conditions per se. Role and the Role × Issue interaction were highly significant and together accounted for 78% of the controlled variance. The Dogmatism × Role interaction was not significant indicating that high or low dogmatics behaved the same irrespective of their assigned role.

The mean amount of yielding for each role by issue across the three manipulated conditions is presented in Table 4. Observation of the means reveals that the role's main effect seems to be a function of differential yielding on one issue—hospital plan. The difference between the average yielding by company or employer representatives and union or employee representatives across the four issues is 2.329. When the hospital plan issue is excluded, the mean difference drops to .197.

Reference to data on perceived defensibility of the built-in starting positions by company or employer and union or employee representatives may provide an explanation for the Role × Issue interaction. Participants were to place each issue on a 5-point scale ranging from "more defensible than other side" to "not as defensible as other side." The position endorsed by the union representative or employee was subtracted from the posi-

TABLE 4 Mean Yielding by Company or Employer and Union or Employee Representatives by Issue

	Wages	Off-Job Training	Paid Vacation	Hospital Plan	Mean by Role
Company or Employer	7.750	7.742	6.675	3.058	6.306
Union or Employee	7.475	6.850	8.433	11.783	8.635
Mean by Issue	7.613	7.296	7.554	7.421	

tion endorsed by the company representative or employer in each dyad. The higher the mean across the 120 contracts in a positive direction, the more defensible was the union's position perceived to be; the higher the mean in a negative direction, the more defensible was the company's position perceived to be. The mean for each issue is as follows:

Wages	Off-job training
+.4298	+.1974
Paid vacation	**Hospital plan**
−.2818	−.6360

The difference between the means is highly significant ($p<.001$). Application of Duncan's multiple-range test indicated that only the mean difference between wages and off-the-job training is not significant or near significant ($p>.10$). The hospital plan issue was thus significantly less defensible to union and employee representatives than the other three issues. It was shown that differential yielding on hospital plan was considerably greater than on any of the other issues.

Table 4 also shows that company or employer representatives yielded less on paid vacation, while union or employee bargainers yielded less on wages and off-the-job training. The union position was considered to be more defensible on wages and off-the-job training, while less defensible on paid vacation and hospital plan. Thus, in a general way, differential yielding by role corresponds to the perceived defensibility of the built-in positions.

Data were not collected concerning reasons for defensibility ratings. However, a general correspondence between the average going rates and the defensibility ratings may be noted. The average going rate for wages and off-the-job training was half the distance between the company and union starting positions. The average going rate for the paid-vacation issue was four steps on the scale from the company starting position, while for hospital plan it was only three steps from the company position. The presumed relation between defensibility, going rates, and differential yielding is more suggestive than conclusive. As such these data suggest hypotheses which may be tested in another setting by, perhaps, manipulating defensibility and determining amount of yielding.

Agreement on the Ranked Importance of the Issues

If the study session was effective in facilitating communication between bargainers, this should be reflected in agreement on the ranked importance of the four issues. The method for determining the extent of agreement between two members of a bargaining dyad was to take the absolute difference between the ranks assigned to each issue by each member and sum the differences. The "agreement scores" were ranked and a Mann-Whitney *U* test was performed. The hypothesis was confirmed. Bargainers who studied the issues before negotiation agreed more on their relative importance than bargainers who planned strategies apart from one another. A z of 2.23 is highly significant ($p<.01$). The difference in amount of agreement between high dogmatics and low dogmatics or between group and individual representatives was slight and nonsignificant.

The amount of time spent discussing each issue corresponded to its average rank in importance. The wage issue was considered to be the most important ($\bar{x}=1.26$) and was discussed longest in debate (8.15 minutes), off-the-job training was second in both importance (2.19) and time to discuss (7.18 minutes), followed by hospital plan (3.03 and 4.13 minutes) and paid vacation (3.52 and 3.65 minutes). The order of ranked importance was not affected by condition or role.

Involvement and the Perception of Compromise as Defeat

In general, representatives wanted themselves or their teams to come out favorably in the negotiations. The overall mean was 1.45 on a 4-point scale. Group representatives wanted their team to come out favorably significantly more than individuals wanted themselves to come out favorably. The means were 1.37 in the case of group representatives and 1.54 for bargainers representing themselves ($t=2.51$, $p<.01$). The differences between the other conditions were small and nonsignificant.

High dogmatics viewed compromise as defeat significantly more than did low dogmatics. The question was asked on a 3-point scale. The means were 2.11 for high dogmatics and 2.37 for low dogmatics ($t=3.36$, $p<.001$). The differences between the other conditions were small and nonsignificant.

DISCUSSION

The results appear to be quite consistent across the measures of conflict resolution used. Strategy experience before bargaining led to a hardening of positions as reflected in measures of agreement and amount of yielding. Bilateral study experience, on the other hand, resulted in faster agreement and more yielding on the part of bargainers. These results were a function of prenegotiation experience apart from the effects of group commitment per se. Whether bargainers represented groups or themselves did not have a significant effect on compromise behavior. That study experience was more effective in facilitating communication may have been revealed in the greater agreement on the ranking of the importance of the issues by bargainers after bilateral study.

The modified Dogmatism Scale was also predictive of conflict resolution. Irrespective of strategy or study prenegotiation experience, high dogmatics were more resistant to compromise than low dogmatics. A postnegotiation question revealed that high dogmatics viewed compromise as defeat more than low dogmatics. The dogmatic subjects behaved in keeping with the theory and evidence presented by Rokeach (1960) and the evidence of Jamias (1964). They were less willing to defect from given positions. Blake and Mouton (1962) and Sherif and Sherif (1965) dismissed the relevance of psychodynamic explanations of behavior in an intergroup situation. The results of this study suggest that these explanations cannot be dismissed so lightly. The low correlation between the modified Dogmatism Scale and the labor-management attitude scale suggests that the former may be tapping a general disposition not related to political or specific content attitudes. Also there were no differences between high- or low-dogmatic union representatives and high- or low-dogmatic company representatives on yielding behavior. It might be interesting to examine the relationship between this scale and extant measures of misanthropy.

Bargainers who represented groups behaved no differently than those who bargained for themselves. A careful attempt was made to maintain group identification during the bargaining session. Bargainers were told, before negotiations, that a team score would be determined and a "winner" and "loser" announced. The results of a postnegotiation question indicated that this manipulation might have been effective. Group representatives wanted their team to come out favorably more than individuals wanted themselves to come out favorably. It is conceivable that such alternative procedures as having all three representatives bargain together as a team or choosing one to represent the team during bargaining might have intensified the salience of representing a laboratory team. However, both alternatives would require a greatly increased number of group sessions and the possibility of unwanted constraints on the bargainers from the bargaining session itself due to the "public" nature of the situation. Only further investigations can clarify this issue.

Experimental studies of intergroup relations have been characterized by the use of short-lived ad hoc groups. The Sherif et al. (1961) boys' camp study is perhaps the only exception. While certain steps were taken in this study to increase group cohesion, group identification or the intensity of competition might have been increased if the groups interacted over a longer period of time. At the current stage of empirical development it is difficult to assess the relevance of findings from simulated groups for groups with their own developmental history.

The implications of this study are clear. While the negotiation situation facing professional diplomats and bargainers is more complicated and more is at stake, these results may be suggestive to those social engineers responsible for creating situations more conducive to agreement. The unilateral attachments of representatives may not lie in their group identifications, but may be the result of a disciplined reticence toward their opponents. When representatives are given positions to defend but compromise is the desired goal, a problem-solving atmosphere, with no sanctions against open discussion from either side, is recommended. However, this should take place before representatives have a chance to develop rationale or a cognitive context for their own position. This may be similar to the situation in labor-management contract negotiations where arbitrators assign starting positions to the contending parties and have them discuss their relative merits in the context of both vantage points. It also appears that efforts aimed at reducing conflict have a better chance of succeeding if carried out by people who are more collaborative in interpersonal relations and who do not view compromise as defeat.

REFERENCES

Bass, B. M. Effects on negotiators of their prior experience in strategy or study groups. Technical Report No. 1, 1963, Contract Nonr 624(14), Office of Naval Research.

Bass, B. M. and Dunteman, G. Biases in the evaluation of one's own group, its allies and opponents. *Journal of Conflict Resolution*, 1963, 7, 16–20.

Blake, R. R. Psychology and the crisis of statesmanship. *American Psychologist*, 1959, 14, 87–94.

Blake, R. R. and Mouton, J. S. Competition, communication, and conformity. In I. A. Berg and B. M. Bass (Eds.), *Conformity and deviation.* New York: Harper & Row, 1961. Pp. 199–229.

Blake, R. R. and Mouton, J. S. The intergroup dynamics of win–lose conflict and problem-solving collaboration in union-management relations. In M. Sherif (Ed.), *Intergroup relations and leadership.* New York: Wiley, 1962. Pp. 94–140.

Blalock, H. M. *Social statistics.* New York: McGraw-Hill, 1960.

Campbell, R. J. *Originality in group productivity: III. Partisan commitment and productive independence in a collective bargaining situation.* Columbus: Ohio State University Research Foundation, 1960.

Crowne, D. P. Family orientation, level of aspiration, and interpersonal bargaining. *Journal of Personality and Social Psychology*, 1966, 3, 641–645.

Deutsch, M. Trust, trustworthiness, and the F scale. *Journal of Abnormal and Social Psychology*, 1960, 61, 138–140.

Deutsch, M. Cooperation and trust: Some theoretical notes. In M. R. Jones (Ed.), *Nebraska symposium on motivation: 1962.* Lincoln: University of Nebraska Press, 1962. Pp. 275–320.

Druckman, D. Dogmatism, prenegotiation experience and simulated group representation as determinants of dyadic behavior in a bargaining situation. Unpublished doctoral dissertation, Northwestern University, 1966.

Edwards, A. L. *Experimental design in psychological research.* New York: Holt, Rinehart and Winston, 1960.

Ferguson, C. K. and Kelley, H. H. Significant factors in overevaluation of own-group's product. *Journal of Abnormal and Social Psychology,* 1964, 69, 223–228.

Gladstone, A. I. Relationship orientation and processes leading toward war. *Background,* 1962, 6, 13–25.

Jamias, J. F. The effects of belief system styles on the communication and adoption of farm practices. Unpublished doctoral dissertation, Michigan State University, 1964.

Lutzker, D. R. Internationalism as a predictor of cooperative behavior. *Journal of Conflict Resolution,* 1960, 4, 426–430.

Mack, R. W. and Snyder, R. C. The analysis of social conflict—toward an overview and synthesis. *Journal of Conflict Resolution,* 1957, 1, 212–248.

Pearson, L. B. *Diplomacy in the nuclear age.* Cambridge: Harvard University Press, 1959.

Rokeach, M. *The open and closed mind.* New York: Basic Books, 1960.

Rusk, D. Parliamentary diplomacy—debate versus negotiation. *World Affairs Interpreter,* 1955, 26, 121–138.

Sherif, M., Harvey, O. J., White, B. J., Hood, W. R., and Sherif, C. W. *Intergroup conflict and cooperation: The robbers cave experiment.* Norman, Okla.: University Book Exchange, 1961.

Sherif, M. and Sherif, C. W. Research on intergroup relations. In O. Klineberg and R. Christie (Eds.), *Perspectives in social psychology.* New York: Holt, Rinehart and Winston, 1965. Pp. 153–177.

Sumner, W. G. *Folkways.* Boston: Ginn, 1906.

Turk, H. and Lefcowitz, M. J. Towards a theory of representation between groups. *Social Forces,* 1962, 40, 337–341.

Vegas, O. V., Frye, R. L., and Cassens, F. P. Learning set as a determinant of perceived cooperation and competition. *American Psychologist,* 1964, 19, 482. (Abstract)

KENNETH K. SERENO
C. DAVID MORTENSEN

The Effects of Ego-Involved Attitudes on Conflict Negotiation in Dyads

Conflicts of one sort or another appear in virtually any social setting where individuals interact to reach some mutually acceptable outcome. And when conflict arises among communicators in small groups, the nature of each individual's attitude toward the topic is apt to be a determinant of any joint decision or outcome. Yet despite the acknowledged importance of attitudes in influencing behavior, few studies have been designed to ascertain how attitudinal structures are related to the processes and outcome of conflict-generating discussion. Most of the literature on attitude change focuses upon responses of subjects who are passive recipients of communication, stresses intrapersonal inconsistency reduction, and does not provide appreciable insight into the dynamics of attitudinal factors as they affect intragroup conflict. As recently as 1966, a review of small group research concludes that very little is known about "the impact of attitudes toward the task and the situation on member and group performance, or on interpersonal relations in the group."[1]

From Kenneth K. Sereno and C. David Mortensen, "The Effects of Ego-Involved Attitudes on Conflict Negotiation in Dyads," *Speech Monographs 36*, 1969, 8–12.

[1]Joseph E. McGrath and Irwin Altman, *Small Group Research* (New York, Holt, Rinehart and Winston, 1966), p. 57.

Similarly, the literature on conflict deals typically with such factors as the need for communication,[2] cooperative versus competitive orientations,[3] threat,[4] hostility,[5] and aggressive versus avoidance behaviors;[6] and with the significance of these factors for processes of bargaining or negotiation.

In conceptualizations of conflict and its resolution, the notion of ego-involvement advanced by Sherif et al. appears to be quite relevant.[7] Though the construct of ego-involvement is not a theory of conflict per se, it provides a basis for predicting conditions under which attitudes—including, presumably, those operating in situations of interpersonal conflict—are susceptible to change. Ego-involvement is defined as the importance or relevance of the topic to an individual as revealed by the person's commitment or stand on an issue. Sherif's social judgment-involvement approach specifies that those persons who are highly involved in their attitudinal stands are less susceptible to change than are those individuals who are not appreciably involved. A person who endorses a moderate position in which he is highly involved, according to Sherif, would be less apt to change his stand than would someone who endorses a more extreme position in which he is less involved. Hence, the critical factor in predicting change is not simply relative extremity of the conflicting attitudinal stands on an issue but rather the intensity or involvement underlying such discrepant positions. Such a theoretical viewpoint clashes with the common belief that extreme attitude positions are necessarily less susceptible to change. It has always seemed sensible to presume that a person who takes

[2]Anatol Rapoport, *Fights, Games, and Debates* (Ann Arbor, University of Michigan Press, 1960).

[3]Morton Deutsch and Robert M. Krauss, "Studies of Interpersonal Bargaining," *The Journal of Conflict Resolution*, VI (1962), 52–76.

[4]*Ibid.*

[5]Theodore M. Newcomb, "Autistic Hostility and Social Reality," *Human Relations*, I (1947), 69–86.

[6]John W. Thibaut and John Coules, "The Role of Communication in the Reduction of Interpersonal Hostility," *The Journal of Abnormal and Social Psychology*, 47 (1952), 770–777.

[7]Carolyn W. Sherif, Muzafer Sherif, and Roger E. Nebergall, *Attitude and Attitude Change: the Social Judgment-Involvement Approach* (Menlo Park, Calif., W. B. Saunders, 1965).

an extreme stand is less likely to abandon or modify his position than is someone who is neutral or who takes a moderate position.

The question, then, is whether the construct of ego-involvement provides a useful predictor of outcome in situations of interpersonal conflict. Sherif's theoretical basis of prediction is, as explained previously, involvement or commitment rather than simply the extremity of attitudinal stands. If the social judgment-involvement approach is relevant to interpersonal decision-making, then in the particular case of two-member groups or dyads, individuals who are extremely opposed but slightly involved should be susceptible to yielding their own stands and reaching some form of mutually acceptable agreement. Conversely, individuals in dyads who hold equally extreme positions but who are highly involved in their stands should be less susceptible to attitudinal change through negotiation.

In this study, the notion of ego-involvement provides the basis for two specific hypotheses. The first concerns the extent of public agreement or consensus reached by opposing two-member groups:

HYPOTHESIS 1: Dyads consisting of slightly involved subjects will reach public agreement with greater frequency than will dyads consisting of subjects who are highly involved.

The second hypothesis extends the reasoning of the first. For subjects to reach public agreement, one or the other or both must abandon their original stands on the issue. If slightly involved subjects reach agreement more frequently than do highly involved subjects, then this difference should be reflected in greater individual attitude changes upon completion of the negotiating process. Therefore:

HYPOTHESIS 2: Dyads consisting of slightly involved subjects will exhibit greater changes between private pretest and posttest responses than will subjects who are highly involved.

PROCEDURE

Subjects were obtained from fundamentals of speech classes at the University of Washington. The method for determining level of ego-involvement consisted of a modification of Sherif's "Own Categories"[8] procedure; on a semantic-differential scale subjects were asked to designate those positions which they found to be *most acceptable, acceptable,* and *nonacceptable.*[9] Three pairs of evaluatively loaded bipolar adjectives (safe/dangerous, wise/foolish, and warranted/unwarranted) were used to evaluate the experimental topic "Legalization of the sale of marijuana." The *most acceptable* positions for each subject on the three bipolar scales were summed. Extreme positive ratings received a score of 1 while extreme negative ratings received a score of 7, the highest possible positive score being 3 and the highest possible negative score being 21.

The experimental treatment was administered only to subjects who endorsed extreme *most acceptable* positions (summed scores of 3 to 6 on the positive, and 18 to 21 on the negative extreme) and who showed either high or low involvement in their stands. Highly involved subjects were operationally defined as those extreme subjects having a minimum latitude of rejection or nonacceptance of 12 (that is, having found at least four of the seven possible positions on each of the three pairs of bipolar scales to be *nonacceptable*) and a maximum latitude of acceptance of 3 (that is, having found no more than one position on each of the three bipolar scales to be *acceptable* in addition to the *most acceptable* position). Slightly involved subjects were operationally defined as those extreme subjects having a latitude of rejection no greater than 6 (that is, having found no more than two of the seven possible positions on each of the three pairs of bipolar scales to be *nonacceptable*).

The experimental treatment was administered five days after

[8]The essence of Sherif's "Own Categories" procedure consists of having a subject sort statements on the issue into a series of separate piles, each pile representing what he considers to be a different stand on the issue. The patterns which result from the subject's sorting of statements and the subject's designation of those piles or stands he considers *most acceptable, acceptable, nonacceptable,* and to which he is *noncommital* indicate his level of ego-involvement.

[9]Lufty N. Diab, "Measurement of Social Attitudes: Problems and Prospects," *Attitude, Ego-Involvement and Change,* ed. Carolyn W. Sherif and Muzafer Sherif (New York, Wiley, 1967), pp. 140–158.

the pretest. Selected subjects were paired randomly in dyads consisting of opposing members who were both either highly or slightly involved. Subjects were told that they would have ten minutes of negotiating time to persuade one another to accept what each thought to be the *most acceptable* stand on the topics.[10] Subjects used a semantic differential that was identical to the one used on the pretest as the basis of their negotiation. Posttest measures consisted of two indices of public agreement and a private expression of attitude on the topic. The measures of public agreement were, first, the number of *dyads* that reached agreement on one or more scales, and second, the total number of *scales* upon which agreement was reached. As a measure of private attitude, subjects independently completed these same scales immediately after the negotiation, *most acceptable* positions being scored identically as the pretest.

RESULTS

The .05 level of significance was required for all statistical tests.

Hypothesis 1 was supported by the data. Dyads consisting of subjects who were slightly involved reached public agreement with greater frequency than did dyads consisting of subjects who were highly involved (see Table 1). While nine of the ten dyads consisting of highly involved subjects failed to reach any agreement, only two of the eighteen dyads consisting of lowly involved subjects were unable to reach agreement on at least one

[10]Subjects were then instructed:

"You can have three possible outcomes. (1) You may not be able to reach any agreement without greatly compromising your personal convictions: if so, then leave the scales blank on the response sheet. (2) You may be able to reach partial agreement without greatly compromising your convictions: if so, then mark an "X" on that position on the scale(s) which corresponds to your joint agreement on the response sheet. (3) You may be able to reach full agreement without greatly compromising your personal convictions; if so, then mark an "X" on all the scales which correspond to your joint agreements on the response sheet.

Remember, any agreement reached must be mutually satisfactory. However, agreement should not be sought at the expense of greatly compromising your personal convictions."

TABLE 1 Frequency of Public Agreement

Level of Involvement	Number of Dyads[1] (HI* n = 10, LI** n = 18)		Number of Scales[2] (HI n = 30, LI n = 54)	
	Agreement	No Agreement	Agreement	No Agreement
High	1	9	2	28
Low	16	2	30	24

[1] χ^2 = 12.95 (corrected for continuity), p. = <.05.
[2] χ^2 = 17.84, p. = <.05.
*HI = High Involvement.
**LI = Low Involvement.

of the three bipolar scales. The chi square (corrected for continuity)[11] of 12.95 was significant (critical χ^2 with 1 df=3.94). Further, dyads consisting of subjects who were slightly involved reached agreement on a larger number of scales than did dyads consisting of subjects who were highly involved. While highly involved dyads reached agreement on only two of thirty scales (10 dyads × 3 scales), slightly involved dyads reached agreement on thirty of fifty-four scales (18 dyads × 3 scales). The resulting chi square of 17.84 was significant (critical χ^2 with 1 df=3.94).

Hypothesis 2 was also supported by the data. Dyads consisting of slightly involved subjects exhibited greater changes between private pretest and posttest responses than did dyads consisting of subjects who were highly involved. Specifically, highly involved subjects did not significantly change their *most acceptable* attitude positions on the topic, while slightly involved subjects did significantly change theirs. These results were in accord with expectations and lent support to the hypothesis (see Table 2). Analysis of covariance[12] was used to directly test the hypothesis, with pretest *most acceptable* scores serving as the

[11] Hubert M. Blalock, *Social Statistics* (New York: McGraw-Hill, 1960), pp. 220–221.
[12] Allen L. Edwards, *Experimental Design in Psychological Research* (New York: Holt, Rinehart and Winston, 1960), pp. 281–300.

TABLE 2 Most Acceptable Mean Scores on Topic "Legalization of Sale of Marijuana"

	n	Pretest	Private Posttest	Difference	t
High Involvement					
Pro toward topic on pretest	10	4.0	4.8	0.8	1.395
Con toward topic on pretest	10	20.5	19.6	−0.9	−1.784
Low Involvement					
Pro toward topic on pretest	18	5.5	7.8	2.3	2.257*
Con toward topic on pretest	18	19.9	14.5	−5.4	−4.340*

*p = <.05; one-tailed test.

adjusting measure. Posttest means for highly and slightly involved subjects who initially favored the topic differed significantly (F=7.048; df=1/25). Posttest means for highly and slightly involved subjects who initially opposed the topic also differed significantly (F=9.850; df=1/25).

DISCUSSION

The findings of the present research attest to the relevance of ego-involvement to conflict negotiation in dyads. Both the frequency of public agreement and the degree of individual or private attitude change was found to be a function of involvement on the topic.

Of significance, also, is the added confirmation of the distinction between extremity of attitude position and the intensity of attitudinal commitment. Recall that all subjects endorsed polarized attitudes positions. Yet significant differences occurred in the responses—both public and private—between highly and slightly involved individuals. In accordance with predictions, slightly involved individuals reached some degree of perceived group agreement with greater frequency than did those dyads composed solely of opposed and highly involved persons; also, slightly involved persons demonstrated significantly greater amounts of individual attitude change than did highly involved subjects.

Though the results of the present research indicate something about the outcome of conflict negotiation under restricted conditions, quite different sorts of outcomes might have occurred if extremity of attitude and degree of ego-involvement had been manipulated in other ways. For instance, what would be the outcome if one member of the pair were highly while the other was slightly involved, or if a highly or slightly involved neutral subject was paired with a highly or slightly involved extreme subject?

Then, too, ego-involvement does not operate in a vacuum. That competitive and cooperative orientations, threat, hostility, and aggressive and avoidance behaviors are variables relevant to conflict behavior has already been noted. It is likely that these variables interact with ego-involvement to affect processes and outcomes of negotiation. Prior research also suggests that information about the group task, perception of opposing parties, goal orientation, time factors, pressures toward conformity and a host of other variables have a bearing upon group processes. How such factors interact with ego-involvement in determining processes and outcomes of conflict await future investigation.

PART IV
Small-Group Conflict

While the previous two parts have dealt with general theories of social conflict and with individual behavior in situations of social conflict, the focus of the next two parts is conflict in particular settings. Extensive analyses have been published on conflict in small groups. Much of this has dealt with short-lived problem-solving groups. Morton Deutsch in "Conflicts: Productive and Destructive," his 1968 Kurt Lewin Memorial Address, discusses destructive and constructive conflicts in much broader contexts than short-lived problem-solving groups. B. Aubrey Fisher in "Decision Emergence: Phases in Group Decision-Making" reports the development of a category system used to evaluate ten problem-solving groups and discusses conflict as one phase in a group's history following an orientation phase and preceding a phase during which conflict is dissipated and decisions emerge.

The family is the most frequently occurring small group. The failure to resolve conflict in the family may be reflected in separation, divorce, and delinquency. Barry has provided an extensive review of the marriage and conflict literature.[1] Robert O. Blood, Jr. in "Resolving Family Conflicts" discusses the sources of family conflict and its resolution.

[1]William A. Barry, "Marriage Research and Conflict: An Integrative Review," *Psychological Bulletin 73*, 1970, 41–54.

Also a frequently occurring group is the classroom. Allan D. Frank in "Conflict in the Classroom" discusses the sources of conflict in the student-teacher relationship and in peer relationships among students in the classroom. The classroom is viewed as a microcosm of society in which unintentional modes of conflict resolution may be learned and in which the suppression of conflict is detrimental to the development of optimum conditions for learning.

The use of small-group conflict to resolve international conflict is described by Leonard W. Doob, William J. Foltz, and Robert B. Stevens in "The Fermeda Workshop: A Different Approach to Border Conflicts in Eastern Africa." Participants in the workshop from Somalia, Ethiopia, and Kenya were involved in this experiment. The workshop has also been described by Doob *et al.*[2] and by Walton.[3]

The constructive use of conflict in organizations is a crucial concern to organizational theorists. The grievance procedure is an institutionalized mode of resolving organizational conflict. Collective bargaining between management and organized labor is a conflict situation. The use of conflict in organizations may be related to productivity. Clagett G. Smith in "A Comparative Analysis of Some Conditions and Consequences of Intra-Organizational Conflict" discusses interpersonal conflict in various types of organizations.

[2]Leonard William Doob *et al.*, eds. *Resolving Conflict in Africa: The Fermeda Workshop* (New Haven: Yale University Press, 1970).

[3]Richard E. Walton, "A Problem-Solving Workshop on Border Conflicts in Eastern Africa," *Journal of Applied Behavioral Science 6*, 1970, 453–489.

MORTON DEUTSCH

Conflicts: Productive and Destructive

It is a great honor and delight for me to receive the Kurt Lewin Memorial Award. As you know, Kurt Lewin has had a profound influence on my life and work. I have been influenced by his value orientations as well as his theoretical orientations. He believed that an intellectually significant social science has to be concerned with the problems of social action and social change and that intelligent social action has to be informed by theory and research. He rejected both a heartless science and a mindless social action. I am proud to have had this remarkable man as a teacher and as a guide.

I wish to discuss the characteristics of productive and destructive conflict and to consider the conditions which give rise to one or another type. Although actual conflicts are rarely purely benign or malign, it is useful for analytic purposes to consider the simple cases. Doing so highlights not only the differences in the outcomes of conflict but also the differences in types of processes by which the outcomes are derived.

From Morton Deutsch, "Conflicts: Productive and Destructive," *The Journal of Social Issues* 25, 1969, 7–41, Kurt Lewin Memorial Address given at the meetings of the American Psychological Association, September 1, 1968, in San Francisco. Preparation of this paper was supported by a contract with the Office of Naval Research, Nonr-4294(00), and a grant from the National Science Foundation, GS-302.

Let me start with the dull but necessary chore of defining some of the key terms that I shall be using. A *conflict* exists whenever *incompatible* activities occur. The incompatible actions may originate in one person, in one group, in one nation; and such conflicts are called *intra*personal, *intra*group, or *intra*national. Or they may reflect incompatible actions of two or more persons, groups or nations; such conflicts are called *inter*personal, *inter*group, or *inter*national. An action which is incompatible with another action prevents, obstructs, interferes with, injures, or in some way makes it less likely or less effective.

A conflict may arise from differences in information or belief (my wife thinks our son's mosquito bites are better treated by calamine lotion, while I think caladryl is better). It may reflect differences in interests, desires or values (I prefer to invest our savings in the stock market while my wife would prefer to spend it on winter vacations). It may occur as a result of a scarcity of some resource such as money, time, space, position (the more closet space that my wife uses for her clothing, the less space there is for my files). Or it may reflect a rivalry in which one person tries to outdo or undo the other.

COMPETITION AND CONFLICT

The terms *competition* and *conflict* are often used synonymously or interchangeably. I believe such usage reflects a basic confusion. Although competition produces conflict, not all instances of conflict reflect competition. Competition implies an opposition in the goals of the interdependent parties such that the probability of goal attainment for one decreases as the probability for the other increases. In conflict which is derived from competition, the incompatible actions reflect incompatible goals. However, conflict may occur even when there is no perceived or actual incompatibility of goals. Thus, if my wife and I are in conflict about how to treat our son's mosquito bites it is not because we have mutually exclusive goals; here, our goals are concordant. The distinction between conflict and competition is not one which I make merely to split hairs. It is an important one and is basic to a theme that underlies this paper: Conflict can occur in a cooperative or competitive context and the processes of conflict resolution which are likely to be displayed will be strongly influenced by the context within which conflict occurs.

I am concerned with psychological or perceived conflict—i.e., conflicts which exist psychologically for the parties involved. I do not assume that perceptions are always veridical nor do I assume that actual incompatibilities are always perceived. Hence, it is important in characterizing any conflict to depict the objective state of affairs, the state of affairs as perceived by the conflicting parties, and the interdependence between the objective and perceived realities. Let me illustrate some of the possibilities of misperception. I may perceive an incompatibility where there is none (my wife's clothes and my files may both be able to fit into our closets even though neither of us believes so); I may perceive an incompatibility as noncontingent but, in reality, it is contingent upon changeable features of the situation (her clothes and my files can both fit if I remove some shelves from the closet that are rarely used); I may experience the frustration and annoyance of incompatible actions without perceiving that they are due to conflict (my closet space may have become cramped and overcrowded because my wife has placed various objects into my space without my being aware of this); or I may perceive an incompatibility but make the wrong attribution so that I perceive the nature of the conflict incorrectly (I may blame my son for having put some of his things in my closet when it was done by my wife).

The possibility that the nature of a relationship may be misperceived indicates that the lack of conflict as well as the occurrence of conflict may be determined by misunderstanding or misinformation about the objective state of affairs. Thus, the presence or absence of conflict is never rigidly determined by the objective state of affairs. Apart from the possibility of misperception, psychological factors enter into the determination of conflict in yet another crucial way. Conflict is also determined by what is valued by the conflicting parties. Even the classical example of pure conflict—two starving men on a lifeboat with only enough food for the survival of one—loses its purity if one or both of the men have social or religious values which can become more dominant psychologically than the hunger need or the desire for survival.

The point of these remarks is that neither the occurrence nor the outcomes of conflict are completely and rigidly determined by objective circumstances. This means that the fates of the particiants in a situation of conflict are not inevitably determined by the external circumstances in which they find themselves. Whether conflict takes a productive or destructive course is thus open to influence even under the most unfavorable objective conditions. Similarly, even under the most favorable objective circumstances, psychological factors can lead conflict to take a destructive course. I am not denying the importance of "real" conflicts but rather I am asserting that the psychological processes of perceiving and valuing are involved in turning objective conditions into experienced conflict.

CONSTRUCTIVE AND DESTRUCTIVE

In the next section, I shall characterize the typical development and course of destructive and constructive conflicts. Here let me clarify what I mean by the value-laden terms *constructive* and *destructive*. At the extremes, these terms are easy to define. Thus, a conflict clearly has destructive consequences if the participants in it are dissatisfied with the outcomes and all feel they have lost as a result of the conflict. Similarly, a conflict has productive consequences if the participants all are satisfied with their outcomes and feel that they have gained as a result of the conflict. Also, in most instances, a conflict whose outcomes are satisfying to all the participants will be more constructive than one which is satisfying to some and dissatisfying to others.

My characterization of destructive and constructive conflicts obviously has its roots in the ethical value "the greatest good for the greatest number." Admittedly, there are still considerable theoretical and empirical difficulties to be overcome before such a value can be operationalized with any generality or precision. It is, of course, easier to identify and measure satisfactions–dissatisfactions and gains–losses in simple laboratory conflict situations than it is in the complex conflicts of groups in everyday life. Yet even in the complex situations, it is not impossible to compare conflicts roughly in terms of their outcomes. In some instances, union-management negotiations may lead to a prolonged strike with considerable loss and ill-will resulting to both parties; in other instances it may lead to a mutually satisfying agreement where both sides obtain something they want. In some cases, a quarrel between a husband and wife will clear up unexpressed misunderstandings and lead to greater intimacy while in others it may produce only bitterness and estrangement.

One more definitional point. It is often useful to distinguish between the "manifest" conflict and the "underlying" conflict. Consider the conflict of an obsessional patient over whether or not she should check to see if she really turned off the stove, or the argument of two brothers over which TV program is to be tuned in, or the controversy between a school board and a teachers' union over the transfer of a teacher, or an international dispute involving alleged infractions of territory by alien aircraft. Each of these manifest conflicts may be symptomatic of underlying conflict: The obsessional patient may want to trust herself but may be afraid that she has impulses which would be destructive if unchecked; the two brothers may be fighting to obtain what each considers to be his fair share of the family's rewards; and so on. "Manifest" conflict often cannot be resolved more than temporarily unless the underlying conflict is dealt with or unless it can be disconnected and separated from the underlying conflict so that it can be treated in isolation.

I shall now turn to the basic questions to which this paper is addressed. What are the characteristic symptoms and courses of conflicts which end up one way or the other? What are the factors which make a conflict move in one direction or the other? I do not pretend that I have complete or even satisfying answers. Nevertheless, I hope that you will agree that these are questions which warrant attention.

THE COURSE OF DESTRUCTIVE CONFLICT

Destructive conflict is characterized by a tendency to expand and to escalate. As a result, such conflict often becomes independent of its initiating causes and is likely to continue after these have become irrelevant or have been forgotten. Expansion occurs along the various dimensions of conflict: the size and number of the immediate issues involved; the number of the motives and participants implicated on each side of the issue; the size and number of the principles and precedents that are perceived to be at stake; the costs that the participants are willing to bear in relation to the conflict; the number of norms of moral conduct from which behavior toward the other side is exempted; and the intensity of negative attitudes toward the other side.

The processes involved in the intensification of conflict may be said, as Coleman (1957, 14) has expressed it, "to create a 'Gresham's Law of Conflict': the harmful and dangerous elements drive out those which would keep the conflict within bounds." Paralleling the expansion of the scope of conflict there is an increasing reliance upon a strategy of power and upon the tactics of threat, coercion, and deception. Correspondingly, there is a shift away from a strategy of persuasion and from the tactics of conciliation, minimizing differences, and enhancing mutual understanding and goodwill. And within each of the conflicting parties, there is increasing pressure for uniformity of opinion and a tendency for leadership and control to be taken away from those elements that are more conciliatory and invested in those who are militantly organized for waging conflict through combat.

THREE INTERRELATED PROCESSES

The tendency to escalate conflict results from the conjunction of three interrelated processes: (a) competitive processes involved in the attempt to win the conflict; (b) processes of misperception and biased perception; and (c) processes of commitment arising out of pressures for cognitive and social consistency.

These processes give rise to a mutually reinforcing cycle of relations which generate actions and reactions that intensify conflict.

Other factors, of course, may serve to limit and encapsulate conflict so that a spiraling intensification does not develop. Here, I am referring to such factors as: the number and strength of the existing cooperative bonds, cross-cutting identifications, common allegiances and memberships among the conflicting parties; the existence of values, institutions, procedures and groups that are organized to help limit and regulate conflict; and the salience and significance of the costs of intensifying conflict. If these conflict-limiting factors are weak, it may be difficult to prevent a competitive conflict from expanding in scope. Even if they are strong, misjudgment and the pressures arising out of tendencies to be rigidly self-consistent may make it difficult to keep a competitive conflict encapsulated.

COMPETITIVE EFFECTS

Elsewhere (Deutsch 1962a, 1965a) I have characterized the essential distinctions between a cooperative and competitive process and described their social psychological features in some detail. Here, I shall only highlight some of the main features of the competitive process. In a competitive encounter as one gains, the other loses. Unlike the cooperative situation where people have their goals linked so that everybody "sinks or swims" together, in the competitive situation if one swims, the others must sink.

Later in the paper, I shall detail some of the factors which lead the parties in a conflict to define their relationship as a competitive one. For the moment, let us assume that they have competitively defined their conflict and let us examine the consequences of doing so and also why these consequences tend to expand conflict. Typically, a competitive process tends to produce the following effects:

1. Communication between the conflicting parties is unreliable and impoverished. The available communication channels and opportunities are not utilized or they are used in an attempt

to mislead or intimidate the other. Little confidence is placed in information that is obtained directly from the other; espionage and other circuitous means of obtaining information are relied upon. The poor communication enhances the possibility of error and misinformation of the sort which is likely to reinforce the preexisting orientations and expectations toward the other. Thus, the ability to notice and respond by the other away from a win–lose orientation becomes impaired.

2. It stimulates the view that the solution of the conflict can only be of the type that is imposed by one side on the other by superior force, deception, or cleverness—an outlook which is consistent with the definition of the conflict as competitive or win–lose in nature. The enhancement of one's own power and the complementary minimization of the other's power become objectives. The attempt to create or maintain a power difference favorable to one's own side by each of the conflicting parties tends to expand the scope of the conflict as it enlarges from a focus on the immediate issue in dispute to a conflict over who shall have the power to impose his preference upon the other.

3. It leads to a suspicious, hostile attitude which increases the sensitivity to differences and threats, while minimizing the awareness of similarities. This, in turn, makes the usually accepted norms of conduct and morality which govern one's behavior toward others who are similar to oneself less applicable. Hence, it permits behavior toward the other which would be considered outrageous if directed toward someone like oneself. Since neither side is likely to grant moral superiority to the other, the conflict is likely to escalate as one side or the other engages in behavior that is morally outrageous to the other side. Of course, if the conflicting parties both agree, implicitly or explicitly, on the rules for waging competitive conflict and adhere to the agreement then this agreement serves to limit the escalation of conflict.

MISJUDGMENT AND MISPERCEPTION

In our preceding discussion of the effects of competition, it was evident that impoverished communication, hostile attitudes, and oversensitivity to differences could lead to distorted views of the other which could intensify and perpetuate conflict. In addition to the distortions that are natural to the competitive process, there are other distortions which commonly occur in the course of interaction. Elsewhere (Deutsch 1962b, 1965b) I have described some of the common sources of misperception in interactional situations. Many of these misperceptions function to transform a conflict into a competitive struggle even if the conflict did not emerge from a competitive relationship.

Here let me illustrate with the implications of a simple psychological principle: *The perception of any act is determined both by our perception of the act itself and by our perception of the context in which the act occurs.* The contexts of social acts are often not immediately given in perception and often they are not obvious. When the context is not obvious, we tend to assume a familiar context—a context which is most likely in terms of our own past experience. Since both the present situations and past experience of the actor and perceiver may be rather different, it is not surprising that they will interpret the same act quite differently. Misunderstandings of this sort, of course, are very likely when the actor and the perceiver come from different cultural backgrounds and are not fully informed about these differences. A period of rapid social change also makes such misunderstandings widespread as the gap between the past and the present widens.

Given the fact that the ability to place oneself in the other's shoes is notoriously underdeveloped in most people and also that this ability is further impaired by stress and inadequate information, it is not astonishing that certain typical biases emerge in the perceptions of actions during conflict. Thus, since most people are motivated to maintain a favorable view of themselves but are less strongly motivated to hold such a view of others, it is not surprising that there is a bias toward perceiving one's own behavior toward the other as being more benevolent and more legitimate than the other's behavior toward oneself. Here I am simply restating a well-demonstrated psychological truth: Namely, the evaluation of an act is affected by the evaluation of its source; the source is part of the context of behavior.

Research, for example, has shown that American students are likely to rate more favorably an action of the United States directed toward the Soviet Union than the same action directed by the Soviet Union toward the United States. We are likely to view American espionage activities in the Soviet Union as more benevolent than similar activities by Soviet agents in the United States.

If each side in a conflict tends to perceive its own motives and behavior as more benevolent and legitimate than those of the other side, it is evident that conflict will spiral upward in intensity. If "Acme" perceives its actions as a benevolent and legitimate way of interfering with actions that "Bolt" has no right to engage in, "Acme" will certainly be amazed by the intensity of "Bolt's" hostile response and will have to escalate his counter-action to negate "Bolt's" response. But how else is "Bolt" likely to act if he perceives his own actions as well-motivated? And how likely he is to respond to "Acme's" escalation with still further counterescalation if he is capable of so doing![1]

To the extent that there is a biased perception of benevolence and legitimacy, one could also expect that there will be a parallel bias in what is considered to be an equitable agreement for resolving conflict: Should not differential legitimacy be differentially rewarded? The biased perceptions of what is a fair compromise makes agreement more difficult and, thus, extends conflict. Another consequence of the biased perception of benevolence and legitimacy is reflected in the asymmetries between trust and suspicion, and between cooperation and competition. Trust, when violated, is more likely to turn into suspicion than negated suspicion is to turn into trust. Similarly, it is easier to move in the direction from cooperation to competition than from competition to cooperation.

[1]Deutsch's choice of the terms "Acme" and "Bolt" recall his studies using a two-person experimental bargaining game. For example see Morton Deutsch and Robert M. Krauss, "The Effect of Threat Upon Interpersonal Bargaining," *Journal of Abnormal and Social Psychology 61*, 1960, 181–189. (Editor's note.)

OTHER PROCESSES LEADING TO MISPERCEPTION

There are, of course, other types of processes leading to misperceptions and misjudgments. In addition to the distortions arising from the pressures for self-consistency and social conformity (which are discussed below), the intensification of conflict may induce stress and tension beyond a moderate optimal level and this over-activation, in turn, often leads to an impairment of perceptual and cognitive processes in several ways: it reduces the range of perceived alternatives; it reduces the time-perspective in such a way as to cause a focus on the immediate rather than the overall consequences of the perceived alternatives; it polarizes thought so that percepts tend to take on a simplistic cast of being "black" or "white," "for" or "against," "good" or "evil"; it leads to stereotyped responses; it increases the susceptibility to fear- or hope-inciting rumors; it increases defensiveness; it increases the pressures to social conformity. In effect, excessive tension reduces the intellectual resources available for discovering new ways of coping with a problem or new ideas for resolving a conflict. Intensification of conflict is the likely result as simplistic thinking and the polarization of thought pushes the participants to view their alternatives as being limited to "victory" or "defeat."

Paradoxically, it should also be noted that the very availability of intellectual and other resources which can be used for waging conflict may make it difficult, at the onset of conflict, to forecast the outcome of an attempt to impose one's preference upon the other. Less inventive species than man can pretty well predict the outcome of a contest by force through aggressive gesturing and other display of combat potential; thus, they rarely have to engage in combat to settle "who shall get what, when." The versatility of man's techniques for achieving domination over other men makes it likely that combat will arise because the combatants have discordant judgments of the potential outcomes. Unlike his hairy ancestors, the "naked ape" cannot agree in advance who will win. Misjudgment of the other side's willingness and capability of fighting has sometimes turned controversy into combat as increased tension has narrowed the perceived outcomes of conflict to victory or defeat.

PROCESSES OF COMMITMENT

It has long been recognized that people tend to act in accord with their beliefs; more recently, Festinger has emphasized in his theory of cognitive dissonance that the converse is also often true: People tend to make their beliefs and attitudes accord with their actions. The result of this pressure for self-consistency may lead to an unwitting involvement in and intensification of conflict as one's actions have to be justified to oneself and to others. The tragic course of American involvement in the civil war in Vietnam provides an illustration.

In an unpublished paper presented over two years ago (1966) I wrote:

> How did we get involved in this ridiculous and tragic situation: a situation in which American lives and resources are being expended in defense of a people who are being more grievously injured and who are becoming more bitterly antagonistic to us the more deeply we become involved in their internal conflict? How is it that we have become so obsessed with the war in South Vietnam that we are willing to jettison our plans for achieving a Great Society at home, neglect the more important problems in South America and India, and risk destroying our leadership abroad? Not so long ago, we had a different view of the importance of Vietnam. In 1954, despite urgent French pleas, President Eisenhower refused to let the American military intervene even if all of Vietnam should fall. Senator Lyndon B. Johnson, at that time, vehemently opposed the use of American soldiers in this far-off land.
>
> Now that we are massively involved in South Vietnam, we hear many different rationalizations of our involvement: Dean Rusk has cited the SEATO treaty commitment, but as Richard N. Goodwin has pointed out in *The New Yorker* (April 16, 1966): "No adviser in the highest councils ever urged action on the basis of the SEATO treaty; none, as far as I know, ever mentioned the existence of such a pledge. And, in fact, there was no such commitment." Efforts to justify our involvement in terms of showing the communists that internal subversion does not pay are also not convincing: Would they not have already learned from Greece, Malaya, the Philippines, the

Congo and Burma, if this was the lesson that had to be taught? Similarly, how persuasive is the "domino theory" when such big dominoes as China, itself, and also such small ones as Cuba have fallen without creating any noticeable domino effect? Nor can we claim "defense of freedom" as our justification when we consider how undemocratic the governments of South Vietnam have been—from Diem's to Ky's.

Why then are we involved in the war in South Vietnam?

Continued Involvement Justifies Past Involvement

The most direct statement of the reason for our continued involvement is the fact that we are involved: Our continued involvement justifies our past involvement. Once involved it is exceedingly difficult to disengage and to admit, thereby, how purposeless and unwitting our past involvement has been. I am stating, in other words, that we are not involved because of any large strategic or moral purpose, and that any such purposes we now impute to our involvement are *ex post facto* rationalizations.

As a nation, we stumbled into the conflict in South Vietnam under the mistaken assumption that "victory might come easily and with little pain." At every step of increasing involvement, we were led to believe that with some small additional help (first economic aid, then military advisers, then the use of American helicopters, then the combat use of American soldiers, then massive air intervention by American planes, then bombing of the North, then massive intervention of American troops, and so on) we would not risk a major conflict. Yet we would help to build an independent, stable country that could stand on its own feet. We have over and over again acted on the tempting assumption that with just a little more investment we would prevent the whole thing from going down the drain.

This type of assumption is one with which we are familiar in connection with the psychology of gambling. We all know of the losing gambler, getting deeper and deeper into a hole, who keeps on betting with the hope that by so doing he will recover his initial losses. Not all losing gamblers submit to the gambler's temptation of course. But those whose sense of omnipotence is at stake, those who are too proud to recognize that they cannot overcome the odds against them are vulnerable to this type of disastrous temptation. Are we, as a nation, so committed to a view of ourselves as omnipotent that we cannot recognize that we are making the wrong gamble?

Gradual and Unwitting Commitment

In addition to the gambler's temptation, I shall describe briefly three other processes of gradual and unwitting commitment. One is the much-discussed process of *dissonance-reduction*. As Festinger (1961) has pointed out: "rats and people come to love the things for which they have suffered." Presumably they do so in order to reduce the dissonance induced by the suffering and their method of dissonance-reduction is to enhance the attractiveness of the choice which led to their suffering: Only if what one chose was really worthwhile would all of the associated suffering be tolerable. Have we not increased what we perceive to be at stake in the Vietnam conflict as it has become more and more costly for us? We are now at the point where we are told that our national honor, our influence as a world leader, our national security are in the balance in the conflict over this tragic little land.

Silvan Tomkins (Tomkins and Izard, 1965) has described a process of *circular, incremental magnification* which also helps to explain the widening of involvement and the monopolization of thought. He suggests that it occurs if there is a sequence of events of this type: threat, successful defense, breakdown of defense and re-emergence of threat, second successful new defense, second breakdown of defense and re-emergence of threat, and so on until an expectation is generated that no matter how successful a defense against a dreaded contingency may seem, it will prove unavailing and require yet another defense. This process is circular and incremental since each new threat requires a more desperate defense and the successive breakdown of each newly improved defense generates a magnification of the nature of the threat and the concurrent affect which it evokes. The increasing and obsessive preoccupation with Vietnam may, in part, reflect just such a process: Time and time again, we have assumed that a new and more powerful defense or assault against the Vietcong would do the trick only to find that a new and more powerful military commitment was required. By now, according to newspaper reports, Vietnam almost monopolizes the thinking of our national leaders and the attention given to more fundamental concerns is minimized.

Situational Entrapment

Let me, finally, turn to an everyday process of unwitting involvement: *situational entrapment*. The characteristic of this process is that behavior is typically initiated under the assumption that the environment is compliant rather than reactive—that it responds as a tool for one's purposes rather than as a self-maintaining system. Well-intentioned actions sometimes produce effects opposite to those intended because the actions do not take into account the characteristics of the setting in which they take place. By now, we are all aware that an unintended consequence of some public health measures in Latin

America was the population explosion. Only now, are we beginning to recognize that some consequences of the types of aid we have given to some underdeveloped countries is to hinder their economic development and to foster a need for ever-increasing aid. Similarly, one may propose that the nature of the American intervention in Vietnam has served to weaken the opposition to the Vietcong, demoralize those in Vietnam who were able and willing to rely on the Vietnamese to solve their problems without foreign control, increase the strength and resolution of the Vietcong, and otherwise produce the responses which would require an increasing involvement and commitment of American resources and men just to prevent an immediate overturn of the situation.

I have used the war in Vietnam to illustrate the process of unwitting involvement in the intensification of conflict. It could also be used to indicate the consequences of a competitive process of resolving our conflicts with Communist China, North Vietnam, and the Vietcong. There has been little in the way of open and honest communication, there has been massive and mutual misperception and misunderstanding, there has been intense mutual suspicion and hostility, there has been derogation of the possibilities of agreement other than those imposed by force, there has been a widening of the scope of the issues in conflict and an escalation of the force employed, and there has been an increasing attempt to polarize loyalties and allegiances about this one area of conflict.

A destructive conflict such as the one in which we have been engaged in Vietnam can be brought to a conclusion because the costs of continuing the conflict become so large in relation to any values that might be obtained through the conflict's continuance that its senselessness becomes compellingly apparent. The senselessness is likely to be most apparent to those who have not been the decision-makers and thus have little need to justify the conflict, and to those who bear the costs most strongly. Destructive conflict can also be aborted before running its full course if there is a strong enough community or a strong third party that can compel the conflicting parties to end their violence. We in the United States are in the unfortunate position that relative to our prestige and power there is neither a disinterested third party nor an international community that is powerful enough to motivate us to accept a compromise when we think our own interests may be enhanced by the outcome of a competitive struggle. Peace in Vietnam might have occurred much earlier if the UN, or even our friends, could have influenced us.

PRODUCTIVE CONFLICT

It has been long recognized that conflict is not inherently pathological or destructive. Its very pervasiveness suggests that it has many positive functions. It prevents stagnation, it stimulates interest and curiosity, it is the medium through which problems can be aired and solutions arrived at; it is the root of personal and social change. Conflict is often part of the process of testing and assessing oneself and, as such, may be highly enjoyable as one experiences the pleasure of the full and active use of one's capacities. Conflict, in addition, demarcates groups from one another and, thus, helps to establish group and personal identities; external conflict often fosters internal cohesiveness. Moreover, as Coser (1956, 154) has indicated:

> In loosely-structured groups and open societies, conflict, which aims at a resolution of tension between antagonists, is likely to have stabilizing and integrative functions for the relationship. By permitting immediate and direct expression of rival claims, such social systems are able to readjust their structures by eliminating the sources of dissatisfaction. The multiple conflicts which they experience may serve to eliminate the causes for dissociation and to re-establish unity. These systems avail themselves, through the toleration and institutionalization of conflict, of an important stabilizing mechanism.

I stress the positive functions of conflict, and I have by no means provided an exhaustive listing, because many discussions of conflict cast it in the role of the villain as though conflict *per se* were the cause of psychopathology, social disorder, war. The question I wish to raise now is whether there are any distinguishing features in the process of resolving conflict which lead to the constructive outcomes? Do lively, productive controversies have common patterns that are distinctive from those characterizing deadly quarrels?

IN THE LITERATURE

I must confess that as I started to work on this paper I had expected to find in the social science literature more help in answering these questions than I have found so far. The writings, for example, on personality development, unfortunately, have little to say about productive conflict; the focus is on pathological conflict. Similarly, the voluminous literature on social conflict neglects productive conflict between groups. It is true that the long-standing negative view of social conflict has yielded to an outlook which stresses the social functions of conflict. Nevertheless, apart from the writings of people connected with the "nonviolence" movement little attempt has been made to distinguish between conflicts that achieve social change through a process that is destructive, from one that is mutually rewarding to the parties involved in the conflict. Yet change can take place either as it has at Columbia, through a process of confrontation which is costly to the conflicting groups, or it can take place through a process of problem-solving, as it has at Teachers College, which is mutually rewarding to the conflicting groups.

My own predilections have led me to the hunch that the major features of productive conflict resolution are likely to be similar, at the individual level, to the processes involved in creative thinking and, at the social level, to the processes involved in cooperative group problem-solving. Let me first turn to the process involved in creative thinking. For an incisive, critical survey of the existing literature I am indebted to Stein (1968).

CREATIVE THINKING

The creative process has been described as consisting of several overlapping phases. Although various authors differ slightly in characterizing the phases, they all suggest some sequence such as the following:

1. An initial period which leads to the experiencing and rec-

ognition of a problem which is sufficiently arousing to motivate efforts to solve it.

2. Second, a period of concentrated effort to solve the problem through routine, readily available, or habitual actions.

3. Then, with the failure of customary processes to solve the problem, there is an experience of frustration, tension, and discomfort which leads to a temporary withdrawal from the problem.

4. During this incubation period of withdrawal and distancing from the problem, it is perceived from a different perspective and is reformulated in a way which permits new orientations to a solution to emerge.

5. Next, a tentative solution appears in a moment of insight often accompanied by a sense of exhilaration.

6. Then, the solution is elaborated and detailed and tested against reality.

7. Finally, the solution is communicated to relevant audiences.

There are three key psychological elements in this process:

1. the arousal of an appropriate level of motivation to solve the problem;

2. the development of the conditions which permit the reformulation of the problem once an impasse has been reached; and

3. the concurrent availability of diverse ideas which can be flexibly combined into novel and varied patterns.

Each of these key elements is subject to influence from social conditions and the personalities of the problem-solvers.

THE AROUSAL OF THE OPTIMAL LEVEL OF MOTIVATION

Consider the arousal of an optimal level of motivation, a level sufficient to sustain problem-solving efforts despite frustrations and impasses and yet not so intense that it overwhelms or that it prevents distancing from the problem. Neither undue smugness nor satisfaction with things as they are nor a sense of helplessness, terror, or rage are likely to lead to an optimal motivation to recognize and face a problem or conflict. Nor will a passive readiness to acquiesce to the demands of the environment; nor will the willingness to fit oneself into the environment no matter how poorly it fits oneself. Optimal motivation, rather, presupposes an alert readiness to be dissatisfied with things as they are and a freedom to confront one's environment without excessive fear, combined with a confidence in one's capacities to persist in the face of obstacles. The intensity of motivation that is optimal will vary with the effectiveness with which it can be controlled: The more effective the controls, the more intense the motivation can be without its having disruptive consequences.

Thus, one of the creative functions of conflict resides in its ability to arouse motivation to solve a problem which might otherwise go unattended: A scholar who exposes his theories and research to the scrutiny of his peers may be stimulated to a deeper analysis when he is confronted with conflicting data and theoretical analysis by a colleague. Similarly, individuals and groups who have authority and power and who are satisfied with the status quo may be aroused to recognize problems and be motivated to work on them as opposition from the dissatisfied makes the customary relations and arrangements unworkable and unrewarding. They may be motivated also by being helped to perceive the possibilities of more satisfying relations and arrangements. Acceptance of the necessity of a change in the status quo rather than a rigid, defensive adherence to previously existing positions is most likely, however, when the circumstances arousing new motivations suggest courses of action that contain minimal threat to the social or self-esteem of those who must change.

Threats Induce Defensiveness

Thus, although acute dissatisfaction with things as they are on the one hand, and the motivation to recognize and work at problems on the other, are necessary for creative solutions, they are not sufficient. The circumstances conducive to creativity are varied but they have in common that "they provide the individidual with an environment in which he does not feel threatened and in which he does not feel under pressure. He is relaxed but alert" (Stein, 1968). Threat induces defensiveness and reduces the tolerance of ambiguity as well as openness to the new and unfamiliar; excessive tension leads to a primitivism and stereotyping of thought processes. As Rokeach (1960) has pointed out, threat and excessive tension leads to the "closed" rather than "open" mind. To entertain novel ideas which may at first seem wild and implausible, to question initial assumptions or the framework within which the problem or conflict occurs, the individual needs the freedom or courage to express himself without fear of censure. In addition, he needs to become sufficiently detached from his original viewpoints to be able to see the conflict from new perspectives.

Although an unpressured and unthreatening environment facilitates the restructuring of a problem or conflict, and, by so doing, makes it more amenable to solution, the ability to reformulate a problem and to develop solutions is, in turn, dependent upon the availability of cognitive resources. Ideas *are* important for the creative resolution of conflict and any factor which broadens the range of ideas and alternatives cognitively available to the participants in a conflict will be useful. Intelligence, the exposure to diverse experiences, an interest in ideas, a preference for the novel and complex, a receptivity to metaphors and analogies, the capacity to make remote associations, independence in judgment, the ability to play with ideas are some of the personal factors which characterize creative problem-solvers. The availability of ideas is also dependent upon social conditions such as the opportunity to communicate with and be exposed to other people who may have relevant and unfamiliar ideas (i.e., experts, impartial outsiders, people with similar or analogous situations), a social atmosphere which values innovation and originality and which encourages the exchange of ideas, and a social tradition which fosters the optimistic view that, with effort and time, constructive solutions can be discovered or invented to problems which seem initially intractable.

Let me note that in my view the application of full cognitive resources to the discovery and invention of constructive solutions of conflict is relatively rare. Resources are much more available for the waging of conflict. The research and development expenditures on techniques of conflict waging or conflict suppression, as well as the actual expenditures on conflict-waging, dwarf the expenditures for peace-building. This is obviously true at the national level where military expenditures dominate our national budget. I would contend that this is also true at the interpersonal and intergroup levels. At the interpersonal level, most of us receive considerable training in waging or suppressing conflict and we have elaborate institutions for dealing with adversary relations and for custodial care of the psychological casualties of interpersonal conflict. In contrast, there is little formal training in techniques of constructive conflict resolution, and the institutional resources for helping people to resolve conflicts are meagre indeed.

COOPERATIVE PROBLEM-SOLVING

In a cooperative context, a conflict can be viewed as a common problem in which the conflicting parties have the joint interest of reaching a mutually satisfactory solution. As I have suggested earlier in the paper, there is nothing inherent in most conflicts which makes it impossible for the resolution of conflict to take place in a cooperative context through a cooperative process. It is, of course, true that the occurrence of cooperative conflict resolution is less likely in certain circumstances and in certain types of conflict than in others. We shall consider some of the predisposing circumstances in a later section.

There are a number of reasons why a cooperative process is likely to lead to productive conflict resolution:

1. It aids open and honest communication of relevant information between the participants. The freedom to share information enables the parties to go beneath the manifest to the underlying issues involved in the conflict and, thereby, to facili-

tate the meaningful and accurate definition of the problems they are confronting together. It also enables each party to benefit from the knowledge possessed by the other and, thus, to face the joint problem with greater intellectual resources. In addition, open and honest communication reduces the likelihood of the development of misunderstandings which can lead to confusion and mistrust.

2. It encourages the recognition of the legitimacy of each other's interests and of the necessity of searching for a solution which is responsive to the needs of each side. It tends to limit rather than expand the scope of conflicting interests and, thus, minimizes the need for defensiveness. It enables the participants to approach the mutually acknowledged problem in a way which utilizes their special talents and enables them to substitute for one another in their joint work so that duplication of effort is reduced. Influence attempts tend to be limited to processes of persuasion. The enhancement of mutual resources and mutual power become objectives.

3. It leads to a trusting, friendly attitude which increases sensitivity to similarities and common interests, while minimizing the salience of differences. However, one of the common pathologies of cooperation (Deutsch, 1962a) is expressed in premature agreement: a superficial convergence in beliefs and values before the underlying differences have been exposed.

It can be seen that a cooperative process produces many of the characteristics that are conducive to creative problem-solving—openness, lack of defensiveness, full utilization of available resources. However, in itself, cooperation does not insure that problem-solving efforts will be successful. Such other factors as the imaginativeness, experience, and flexibility of the parties involved are also determinative. Nevertheless, if the cooperative relationship is a strong one it can withstand failure and temporarily deactivate or postpone conflict. Or, if it cannot be delayed, cooperative relations will help to contain destructive conflict so that the contest for supremacy occurs under agreed upon rules.

CONTROLLED COMPETITIVE CONFLICT

So far, my discussion has centered on unregulated conflict. I have considered characteristics of a destructive competitive process in which the outcomes are determined by a power struggle and also those of a cooperative process in which the outcomes are determined by joint problem-solving. However, it is evident that competitive conflict, because of its destructive potential, is rarely unregulated. It is limited and controlled by institutional forms (e.g., collective bargaining, the judicial system), social roles (mediators, conciliators, referees, judges, policemen), social norms ("fairness," "justice," "equality," "nonviolence," "integrity of communication," etc.), rules for conducting negotiations (when to initiate and terminate negotiations, how to set an agenda, how to present demands, etc.), and specific procedures ("hinting" versus "explicit" communication, public versus private sessions, etc.). These societal forms may be aimed at regulating how force may be employed (as in the code of a duel of honor or in certain rules of warfare), or it may be an attempt to ascertain the basic power relations of the disputants without resort to a power struggle (as is often the case in the negotiations of collective bargaining and international relations), or it may be oriented toward removing power as the basis for determining the outcome of conflict (as is often the case in judicial processes).

With regard to regulated conflict, it is pertinent to ask what are the conditions which make it likely that the regulations will be adhered to by the parties in conflict? In a duel of honor, when would a duelist prefer to die rather than cheat? These questions, if pursued along relevant intellectual lines would lead to an examination of different forms of rule violation and social deviance, their genesis and control. Such an investigation is beyond the scope of this paper. However, it seems reasonable to assert that adherence to the rules is more likely when: (a) the rules are known, unambiguous, consistent, and unbiased; (b) the other adheres to the rules; (c) violations are quickly known by significant others; (d) there is significant social approval for adherence and significant social disapproval for violation; (e) adherence to the rules has been rewarding while uncontrolled conflict has been costly in the past; and (f) one would like to be able to employ the rules in future conflicts. Undoubtedly, the most critical influence serving to encapsulate and control competitive conflict is the existence of common membership in a community which is strong enough to evoke habitual compliance to its values and procedures and also confident enough of its strength to tolerate internal struggles.

There are several productive possibilities which inhere in regulated conflict. It provides a basis for resolving a conflict when no other basis for agreement can be reached: "First choice" goes to the winner of the contest. However, the winner is not necessarily the sole survivor as may be the case in an uncontrolled test of power. The values and procedures regulating the conflict may select the winner on some other basis than the relative combat strength of the contestants. A conflict between husband and wife or between the United States and one of its citizens may be settled by a judicial process which permits the contestant with a stronger legal claim to win even though his physical prowess may be weaker. Or, the rules may make the contest one of intellectual rather than physical power. Thus, by the regulation of conflict a society may encourage the survival of certain values and the extinction of others because the rules for conducting conflict reflect the values of the society.

Also, insofar as a framework for limiting a conflict exists it may encourage the development of the conflict sufficiently to prevent "premature cooperation." The fear of the consequences of unrestrained conflict may lead to a superficial, unsatisfying, and unstable agreement before the underlying issues in the conflict have been worked through. The freedom to push deeper into a conflict because some of its potential dangers have been eliminated is, of course, one of the characteristics of creative conflict resolution. However, for the conflict to be contained as it deepens, there must be a community which is strong enough to bind the conflicting parties to the values and procedures regulating conflict. If the direct or mediated cooperative interests of the conflicting parties are weak, the control process is likely to fail or be subverted; the agreements arrived at will be challenged and undermined; conflict will escalate and take a destructive turn. Effective regulation presupposes a firm basis of confidence in the mutual allegiance to the procedures limiting conflict.

CONDITIONS WHICH INFLUENCE THE COURSE OF CONFLICT RESOLUTION

I now turn to a consideration of the factors which tend to elicit one or the other process of conflict resolution. First, I shall consider the question: What gives rise to a destructive or constructive course of conflict? Next, I shall consider the more difficult question: What can be done to change a destructive conflict into a constructive one?

FACTORS DETERMINING THE COURSE OF CONFLICT

There are innumerable specific factors which may influence the course which a conflict takes. It is useful to have some simplifying outline that highlights central determinants and permits a proliferation of detail as this becomes necessary.

Process

In the preceding sections, I have indicated that the characteristic strategies and tactics elicited by cooperative and competitive processes tend to be self-confirming and self-perpetuating. The strategy of power and the tactics of coercion, threat, and deception result from and result in a competitive orientation. Similarly, the strategy of mutual problem-solving and the tactics of persuasion, openness, and sharing elicit and are elicited by a cooperative orientation. However, cooperation which is reciprocated by competition is more likely to end up as mutual competition than mutual cooperation.

Prior Relationship

The stronger and the more salient the existing cooperative as compared with the competitive bonds linking the conflicting parties, the more likely it is that a conflict will be resolved cooperatively. The total strength of the cooperative bonds is a function of their importance as well as their number. There are obviously many different types of bonds that could be enumerated: superordinate goals, mutually facilitating interests, common allegiances and values, linkages to a common community, and the like. These bonds are important to the extent that they serve significant needs successfully. Thus, experiences of successful prior cooperative relationships together enhance the likelihood of present cooperation; experiences of failure and disillusionment in attempts to cooperate make it unlikely. On the other hand, the past experience of costly competitive conflict does not necessarily enhance the probability of cooperation, although this is a possible result.

The Nature of the Conflict

Here I wish to highlight several major dimensions of conflict: the size (scope, importance, centrality), rigidity, and interconnectedness of the issues in conflict.

Roger Fisher (1964), in a brilliant paper entitled "Fractionating Conflict," has pointed out that "issue control" may be as important as "arms control" in the management of conflict. His thesis is the familiar one that small conflicts are easier to resolve than large ones. However, he also points out that the participants may have a choice in defining the conflict as a large or small one. Conflict is enlarged by dealing with it as a conflict between large rather than small units (as a conflict between two individuals of different races or as a racial conflict), as a conflict over a large substantive issue rather than a small one (over "being treated fairly" or "being treated unfairly at a particular occasion"), as a conflict over a principle rather than the application of a principle, as a conflict whose solution establishes large rather than small substantive or procedural precedents. Many other determinants of conflict size could be listed. For example, an issue which bears upon self-esteem or change in power or status is likely to be more important than an issue which does not. Illegitimate threat or attempts to coerce are likely to increase the size of the conflict and thus increase the likelihood of a competitive process.

"Issue rigidity" refers to the availability of satisfactory alternatives or substitutes for the outcomes initially at stake in the conflict. Although motivational and intellectual rigidity may lead the parties in conflict to perceive issues more rigidly than reality dictates, it is also evident that certain issues are less conducive to cooperative resolution than others. "Greater power over the other," "victory over the other," "having more status than the other" are rigid definitions of conflict since it is impossible on any given issue for both parties in conflict to have outcomes which are superior to the other's.

Many conflicts do not, of course, center on only one issue. If the issues are separable or sufficiently uncorrelated, it is possible for one side to gain on one issue and the other side to find satisfaction in another issue. This possibility is enhanced if the parties do not have the same evaluations: Issue A is important to one and not the other, while the reverse is true for issue B.

The Characteristics of the Parties in Conflict

Ideology, personality, and position may lead to a more favorable evaluation of one process than the other. The strategy and tactics associated with competitive struggle may seem more manly or intriguing than those associated with cooperation: Consider the contrasting popular images of the soldier and of the diplomat. Similarly, the characteristics of the individual parties to a conflict will help determine the size and rigidity of the issues that they perceive to be in conflict and also their skill and available resources for handling conflict one way or another.

In addition, conflict and dissension within each party may affect the course of conflict between them. Internal conflict will often either increase external belligerence as a tactic to increase internal cohesiveness or lead to external weakness and possibly tempt the other side to obtain a competitive advantage. Internal instability also interferes with cooperative conflict resolution by making it difficult to work out a durable, dependable agreement.

Estimations of Success

Many conflicts have an unplanned, expressive character in which the course of action taken is an expression both of the quality of the relationship between the participants and of the characteristics of the individual participants. Other conflicts are guided by an instrumental orientation in which courses of action are consciously evaluated and chosen in terms of how likely they are to lead to satisfying outcomes. Many factors influencing the estimations of success of the different processes of conflict resolution could be listed. Those who perceive themselves to have a clear superiority in power are likely to favor an unregulated competitive process; those who perceive themselves as having a legal superiority in "rights" are likely to favor adversary relations that are regulated by legal institutions; those who are concerned with the long-range relationships, with the ability to work together in the future are more likely to favor a cooperative process. Similarly, those who have been excluded from the cooperative process and expect the regulations to be stacked against them may think of the competitive process as the only one offering any potential of satisfaction.

Third Parties

The attitudes, strength, and resources of interested third parties are often crucial determinants. Thus, a conflict is more likely to be resolved cooperatively if powerful and prestigious third parties encourage such a resolution and help to provide problem-solving resources (institutions, facilities, personnel, social norms, and procedures) to expedite discovery of a mutually satisfactory solution.

CHANGING THE COURSE OF CONFLICT

From much that I have stated earlier, it is evident that I believe that a *mutually* cooperative orientation is likely to be the most productive orientation for resolving conflict. Yet it must be recognized that the orientations of the conflicting parties may not be mutual. One side may experience the conflict and be motivated to resolve it; the other side may be content with things as they are and not even aware of the other's dissatisfaction. Or both may recognize the conflict but one may be oriented to a win-lose solution while the other may be seeking a cooperative resolution. We have suggested earlier that the usual tendency for such asymmetries in orientation is to produce a change toward mutual competition rather than mutual cooperation. It is, after all, possible to attack, overcome, or destroy another without his consent but to cooperate with another, he must be willing or, at least, compliant.

How can Acme induce Bolt to cooperate in resolving a conflict if Bolt is not so inclined or if Bolt perceives his interests as antagonistic to Acme's? There is, obviously, no single answer to this question. What answer is appropriate depends upon such factors as: the nature of the conflict, the relative power of Acme and Bolt, the nature and motivation of Bolt's noncooperation, the particular resources and vulnerabilities of each party, and their relationships to third parties. However, it is evident that the search for an answer must be guided by the realization that there are dangers in certain types of influence procedures. Namely, they may boomerang and increase open resistance and alienation or they may merely elicit a sham or inauthentic cooperation with underlying resistance. Inauthentic cooperation is more difficult to change than open resistance because it masks and denies the underlying alienation.

Let me offer some hypotheses about the types of influence procedures which are likely to elicit resistance and alienation:

1. *Illegitimate techniques* which violate the values and norms governing interaction and influence that are held by the other are alienating (the greater the violation, the more important and the more numerous the values being violated, the greater will be the resistance). It is, of course, true that sometimes an adaptation-level effect occurs so that frequently violated norms lose

their illegitimacy (as in parking violations); at other times, the accumulation of violations tends to produce an increasingly negative reaction.

2. *Negative sanctions* such as punishments and threats tend to elicit more resistance than positive sanctions such as promises and rewards. What is considered to be rewarding or punishing may also be influenced by one's adaptation level; the reduction of the level of rewards which are customarily received will usually be viewed as negative.

3. Sanctions which are *inappropriate* in kind are also likely to elicit resistance. Thus, the reward of money rather than appreciation may decrease the willingness to cooperate of someone whose cooperation is engendered by affiliative rather than utilitarian motives. Similarly, a threat or punishment is more likely to be effective if it fits the crime than if its connection with the crime is artificial. A child who breaks another child's toy is punished more appropriately if he has to give the child a toy of his own as a substitute than if he is denied permission to watch TV.

4. Influence which is *excessive* in magnitude tends to be resisted; excessive promise or reward leads to the sense of being bribed, excessive threat or punishment leads to the feeling of being coerced.

These factors summate. Illegitimate threat which is inappropriate and excessive is most likely to elicit resistance and alienation while an appropriate legitimate reward is least likely to do so. Inauthentic cooperation, with covert resistance, is most likely when resistance is high and when bribery or coercion elicits overt compliance.

WHAT ACTION INDUCES COOPERATION?

I have, so far, outlined what one should *not* do if one wants to elicit authentic cooperative conflict resolution. Let me turn now to the question of what courses of action can be taken which are likely to induce cooperation. In so doing, I wish to focus on a particularly important kind of conflict: conflict between those groups who have considerable authority to make decisions and relatively high control over the conventional means of social and political influence, and those groups who have little decision-making authority and relatively little control over the conventional means of influence.

Although there have always been conflicts between the ruler and the ruled, between parents and children, and between employers and employees, I suggest that this is the characteristic conflict of our time. It arises from the increasing demand for more power and prosperity from those who have been largely excluded from the processes of decision-making usually to their economic, social, psychological and physical disadvantage. The racial crisis in the United States, the student upheavals throughout the world, the revolutionary struggles in the underdeveloped areas, the controversies within and between nations in Eastern Europe, and the civil war in South Vietnam—all of these conflicts partly express the growing recognition at all levels of social life that social change is possible, that things do not have to remain as they are, that one can participate in the shaping of one's environment and improve one's lot.

ROLE SATISFACTION

It is evident that those who are satisfied with their roles in and the outcomes of the decision-making process may develop both a vested interest in preserving the existing arrangements and appropriate rationales to justify their positions. These rationales generally take the form of attributing superior competence (more ability, knowledge, skill) and/or superior moral value (greater initiative, drive, sense of responsibility, self-control) to oneself compared to those of lower status. From the point of view of those in power, lack of power and affluence is "little enough punishment" for people so incapable and so deficient in morality and maturity that they have failed to make their way in society. The rationales supporting the status quo are usually accompanied by corresponding sentiments which lead their possessors to react with disapproval and resistance to attempts to change the power relations and with apprehension and defensiveness to the possibility that these attempts will succeed. The apprehension is often a response to the expectation that the change will leave one in a powerless position under the control of those who are incompetent and irresponsible or at the mercy of those seeking revenge for past injustices.

If such rationales, sentiments and expectations have been developed, those in power are likely to employ one or more defense mechanisms in dealing with the conflict-inducing dissatisfactions of the subordinated group: *denial,* which is expressed in a blindness and insensitivity to the dissatisfactions and often results in an unexpected revolt; *repression,* which pushes the dissatisfactions underground and often eventuates in a guerrilla-type warfare; *aggression,* which may lead to a masochistic sham cooperation or escalated counter-aggression; *displacement,* which attempts to divert the responsibility for the dissatisfactions into other groups and, if successful, averts the conflict temporarily; *reaction-formation,* which allows expressions of concern and guilt to serve as substitutes for action to relieve the dissatisfaction of the underprivileged and, in so doing, may temporarily confuse and mislead those who are dissatisfied; *sublimation,* which attempts to find substitute solutions—e.g., instead of increasing the decision-making power of Harlem residents over their schools, provide more facilities for the Harlem schools.

WHAT CAN A LESS POWERFUL GROUP DO?

What can a less powerful group (Acme) do to reduce or overcome the defensiveness of a more powerful group (Bolt) and to increase the latter's readiness to share power? Suppose, in effect, that as social scientists we were consultants to the poor and weak rather than to the rich and strong, what would we suggest? Let me note that this would be an unusual and new position for most of us. If we have given any advice at all, it has been to those in high power. The unwitting consequence of this one-sided consultant role has been that we have too often assumed that the social pathology has been in the ghetto rather than in those who have built the walls to surround it, that the "disadvantaged" are the ones who need to be changed rather than the people and the institutions who have kept the disadvantaged in a submerged position. It is not that we should detach ourselves from "Headstart," "Vista," and various other useful training and remedial programs for the disadvantaged. Rather, we should have an appropriate perspective on such programs. It is more important that the educational institutions, the economic and political systems be changed so that they will permit those groups who are now largely excluded from important positions of decision-making to share power than to try to inculcate new attitudes and skills in those who are excluded. After all, would we not expect that the educational achievements of black children would be higher than they are now if school boards had more black members and schools had more black principals? Would we not also expect that the occupational attainment of blacks would be higher (and their unemployment rate lower) if General Motors, AT&T, and General Electric had some black board-members and company presidents as well as white ones? Again, would we not expect more civil obedience in the black community if Charles Evers rather than James Eastland were chairman of the Senate Judiciary Committee and if the House had barred corrupt white congressmen as well as Adam Clayton Powell? Let us not lose sight of what and who has to be changed, let us recognize where the social pathology really is!

ATTENTION, COMPREHENSION, ACCEPTANCE

But given the resistance and defensiveness of those in high power, what can we recommend to those in low power as a strategy of persuasion? As Hovland, Janis, and Kelley (1953) have pointed out, the process of persuasion involves obtaining the other's *attention*, *comprehension*, and *acceptance* of the message that one is communicating. The process of persuasion, however, starts with the communicator having a message that he wants to get across to the other. He must have an objective if he is to be able to articulate a clear and compelling message. Further, in formulating and communicating his message, it is important to recognize that it will be heard not only by the other, but also by one's own group and by other interested audiences. The desirable effects of a message on its intended audience may be negated by its unanticipated effects on those for whom it was not intended. I suggest that the following generalized message contains the basic elements of what Acme must communicate to Bolt to change him and, in addition, it is a message which can be overheard by other audiences without harmful consequences. Admittedly, it must be communicated in a way which elicits Bolt's attention, comprehension and acceptance of its credibility rather than in the abstract, intellectualized form in which it is presented below. And, of course, the generalized objective of equality must be detailed in terms of specific relations in specific contexts.

I am dissatisfied with our relationship and the effects it has. I think it can be improved in ways which will benefit you as well as me. I am sufficiently discontent that I can no longer continue in any relationship with you in which I do not participate as an equal in making the decisions which affect me as well as you, except as a temporary measure while we move toward equality. This may upset and discomfort you but I have no alternative other than to disengage myself from all forms of inauthentic cooperation: My dignity as well as pressure from my group will no longer allow me to engage in this self-deception and self-abasement. Neither coercion nor bribery will be effective; my self-respect and my group will force me to resist them. I remain prepared to cooperate with you as an equal in working on joint problems, including the problems involved in redefining our relationship to one another. I expect that changing our relationship will not be without its initial difficulties for both of us; we will be uncertain and perhaps suspicious, we will misunderstand and disagree and regress to old habits from time to time. I am willing to face these difficulties. I invite you to join with me to work toward improving our relationship, to overcome your dissatisfactions as well as mine. I believe that we both will feel more self-fulfilled in a relationship that is not burdened by inauthenticity.

It would take too long to detail all of the elements in this message and their rationales. But essentially the message commits Acme irreversibly to his objective—self-esteem and social esteem are at stake; he will be able to live neither with himself nor his group if he accepts an inferior status. This is done not only in words but also by the style of communicating which expresses a self-confident equality and competence. It provides Bolt with the prospect of positive incentives for changing and negative ones for not changing; Acme maintains a cooperative stance throughout and develops in action the possibility of a true mutual exchange by expressing the awareness that dissatisfactions are not one-sided. It also inoculates against some of the expected difficulties involved in change. It should be noted that Acme's statements of the threats faced by Bolt if change is not forthcoming (the instrumental threat of noncooperation, the moral threat that the status quo violates important social norms concerning human dignity and authenticity, the threat of resistance to coercion) are neither arbitrary, illegitimate, coercive, nor demanding to Bolt—i.e., they are not strongly alienating.

RAGE OR FEAR HANDICAPS

Rage or fear in the low power group often makes it impossible for them to communicate a message of the sort that I have described above. Rage leads to an emphasis on destructive, coercive techniques and precludes offers of authentic cooperation. Fear, on the other hand, weakens the commitment to the steps necessary to induce a change and lessens the credibility that compliance will be withdrawn if change does not occur. Although it is immediately destructive, rage is potentially a more useful emotion than fear since it leads to bold actions which are less damaging to the development of a sense of power and, hence, of self-esteem. And these latter are necessary for authentic cooperation. Harnessed rage or outrage can be a powerful energizer for determined action and if this action is directed toward building one's own power rather than destroying the other's power, the outrage may have a socially constructive outcome.

In any case, it is evident that when intense rage or fear are the dominant emotions the cooperative message that I have outlined is largely irrelevant. Both rage and fear are rooted in a sense of helplessness and powerlessness: They are emotions associated with a state of dependency. Those in low power can overcome these debilitating emotions by their own successful social action on matters of significance to them. In the current slang, they have got to "do their own thing," it cannot be given to them nor done for them. This is why my emphasis throughout this discussion has been on the sharing of power, and thus increasing one's power to affect one's fate, rather than on the sharing of affluence. While the sharing of affluence is desirable, it is not sufficient. In its most debilitating sense, "poverty" is a lack of power and not merely a lack of money. Money is, of course, a base for power but it is not the only one. If one chooses to be poor, as do some members of religious or pioneering groups, the psychological syndrome usually associated with imposed poverty—a mixture of dependency, apathy, small time perspective, suspicion, fear, and rage—is not present.

AUTHENTIC COOPERATION

Thus, the ability to offer and engage in authentic cooperation presupposes an awareness that one is neither helpless nor powerless, even though one is at a relative disadvantage. Not only independent action but also cooperative action requires a recognition and confirmation of one's capacity to "go it alone" if necessary. Unless one has the freedom to choose not to cooperate, there can be no free choice to cooperate. "Black power" is, thus, a necessity for black cooperation—of black cooperation with blacks as well as with whites. Powerlessness and the associated lack of self- and group-esteem are not conducive either to internal group cohesiveness or to external cooperation. "Black power" does not, however, necessarily lead to white cooperation. This is partly because, in its origin and rhetoric, "black power" may be oriented against "white power" and thus is likely to intensify the defensiveness of those with high power. When "black power" is primarily directed against "whitey" rather than for "blacks," it is of course to be expected that "whitey" will retaliate. The resulting course of events may provide some grim satisfaction to those despairing blacks who prefer to wield even short-lived destructive power rather than to be ineffectual and to those whites who prefer to be ruthless oppressors rather than to yield the psychic gains of pseudo-superiority.

However, even if "power" is "for" rather than "against" and provides a basis for authentic cooperation, cooperation may not occur because it is of little import to the high power group. It may be unaffected by the positive or negative incentives that the low power group control; it does not need their compliance. Universities can obtain new students; the affluent nations no longer are so dependent upon the raw materials produced in the underdeveloped nations; the white industrial society does not need many unskilled Negro workers.

WHAT CAN THE GROUP DO FOR ITSELF?

What can the low power group do in such situations? First of all, theoretically it may be possible to "opt out" more or less completely—to withdraw, to migrate, to separate so that one is no longer in the relationship. However, as the world and the societies composing it become more tightly knit, this option becomes less and less available in its extreme forms. Black communities can organize their own industries, schools, hospitals, shopping centers, consumer cooperatives, and the like but only if they have resources, and these resources would be sharply curtailed if their relationship with the broader society were completely disrupted. Similarly, students can organize their own seminars, their own living communes, their own bookstores, but it would be difficult for them to become proficient in many of the sciences and professions without using the resources available in the broader academic community. Self-imposed "apartheid" is self-defeating. "Build baby build" is a more useful slogan than "out baby out" or "burn baby burn."

Through building its own institutions and developing its own resources, a low power group makes itself less vulnerable to exploitation and also augments its power by providing itself with alternatives to inauthentic cooperation. In so doing, it increases the likelihood that those in high power will be responsive to a change—the positive incentives for changing and the negative incentives for not changing take on greater value. Moreover, such self-constructive action may help to reduce the fears and stereotypes which underlie much of the defensiveness of high power groups.

In addition to the strategy of developing one's own resources and building one's own institutions, there are still other strategies that can be followed by a low power group in the attempt to influence a reluctant or disinterested high power group. The various strategies are not incompatible with one another. I list several of the major ones: (a) augment its power by collecting or activating subgroups within the high power group or third parties as allies; (b) search for other kinds of connections with the high power group which, if made more salient, could increase its affective or instrumental dependence upon the low power group and thus change the power balance; (c) attempt to change the attitudes of those in high power through education and moral persuasion; (d) use existing legal procedures to bring pressures for change; and (e) use harassment techniques to increase the other's costs of adhering to the status quo.

The effectiveness of any strategy of influence is undoubtedly much determined by the particular circumstances so that no strategy can be considered to be unconditionally effective or ineffective. Nevertheless, it is reasonable to assume that low power groups can rarely afford to be without allies. By definition, a low power group is unlikely to achieve many of its objectives unless it can find allies among significant elements within the high power group or unless it can obtain support from other ("third party") groups that can exert influence on the high power group. There is considerable reason to expect that allies are most likely to be obtained if: (a) they are sought out rather than ignored or rejected; (b) superordinate goals, common values and common interests can be identified which could serve as a basis for the formation of cooperative bonds; (c) reasonably full communication is maintained with the potential allies; (d) one's objectives and methods are readily perceived as legitimate and feasible; (e) one's tactics dramatize one's objectives and require the potential allies to choose between acting "for" or "against" these objectives and, thus, to commit themselves to taking a position; and (f) those in high power employ tactics, as a counter-response, which are widely viewed as "unfitting" and thus produce considerable sympathy for the low power group.

CIVIL DISOBEDIENCE

There is no time here to elaborate on procedures and tactics of building allies; this is what politics is all about. However, let me just comment about the nonviolent, civil disobedience, confrontation tactics which have been employed with considerable success by civil rights and student groups. These methods have tended, with continuing usage, to have less effect in arousing public response and sympathy for the low power groups involved. In part, this is because many of those in high power have learned that to employ coercion as a response to a nonviolent tactic of civil disobedience is self-defeating; it only serves to swing much of the hitherto uninvolved public behind the demonstrators. This is, of course, what happened in Selma and Birmingham as well as at Columbia University and Chicago when unfitting force was used. These techniques also have become less effective because repeated usage vulgarizes them; a measure which is acceptable as an unusual or emergency procedure becomes unacceptable as a routine breeder of social disruption. Let me note parenthetically that I have discussed "nonviolent, confrontation" tactics as a method for gaining allies and public support rather than as a procedure for directly changing the attitudes of those in high power who are strongly committed to their views. I have seen no evidence that would suggest it has any significant effects of the latter sort.

Finding allies and supporters is important not only because it directly augments the influence of a low power group but also because having allies enables the low power group to use each of the other change strategies more effectively. I shall not discuss the other strategies in detail but confine myself to a brief comment about each. A low power group can increase the dependence of a high power group on it by concentrating its power rather than by allowing it to be spread thinly. Thus, the political power of the Negro vote could be higher if it were able to decide the elections in a half-dozen states such as New York, California, Pennsylvania, Illinois, Ohio, and Michigan than if the Negro vote was less concentrated. Similarly, their economic power would be greater if they were able to obtain control over certain key industries and key unions rather than if they were randomly dispersed.

Education, moral persuasion, and the use of legal procedures to bring about social change have lately come into disrepute because these strategies do not bring "instant change" nor do they produce as much *esprit de corps* as strategies which give rise to direct action techniques. Nevertheless, it would be a mistake to underestimate the importance of beliefs, values and the sense of legitimacy in determining individual and social action. Similarly, to engage in anti-intellectualism or to ignore the significance of intellectual work in establishing true knowledge is an error. Truth threatens arbitrary power by unmasking its unreasonableness and pretensions. Anti-intellectualism is a tool of the despot in his struggle to silence or discredit truth. Also, it would be a mistake to ignore the tremendous changes in beliefs and values concerning human relationships which have occurred during the recent past. Much of the evil which now occurs is not a reflection of deliberate choice to inflict such evil but rather the lack of a deliberate choice to overcome self-perpetuating vicious cycles. Obviously, a considerable educational effort is needed to help broaden the understanding of conflict and to accelerate growth in the ability to include others in the same moral community with oneself even though they be of rather different social, economic and ethnic background.

HARASSMENT

Harassment may be the only effective strategy available to a low power group if it faces an indifferent or hostile high power group. Although sharp lines cannot be drawn, it is useful to distinguish harassment, obstruction, and destruction from one another. *Harassment* employs legal or semilegal techniques to inflict a loss, to interfere with, disrupt or embarrass those with high power; obstruction employs illegal techniques to interrupt or disrupt the activities and purposes of those in high power; destruction employs illegal, violent techniques to destroy or to take control over people or property. Obstructive and destructive techniques invite massive retaliation and repression which, if directed against harassment techniques, would often seem inappropriate and arouse sympathy. However, a clearly visible potential for the employment of obstructive and destructive techniques may serve to make harassment procedures both more acceptable and more effective.

There are many forms of harassment which can be employed by low power groups: consumer boycotts; work slowdowns; rent strikes; demonstrations; sit-ins; tying up phones, mail, government offices, businesses, traffic, etc. by excessive and prolonged usage; ensnarling bureaucratic systems in their own red tape by requiring them to follow their own formally stated rules and procedures; being excessively friendly and cooperative; creating psychological nuisances by producing outlandish behavior, appearances and odors in stores, offices and other public places; encouraging contagion of the ills of the slum (rats, uncollected garbage, etc.) to surrounding communities; etc. Harassment, as is true for most procedures, is undoubtedly most effective when it is employed to obtain well-defined, specific objectives and when it is selectively focused on key persons and key institutions rather than when it is merely a haphazard expression of individual discontent.

IN CONCLUSION

As I review what I have written in this last section, where I have functioned as a self-appointed consultant to those in low power, I am struck by how little of what I have said is well-grounded in systematic research or theory. As social scientists we have rarely directed our attention to the defensiveness and resistance of the strong and powerful in the face of the need for social change. We have not considered what strategies and tactics are available to low power groups and which of these are likely to lead to a productive rather than destructive process of conflict resolution. We have focused too much on the turmoil and handicaps of those in low power and not enough on the defensiveness and resistance of the powerful; the former will be overcome as the latter is overcome.

Is it not obvious that with the great disparities in power and affluence within nations and between nations that there will be continuing pressures for social change? And is it not also obvious that the processes of social change will be disorderly and destructive unless those in power are able or enabled to lower their defensiveness and resistance to a change in their relative status? Let us refocus our efforts so that we will have something useful to say to those who are seeking radical but peaceful social change. Too often in the past significant social change in the distribution of power has been achieved at the cost of peace; this is a luxury that the world is no longer able to afford.

REFERENCES

Coleman, J. S. *Community conflict.* New York: Free Press, 1957.

Coser, L. *The functions of social conflict.* New York: Free Press, 1956.

Deutsch, M. Cooperation and trust: some theoretical notes. In M. R. Jones (Ed.), *Nebraska symposium on motivation.* Lincoln: University of Nebraska Press, 1962. (a)

Deutsch, M. A psychological basis for peace. In Q. Wright, W. M. Evan, and M. Deutsch (Eds.), *Preventing World War III: some proposals.* New York: Simon & Schuster, 1962. (b)

Deutsch, M. Conflict and its resolution. Presidential address before the Division of Personality and Social Psychology of the American Psychological Association, September 5, 1965. (a)

Deutsch, M. A psychological approach to international conflict. In G. Sperrazzo (Ed.), *Psychology and international relations.* Washington, D.C.: Georgetown University Press, 1965. (b)

Deutsch, M. Vietnam and the start of World War III: some psychological parallels. Presidential address before the New York State Psychological Association, May 6, 1966.

Deutsch, M. *The resolution of conflict.* New Haven: Yale University Press (in preparation).

Festinger, L. The psychological effects of insufficient reward. *American Psychologist,* 1961, 16, 1–11.

Fisher, R. Fractionating conflict. In R. Fisher (Ed.), *International conflict and behavioral science: the Craigville papers.* New York: Basic Books, 1964.

Hovland, C. I., Janis, I. L. and Kelley, H. H. *Communication and persuasion.* New Haven: Yale University Press, 1953.

Rokeach, M. *The open and closed mind.* New York: Basic Books, 1960.

Stein, M. *The creative individual.* In manuscript, 1968.

Tomkins, S. S. and Izard, C. C. (Eds.), *Affect, cognition, and personality.* New York: Springer Publishing Co., 1965.

B. AUBREY FISHER

Decision Emergence: Phases in Group Decision-Making

The study of small groups long has been a major interest in the behavioral sciences. Since the famed Hawthorne studies,[1] researchers fruitfully have probed the socio-emotional dimension of groups attempting to explain, among other things, the "Hawthorne effect." Unfortunately, in-depth research of task behavior has not kept pace. McGrath and Altman, following an intensive study of small group research, called for "more attention to analysis of the behavior of groups—their interaction—as opposed to the products or outcomes of that behavior."[2] For those whose primary interest is the process of speech communication, the need for careful analysis of the group interaction process is acute.

This study is concerned with the group task of decision-making—typically, but not necessarily, problem-solving. Without sufficient insight into the nature of a group's interaction

From B. Aubrey Fisher, "Decision Emergence: Phases in Group Decision-Making," *Speech Monographs 37*, 1970, 53–66.

[1]For a comprehensive account of the Hawthorne studies, See F. J. Roethlisberger and William J. Dickson, *Management and the Worker* (Cambridge: Harvard University Press, 1946).

[2]Joseph E. McGrath and Irwin Altman, *Small Group Research: A Synthesis and Critique of the Field* (New York: Holt, Rinehart and Winston, 1966), p. 3.

process, the typical approach[3] to group decision-making has followed John Dewey's[4] pattern of reflective thinking for individuals. However, Kelley and Thibaut,[5] among others, have warned against substituting an individual process for the group process.

There have been few attempts to test theoretical conceptions of group task behaviors systematically. Among the most notable of such conceptions are Bales and Strodtbeck's[6] three-phase progression of group development, Bennis and Shepard's[7] four levels of work, and Scheidel and Crowell's[8] spiral process of idea development. Each of these studies, however, possesses serious limitations. Bales and Strodtbeck, for example, reported that groups concentrated on different kinds of problems across time but they did not discuss the interaction process which the groups used to solve those problems. Bennis and Shepard's study was concerned primarily with delineating those socio-emotional variables which obstruct efficient task completion. Only Scheidel and Crowell observed the verbal behavior related specifically to task accomplishment—notably decision-making. Unfortunately, these authors did not report observing aspects of the time dimension which McGrath and Altman consider "absolutely crucial for understanding small group phenomena."[9]

[3]See, for example, J. F. Dashiell, "Experimental Studies of the Influence of Social Situations on the Behavior of Individual Human Adults," *A Handbook of Social Psychology*, ed. C. Murchison (Worcester: Clark University Press, 1935), p. 1131; James G. March and Herbert A. Simon, *Organizations* (New York: Wiley, 1958), p. 179; and Abraham Zalenik and David Moment, *The Dynamics of Interpersonal Behavior* (New York: Wiley, 1964), p. 152.

[4]See John Dewey, *How We Think* (Boston: D. C. Heath, 1910) and *Logic: The Theory of Inquiry* (New York: Holt, Rinehart and Winston, 1938).

[5]Harold H. Kelley and John W. Thibaut, "Experimental Studies of Group Problem Solving and Process," *Handbook of Social Psychology*, ed. Gardner Lindzey (Reading, Addison-Wesley, 1954), 2, 738–741.

[6]Robert F. Bales and Fred L. Strodtbeck, "Phases in Group Problem-Solving," *Journal of Abnormal and Social Psychology*, 46 (1951), 485–495.

[7]Warren G. Bennis and Herbert A. Shepard, "A Theory of Group Development," *Human Relations*, 9 (1956), 415–437.

[8]Thomas M. Scheidel and Laura Crowell, "Idea Development in Small Discussion Groups," *Quarterly Journal of Speech*, 50 (1964), 40–45.

[9]McGrath and Altman, p. 73.

The purpose of the present investigation, then, was to discover the nature of the interaction process across time leading to group consensus on decision-making tasks. A pilot study involving intensive observation of classroom and non-classroom group discussions revealed several general characteristics of task behavior consistent among all groups. First, an accumulation of verbal cues, reinforcing or resisting the group's tendency to arrive at decisions, determine the ultimate but gradual emergence of those decisions. Second, this pattern of verbal cues operates independently from the group's social dimension or level of cohesiveness. Third, a linear problem-solving agenda suitable for individual decision-making was not typically evident. Groups who consciously elected to use such a system typically reached decisions despite, rather than because of, that system.

These group characteristics from the pilot study suggested that group members perceive several alternatives for accomplishing their tasks. As discussions progress, these alternatives are debated, refined, accepted, changed, rejected, etc., until the final task product evolves from their deliberations—largely through a "method of residues" or elimination of available alternatives. Although they did not discuss the interaction process involved, Kelley and Thibaut[10] believed that group decision-making involved a process of choosing among alternatives. The present investigation of the interaction process characteristic of decision-making small groups proceeded from these preliminary observations.

METHOD

Selection of Groups

After careful examination of available groups and the purposes of the investigation, the following criteria were used to select groups for observation:

1. The group's goal is to achieve consensus on decisions.
2. The group's interaction is primarily verbal.

[10]Kelley and Thibaut, p. 744.

3. The group operates in a developing or emergent context.
4. The entire history of the group is available for study.
5. A written record of the group's task performance is available.
6. The group successfully accomplished its task.
7. The group is not formed within a classroom context.

Despite these common characteristics, the ten selected groups displayed a variety of dissimilarities. They varied in size from four to twelve members, in duration from twenty-five minutes to over thirty hours, in composition from all males to all females, in age from teens to the sixties. These differences imply a diversity of social structures, role relationships, leadership methods, and decision quality, among others. The maturity and attitudes of the members, their experience and expertness with using the group method, and so forth also varied. The present study purposely did not attempt to control variables in the social dimension. Since the purpose was to discover patterns of verbal task behavior regardless of socio-emotional structures and individual differences among participants, the diversity of social dimensions among the groups was vital.

Content Analysis: The Category System

Audiotapes of the verbal interaction of each group's entire history were transcribed and submitted to content analysis using an original category system expressly designed to exclude forces of the socio-emotional dimension apparent in the interaction. Any interaction considered to be serving purely a procedural or socializing function, i.e., non-task function, was coded into an "et cetera" category and excluded from the data.

The concept of *decision proposal* is central to the operation of the category system. Identifying the specific decision alternative being considered by the group anchors verbal interaction to the subject matter of the discussion. Verbal interaction, as defined by this study, then, processes information pertinent to a specific decision proposal and leads to its eventual acceptance or rejection by the group. The difference between task-function categories is the difference between functions performed on the decision proposal. If one assumes that a group reaches consensus via interaction, then the observed patterns of interaction functioning on a group's perception of decision proposals should reveal how groups use interaction to achieve consensus on those decision proposals. The categories, taken together, comprise a list of all possible task functions which verbal behavior can perform.

The *unit* of interaction is defined as a given instance of the performance of a task function on a decision proposal regardless of its length or intensity. The distinction between two units of interaction, therefore, is the interruption of one individual's contribution by another individual or the crossing of function categories within an individual's contribution. Defining the unit as a function attempt rather than a thought-unit, then, results in dispersing the data from interaction analysis among group members. In general, "n" units may be interpreted as nearly "n" individual comments containing "n" different attempts to direct the group's perception of a decision proposal.

The category system described each unit of interaction along several dimensions, each of which contains mutually exclusive and exhaustive categories.

Dimension One:
- A—Asserted
- S—Seeking

Dimension Two:
- 1—Interpretation
- 2—Substantiation
- 3—Clarification
- 4—Modification
- 5—Summary
- 6—Agreement

Dimension Three:
(applicable to "1" and "2" categories only)
- f—Favorable toward the proposal
- u—Unfavorable toward the proposal
- a—Ambiguous toward proposal

Additional Symbols:

O_n—Origin of a decision proposal

(D_n)—Reintroduction of a proposal

Hence, a unit coded "A210$_3$" would indicate an asserted contribution introducing into the discussion and favorably substantiating decision proposal number three. Agreement among minimally trained coders using the system exceeded .86 in several checks for reliability of the category system.

Content Analysis: Static and Contiguity Analyses

After the transcripts of verbal interaction were coded into units of the category system, each group was arbitrarily divided into five-minute segments. Each coded comment in each segment for each group was then transferred to a contiguity table for analysis, adopting a procedure used by Scheidel and Crowell.[11] The "contiguity analysis," utilizing the units as both rows and columns in the table, identified each contiguous pair of function units. That is, the rows of the table indicated the antecedent unit of each pair; the column indicated the subsequent. Therefore, each cell in the table included the frequency with which the column-unit immediately followed the row-unit during that five-minute segment of time. Since an inspection of the data revealed nearly all the units to be assertions, the contiguity table did not distinguish between asserted and seeking comments.

A "static analysis," i.e., the total number of units in each category in each segment, is available from the contiguity table by using the marginal totals of the rows—the antecedent units. But the contiguity analysis of this study provides, in addition, a key to group interaction not available with most category systems. Units quantifying contiguous pairs of function attempts typically indexed interaction between pairs of members when the system was applied to the group transcripts. Weick[12] considers the "interact," as well as the "act," an essential unit of

[11]Scheidel and Crowell, pp. 142–143.

[12]Karl E. Weick, *The Social Psychology of Organizing* (Reading, Addison-Wesley, 1969), pp. 45–48.

collective structure. McGrath and Altman apparently concur in stating, "there are strong conceptual reasons for preferring dyadic or polyadic units (interacts of two or more group members)."[13] The present study attempts to consider both "acts" and "interacts" within its scope of interaction analysis. Thus, static analysis of the data provides units of "acts," and contiguity analysis of the data provides units of "interacts."

Division into Phases

Since the pilot study indicated a changing pattern of verbal cues reinforcing or resisting the group's tendency to arrive at a decision, the data from the third dimension of the category system were observed for each five-minute segment of each group. A consistent four-phase pattern emerged from a study of the proportional fluctuation of interaction units favorable, unfavorable, and ambiguous toward the decision proposals. In the early stages of the discussion, both favorable attitudes and ambiguous attitudes were expressed with greater frequency than unfavorable attitudes. Then, as the proportion of ambiguous units declined, unfavorable units increased to surpass the proportional frequency of ambiguous ones. In a third phase, unfavorable units declined while the proportional frequency of ambiguous units rose above the frequency of unfavorable ones.

[13]McGrath and Altman, p. 74.

TABLE 1 Results of Content Analysis for Phase One

		Subsequent Units							
		1f	1u	1a	2f	2u	2a	3	6
Antecedent Units	1f	19	12	14	16	4	10	21	14
	1u	7	12	11	16	6	5	8	19
	1a	16	13	29	6	9	20	15	18
	2f	17	11	5	25	16	12	25	17
	2u	6	6	10	11	8	7	18	9
	2a	3	6	13	9	7	13	22	17
	3	18	10	20	27	17	16	154	24
	6	21	13	16	14	9	11	25	XX

Total pairs of units categorized = 1008.

TABLE 2 Results of Content Analysis for Phase Two

Antecedent Units	Subsequent Units: 1f	1u	1a	2f	2u	2a	3	6
1f	37	18	13	10	9	6	10	21
1u	16	22	4	12	7	5	10	18
1a	11	8	10	9	6	3	13	7
2f	13	15	10	34	20	12	19	23
2u	7	10	5	28	17	12	7	6
2a	5	3	2	9	10	9	13	3
3	12	10	8	23	10	13	122	3
6	18	8	7	23	9	1	4	XX

Total pairs of units categorized = 848.

TABLE 3 Results of Content Analysis for Phase Three

Antecedent Units	Subsequent Units: 1f	1u	1a	2f	2u	2a	3	6
1f	53	28	35	35	14	14	25	19
1u	20	12	18	20	5	9	9	4
1a	39	11	42	24	11	21	19	8
2f	36	19	25	47	28	19	26	34
2u	13	7	9	31	6	8	9	4
2a	9	5	22	31	7	24	34	11
3	33	9	15	26	7	10	170	6
6	16	8	8	22	7	9	7	XX

Total pairs of units categorized = 1312.

TABLE 4 Results of Content Analysis for Phase Four

Antecedent Units	Subsequent Units: 1f	1u	1a	2f	2u	2a	3	6
1f	72	7	13	26	3	4	20	23
1u	6	2	1	5	0	2	1	0
1a	15	1	7	8	1	1	3	2
2f	23	2	8	44	4	9	20	15
2u	3	0	1	10	1	0	2	0
2a	3	0	2	10	0	5	2	1
3	23	5	2	9	4	1	70	7
6	18	0	4	11	1	1	5	XX

Total pairs of units categorized = 549.

In the final phase, favorable units rose sharply, and both ambiguous and unfavorable units declined sharply.

This four-stage pattern appeared in each of the ten groups studied with slightly varying degrees of distinction between phases. In all ten groups, the distinctions between the first and second and between the third and fourth phases were clearly evident. The distinction between the second and third phases was not so clear-cut in all ten groups. Distinguishing the four phases, then, does not imply the presence of clearly discrete phases of progression. Rather, the phasic progression reflects a continuous and gradual change of interaction patterns.

Quantitative Analysis

Each of the ten groups was separated into four phases on the basis of the variations in the third dimension (favorability). The data from all ten groups were then collapsed into the four phases and transferred to contiguity and static analysis tables utilizing the four phases as the rows and the various combinations of units and pairs of units as the columns. Three tables for contiguity analysis and three tables for static analysis were formed by collapsing all the units into each of the three dimensions. Thus, 109 categories of interaction appeared as column headings in the six tables.

The Pearson chi-square test of association[14] was selected to determine whether the four phases were independent of the categories of content analysis. So that the tests for independence would indicate which categories of interaction distinguished between which phases, each of the 109 categories from static and contiguity analysis was systematically tested for every possible combination of two phases by replicating two-by-two contingency tables. The frequency of each category was compared against the combined frequencies of all other categories in phases one and two, one and three, one and four, two and three, two and four, and three and four. In this fashion each category was compared across all four phases using six contingency ta-

[14]A complete description of this test and its applications is found in William L. Hays, *Statistics for Psychologists* (New York: Holt, Rinehart and Winston, 1963), pp. 589–603.

bles for each category-unit. Each rejected null hypothesis, then, aids in distinguishing more precisely, on the basis of the category system, the interaction patterns of the four phases.

RESULTS

The tables reveal some categories to be barren of information. In addition to the category of "seeking," the number of units coded into the "modification" (4)[15] and "summary" (5) categories were too few to warrant attention. Thus, all such units, including all interacts which contained either as the antecedent or subsequent unit, were eliminated from further consideration. Of the 3,717 units remaining, phase one contained 1,008 and phase two contained 848 (see Tables 1 and 2). Phase three appeared to be the longest phase typically with 1,312 units (see Table 3). Conversely, phase four was typically the shortest with only 549 units (see Table 4). The table for this final phase is the only one with empty cells. The extremely low frequency of interaction units expressing unfavorable attitudes toward decision proposals (1u, 2u) resulted in these null cells.

Of the 654 null hypotheses of independence of category-units and phases, 217 were rejected with results beyond the .05 level of significance. Table 5 shows the units for which significant chi-square results were obtained between each pair of phases. Of the 217 rejected hypotheses, 40 are labelled questionable because of an expected frequency less than ten.[16] Nearly all of these 40 are the result of low frequencies of unfavorable (u, 1u, 2u) or ambiguous (a, 1a, 2a) category units in phase four.

DISCUSSION

The results of the chi-square tests indicate that the four phases can be differentiated on the basis of an interaction pat-

[15]Letters and numbers in parentheses indicate the coding symbol used to delineate that function category within the category system.

[16]Hays, p. 597, indicates that a conservative rule of thumb for contingency tables with a single degree of freedom is a minimum expected frequency of ten.

tern characteristic of each phase. The following is a description of the distinctive interaction pattern found for each phase:

Phase One

Significantly more clarification (3) and agreement (6) occurred in phase one than in any of the other three phases. It appears that a group's early problems of socializing and developing a socio-emotional climate conducive to task accomplishment affected the task interaction patterns in the early phase. As each member was unaware of his initial social position in the group, he did not quickly or strongly assert himself or his opinions. Consequently, he made assertions tentatively in order to "test" the group.

The categories of interaction antecedent to agreement (6) substantiates this explanation. For instance, members agreed with significantly more ambiguous comments (a/6) and ambiguous interpretations (1a/6) in the first phase. The frequency of ambiguous comments following agreement (6/a) was also significantly greatest in the first phase. Interestingly, members also agreed more often with unfavorable comments (u/6) in the first phase than in either of the latter two phases. And unfavorable comments followed agreement (6/u) more often in the first phase than in either of the last two.

Indicative of the tendency to agree to nearly everything in the early phase is the discovery that agreement followed clarification (3/6) more often in phase one than in either of the next two phases. Clarification also followed agreement (6/3) most often in the first phase. Agreement may function in phase one, then, not so much to reinforce opinions and beliefs as to encourage social facilitation or to avoid disrupting the developing social climate.

Group members in phase one tended to search tentatively for ideas and directions to aid their decision-making efforts. Since the members were unaware of the direction the group would ultimately pursue, fewer favorable comments (f, 1f, 2f) appear in this phase than in any other, and more unfavorable comments appear than in either phase three or four. The first phase also contains fewer unfavorable comments reinforced by unfavorable comments (u/u) than either of the next two phases.

Favorable comments were least reinforced in phase one, i.e., favorable interpretation followed by favorable interpretation (1f/1f), perhaps because of the members' tentative opinions, typical of task communication in a developing social structure. Fewer favorable comments followed other favorable comments (f/f) in phase one than in either phase three or phase four. Tentative opinions, of course, do not demand substantiation. Thus, significantly fewer substantiation units (2) appear in phase one than in either of the final two phases.

Attitude reinforcement, for the purposes of this study, is defined as an antecedent unit followed by either agreement or a unit expressing the same attitude toward the decision proposal. Indicative of the tentative nature of early task communication is the random pattern of attitude reinforcement. That is, group members do not reinforce predominantly one attitude toward decision proposals. Rather, they reinforce significantly more ambiguous comments (a/a) than in phases two or four. On the other hand, when compared with either the third or fourth phase, phase one contains more unfavorable comments reinforced by agreement (u/6) and other unfavorable comments (u/u).

Unexpectedly, members also reinforced favorable units less often in the earliest phase. For example, phase one contains significantly fewer favorable interpretation comments reinforced by other favorable interpretation (1f/1f). When compared to either phase three or phase four, the first phase contains less reinforcement of favorable comments with favorable comments (f/f). Several factors can account for these data. First, each of the other phases contains more favorable comments (f, 1f, 2f) than does the first, undoubtedly because the group progressively approaches consensus. Second, since reinforcement is sporadic rather than systematic, the first phase includes proportionately more reinforcement of unfavorable and ambiguous comments.

TABLE 5 Significant Differences Among Phases Based on Units of Interaction

	Phases			
Unit	One	Two	Three	Four
(Reinforced Agreement)				
1f/1f		>1	>1	>1,2,3
1f/2f			>2	>1,2,3
1f/6				>1,3
2f/1f				>1,2
2f/2f				>1,2*,3
6/1f				>3
6/2f		>1		
f/f			>1	>1,2,3
f/6				>1,3
6/f		>3		>3
(Reinforced Disagreement)				
1u/1u		>1,3,4		
1u/2u		>4*		
1u/6	>3,4*	>3*,4*		
2u/2u		>1,3,4*		
2u/6	>4*	>4*		
6/1u	>4	>4*		
u/u	>3,4	>1,3,4		
u/6	>3,4	>3,4		
6/u	>3,4	>4*	>4*	

	Phases			
Unit	One	Two	Three	Four
(Expressed Attitudes)				
1f		>1	>1	>1,2,3
1u	>4	>3,4	>4	
1a	>2,4		>2,4	
2f		>1	>1	>1,2,3
2u	>4	>1,3,4	>4	
2a	>2,4		>2,4	
f		>1	>1	>1,2,3
u	>3,4	>1,3,4	>4	
a	>2,4		>2,4	
(Tenacity of Attitudes)				
1/1			>1	>1,2
1/2			>1,2	
1/6	>3	>3		>3
2/1			>1,2,4	
2/2		>1	>1	>1
6/1	>3			
1			>1,2	>1,2
2		>1	>1,4	

(Reinforced Ambiguous Disagreement)				
1a/1a	>2,4		>2,3	
1a/2a	>2,4*		>2,4*	
1a/6	>3,4*			
2a/1a	>2*		>2,4*	
2a/6	>2*,4*			
6/1a	>3			
6/2a	>2*			
a/a	>2,4		>2,3	
a/6	>2,3,4			
6/a	>2,3,4			
(Overt Conflict)				
1u/1f		>1		
2f/1u		>4*	>4*	
2f/2u		>4*	>4	
2u/2f		>1	>1	
f/u		>1,4	>4	
u/f		>1,4		
(Ambiguous Conflict)				
1f/1a			>1	
1a/1f			>1,2	
1a/2f			>1	
2f/1a			>1	>1*
2a/2f			>1,2	
f/a			>1,2	
a/f			>1,2	>1,2
1f/3				>2,3
1u/3		>4*		
2f/3			>4	
2u/3	>3,4*			
2a/3	>4*	>4*	>4	
3/1f	>4			>2
3/1a				>1*
3/2u	>3			
3/2a	>4	>4*		
3/6	>2,3	>4*		
6/3	>2,3,4			
3/2	>3,4	>3,4		
3	>2,3,4			
6	>3,4	>3		
(Et cetera)				
1u/1a			>2*,4*	
1a/1u	>4*			
2u/2a	>4*	>4*		
2a/2u	>4*	>4*		
u/a		>4	>4	>1
a/u	>3,4	>4	>4	

*. . . Questionable result (ef < 10).

Hence, there is proportionately less reinforcement of favorable comments. Such explanations, while justified statistically, add little to our understanding of group task interaction.

The function of ambiguous units provides the key to understanding the first phase. More ambiguous comments (a, 1a, 2a) are contained in phase one than in any other phase except the third, which is also characterized by ambiguity. Many ambiguous comments in the first phase probably reflect favorable attitudes toward decision proposals. That is, since favorable attitudes assert themselves with increasing intensity throughout the four phases, they must appear in phase one in rudimentary form. Since favorable comments are observed relatively infrequently in the first-phase, they are probably expressed as ambiguous attitudes. As the issues become clarified and as the social climate becomes more conducive to the honest statement of one's true position, those opinions appear as favorable units.

Characteristic of the first phase, then, is getting acquainted, clarifying, and tentatively expressing attitudes. Bales and Strodtbeck[17] described the initial stage of their three-phase group development as emphasizing problems of orientation. Schutz[18] also characterizes his initial stage of "inclusion" as a period of members orienting themselves to the group atmosphere and testing ambiguous "goblet issues" of questionable relevance. The task activity of Tuckman's[19] first phase, "forming," is also characterized by orientation. The present data reveal characteristics consistent with these descriptions of group development. Therefore, the first phase of this decision-making model will be called the *orientation phase*.

Phase Two

The period in a group's history of task behavior following the orientation phase is characterized by dispute. For example, more

[17]Bales and Strodtbeck.

[18]William C. Schutz, "Interpersonal Underworld," *Harvard Business Review, 36* (1958), 123–135.

[19]Bruce W. Tuckman, "Developmental Sequence in Small Groups," *Psychological Bulletin, 63* (1965), 384–399.

unfavorable (u) and unfavorable substantiation (2u) units are contained in the second phase than in any other phase, and more unfavorable interpretation (1u) units appear in phase two than in the two succeeding phases.

In the orientation phase, members tentatively formulate opinions. By the second phase, they are much more definite. Along with the highest level of unfavorable comments in phase two, the number of favorable (f), favorable interpretation (1f), and favorable substantiation (2f) units increased significantly from the orientation phase. But ambiguous (a), ambiguous interpretation (1a), and ambiguous substantiation (2a) units are significantly fewer than in phases one or three. The members in the second phase are aware of the direction the groups' task behavior is heading, of the relevant decision proposals which are emerging from the group deliberations. Thus, members typically express either a favorable or an unfavorable attitude toward those decision proposals rather than an attitude of ambiguity.

With polarization of attitudes comes disagreement. Comparing the orientation phase with the second phase reveals a significant increase in the frequency of unfavorable interpretation followed by favorable interpretation (1u/1f) and unfavorable substantiation followed by favorable substantiation (2u/2f). Ideational conflict is further evidenced by more unfavorable comments followed by favorable comments (u/f) than in either the first or the last phase.

Characteristic of second phase conflict is the greater tendency to disagree with unfavorable than with favorable comments. That is, unfavorable units are resisted in phase two by subsequent favorable units (1u/1f, 2u/2f). No unquestioned significant difference was found between phase two and any other phase in the frequencies of favorable interpretation and favorable substantiation followed by any unfavorable comment (1f/1u, 1f/2u, 2f/1u, 2f/2u). However, collapsing interpretation and substantiation indicates a significantly greater number of favorable units followed by unfavorable units (f/u) in phase two.

Not only are comments in the second phase less ambiguous, they are also expressed more tenaciously. Phase two is characterized by attempts to persuade dissenting members. It contains a smaller proportion of interpretation units (1) than either phase three or phase four. Argument form, i.e., premises and data leading to a conclusion, is the appropriate form for debate, and the significantly greater number of substantiation units (2, 2/2) indicates the argumentative quality of this phase, unlike orientation.

The reinforcement schedule of the second phase leads to the inference that coalitions have been formed. While reinforcement was random in the orientation phase, it is bimodally distributed in the second phase. The frequency of favorable interpretation comments following favorable interpretation comments (1f/1f), for example, increased significantly from the orientation phase. And only the fourth phase contains significantly more favorable comments followed by other favorable comments (f/f). But unfavorable comments reinforced by other unfavorable comments (u/u) and unfavorable interpretation reinforced by unfavorable interpretation (1u/1u) and unfavorable substantiation units reinforced by unfavorable substantiation (2u/2u) occurred with significantly greater frequency in the second phase than in either phase three or four. On the other hand, ambiguous units (a, 1a, 2a) appeared less frequently in phase two and were subsequently not reinforced.

The reinforcement pattern indicates the presence of coalitions formed from ideational polarization. Because of the nature of the category system and the unit measuring interaction, whenever a dyadic unit (e.g., 1f/1f, 1u/1u, etc.) appears, it typically indicates an interaction between two members. The dyadic units most prevalent in phase two imply coalitions of individuals. In other words, two coalitions are present in the second phase—one favoring and one opposing those decision proposals which ultimately achieve consensus. Of course, these coalitions are relevant only to the extent that they involve attitudes toward decision proposals. In no way do the data from this study preclude the presence of other coalitions. Coalitions that are idiosyncratic to a particular group or that characterize unsuccessful groups or that result from socio-emotional pressures are not necessarily revealed by these data.

The second phase, therefore, is characterized by dissent. Polarization of attitudes points to this conclusion. The rise of dyadic interactions of favorable and unfavorable units is indicative of dissent, as is the increase of substantiation and substantiation dyads. Because of these distinguishing characteristics, phase two could be called the phase of controversy, argument, or conflict. The most descriptive of these terms is conflict—hence, the *conflict phase.*

Phase Three

Conflict and argument dissipate during phase three. For example, unfavorable substantiation (2u) and interpretation (1u) are significantly fewer than in the conflict phase. And phase three contains fewer unfavorable units (u) than either of the earlier phases. Consequently, unfavorable opinions, liberally reinforced in the conflict phase, receive less reinforcement (1u/1u, 2u/2u, u/u) in the third phase.

But residues of conflict remain, indicating that the reduction of conflict is gradual. More unfavorable substantiation followed by favorable substantiation (2u/2f), for example, appears in phase three than during orientation. And the argument form, typical of ideational conflicts, appears more often in the third phase than during orientation. That is, more dyadic interactions of substantiation (2/2) appear in phase three. Perhaps more importantly, phase three contains more interpretation followed by interpretation (1/1) and favorable comments followed by other favorable comments (f/f). While conflict may yet exist in the third phase, the members do not defend unfavorable attitudes so tenaciously against persuasive attempts.

Conflict, denoted by the bimodal distribution of favorable and unfavorable units, is lower in the third phase than in any other except for the final phase. Only when associated with the fourth phase is phase three found to contain more unfavorable units (u, 1u, 2u), fewer favorable units (f, 1f), less positive reinforcement of favorable attitudes (f/f), and more negative reinforcement (f/u). Thus, the level of conflict in phase three is significantly lower than in either preceding phase but somewhat higher than in the final phase.

The hallmark of the third phase is the recurrence of ambiguity. More ambiguous units (a, 1a, 2a) appear in phase three than in either the conflict phase or the fourth phase. As in the orientation phase, ambiguous units are reinforced in significantly greater proportion than in phases two or four; i.e., ambiguous interpretation followed by ambiguous interpretation (1a/1a), ambiguous substantiation followed by ambiguous interpretation (2a/1a), and ambiguous interpretation followed by ambiguous substantiation (1a/2a). Thus, ambiguity, prominent in the orientation phase, declines in the conflict phase, and reasserts itself in the third phase.

But while the *level* of ambiguity and reinforcement of ambiguity is not significantly different from the orientation phase, the *function* performed by ambiguity in phase three is. The discussion above of the orientation phase suggested that ambiguity served as the initial expression of tentatively favorable attitudes. This explanation of ambiguity is not appropriate to the third phase. For example, phase three contains fewer reciprocal reinforcement patterns (a/6 and 6/a, 1a/6 and 6/1a); groups are no longer searching for attitude direction. This direction was plotted in the orientation phase and debated in the conflict phase. In the third phase, task direction is no longer an issue. Hence, phase three contains significantly fewer dyadic interactions including clarification units (3/6, 6/3, 2u/3, 3/2, 3/2u), and significantly more favorable units (f) and favorable interpretation units (1f), and receive more positive reinforcement (1f/1f, f/f). Hence, ambiguity's role in phase three is not that of tentative attitude expression.

The key to the function of ambiguity in the third phase lies in associating phase three with the conflict phase. The earlier phase was typified by negatively reinforced attitudes bimodally distributed between favorable and unfavorable units. The preceding discussion has indicated that phase three contains fewer unfavorable units (u, 1u, 2u) and fewer positive reinforcement patterns of unfavorable attitudes (u/u, 1u/1u, 2u/2u). But ambiguous units (a, 1a, 2a) and positive reinforcement of ambiguous units (1a/1a, 2a/1a, 1a/2a) increased. Further comparison with the conflict phase reveals that the negative reinforcement of favorable units is fundamentally different in the third phase. That is, the third phase contains more favorable units followed by ambiguous units (f/a) and ambiguous units followed by favorable units (a/f, 1a/1f, 2a/2f). These same units also distinguish the third phase from the orientation phase, lending credence to the inference that ambiguity functions differently in phase three.

Ambiguity, then, functions in the third phase as a form of modified dissent. That is, the group members proceed to change their attitudes from disfavor to favor of the decision proposals through the mediation of ambiguity. Only the most naive observer of human behavior would speculate that attitude change would be abrupt, particularly after these members had, during the conflict, publicly committed themselves to positions unfavorable to the decision proposals. Thus, dissent proceeds to assent via ambiguity. The conflict phase was characterized by dissent in the form of comments unfavorable to the decision proposals. The succeeding phase is characterized by dissipating dissent in the form of comments ambiguous toward the decision proposals.

The two coalitions present in the conflict phase also dissipate during the third phase. The dissenting coalition turns to ambiguous comments as a form of dissent. But since this dissipation of conflict is gradual and marked by ambiguity, the question concerning the point in time at which decisions are made must remain unanswered. In all likelihood, the group participants are as unaware as the observer of this point in time. In the absence of apparent conflict, decisions may appear to have been reached. But the ambiguous attitude, while not unfavorable, is not yet favorable. As disfavor dissipates to ambiguity, though, favorable attitudes increase concomitantly. This characterization of the third phase prompts the label *emergence phase.*

Phase Four

While groups tend to reach decisions during the emergence phase, members become increasingly aware of those decisions in the final phase. Argument is no longer important in phase four. Significantly more interpretation (1) is evident in the final phase than in either of the first two, and more favorable interpretation (1f) than in any preceding phase. Although the final phase contains more favorable substantiation (2f) than in any other phase, substantiation (2) is proportionately greater in the emergence phase. The argument form as a unit of interaction (2), then, characteristically favors the decision proposals in the final phase. That is, fewer unfavorable substantiation units (2u) are contained in the final phase, and fewer ambiguous substantiation (2a) units appear in the final phase than in either phase one or three. Thus, the argument form appears in phase four but characteristically favors the consensus decisions.

Comments favoring the decision proposals are constantly reinforced in phase four. When compared with every other phase, the final phase contains more dyadic interactions reinforcing favorable attitudes (f/f, 1f/1f, 1f/2f, 2f/2f). Excluding the emergence phase, the final phase also contains more favorable substantiation units followed by favorable interpretation units reinforced by agreement (f/6, 1f/6). This preponderance of interaction favoring the decision proposals and reinforcing those favorable attitudes earmarks the final phase of group deliberations.

Dissent has all but vanished in phase four. The final phase contains the fewest unfavorable attitudes (u, 1u, 2u) and less positive reinforcement of unfavorable attitudes (u/u, u/6, 2u/6). Except for the orientation phase, the final phase contains the fewest dyadic interactions of negative reinforcement (f/u, 2f/1u, 2f/2u). But while the low level of conflict during orientation reflected a conscious avoidance of conflict, in the final phase it reflects unity of opinion among group members. Analysis of the interaction also reflects this difference between the first and fourth phases. That is, phase four contains a significantly greater number of units favoring decision proposals (f, 1f, 2f).

Ambiguous dissent, characterizing the emergence phase, also dissipates in the final phase. For example, phase four contains fewer ambiguous units (a) and less reinforcement of ambiguous attitudes (a/a, 1a/1a). Yet some modified dissent remains. The frequency of favorable units following ambiguous units (a/f), for example, is greater in the final phase when it is compared with either of the first two phases. Of course, the gradual dissipation of dissent indicates that some residues from the emergence phase would probably appear in the succeeding phase, particularly early in the latter phase. Then, too, the low frequency of favorable comments in the orientation phase and the low frequency of ambiguous comments in the conflict phase make these particular interphase comparisons less meaningful. With the very high frequency of favorable comments and extremely low frequency of ambiguous and unfavorable comments in the final phase, one can safely conclude that the dissipation of dissent—modified or unmodified—is virtually complete.

This characteristic pattern of predominantly favorable attitudes consistently receiving positive reinforcement distinguishes the final phase of the group histories. Pervading the final stage is a spirit of unity. All members are in agreement and strive to show that agreement through positive reinforcement. Dissenting opinions, either unfavorable or ambiguous, have all but vanished. If decisions emerged during the emergence phase, they are reinforced during this final phase. Hence, the final phase bears the name characteristic of its dyadic interaction patterns—the *reinforcement phase.*

CONCLUSION

I would be among the first to suggest that the four phases of orientation, conflict, emergence, and reinforcement will not necessarily be present in all task-oriented small groups. Certainly, task groups subject to external legitimate controls would modify the "natural" context characteristic of the groups studied and might consequently affect the groups' interaction processes. Then, too, permanent groups might deviate from the four-phase pattern in subsequent task performances. The nature and extent of such differences point to the need for further research.

But while this four-phase model of "decision emergence" does not pretend to be applicable to all decision-making groups in all situations, the present study does demonstrate that the process of interaction is susceptible to study and analysis apparently free from overt influences of the socio-emotional dimension. This study demonstrates further that the interaction patterns of task behavior follow a consistent pattern of progression across time as groups make decisions despite the presence of social variables idiosyncratic to specific groups. Of course, the relative length of each phase may differ idiosyncratically among groups, but there is some evidence to believe that the proportionate amount of task behavior does not vary significantly with the social structures of groups.[20] Thus, inductively applying this model to similarly unstructured decision-making groups seems plausible.

Further research into task behavior utilizing this category system would probably benefit from several revisions of the system. I suggest that the categories of modification (4) and summary (5) be omitted from further applications of this system.[21] The category system might also differentiate between "bivalued" attitudes and "neutral" attitudes in the ambiguous (a) category in the system's third dimension. An additional category of "disagreement" might also be added to complement the category of "agreement" (6). One should keep in mind that this category system was not intended to be a system for comprehensive observation of group behavior. It was developed to serve only the limited purpose of observing more closely the interaction patterns of verbal task behavior free from the overt influences of the socio-emotional dimension.

Perhaps the major contribution of this study is its emphasis on the process of interaction; that is, on determining how communication patterns mediate input variables into a group product. This study demonstrates that interaction patterns can be observed directly and the nature of group task completion from the vantage point of verbal behavior can be understood more clearly.

[20]See, for example, R. Victor Harnack, "An Experimental Study of the Effects of Training in the Recognition and Formulation of Goals upon Intra-Group Cooperation," *Speech Monographs*, 22 (1955), 31–38.

[21]Subsidiary to the present study was a theory regarding the progressive but largely indirect modification of decision proposals. Since this theory is not strictly within the scope of this report, it is not reported here.

ROBERT O. BLOOD, JR.

Resolving Family Conflicts

INTRODUCTION

Aside from the inner conflicts of the individual person, the family is the smallest arena within which conflict occurs. Since the scale of conflict is so much smaller than occurs between the great powers of the world, can the ways in which families resolve their conflicts ever apply to international conflict?

The present article deals primarily with the inherent characteristics of family conflict, some of them diametrically opposite to international conflict. Nevertheless, the study of small-scale conflict seems most likely to yield new hypotheses relevant to large-scale conflict if the family is studied on its own terms. Were we to limit ourselves to facets of obvious relevance, new ways of looking at international conflict might be missed. In any case, a general theory of conflict must eventually embrace all ranges of social systems, from the largest to the smallest. Hence family conflict has potential interest for its similarities with, and its differences from, large-scale conflict.

Conflict is a widespread and serious problem in the contemporary American family. Roughly, one marriage in every four ends

From Robert O. Blood, "Resolving Family Conflicts," *The Journal of Conflict Resolution* 4, 1960, 209–219.

in divorce, which is usually preceded, and often caused, by the failure of family members to avoid or solve their conflicts. Many additional families survive their periods of stress only at great cost to their physical and mental health. Many a husband's ulcers, a wife's headaches, and a child's nervous tics are traceable to domestic tension and warfare.

How does it happen that conflict afflicts so many families?

SOURCES OF FAMILY CONFLICT

Families everywhere tend to have certain characteristics which lay them open to potential conflict.

Compulsion

For one thing, a family is not a voluntary organization (except for the husband and wife). Children do not choose their parents. When the going gets tough, they cannot resign their membership. Even the parents are under heavy pressure to stick with the group no matter what.

Such involuntary participation tends to intensify conflict, once it originates. Because they have to continue living in the same house year in and year out, family members can develop deep antipathies for one another. What began as a mere conflict of interest easily turns into emotional hatred through the accumulation of grievances between two family members. Once such hostility has arisen, conflict often becomes self-perpetuating.

Intimacy

The conflict potentialities inherent in the involuntary membership of the family are accentuated by the intimacy of contact within the family. In school or church or business, physical distance and social formality are maintained at some minimum level. Moreover, contact is restricted to a limited range of relationships, such as teacher-pupil, priest-parishioner, or boss-secretary.[1]

By contrast, relationships within the family are functionally

[1]This is what Talcott Parsons calls "functionally specific relationships" (8).

diffuse. Family members lay all sorts of claims on one another for economic maintenance, recreational companionship, sexual responsiveness, sympathetic understanding, love and affection, etc. The comprehensiveness of these claims points to additional potential sources of conflict.

When conflict does occur within the family, it lacks the restraint imposed by concern for public opinion. If a man's home is his castle, it is also the place where his dungeons of despair are. A man who would never strike a woman in public finds his fury uncontrollable when goaded by a nagging wife behind closed doors. A child who would be patiently admonished in a public park needs a pillow in his pants for the same behavior at home. The very privacy, which makes possible the most uninhibited embrace within the bedroom, permits an equally uninhibited tongue-lashing. Intimacy of contact, therefore, contributes to both the extensity and the intensity of conflict within the family.

Smallness

While families everywhere are characterized by compulsory membership and intimate contact, the American family's small number of children further magnifies the problem of conflict, especially between siblings. In a large family, one child's share of his mother's attention and affection is so limited that it matters little whether he has it or not. In a two-child family, however, one child can monopolize the parent simply by vanquishing his sole sibling. Under these circumstances sibling rivalry becomes acute.

Similarly, among three siblings, the inherent instability of the triad typically leads the two older children to battle for the pawn. Again limited size dictates who the potential enemy shall be, makes him highly visible in the small group, and leads to the development of long-term feuds.

Change

The above family features would not be so bad were it not for the rapidity with which the family situation changes. Given fixed ingredients, a stable equilibrium might be sought. But families change so fast that a moving equilibrium is the best that can be hoped for.

Families change rapidly in size. Census figures show that newlyweds typically have hardly more than a year in which to work out their marital relationship before it is altered by the nausea of pregnancy. Then the children come every two years—bing, bing, bing. A decade and half later they leave for college or its working-class equivalents with similar rapidity (5).

Meanwhile the family may have maintained the same size, but the needs of its members were rapidly changing. Every time a new child starts to crawl, to climb, to wander across the street, to go to school, to experience puberty, or to drive a car, the pattern of family living must be readjusted. The changing "developmental tasks" of growing individuals create corresponding "family developmental tasks." Even parents' needs change as, for example, when the mother loses her figure or the father fails to get the raise he expected. Since the American family specializes in personality development and personal need fulfillment, such individual changes tend to disrupt the family equilibrium.

Given so many potentialities for conflict, what mechanisms exist for preventing the total disruption of what is so often called the "basic unit" in society?

NORMATIVE MECHANISMS FOR PREVENTING FAMILY CONFLICT

No society can afford to turn its back on family conflict. The family is too indispensable a unit of social structure and too necessary a means for the transmission of culture to the oncoming generation to be allowed to fall apart.

Consequently, every society tends to develop patterned ways of inhibiting the emergence of conflict. With the passage of time, these mechanisms tend to acquire the force of norms. That is, social pressures are mobilized to increase the likelihood that these mechanisms will be utilized, and social sanctions are imposed on those who violate them.

Different preventive mechanisms are found in various societies, depending partly on the points at which their family system is especially vulnerable to conflict. The following analysis classifies particular taboos and requirements in broad categories of general interest.

1. Avoidance of Probable Sources of Conflict. Many societies have devices for keeping apart potential or actual family members who otherwise would be likely to come into conflict with each other. By "potential family members" are meant couples who are not yet married. Societies have many ways of screening out those most predisposed to conflict. The traditional "publishing of the banns" allowed triple opportunities for objections to be raised to an inappropriate partnership. The formal engagement notifies parents and friends of the couple's intentions, providing a last opportunity for pressures to be brought to bear in disapproved cases. Studies of broken engagements show that such pressures often successfully prevent what would presumably be conflict-laden marriages (4, pp. 275–76).

Studies of "mixed marriages" of many sorts show a greater incidence of conflict due to the contrasting cultural values, expectations, and behavior patterns of the partners (6). Church organizations mobilize their resources to discourage interfaith marriages, and informal social pressure tends to prevent heterogamous marriages across racial, national, or class boundaries. Although a majority of all mixed marriages succeeds, such social pressures presumably break up in advance those mixed marriages which would be least likely to succeed.

New preventive mechanisms in our society are marriage education and premarital counseling. An estimated 10 percent of American college students now take a course in preparation for marriage, one of whose main purposes is to rationalize the process of mate selection through emphasizing numerous ways of testing compatibility (3). Most such courses operate on the premise that young people are liable to contract incompatible marriages if they are not careful. Hence the chief value of compatibility testing is to detect which relationships are incompatible.

One of the main functions of premarital counseling, similarly, is to provide couples in doubt with an opportunity to look objectively at the conflicts already apparent in their relationships and to provide them with emotional support as they go through the process of deciding to avoid each other in the future.

Two legal moves designed to avoid domestic difficulties are almost universal among the fifty states. One of these is the five-day waiting period between the time of applying for a marriage license and the date of the wedding. This provides an opportunity for those intoxicated with wine or perfume to sober up and reconsider. Similarly, the age at which couples can marry without the blessing of their parents has been increased to eighteen for the bride and twenty-one for the groom. Since teen-age marriages have a conspicuously higher divorce rate, raising the minimum age probably reduces the number of marriages which get off to a bad start.

Once the marriage has been contracted, one of the widespread sources of difficulty is the in-law relationship. Since marriage involves a drastic shift in allegiance from parents to spouse, newlyweds often have ambivalent feelings which are reflected in interspousal jealously and conflict. This marital tension makes it correspondingly difficult for couples to get along with their parents-in-law.

Our society reduces friction in this area by warning couples not to move in with their in-laws if they can possibly avoid doing so. Some societies prescribe even stricter avoidance by restricting or prohibiting social intercourse with the mother-in-law. Especially taboo is the familiarity of joking with the mother-in-law. Reserve and formality are frequently required. Sometimes complete avoidance is the rule—one must neither talk with nor even look at the mother-in-law.[2] Although there may be social losses, such mechanisms of avoidance effectively rule out the possibility of conflict between potentially hostile individuals.

2. Allocation of Rights and Duties to Particular Roles. A second way in which societies prevent conflict is by distribut-

[2]Most of the cross-cultural examples in this paper are drawn from George P. Murdock (7).

ing the authority, privileges, and responsibilities of family members according to a fixed pattern. In so doing, these societies predetermine the outcome. In fact, they short-circuit the conflict process completely because they take the issue out of the area of legitimate controversy. Henceforth only in socially deviant families does conflict ever occur over the allocated matters. For example, the incest taboo allocates sexual privileges exclusively to the husband and wife. Murdock and other anthropologists believe that the reason why this allocation pattern is found universally is because it is essential to family harmony (7, pp. 295–96). It functions to prevent sexual jealousy and rivalry within the family which would exist if more than one member of the family were allowed access to the same sexual partner.

Similarly, authority in the family is seldom distributed evenly among family members or (vaguer yet) left to each new family to decide for itself. Almost every society centralizes legitimate power in one role, usually that of the father. This is not to say that the wife and children are necessarily excluded from consultation in the decision-making process. Indeed, consideration for the wishes of the members of his family may be enjoined on the patriarch. However, a patriarchal family system specifies that in a showdown—when husband and wife cannot agree on mutually exclusive alternatives—the husband's wishes should prevail. The beauty of this system lies not in male superiority but in the fact that a ready out is available from any deadlock which may arise. It could as easily be the wife (and is in a few societies). It is handy, however, to have a way of avoiding prolonged crises within the family.

Authority need not be allocated entirely to one role. Each partner may have certain areas of family living in which he has autonomous jurisdiction. For example, most Detroit husbands make the final decision about what car to buy, while the typical wife decides how much money to spend on food for the family.[3] Whenever people grow up expecting the husband or the wife to

[3]All references to Detroit families are drawn from the writer's 1955 interview study of 731 housewives (a representative sample of the Detroit Metropolitan Area) (2).

make decisions on their own in the "proper" areas, those areas are effectively removed from the domain of conflict.

Herein lies the problem of the democratic family. Whenever two or more family members believe they ought to share in making a certain decision, they have added another potential conflict to their portfolio. The American family has been drifting in the direction of a "companionship" ideology, which specifies that an increasing number of decisions should be made jointly. A good example is the family vacation, which 66 percent of all Detroit housewives report is planned fifty-fifty. In the long run, mutual planning is likely to produce results which at least partly please both partners. And, according to our democratic philosophy, this is an improvement over the old system of fully pleasing one partner at the expense of the other.

But the process may be painful. The trend "from institution to companionship" has opened a whole Pandora's box of potential new conflicts. These do not necessarily materialize; under the classical patriarchate, they could not.

The blurring lines in the division of labor similarly open the way to more conflict. In a time when women did the dishes without question, dish-washing was not a topic for cartoons (symptoms of sore spots in any society). But, as men and women alike begin to wonder whether and how much men should help out in the kitchen, a new area of controversy is added to the list. Thus a clearly defined division of labor, like a clear-cut allocation of authority, may be a social device for preventing conflict.

3. Equality of Treatment Within the Family. The allocation of authority to particular members of the family does not mean the right to wield it arbitrarily. Despotic power creates unrest within the body domestic just as much as in the body politic. To prevent such unrest, the centralization of authority must be coupled with a bill of rights for the weaker family members to protect them from discriminatory treatment.

The exercise of power within the family takes two forms: (1) influencing or forcing the individual to alter his behavior (either by doing something he does not want to do or by stopping what he would like to do) and (2) granting or withholding favors. Even though the ability to exercise both types of power may be vested primarily (or ultimately) in the father, it is well to remember that the mother is a powerful figure for her children, especially when they are small. Indeed, every member of the family has the power to grant or withhold his attention, love, and respect regardless of how weak he may be in other respects. Therefore, when we speak of the necessity of equal treatment, we are not referring to the father alone.

How does equal treatment manifest itself in the family? The illustrations are endless. If Johnnie gets a story before he goes to bed, so must Jane. If he has to pick up the living room floor, she has to be forced to do her share. If Tom gets to use the family car on Friday, then Dick has a right to it on Saturday. Children and parents alike recognize the justice of such claims and can appeal to the moral value of fair play to secure equality. Insofar as equality is achieved, conflict tends to be avoided.

The administrative problem is complicated, however, by the fact that siblings are rarely of the same age. As a result, the principle of equality cannot always mean uniformity of treatment at any particular time. If John stays up until 9:00 P.M., that does not mean Jane can—being two years younger, she must have extra sleep. Accepting such seeming discrepancies is not easy for younger children. However, parental emphasis on the idea that, "when you are ten years old, you will be able to stay up until 9:00 P.M. too" is often effective.

Age-graded equality is likely to prevent conflict especially well when the system for moving from one notch to the next is clearly understood by all concerned. For instance, if every child's allowance automatically increases a nickel on his birthday, the younger siblings can feel confident that they will receive their "just deserts" when the proper time comes.

In the light of what was said earlier about the conflict-preventing function of the incest taboo, it is apparent that the custom of polygyny presents very serious problems. Whenever there are several wives but only one husband, the danger of jealousy and conflict among the wives is very acute. It is not surprising, therefore, that polygynous societies have devised all three types of measures for preventing the outbreak of such conflict. (1) Avoidance is achieved by placing each wife and her children in a separate hut. (2) Authority over subsequent wives is usually allocated to the first wife—her position is thereby less threatened, and the loss of exclusive wifehood is offset by the addition of maid service. (3) More important for our present purposes is the common requirement that the man treat his wives equally, that he not play favorites among them. This often takes the form of requiring the husband to follow a strict schedule of rotation among his wives, spending an equal number of nights with each in turn. No society can effectively control the warmth or coolness with which he treats an unpopular wife; however, this merry-go-round rule at least spares her the humiliation of public knowledge of her husband's disfavor.

Equality of treatment is not an easy achievement, especially where intangibles like affection and attention are involved. Only the childless couple can completely avoid conflict from this source. As soon as the first child arrives, competition for the time and interest of the mother is created. Since she does not have enough time to go around, she must be prepared to say to her son, "I played with you last night, so tonight you should not object to my going out with your father." Even the child whose oedipal wishes have not been effectively resolved may accept such a statement if the norm of family equality has been adequately learned.

Avoidance, allocation, and equality—not separately but in combination—are the inventions which cross-cultural research shows to have been practical ways by which societies have prevented family conflict.

INSTRUMENTAL MECHANISMS FOR RESOLVING FAMILY CONFLICTS

Despite the existence of preventive mechanisms, and wherever those mechanisms do not exist, conflict occurs. The means of ending those conflicts seem far less often culturally prescribed. Rather there seem to be a number of optional procedures, in the United States at least, which are available to families as ways out of their dilemmas. These mechanisms are instrumental in the sense that they can be employed as means to achieve certain ends, if the family so desires.

1. Increased Facilities for Family Living. When conflict results from scarce facilities, it is sometimes possible to satisfy both the conflicting parties by increasing the resources at the family's disposal. For example, sibling jealousy often originates from the mother's preoccupation with the new baby on her return from the hospital. An extra "mother" in the form of grandmother or nurse relieves the real mother of part of her work load so that she can give more attention to her displaced child.

Those societies with an extended family system have built-in grandmothers, aunts, and cousins who flexibly replace the mother when her attention is unavailable. Ethnographers report a general lack of sibling rivalry under this multiple mothering.

Conflict in the American home often centers around the use of scarce physical facilities. The current trends to a second car, a second television set, and a second telephone result not only in increased profits for the corresponding manufacturers but in decreased tension for family personnel who can now use parallel facilities simultaneously instead of having to compete for control of single channels. Similarly, the new-fangled recreation room provides the rest of the family with a retreat when daughter decides to throw a party in the living room, taking the tension off competition for "the only room in the house where I can entertain my friends."

2. Priority Systems for the Use of Limited Facilities. When enlargement of facilities is impossible, family conflict often becomes chronic—there is perpetual tension between family members, perennial jockeying for position, and fear that the competitor is getting ahead or taking advantage. Such feuding can often be seen among young children and is difficult to end by

rational means. With older family members, war weariness may eventuate in a desire for peace at any price. Conflict may then be ended by facing the issues and arriving at decisions in some fashion or other.

The product of such decision-making is often a priority system governing the use of the scarce facility. If the bone of contention is the television set, a schedule for the whole week, born of a major showdown, may take the place of petty conflict "every hour on the hour." If the scarcity has been financial, the record of decisions takes the form of a budget. Here the mutual recriminations sparked by overdrawn bank accounts can be obviated by advance planning about where the money is to be spent.

The beauty of a budget, as of any other system, is that personal control ("I say you must") is replaced by impersonal control ("The budget says you must"). The process of agreeing on a budget is still liable to plenty of conflict, but, once formulated, a budget tends to divert attention from the hostile antagonist to the operational code.

3. Enlargement of Areas of Autonomy. Analogous in many ways to the method of effecting an absolute increase in the facilities available to family members is the chopping-up of existing facilities into smaller units which can then be made available exclusively to different members of the family. This results in a relative increase in the facilities at the disposal of the individual without the necessity of securing the consent of other family members. Hence potential conflict is avoided. For example, some couples plague themselves with difficulty by trying to arrive at joint decisions about the disposition of the scarce commodity of money. Worse yet, each partner may endlessly reproach the other for the petty expenditures he has already made. Such bickering can be ended by granting each partner an allowance to be spent as he sees fit without the necessity of accounting to the other for his whims and fancies. This innovation correspondingly restricts the area in which decision-making (and potential conflict) must occur to more critical areas of financial management.

The method of granting autonomy is not limited, however, to the use of scarce facilities. The problem of adolescent-parent conflict may be resolved by judicious increases in the amount of autonomy granted the teen-ager. Some parents clash head-on with their high-school sons and daughters in attempting to curb their adoption of the latest fads in dress and speech. Certainly, the easiest way out of this dilemma is to recognize that teen-agers are old enough to decide for themselves what to wear and how to talk.

Similarly, conflict may result from undue stress on total-family activities. The mother who worries about finding recreation which both her four-year-old and her fourteen-year-old will enjoy may be troubling herself unduly, since almost anything she chooses evokes dissent from one child or the other. Autonomy under such circumstances need not mean a complete atomization of the family but simply a willingness of a subgroup within the family to enjoy singing nursery rhymes without feeling the necessity of compelling disinterested members to join.

4. Safety Valves for Reducing Tension Between Family Members. Insofar as conflict within the family is precipitated or accentuated by accumulated interpersonal resentment, various means are available for reducing the level of this tension. Vacations are one such resource. Of course, a family may find plenty of things to quarrel about on a vacation, but at least they are new issues. As far as the old problems are concerned, a change of scenery makes it possible to forget about them for a while, and on return they may even have lost their power to provoke antagonism.

A change in personnel may be just as effective. Adding a pal or two for the morning play period may so restructure relationships within the sibling group that the old feuds are disrupted at least for the time being.

For some purposes, however, it is most effective to get away from the family group completely. One reason we speak of harried housewives but not of harried husbands is that wives (and especially mothers) are so often tied down to the four walls and the four faces of the home. The piling-up of petty irritations into peaks of tension results in perennial irritability and conflict-proneness. Then little issues provoke major crises because of the loading of accumulated tension.

Under these circumstances escape mechanisms are not childish but sensible. Getting out of the house produces a sense of relief. A television farce or romance produces the right kind of distraction. Even "going home to mama" may be useful provided mama does not take daughter's troubles too seriously.

There may be corresponding value in masculine and children's expeditions. The husband's "night out with the boys" may be resented by his wife but is likely to result in a new look in marital relations. And the children need not always be on the receiving end for personnel changes but may find welcome escape from the network of conflict by visiting their friends in return.

There is also what the psychologists call "catharsis"—the reduction of tension through telling one's troubles to someone else. There is little doubt that "unloading" one's difficulties on someone else genuinely lightens the burden of conflict for most people. In so doing, it reduces the necessity for purposeless vindictiveness which prolongs the conflict. In effect, catharsis (like the other safety valves) helps to break the vicious circle of attack and retaliation which so often characterizes families with a long history of conflict.

The only problem involved in the use of catharsis is the selection of the target. Among the shoulders which might conveniently be cried on are those of the husband (provided he is not the antagonist in the conflict), the mother, and the neighbor. Providing a sympathetic ear for the spouse is one of the major steps in accomplishing what I like to call the "mental hygiene function" of marriage. Mothers and neighbors can usually be counted on to be sympathetic—but sometimes too much so, tending to jump into the conflict, too, starting a mobilization race on both sides.

Because of these dangers in lay friendships, couples in serious conflict sometimes find it useful to turn to a professional third party, for instance, a clergyman, doctor, or family counselor. These functionaries are accustomed to providing people with discreet opportunities for catharsis.

Whatever the specific safety valve opened, the reduction of the head of steam facilitates the tolerance of frustration and a patient approach to finding satisfactory solutions to the basic sources of conflict.

PROCESSES OF RESOLVING FAMILY CONFLICT

So far we have been ducking the main issue of what happens when two parties to a family conflict collide head-on. To treat this problem, it is necessary to assume that the two partners (for it is most often the husband and wife who find themselves in this position) think of each other as equals. Hence the problem cannot be solved by appeal to differential authority.

One obstacle to resolving family conflict is that it is often dyadic in nature. Hence voting is impossible. Or at least there is no way to break the inevitable tie. Some families have found that conflicts of limited importance can be settled by ordinary voting procedures—especially if there is an odd number of children in the family. But this easy way out is available at best during a small fraction of the total family life-cycle.

What, then, to do in case of a deadlock?

Discussion

The natural first step is to talk things over, to outline the various possible solutions, to weigh the pros and cons in an attempt to arrive at some sort of solution. This process of decision-making has been studied and analyzed too well elsewhere to need detailed treatment here (1, pp. 225–51). Suffice it to say that there are three major types of solutions which can be reached (1) *consensus*—that is, mutual agreement by both partners that a vacation at the lake would be best for both of them; (2) *compromise*—one week at the lake and one week in the mountains so that both partners gain part and lose part of their objectives; (3) *concession*—two weeks in the mountains, not because the wife is convinced that that would be most enjoyable, but because she decides to end the conflict by dropping her own demands.

Most families solve most of their problems by such processes of communication followed by decision-making.

Mediation

Occasionally, couples need outside help in arriving at a decision. Here relatives and friends can seldom qualify because they are usually more closely aligned with one partner than the other. Hence professional personnel are almost the only resort.

The function of the third party in this case is seldom to take over the decision-making process. Rather he acts as a catalytic agent, enabling the couple to become more objective and more rational by his very presence. If conflict is serious and hostile feelings have accumulated, he may work with each partner separately for a long time. Only after self-insight and mutual empathy have been achieved might it be productive for the couple to be seen jointly. Meanwhile the couple may discover on their own that they have already acquired the ability to settle their conflict, aided by the new skills and understandings gained in counseling. Even when only one partner turns to a third party, the beneficial repercussions of the counselor's collaboration may be felt throughout the family.

Accommodation

In one sense, accommodation might be listed as a type of decision. More accurately, however, it represents the recognition of a failure to agree. In the classic phrase, we "agree to disagree" or to "live and let live." In the specific case of the summer vacation, this could mean separate vacations for husband and wife (though so much autonomy runs heavily counter to American mores).

It is not always possible for the parties to a family conflict to go their separate ways. If the issue at hand is the need for a new car, one either gets one or one does not. But if John likes to play tennis while Mary likes to go to concerts, Mary could accommodate herself to going it alone while John finds a different partner.

Essentially accommodation involves adopting a philosophical attitude of resignation—coming to the conclusion that further attempts to influence the partner are just not worth the conflict they provoke. Hence expectations of mutuality are abandoned in favor of accepting the partner as he is.

Separation

If neither discussion, mediation, nor accommodation succeeds in settling family conflict, the last resort is separation. In a sense, separation does not really settle conflict at all, but it usually does end it. If the antagonists are no longer within shooting distance of each other, their attention is soon likely to be diverted from the point at issue.

The term "separation" is usually applied to husband and wife. If they cannot live together in peace, few there are who would force them to go on living in conflict. Even those groups who are most opposed to divorce and remarriage recognize that separating the marriage partners is sometimes preferable to prolonging the agony.

Separation can also occur between parents and children. The military academies of this country are populated by boys whose parents were unable to arrive at peace treaties with them. And the older adolescent who leaves home for college, job, or marriage sometimes only thus terminates his or her revolutionary war.

Separation is the most drastic way out of family conflict, yet those who have tried it often say that peaceful loneliness is an improvement over perpetual conflict.

CONCLUSION

Returning now to the question of the similarities and differences between family conflict and conflict in other settings, it is apparent that the sources of family conflict are largely distinctive. Families are uniquely small and intimate. The structure and developmental tasks of the family are transformed with unusual speed. Only in the involuntary nature of world society is there a close analogy.

Much as the sources of conflict may differ between the family and the world community, the mechanisms for preventing and resolving conflict have more in common. International "mechanisms of avoidance" include the United Nations Emergency Force sealing the border between Israel and Egypt and the proposals for disengagement in Central Europe. The "allocation of authority" to a world court and a world government would alter the naked struggle of sovereign nations among themselves. "Equality of treatment" is just as difficult a problem among nations differing in size, wealth, and maturity as among children differing in age. However, the admission of all nations to membership in the United Nations might achieve minimal equality and bring excluded nations within the sphere of authority of the international organization. Rotation systems in key international offices tend to reduce international jealousy.

"Increased facilities" for international living are provided through economic development, reducing the envy of the "have" nations by the have-nots. "Priority systems" for the use of limited facilities apply to such international waterways as rivers and harbors on which multiple countries depend. "Enlargement of areas of autonomy" reduces international conflict as colonial powers become independent. International "safety valves" include the opportunities for catharsis provided by the open forum of the General Assembly and by smaller-scale talks at or below the summit.

Big-power rivalry between East and West is closely analogous to the conflict between husband and wife. Voting has little value when the conflicting parties perennially deadlock or veto each other. The focus under such circumstances must be on the same processes that enable families to resolve their deadlocks. Discussion through negotiation and diplomatic talks may lead to consensus, compromise, or concession internationally as well as familially. The General Secretary of the United Nations has increasingly become an international mediator, as have many of the smaller powers. Accommodation to the status quo has been the outcome of many an international crisis that for a time threatened to disturb the peace. But separation, in a shrinking world, is one process not open to national societies, for, much as they may dislike each other, they must go on forever living in the same international "house."

REFERENCES

1. Blood, Robert O., Jr. *Anticipating Your Marriage.* New York: Free Press, 1955.
2. Blood, Robert O., Jr., and Wolfe, Donald M. *Husbands and Wives: The Dynamics of Married Living.* New York: Free Press, 1960.
3. Bowman, Henry A. *Marriage Education in the Colleges.* New York: American Social Hygiene Association, 1949.
4. Burgess, Ernest W., and Wallin, Paul. *Engagement and Marriage.* Philadelphia: Lippincott, 1953.
5. Glick, Paul. "The Life Cycle of the Family," *Marriage and Family Living,* XVII (1955), 3–9.
6. Landis, Judson T. "Marriages of Mixed and Non-mixed Religious Faith," *American Sociological Review,* XIV (1949), 401–7.
7. Murdock, George P. *Social Structure.* New York: Macmillan, 1949.
8. Parsons, Talcott. "The Social Structure of the Family." In Ruth Nanda Anshen (ed.), *The Family: Its Function and Destiny.* New York: Harper & Row, 1949.

ALLAN D. FRANK

Conflict in the Classroom

In this book and elsewhere conflict has been examined from a number of different points of view, including economics, political science, sociology, social psychology, anthropology, human communication theory, history, psychology, systems theory, and game theory. It appears that a distinct, cross-disciplinary field committed to the study of human conflict is well past the formative stage. What is proposed here is an examination of conflict and conflict resolution from the perspective of instructional theory and practice. To the writer's knowledge no systematic attempt toward this end has materialized to date.

Since social conflict, by definition, requires interaction in a social context, it seems necessary to examine the classroom setting to determine if the required social variables are present to warrant application of conflict theory to that setting.

THE CLASSROOM AS A SOCIAL SYSTEM

Much of conflict theory focuses on struggles between relatively well-defined, stable, and cohesive groups in which members clearly perceive their own group membership. Examples are nations, states, labor and management organizations, political parties, and professional, social, and religious organizations. It is doubtful that a classroom fits the usual definitions of "groups" or "parties" in a conflict cited in the literature on social conflict (such as Lewis Coser's *The Functions of Social Conflict*). This being the case, there may be a real difficulty in pursuing an analysis of social conflict in the classroom. Since conflict takes place either within a larger social system, or between smaller social systems, it is necessary to locate one or both of these phenomena in the classroom prior to discussing "social conflict in the classroom." If it can be established that a classroom is a total social system and/or a number of smaller social subsystems, then the analysis can get under way. This involves finding satisfactory answers to these questions:

1. Is the classroom a social system?
2. Is the classroom a *unique* social system?
3. Given that it is a social system, is the classroom a *type* of social system that can be analyzed using conflict theory and principles?

Is the Classroom a Social System?

It would be easy to infer that just because 20 to 40 students meet regularly in the same room that they are a functioning social unit. However, it would be a mistake to accept this inference outright. As the ensuing discussion will illustrate, it is erroneous to assume that a group of persons in close physical proximity necessarily constitutes a social system. With this disclaimer aside, evidence which helps to define the classroom as a social system will be examined.

Bruner characterizes the instructional process as "essentially social," and maintains that students must have "minimal mastery of social skills" in order to become effectively involved in the instructional process.[1] Withall and Lewis when discussing social interaction in the classroom state:

> The statement by Thelen and Tyler (1950) that "realization of the very great influence of the classroom group upon individual learning

[1]Jerome S. Bruner, *Toward a Theory of Instruction* (New York: W. W. Norton, 1968), p. 42.

follows from a consideration of the implications of much of the recent research in social psychology" can be regarded as a kind of prologue to the period in which educational research began to capitalize on a view of the classroom group as a social milieu in which learning and instruction occurred.[2]

Writing from the perspective of T-Group theory, Miles states:

> Perhaps the fundamental contribution of T-Group practice [to the classroom] is a clear sense that the classroom is a miniature social system with regularities and predictable features which both aid and hinder learning.[3]

Further support comes from a recent work by Clark, Erway, and Beltzer.[4] The authors' basic theme is that classrooms are social units, complete with a communication system and various subsystems, and hence the teacher and students must understand the system and subsystems in order for effective learning to take place. Since modern instructional theory seeks to emphasize rather than question the premise that the classroom is a social system, there appears to be no need to cite additional evidence.

Is the Classroom a Unique Social System?

While it is probably true that classroom learning is essentially a social experience which takes place in a social system, there is support for the position that this social system is, in some respects, unique.

The classroom is somewhat unique in terms of its purposes and membership. Classrooms can be viewed as collective, formal learning situations, set up and controlled by adults, to facilitate students' progress toward educational goals selected by adults.

[2]John Withall and W. W. Lewis, "Social Interaction in the Classroom," in *Handbook of Research on Teaching*, ed. N. L. Gage (Chicago: Rand-McNally, 1963), pp. 700–701.

[3]Matthew B. Miles, "The T-Group and the Classroom," *T-Group Theory and Laboratory Method*, eds. Leland P. Bradford, Jack R. Gibbs, and Kenneth D. Benne (New York: Wiley, 1964), p. 469.

[4]Margaret Clark, Ella Erway, and Lee Beltzer, *The Learning Encounter: The Classroom as a Communications Workshop* (New York: Random House, 1971).

Such a social system is unique in the sense that members exercise little control over the makeup and goal-orientation of their group.

Note also, that group membership is determined almost totally by non-members. In most instances members do not control who should be included or excluded from the group. Indeed, individual membership may be either totally involuntary (required course) or a result of insufficient flexibility in class scheduling to allow students to join "voluntary" groups in "elective" courses. A student might, then, be in a class simply because it fits into his "schedule." The student's very presence in school may be the result of a state law or a desire to avoid the military draft.

So much for the uniqueness of the physical membership in the classroom. What about psychological membership? First, there are the psychological effects of the required membership mentioned above. A student in a "required" course or in a course that merely "fits his schedule" may never be able to accept as his own the objectives and values which guide the social interaction in that classroom. It is probably true that most classrooms contain members who, though physically present, have psychologically withdrawn from the social system by rejecting any one or more of the following: the classroom's learning outcomes, the value system of the classroom, the teacher, other members. Such a student would probably not perceive himself as a member of the classroom social unit.

The classroom is also unique in terms of the personal traits of its members. The most obvious factor here is the age difference between the teacher and the students. The teacher is normally viewed by students as an adult from a *different* generation, and frequently he is perceived as a parent-substitute or some other symbol of adult authority. With regard to the students, they are normally younger than the teacher, but they normally vary greatly in their level of maturity. In a figurative sense, "men and women" sit alongside of "boys and girls." In terms of physical, social, mental, and philosophical development, differences could well outweigh similarities, and it should be noted that group stability and cohesiveness are derived from identifiable similarities of values and objectives. If we add to this mix the characteristic instability of social relationships among youth, we arrive at a view of a social system which is characterized by such words as "heterogenous," "unstable," and "potential for generational conflict."

Another unique characteristic of the "classroom society" is the presence of a number of subgroups or subsystems in the classroom. At the simplest level of analysis, there are subgroups of "two" consisting of a teacher and each student operating separately in a competitive environment. Students can be perceived as individuals competing with other individuals who happen to be in the same room for grades, smiles, favorable reports to parents, and other prizes, all of which are awarded by the teacher. Such a point of view may account for much of the social behavior in a classroom, and is supported by research in teaching which notes the dominance of teacher-student dyadic interaction in the classroom.

Going beyond the dyad to subgroups made up of several persons, one cannot speak specifically of the various subgroups within a given classroom, but some of them might well be built around such factors as: acceptance/rejection of the classroom's learning objectives and values, academic achievement levels, socioeconomic background, race or national origin, occupational aspirations, sex, common out-of-class interests, and other bases for friendship choices. In some instances, outside-of-class subgroups enter a classroom in whole or part, thus making the social unit even more complex. A given student may have an overriding allegiance to some outside-of-class group, or he may feel more a part of some in-class subgroup than the class as a whole.

Clark, Erway and Beltzer observe that "Almost every communication system contains many simultaneously operating subsystems."[5] Throughout their book, these authors explain and illustrate how these subsystems form and how they interact with

[5]*Ibid.*, p. 10.

each other, with the teacher, with a student, and with the total classroom social system. It is clear that the classroom should not be viewed as one social system, but rather as a multiplicity of systems ranging in size from one to the entire classroom. These subgroupings not only function separately and simultaneously, but also interact with each other. Such a social system is very complex, which makes it difficult to predict what social behaviors will be produced by an event when the social system is in a given state. The classroom social system, then, does appear to possess unique characteristics.

Can the Classroom Social System Be Analyzed Using Conflict Theory?

Having established that the classroom can be perceived both as a social system (though a unique one) and as a cluster of interacting subsystems, the analysis of conflict in the classroom can get underway. Before proceeding, the two segments "classroom as a social system" and "social conflict" should be interrelated to determine if such an analysis is feasible.

Coser defines social conflict as follows:

> For the purposes of this study, it [social conflict] will provisionally be taken to mean a struggle over values and claims to scarce status, power, and resources in which the aims of opponents are to neutralize, injure, or eliminate their rivals.[6]

Such a definition, and discussions leading from it, tend to deal with struggles between relatively well-defined, stable, and cohesive groups in which members clearly perceive their own membership. Can this definition, and the conflict theory surrounding it, be applied to the classroom setting?

If we put aside the notion that classroom conflict invariably involves a conflict between the teacher as a representative of one social system and a cohesive stable social system made up of all students in the classroom, then we will have taken a large step toward an affirmative answer to the question posed above.

[6]Lewis Coser, *The Functions of Social Conflict* (New York: The Free Press, 1956), p. 8.

If we further perceive a variety of potential pairings for classroom conflict, then we are another step closer to an affirmative answer. Possible pairings include: teacher-student, student-student, teacher-entire class, student-subgroup, teacher-subgroup, student-class, and subgroup-subgroup.

However, even with these qualifications Coser's definition seems to fit the classroom social situation a bit uncomfortably. Its sociological orientation toward struggles between political and social groups within an entire society is too broad a perspective for use in this analysis. Deutsch's definition seems to fit better because it focuses on smaller units of social interaction. He writes:

> A conflict exists whenever incompatible activities occur. An action which is incompatible with another action prevents, obstructs, interferes with, injures, or in some way makes it less likely or less effective. Conflicts may arise from differences in interests, desires, or values, or from scarcity of some resource such as money, time, space, position, or it may reflect a rivalry in which one person tries to outdo or undo the other.[7]

Coser's and Deutsch's definitions are not basically incompatible. They represent a sociological and social psychological perspective, respectively. Coser's definition presupposes larger social units than Deutsch's. Deutsch's definition can also be viewed as a more specific spelling out of the dimensions of conflict described in Coser's. His specifics will be most useful in analyzing the classroom situation. The writer will have a composite of both definitions in mind whenever he uses the terms "conflict" and "social conflict."

The evidence presented during the discussion of the classroom as a social unit points to two conclusions: (1) Classrooms are sufficiently similar to the other social settings in which most conflict research has been conducted so that research findings and derived principles from these other situations can be applied to the classroom, provided that relevant restrictions and differences are noted. (2) The classroom can be treated like any other

[7]Morton Deutsch, "Conflicts: Productive and Destrictive," p. 156 of this book.

social system when performing an analysis of sources of social conflict.

JUSTIFICATION AND RATIONALE FOR THE ANALYSIS OF CLASSROOM CONFLICT

In this section three tasks will be pursued: (1) examination of the potential value of conflict theory for improving classroom teaching, (2) establishing the focus of this analysis on the classroom as a social setting, (3) integration of various theoretical perspectives as they relate to potential sources of conflict in the classroom. The last two sections will discuss sources of conflict in the classroom, and some conclusions and suggestions for further research.

At this point it should be noted that by education and experience, the writer is best qualified to deal with the secondary- and college-level classroom, hence, the focus will be on seventh grade through the fourth year of college. In most instances references to grade level will be made only when the nature of the statement warrants it, and although such factors as age and maturity may be significant variables in any analysis of conflict, no systematic consideration of these two variables will be attempted.

This analysis will be restricted almost exclusively to *interpersonal* conflict in the classroom and will refer to *intrapersonal* conflict only in the context of how it may be a source of interpersonal conflict.

Potential Value of Conflict Theory to the Classroom

Here it will be shown that since social conflict among youth involves a higher affective investment than among adults, the study of social conflict and conflict resolution in the schools would most appropriately take place within an educational focus which has been labeled as *affective education.* It will also be shown that, paradoxically, while affective education and "social conflict education" are valuable and necessary, they are both generally neglected in the schools.

Affective Investment in Conflict. Although it is erroneous to assume that participants in a conflict invariably have an affective investment in it, this approach to analysis will assume a high level of affective investment in classroom conflicts. This assumption is based on evidence which indicates that younger persons have more of a tendency to respond emotionally to social events involving tension, frustration, aggression, and conflict than do older persons. It should be noted that all subsequent statements concerning affective and conflict behavior are made with the knowledge that they pertain only to our own culture.

This tendency to respond emotionally to social events is discussed in a book written as a group project of the Committee on Adolescence of the Group for the Advancement of Psychiatry.[8] Commenting on response characteristics of adolescents (persons between 10 and 20 years old) they make such observations as:

1. This growth interval [ages 10 to 20] is characterized by increases in youth activity, aggressiveness, mobility, and social interaction.[9]

2. The basic instinctual forces are given considerable impetus by the physiological changes of puberty. One manifestation of this is an increase in energy, which often overrides the thought processes and control mechanisms and discharges itself through action. Adolescents are thus prone to act impulsively in all sorts of ways, many of which will appear pathologic.[10]

3. The teenager has become very conscious of his special status. He is eager for the accompanying privileges, impatient or downright defiant of the restrictions, and not a little cocky about the vaguely defined power his group wields.[11]

4. One of the unique characteristics of adolescence, in both phases, [beginning and end] is the recurrent alternation of spisodes of disturbed behavior with periods of relative quiescence.

[8]Group for the Advancement of Psychiatry, Committee on Adolescence, *Normal Adolescence* (New York: Scribner's, 1968).

[9]*Ibid.*, p. 17.

[10]*Ibid.*, p. 25.

[11]*Ibid.*, p. 39.

These episodes have the qualities both of rebellion and experiment.[12]

At other places in this work the authors cite such phenomena as alienation from the adult culture and rejection of adult values, intense interest in moral and philosophical questions, a struggle to throw off dependence on adults and to gain adult status. Looft lists what he labels as "well-documented characteristics of youth in Western cultures." He mentions specifically: "attention-attracting behaviors, the influence of peers, short-lived romantic affairs, and their impermanent interpersonal relations."[13] Although the intensity of these phenomena vary with age, what emerges is a composite for 10- to 20-year-olds characterized by intense energy, aggressiveness, impulsiveness, impermanence and instability of social relationships, and struggle against the existing culture.

Writing from a different perspective McLuhan comments on the effects of television viewing on the emotional involvement of young people in social events:

> The young people who have experienced a decade of TV have naturally imbibed an urge toward involvement in depth that makes all the remote visualized goals of usual culture seem not only unreal but irrelevant, and not only irrelevant but anemic. It is the total involvement in all-inclusive *nowness* that occurs in young lives via TV's mosaic image.[14]

It does appear that young people tend to respond more emotionally to social events than do adults. Indeed, one of the marks of adult maturity is a balanced relationship between the emotions and rational control systems, which allows for emotional responses without permitting them to overwhelm reason. Since research in social conflict focuses primarily on the adult world it is not surprising that Coser states:

> Realistic conflict need not be accompanied by hostility and aggres-

[12] *Ibid.*, p. 61.

[13] William R. Looft, "Egocentrism and Interaction in Adolescence," *Adolescence 6*, no. 24 (Winter 1971), 488.

[14] Marshall McLuhan, *Understanding Media: The Extensions of Man* (New York: McGraw-Hill, 1965), p. 335.

siveness. "Tensions" in a psychological sense are not always associated with conflict behaviors. Yet it might be "useful" to hate the opponent.[15]

What emerges in discussions of the role of affect in conflict is an image of a mature adult who is capable of monitoring his feelings in such a way as to increase his chances of prevailing in a conflict situation. In view of the evidence presented considering the emotional responses of the young to social events, such mature monitoring of the emotions would be most rare in classroom situations, and hence, affective investment would almost invariably accompany conflict. If this conclusion stands then we can proceed to place considerations of classroom conflict primarily within the affective domain of instruction.

AFFECTIVE EDUCATION: VALUE AND NEGLECT. The affective domain of instruction has been traditionally ignored in our educational system and dealing with classroom conflict and teaching about social conflict can be one step toward achieving better balance between the cognitive/affective emphases in classroom instruction.

Interestingly enough two influential statements[16] on this theme of cognitive and affective domains of instruction have been published, and both are steps in a sequential process to provide statements of educational goals in the cognitive, affective and psychomotor domains of instruction. At this point, then, a case will be made for more emphasis on affective goals of instruction, to be followed by statements supporting the need to deal with and teach about social conflict in the classroom.

Karathwoh *et al.* point to the lack of emphasis on affective educational goals:

> It is not entirely fair to imply that evaluation of the attainment of affective objectives is completely absent from the regular activities of

[15]Coser, *op. cit.*, p. 59.

[16]Benjamin S. Bloom, ed., *Taxonomy of Educational Objectives; The Classification of Educational Goals, Handbook I: Cognitive Domain* (New York: Longmans, Green, 1956); and David R. Krothwohl, Benjamin S. Bloom, and Bertram B. Masia, *Taxonomy of Educational Objectives; The Classification of Educational Goals, Handbook II: Affective Domain* (New York: McKay, 1964).

schools and teachers. Undoubtedly almost every teacher is on the alert for evidence of desirable interests, attitudes, and character developments. However, most of this is the noting of unusual characteristics or dramatic developments when they are almost forced on the teacher's attention. What is missing is a systematic effort to collect evidence of growth in affective objectives which is in any way parallel to the very great and systematic efforts to evaluate cognitive achievement.[17]

They conclude this part of their discussion with this statement:

> . . . under some conditions the development of cognitive behaviors may actually destroy certain desired affective behaviors and that, instead of a positive relation between growth in cognitive and affective behavior, it is conceivable that there may be an inverse relation between growth in the two domains.[18]

An example of this inverse relationship might be courses in appreciation of art, music, and literature which can either create an aversion to the art form or a lessened interest in it.

The editor's introduction to a recent work by George Isaac Brown contains further evidence of the neglect of affective education while calling for more emphasis on it in the schools. The editor (Stuart Miller) writes:

> It is obvious that we have wandered away from this tradition [education for the whole man]. Everywhere we hear cries that education is "irrelevant." Millions of American children find that our system doesn't work for them: they fail in it, they drop out, they protest, or they are thrown out. Surely there are many reasons for discontent with the present educational system, and surely the reasons for this discontent will have to be attacked in a great variety of ways. But one cannot help thinking that an underlying reason for this discontent is the school's lack of attention to the total human needs of their students: specifically their emotional, physical, and spiritual needs.[19]

The call for more emphasis on affective educational goals comes from several sources. The mere act of publishing *Handbook II: Affective Domain* constitutes an endorsement, by the authors, of the importance of affective educational outcomes.

[17]Krothwohl, Bloom, and Masia, *op. cit.*, pp. 15–16.

[18]*Ibid.*, p. 20.

[19]George Isaac Brown, *Human Teaching for Human Learning: An Introduction to Confluent Education*, ed. Stuart Miller (New York: Viking, 1972).

Writing in the area of measurement and evaluation Gronlund states:

> The least tangible objectives are those in the realm of attitudes, appreciations, interests, and facets of adjustments . . . The general tendency in the past has been to avoid the less tangible outcomes of instruction and to concentrate on improving the methods of evaluating knowledges and skills. . . . Although learning outcomes in these less tangible areas are more difficult to identify and evaluate, the importance of these objectives seems to justify the additional effort required. Improvement in the entire educational process is more likely to result from efforts to identify and evaluate *all* important outcomes of instruction than from attempts to improve instruments for evaluation in a highly tangible but limited area.[20]

Writing from the perspective of T-Group Theory Miles observes:

> We note here an interesting paradox. American adults are beginning to spend large amounts of money to understand "human relations" in their work; American children are to be forbidden such learning because it is not "subject matter," because it is the province of the family, the church, or the social agency, or because it is somehow irrelevant to "national survival."[21]

Later in the same work he concludes:

> No amount of official classroom concern with cognitive changes can obscure the fact that the child, like the adult T-group member, is always learning as a whole person. Attitudinal, value-related, and behavioral changes are proceeding simultaneously with the cognitive changes. From a broader standpoint . . ., the schools must be as concerned with man feeling, doing, and acting—alone or with others—as they are with man thinking.[22]

Writing in 1970, Egan highlights a serious deficiency in our educational system:

> One disturbing reason [for the spread of the encounter-group phenomena], is the general failure of education as we know it in the United States to be a vehicle of putting people in growthful contact with one another. Fuller interpersonal living is not ordinarily one of

[20]Norman E. Gronlund, *Measurement and Evaluation in Teaching* (New York: Macmillan, 1965), pp. 22–23.
[21]Miles, *op. cit.*, p. 453.
[22]*Ibid.*, p. 405.

the fruits of eight, twelve, or sixteen years of formal education. Therefore, encounter groups as we know them are to this extent remedial, and they will remain remedial until education grows up emotionally.[23]

Glasser,[24] writing from the viewpoint of reality therapy, identifies two basic human needs: the need for love and the need for self-worth. He insists that it is the schools' responsibility to help students learn how to give and receive love. His book as a whole can be viewed as a call for more attention to affective education. There seems, then, to be ample support for the conclusion that affective educational goals should receive more emphasis in the classroom.

Training in Conflict Resolution: Value and Neglect

A case will now be made for including learning outcomes related to the study of social conflict and conflict resolution.

Blake and Mouton whose article appears in Part II call directly for specially designed methods for classroom study of social conflict and conflict resolution:

> Classroom learning methodologies that could enable men to gain insights regarding conflict and acquire skills for resolving it seem to be impoverished. To aid men in acquiring both the conceptual understanding for managing conflict and the skills to see their own reactions in situations of conflict, man-to-man feedback seems to be an essential condition.[25]

Deutsch, whose article is also published in this volume, laments that "there is little formal training in techniques of constructive conflict resolution"[26] and later concludes that "a considerable educational effort is needed to help broaden the understanding of conflict. . . ."[27]

A review of some of the literature in relevant areas of re-

[23]George Egan, *Encounter: Group Process for Interpersonal Growth* (Belmont, Calif.: Brooks/Cole, 1970), second page of preface.

[24]William Glasser, *Schools Without Failure* (New York: Harper & Row, 1969).

[25]Robert R. Blake and Jane Srygley Mouton, "The Fifth Achievement," p. 92 of this book.

[26]Deutsch, *op. cit.*, p. 175.

[27]*Ibid.*, p. 194.

search uncovers no evidence that training in conflict resolution is being undertaken in more than a handful of schools. Several schools offer college level courses in social conflict and conflict resolution, and some urban school districts conduct in-service programs in conflict management which are tied in mainly to racial conflict. Although the absence of published reports concerning ongoing programs of "social conflict education" in the schools does not constitute direct evidence of neglect, it is highly suggestive.

Admittedly one cannot cite an abundance of evidence calling for teaching social conflict and conflict resolution in the classroom. But the evidence presented in this section and elsewhere does point to certain conclusions, however tentative:

1. Potential for social conflict exists in classrooms.
2. Lack of attention to affective variables in the classroom situation reduces the effectiveness of the learning environment, and conflict is viewed here from a predominantly affective standpoint.
3. Teachers are inadequately prepared to deal effectively with conflict situations in the classroom.
4. Human relations training in general, and training in conflict resolution in particular, would prepare students to function more effectively as social beings in an increasingly complex and conflict-prone culture.
5. Conversely, denial of such training to students is a denial of the social-emotional dimension of their being.
6. There is ample evidence to suggest that training in modification of social behaviors can be accomplished in educational settings, provided that the settings are modified sufficiently to produce such results.

At this point the writer can no longer withhold a few value judgments which became increasingly intense as he reviewed some of the recent publications concerning affective education and conflict resolution. An incredible paradox seemed to develop. On the one hand, all but the more recent writers in the area of conflict resolution have generally viewed conflict as harmful, and both recent and earlier writers point to the increasing prevalence of conflict and to the dangers of continued neglect in training human beings to handle harmful conflict. On the other hand, some critics of the educational system charge that much of education is (1) irrelevant, (2) warped by overemphasizing man's cognitive dimension while ignoring his affective side, and (3) oblivious to its potential for helping young people to develop interpersonal competence in relating to other human beings. As the evidence mounted to establish that affective education, and particularly education in conflict resolution, is desperately needed at all levels of education, an equally imposing array of evidence strongly suggests that, for the most part, the schools have not grown up emotionally and continue to stuff students' heads with cognitive matter which, at best, has no positive effects on their affective growth, or at worst, the "stuffing process" itself mutilates students' self-concepts and their emotional-attitudinal response systems.

Although there has been over a half-century of attack on the educational model which makes teaching the process of filling containers (students) with "academically respectable" content (non-human, intellectual stuff), so that each container can be stamped Grade "A," "B," "C," "D," or "E" after the contents of each container are spilled out for examination, this model not only persists, but remains dominant. No one knows how many personalities and self-concepts have been ground to pieces in the process. No one knows to what extent the schools train students to be self-centered and self-seeking, overly competitive, socially insensitive, antisocial, anti-authority, conforming, anxiety-prone, and conflict-prone. Who can tell to what extent the "correct-answer-syndrome" so prevalent in the schools creates persons with a "low tolerance for ambiguity" which may be a major source of human conflict?

Let those who maintain that affective education does not belong in the schools examine some of the fruits of their harvest as listed above. They may also wish to consider the millions of dollars spent annually by business and industry on "human relations training," which is designed to undo the damage which the schools have either inflicted or at least which they have left untouched. Do the schools create increasing numbers of "Grade A" containers who are flops as human beings? That's a crucial question to ponder.

Affective education and education in conflict resolution deserve a central position in curricula and in the instructional process. The emphasis on conflict *resolution* is not meant to imply that social conflict is inherently harmful. Conflict can have constructive effects on people and on relationships between people. If so, let's teach young people why this is so and how to achieve the constructive results. Conflict can also have harmful effects on persons and on relationships between people. If this is so, let's teach students how to minimize negative effects and how to avoid or resolve potentially dangerous and harmful conflicts through communication. To do less for youth is to deny their humanness and to deny them an opportunity to create social systems that are less conflict-prone and more successful in conflict management.

Focus of the Analysis

The social system to be analyzed is a classroom whose members are preadolescent or adolescent students and at least one teacher. The student members will be perceived as within the range of 10 to 20 years old. The term *prolonged adolescence* is used by the Committee on Adolescence, Group for the Advancement of Psychiatry[28] to describe the college student as a person who possesses all the physical and many of the intellectual and social prerequisites for adulthood, but whose passage to full adulthood is delayed by a continuing dependency relationship with respect to parents and school. Hence the term *adolescence* can be used descriptively with respect to students under the age of 21 who are enrolled in college classes.

It is obvious that classrooms are located in school buildings, school buildings in a school system, school systems in a com-

[28]Committee on Adolescence, Group for the Advancement of Psychiatry, *op. cit.*

munity, communities in a state, states in a society with a unique culture and value system, and finally that students and teachers live in homes. It is also apparent that each of these segments interact with each other and that each of the segments outside the classroom influence the social setting within the classroom. To pursue a line of analysis involving all of these segments would fill several volumes and hence it will not be attempted here. The focus of this analysis will, therefore, be on the classroom. References to outside social units will be made only when needed to analyze the classroom situation.

The classroom will be perceived as a collective formal learning situation in which emphasis is placed on the cognitive goals of education. It will be useful here to summarize an analysis of differences between the classroom (as defined above) and the T-group as accomplished by Miles.[29] His summary of the characteristics of the classroom accurately depicts the writer's view of the classroom as devoid of affective education and inept at managing conflict. The summary of the T-group accurately depicts the direction the writer hopes classrooms will move to incorporate affective education and the teaching of conflict resolution at all levels in the educational system.

[29]Miles, *op. cit.*, pp. 452–474.

Summary of Differences Between Classroom and T-Group

Classroom	T-Group
1. purposes	
a. Internalization of publicly dictated subject matter—emphasis on events and relationships removed in time and space from classroom.	a. Group decides what it wishes to learn—emphasis on here and now.
b. Stresses cognitive learnings endorsed by culture. Group process not of direct interest—viewed as a tool to promote cognitive learning.	b. Stress on cognitive, affective and behavioral learnings. Group process a main topic of direct study.

Summary of Differences Between Classroom and T-Group (cont.)

Classroom	T-Group
1. purposes	
c. Purpose of learnings is to prepare the immature student to function as an adult *later*. The interpersonal here-and-now not discussed *officially*.	c. Purpose of learnings is to prepare group members to function better "back home" immediately, by analysis of the here-and-now of interpersonal relations.
d. Classroom purposes externally given and usually less ambiguous than T-group goals.	d. T-group goals internally derived; often deliberately ambiguous and abstract to force attention on the here-and-now.
2. context and design factors	
a. Accountability to the public (school board, community, parents, and students) hence teachers have few opportunities to experiment with role.	a. Accountability to immediate situation only—maximum opportunities for role experimentation by trainer.
b. Group consists of 20–40 children, requiring a more stable control system—hard to respond to individual needs. Can be many uninvolved members.	b. Group consists of 8–20 adults, requiring minimal control. Stress on individual needs. Few uninvolved members.
c. Age range 2–3 years and teacher's greater age gives her status and authority.	c. Age range up to 30–40 years. Trainer seen as a peer and earns status.
3. client population	
a. Focus on education, not reeducation (except for remedial work). Student has little to unlearn prior to learning.	a. Focus on reeducation. Client has much to unlearn prior to learning.
b. Membership involuntary. Wide range of individual differences encourages arbitrary control methods and standardized approaches to content. Also gives rise to movement to individualize instruction.	b. Membership voluntary. Groups normally highly homogeneous.

Summary of Differences Between Classroom and T-Group (cont.)

Classroom	T-Group
4. Guiding Agent Role	
a. Teacher's role clear and behavior explicit—only teacher teaches. Teacher is authority—gap between teacher and student.	a. Trainer's role often ambiguous. Members teach each other. No gap—no designated authority.
b. Teacher role is central in the class and remains central. No feeling that control function should be shared or that teaching methods need validation from group.	b. Trainer role central at start, but he actively works to transfer control to group. Methods require group validation.
5. Group Process	
a. Official classroom interactions tend to be predominantly dyadic, teacher-student types, with minimal student-student interaction. Most interactions funneled through teacher.	a. Interaction predominantly between members. Trainer works to direct interactions away from himself to group.
b. Range of acceptable behaviors is narrow and tied to cognitive goals. Classroom norms taboo use of here-and-now events as legitimate content.	b. Wide range of acceptable behaviors tied to cognitive, affective, and behavioral goals. Here-and-now events main content.
c. Methods of logical and scientific inquiry applied to cognitive content areas but not to analyze here-and-now interpersonal events. Interpersonal events viewed as necessary but distressing accompaniments of teaching, or as a means of achieving cognitive goals. As content moves further away from students' direct experience, direct examination of group process seems less necessary.	c. Methods of logical and scientific inquiry developed for purpose of analyzing here-and-now interpersonal events.

Miles's summary and the writer's earlier discussion of "The Classroom as a Social System," taken together, constitute a general description of the classroom which will be useful in identifying variables which can be examined when pursuing an analysis of classroom conflict. This general description alludes to a number of theoretical perspectives which are commonly used when discussing learning-oriented classroom interactions. A discussion of these perspectives and how they relate to the analysis of classroom conflict appears in the subsequent paragraphs.

Theoretical Perspectives for the Analysis of Classroom Conflict

Learning-oriented classroom interactions have been discussed by writers in a number of different fields, including: psychology of adolescence, social psychology, educational psychology, measurement and evaluation, behavioral objective formulation, and instructional theory. Each of these perspectives points to variables in the classroom which have potential for precipitating social conflict. These variables can be perceived as being contained within some of the topics pursued by writers in the different fields mentioned above. The topics most relevant to an analysis of social conflict appear to include the following:

1. Social-response characteristics of adolescents
2. Interpersonal communication variables operative in the classroom's social system and subsystems
3. Selection and statement of educational objectives
4. Motivation of students to work toward achievement of objectives
5. Selection and sequencing of learning experiences designed to achieve objectives
6. Teaching method
7. Choice of criteria and application of same to measure and evaluate progress toward objectives
8. Selection of criterion levels which specify the minimum level of acceptable performance the students must attain in pursuit of objectives

9. Passing judgment on students' performance levels by "grading" them

While all of these topical areas may not prove to be equally relevant to an analysis of social conflict, evidence from each will be examined to determine whether potential sources of conflict can be identified within the confines of any of them. In brief, the procedure will be as follows:

1. A proposition or principle of social conflict concerning sources of conflict which appears to be applicable to the classroom situation will be identified.
2. Evidence from all topical areas will be examined to determine the probability that the principle or proposition can be expected to be operative in the classroom.
3. A tentative conclusion or hypothesis concerning sources of classroom conflict will be stated.

Since there is almost no published research on the analysis of classroom conflict (as pursued here), the evidence cited will normally not lead to conclusions, but rather to hypotheses that hopefully will stimulate research in this area. Where the evidence seems adequate, tentative conclusions will be offered.

SOURCES OF CONFLICT IN THE CLASSROOM

It would be a mistake for the reader to assume that this section will list sources of conflict which invariably produce conflicts in the classroom. The principle of multiple causality points to a more complex analysis, for any given sources, separately or in combination, may or may not lead to social conflict. Sources often interact with each other and with other variables in the social environment to influence their ultimate translation or non-translation into social conflict behaviors. When one views patterns of causal factors, with interaction within and between patterns, it becomes no simple task to designate which sources, in what combination, at what moment would most probably produce social conflict behaviors. Mack and Snyder in their overview of conflict theory observe that "the presence or persistence of underlying source factors does not necessarily mean that conflict, as defined, will arise."[30]

According to Mack and Snyder, when sources produce events which satisfy five preconditions for conflict then a conflict can be said to exist. The reader is referred to pages 35–37 of this volume for the authors' discussion of the preconditions, which together comprise their definition of social conflict. Mack and Snyder further indicate that ". . . particular sources which result in the analytic preconditions do not account for the origin, form, intensity, duration, reduction, or resolution of conflict."[31] They make a distinction between "sources" and "conditions" of conflict when they describe the term *conditions* as follows:

> . . . certain elements inherent in the nature of parties to conflict, in the interaction relationships between parties, and in the social context will often account for the origin, form, intensity, duration, limits, and resolution of conflict. Conditions are not, then, a special category of factors but a way of viewing the impact of the elements to be discussed in succeeding sections.[32]

To sum up, the existence of sources of conflict may or may not lead to a conflict situation. However, the impact of these sources in terms of leading to conflict/non-conflict, and in terms of the types of conflict behaviors produced, will be influenced by the conditions of conflict which Mack and Snyder discuss in their selection.

The above discussion of conditions of conflict can be viewed as another restriction on moving from identification of potential sources on to predictions of the existence and nature of conflict attributed to the sources. To pursue an analysis of both conditions and sources of conflict is well beyond the focus of this section and would further complicate an already complex analysis. Hence potential sources of conflict in the classroom will be identified and related to relevant propositions, while

[30] Raymond W. Mack and Richard C. Snyder, "The Analysis of Social Conflict–Toward an Overview and Synthesis," p. 41 of this book.

[31] *Ibid.*, p. 46.

[32] *Ibid.*

keeping in mind the limitations of such a line of analysis imposed by the concepts "multiple causality" and "conditions of conflict."

In the remainder of this section, principles and propositions concerning potential sources of social conflict will be related to the classroom situation. It should be understood that these principles and propositions are not "truths," but rather premises with varying degrees of supporting evidence. The premises that have been identified fall roughly into three groups: intrapersonal, interpersonal, and social context.

Intrapersonal Sources of Interpersonal Conflict

PROPOSITION 1: Intrapersonal conflict between aggressive impulses and socially sanctioned moral norms of behavior leads to projection of aggression on external groups.[33]

The Committee on Adolescence, Group for the Advancement of Psychiatry (hereafter referred to as "Committee on Adolescence") emphasizes that adolescence is characterized by a struggle for independence from adult control which is frequently accompanied by aggressive impulses and rebellion. When discussing adolescent rebellion they write:

> At first the rebellion tends to be primarily verbal. With repeated self-assertion, however, the adolescent's effort to achieve independence tends to take the form of action, at times rebellious and at times constructive.[34]

Aggressive impulses mentioned by the Committee on Adolescence include: "a welling up of negativism, stubbornness, unruliness, and disobedience,"[35] and "increased sexual and aggressive urges."[36] Such aggressive impulses lead almost inevitably to intrapersonal conflict between the impulse and some internalized social norm. As the Committee on Adolescence observes:

[33] *Ibid.*, p. 58.
[34] Committee on Adolescence, *op. cit.*, p. 68.
[35] *Ibid.*, p. 58.
[36] *Ibid.*, p. 25.

> . . . the problem for society persists: how to fit new organisms into the older cultural context, how to make individuals achieve the kinds of discipline over their sexual and aggressive drives which are prescribed, preferred or adaptive in a specific society and culture.[37]

Assuming that students have normal aggressive impulses and that they have internalized social norms which are reinforced with pressures toward "self-discipline," one can expect to find abundant instances of intrapersonal conflict in the classroom. If proposition one holds, then one would further expect adolescents to perceive others in the classroom as being aggressive towards them. Although it would be possible to cite research that students perceive other students and teachers as being aggressive towards them, this would not prove that the perception is caused by this type of intrapersonal conflict.

What should be emphasized here is that this type of intrapersonal conflict might well be particularly intense in the adolescent. The adolescent is particularly vulnerable because his struggle for independence is characterized by swings between independence from and dependence on adults. His drive toward independence gives rise to some of his aggressive impulses, while his lingering need for dependence makes violation of accepted social norms more painful for him.

The teacher, then, can expect that many students in the 10–20 age group will be undergoing the type of intrapersonal conflict described above, with consequent projection of aggression on others. One would expect the intensity and frequency of the conflict to subside as the adolescent moves toward the late teens. The Committee on Adolescence observes that toward the end of adolescence, earlier psychological disequilibrium is replaced by relative equilibrium in that a balance is achieved between aggressive impulses and rational control mechanisms.[38] The Committee also observes that some individuals undergo a period of *protracted adolescence* which they describe as follows:

[37] *Ibid.*, p. 35.
[38] *Ibid.*, p. 62.

The offset is markedly delayed because the conflicts and behavior typical of adolescence persist and become a "way of life."[39]

Hence, this type of intrapersonal conflict could be operative in students through the senior year of college. This conclusion is supported additionally by the Committee's view that college students are adolescents in the last stage of development. The Committee notes that even at the college level "some adolescents go through a rather extreme phase . . ."[40] which seems to indicate that although college-age students typically are arriving at a state of psychological equilibrium, there are still some who are witnessing severe intrapersonal conflict.

The consequences for the classroom are clear: Perceptions of aggression in others and in other subgroups, could, through the mechanism of the self-fulfilling prophecy,[41] trigger a high incidence of aggression among the communication sub-systems in the classroom and the frequency and intensity of such aggression would be inversely proportional to age. Aggressive impulses do not necessarily lead to overt aggression, nor does aggression inevitably lead to conflict, but as the impulses are present in a greater proportion of students, and as their intensity increases, it can be hypothesized that the probability of interpersonal conflict would increase.

HYPOTHESIS 1: As the number of adolescent students in a class experiencing intrapersonal conflict between aggressive impulses and adult-sanctioned behavioral norms increases, and as the intensity of the intrapersonal conflict increases, the probability of interpersonal conflict will increase.

PROPOSITION 2: Pressure for self-consistency may lead to an unwitting involvement in and intensification of conflict as one's actions have to be justified to oneself and to others.[42]

This proposition was formulated from Deutsch's discussion

[39]*Ibid.*, p. 63.

[40]*Ibid.*, p. 81

[41]For a discussion of the self-fulfilling prophecy, see Robert Rosenthal and Lenore Jacobson, *Pygmalion in the Classroom, Teacher Expectation and Pupils' Intellectual Development* (New York: Holt, Rinehart, and Winston, 1968).

[42]Deutsch, *op. cit.*, p. 166.

of Festinger's theory of cognitive dissonance which explains the need for self-consistency, more specifically, the need to make one's actions agree with one's beliefs. It appears that, here too, adolescents could be particularly vulnerable. Three factors tend to make this so. They are the adolescents' tendency to (1) engage in impulsive actions, (2) rebel against adult authority to achieve independence, and (3) reject perceived adult hypocrisy. The first two were discussed earlier, but with regard to the third, the Committee on Adolescence observes:

> With the capacity to view their parents and society with new objectivity, the failings and hypocrisies seem to stand out with blinding clarity to the adolescent. . . .[43]

They conclude that "The adolescent shows great concern for the moral probity of parents and other adults and constantly compares words with deeds."[44] The Committee also discusses "idealism" and "serious interest in ethics and religion" as characteristics of late adolescence.

The adolescent then can be described on a general level as prone to impulsive actions often motivated by his drive for independence, and as being highly idealistic and reluctant to view himself as hypocritical. Placed in the context of the classroom, one would expect adolescents to make impulsive statements and his peers might well insist that he should "put up or shut up." Or, the adolescent might engage in impulsive actions which violate his "idealism" and adult-sanctioned ethical-religious standards. Viewing this cognitive dissonance in the context of the adolescents' repugnance toward hypocrisy, one could make a case that the pressure for self-consistency would not only be intense among adolescent students, but also that the pressure would occur frequently. Given the extremely powerful influence of the peer group during this period of life, there would be strong pressure to justify one's actions not only to oneself, but to others (specifically peers).

Anyone who has taught students in the 10–20 age range

[43]Committee on Adolescence, *op. cit.*, p. 88.
[44]*Ibid.*, p. 89.

can recall many instances of what the Committee on Adolescence describes as "adolescent uncertainty garbing itself in arrogance and super-certainty, and using that easiest way of seeming to be an individual—to be 'against.' "[45] Anyone who has taught adolescents over a period of time has probably observed numerous instances of adolescents getting themselves psychologically "cornered" through impulsive statements and actions. In almost every instance there would probably be evidence of a strong "pressure for self-consistency" which led to either extreme acts to jibe with earlier extreme statements, or elaborate rationalizations to justify earlier extreme acts. The adolescent appears to be highly susceptible to such psychological cornering which can force him into interpersonal conflicts or the intensification of existing conflicts, neither of which he may desire. It appears particularly difficult for the adolescent to "back down" once his impulsive verbalizations or acts, coupled with his "arrogance" and "challenges to adult authority," lead him toward conflict with others. It would seem that this is almost inevitable for adolescents who are simultaneously pulled by a strong impulse to act, a strong need to justify actions to self and others, and a strong need for self-consistency (the avoidance of hypocrisy).

HYPOTHESIS 2: Adolescent students are more likely, than any other age group, to become involved either in interpersonal conflicts in the classroom, or in the intensification of existing conflicts, due to the relatively stronger pressure for self-consistency operating on them.

Interpersonal Sources of Conflict

PROPOSITION 3: Social conflict is normally accompanied by a felt or actual discrepancy in the power relations of the parties.[46]

From the perspective of conflict theory, a felt need to readjust power relationships and subsequent actions stemming from this need are viewed as sources of conflict, while at the same time, the accomplishment of such readjustment is viewed as a func-

[45] *Ibid.*, p. 82.
[46] Mack and Snyder, *op. cit.*, p. 33.

tion of social conflict which may lead to constructive effects on the interpersonal relationships between the parties. Although the main imbalance of power appears to be between students and teachers, there is also some evidence of power imbalance among the various subgroups in the classroom, hence both will be examined.

The classroom teacher possesses considerable power as evidenced by such common factors as:

1. Receiving support from the building principal, the general school administration, the school board, and in some instances from state laws, parents and the community-at-large, in enforcing "rules of conduct"
2. Giving and grading tests
3. Assigning grades
4. Writing descriptions of "disruptive behavior" which are placed in students' permanent records
5. Removing a student from the classroom or switching him to another classroom on academic or behavioral grounds
6. Determining the objectives, learning experiences, and achievement standards which are utilized in the classroom

These are some of the powers which are assigned almost routinely to teachers. In very few instances do students participate in any significant way in the assignment and execution of these powers which have not only short-range effects on their personal and academic lives in school, but also may have long-range effects on their future success and happiness.

Glasser has the relative "powerlessness" of students clearly in mind when he writes:

> The children realize that they have no part in making decisions about their behavior or their participation in school. Taught formally from kindergarten about the value of our democratic way of life, children learn from experience that the major premise of a democratic society—that the people involved in any endeavor help determine its rules—does not apply to them.[47]

[47]Glasser, *op. cit.*, p. 37.

He then recommends that "children should have a voice in determining both the curriculum and the rules of their school."[48]

Pursuing the theme that rebellious behavior in high school is one probable result of "expressive alienation," Stinchcombe states:

> The system of symbols on which school authority depends are those of age-grading, that is, symbols that distinguish adults from children and justify school authority by pointing to age differences. When these symbols fail to elicit loyalty because the student rejects the picture of himself as an adolescent, expressive alienation results.[49]

Discussing the systematic exclusion of adolescents from real participation in school and in society, Frantz observes:

> Excluded as a partner in modern society, the adolescent is faced with the prospect of growing up in exile with the status of a "nobody," finding himself unneeded, unnecessary, and unable to take part even in the decision-making which concerns him—yet being expected to exhibit responsible behavior. . . .[50]

Some indication of faculty resistance to college students' demands for a more significant role in educational decision-making can be seen in Sanford's comments about faculty responses to proposed student-involvement in curricular decisions. He writes:

> In many discussions of student power, the question of where it will all end comes up, and then the fear is expressed that students may actually assault that great citadel of faculty power—the curriculum itself.
>
> There is no reason in educational theory why students should not have a voice in the deliberations of all university committees and boards, including those that choose presidents, hire and promote faculty, and design curricula. . . .
>
> Curricula should be based not on power but on educational theory and knowledge. Most university faculty, unfortunately, are not in-

[48] *Ibid.*

[49] Arthur L. Stinchcombe, *Rebellion in a High School* (Chicago: Quadrangle, 1964), p. 9.

[50] Catherine Frantz, "The Adolescent's Non-Role in Society," *Education 91*, no. 2 (November–December 1970), 139.

terested in education [educational theory] and do not know how to discuss the subject.[51]

That students want some of the power that faculty seem reluctant to share is evident in this statement by Hirschlein and Jones:

> Junior high, high school, and college youths are crying for relevance. Each wants and must have a role in planning his own curriculum. Each must have the freedom to pursue objectives that have meaning for him.[52]

If we stopped at this point, we could conclude, at least tentatively, that the usual classroom situation is characterized by "a felt or actual discrepancy in the power relations of the parties." However a stronger case can be made by investigating the potency of the teacher's power and styles of its application and probable responses of students to these applications.

Grading and testing are probably among the most potent of the teacher's powers. Burns, when reviewing some of the more common arguments against grading, maintains that grading and related testing permit or cause:

1. A large number of learners to be permanently condemned to failure
2. Tests to be used for punishment
3. Non-essential factors to be considered as subject-matter achievement
4. Vast areas of disharmony between teachers and students, schools and students, learning and students, and parents and their children
5. Gray hairs and ulcers[53]

Underscoring the importance assigned to students' grades, Glasser makes a series of observations:

[51]Nevitt Sanford, "The Campus Crisis in Authority," *Educational Record 51*, no. 2 (Spring 1970), 114.

[52]Beulah M. Hirschlein and John G. Jones, "Why Johnny Can't Feel," *Education 91*, no. 1 (September–October 1970), 51.

[53]Richard W. Burns, "The Practical Educational Technologist: Measuring Objectives and Grading," *Educational Technology 8*, no. 18 (September 1968), 13–14.

> Today, grades are the be-all and end-all of education. The only acceptable grades are good ones, and these good grades divide the school successes from the school failures. Grades are so important that they have become a substitute for education itself.[54]
>
> Grades have become moral equivalents. A good grade is correlated with good behavior, a bad grade with bad behavior, a correlation that unfortunately is very high.[55]
>
> Grades, therefore, have become a substitute for learning, the symbolic replacement of knowledge. One's transcript is more important than one's education.[56]
>
> Grades are the currency of education. The highest grades are worth the most in terms of honors and entrance into better schools at every level.[57]
>
> As long as we label people failures at some time in their lives and then damn them for the rest of their lives for this failure through grades, we will perpetuate misery, frustration, and delinquency.[58]

The evidence cited above clearly indicates that the processes of testing and grading invest great power in the hands of teachers. If we add to this the fact that teachers select the objectives to be pursued, the learning experiences related to the objectives and the criterion levels that determine success or failure, it becomes apparent that the teacher exercises immense influence over the present and future lives of his students. In addition, the teacher's subjective evaluations of a student's conduct can have impact on a student's future attempts to enter post-high school education or the job market. Hence, the demonstrated potency of the teacher's power serves to emphasize the extent of the power imbalance between teachers and students. Various teaching and control strategies tend to tip the imbalance even more in the favor of teachers.

With regard to basic approaches to teaching, one can find evidence in the literature on teacher effectiveness that teachers vary in the extent to which they share power with students. Two extremes investigated by Flanders are the teacher who domi-

[54]Glasser, *op. cit.*, p. 60.
[55]*Ibid.*
[56]*Ibid.*, p. 61.
[57]*Ibid.*
[58]*Ibid.*, p. 64.

nates the classroom through direct influence attempts and the teacher who influences indirectly through encouraging student participation. It would be erroneous to speak of two "types of teachers." Rather, one envisions two extremes on a continuum, with variations among teachers with respect to flexibility of movement along the continuum and preference for one extreme.

On the whole, teachers appear to prefer the dominating end of the continuum. Gump discusses this tendency when comparing the "dominating" tendencies of parents and teachers. He writes:

> Teachers, more often than parents, take the initiative in starting interaction, usually seek to move the child rather than to respond to his interest, and deal almost exclusively with the "business at hand." In brief, teachers dominate children more than parents.[59]

Flanders studied some of the effects of direct and indirect teacher influence. He lists some of the characteristics that distinguished the most indirect teachers from the most direct teachers, as follows:

> First, indirect teachers were more alert to, concerned with, and made greater use of statements made by students.
>
> Second, the most indirect teachers asked longer, more extended questions, and did this about four times more frequently than did the most direct teachers.
>
> Third, the most direct teachers had more discipline problems and found it necessary to interrupt giving directions in order to criticize students three times more often than did the most indirect. . . . It was the tester's impression that sustained and rigidly employed patterns of above-average direct influence invited student resistance.[60]

When discussing the results of his study, Flanders emphasizes that all teachers use both direct and indirect influence over a

[59]Paul V. Gump, "Environmental Guidance of the Classroom Behavioral System," *Contemporary Research on Teacher Effectiveness*, eds. Bruce J. Biddle and William J. Ellena (New York: Holt, Rinehart, and Winston, 1964), p. 177.

[60]Ned A. Flanders, "Some Relationships Among Teacher Influence, Pupil Attitudes, and Achievement," *Contemporary Research on Teacher Effectiveness*, eds. Bruce J. Biddle and William J. Ellena (New York: Holt, Rinehart, and Winston, 1964), pp. 209–210.

period of time, but that teachers vary in the extent and frequency of their movement across the continuum. Behavioral flexibility appeared to be a significant variable affecting the results. Flanders concludes:

> Teachers who were able to provide flexible patterns of influence, by shifting from indirect to direct with the passage of time, created situations in which students learned more. The students of teachers who were unable to do this learned less.[61]

Earlier in his study, he had observed:

> It is now known that, in the indirect classrooms, students learned more and possessed more constructive and independent attitudes than in the direct. Furthermore, the indirect teachers were more flexible than the direct teachers in that they made more dramatic changes in their patterns of influence in the various time-use activity categories.[62]

To sum up, teachers, on the whole, tend to prefer the dominating end of the influence continuum. This can be roughly equated with a general reluctance to share power with students. In addition, teachers characterized by strong preference for direct influence strategies and behavioral inflexibility tend to provoke student resistance to their influence attempts. This approach to teaching would probably do much to exaggerate the power discrepancy, as there is present not only a reluctance to share power, but also positive attractions to centralizing power in the teacher and to the wielding of power.

A study by Rafalides and Hoy examined the effects of two types of control orientations in 45 high schools. The control orientation was a school-wide phenomenon as identified from questionnaires completed by 3000 teachers and administrators. Since it is probable that the dominant student control orientation in a school will have impact on the classroom teacher's control strategies, the effects of the custodial orientation are further evidence of how teacher methods can widen the student-teacher power gap. They describe *custodialism* as a school

[61] *Ibid.*, p. 219.
[62] *Ibid.*, p. 215.

having certain characteristics, which have been paraphrased as follows:

1. School organization is autocratic.
2. Pupil-teacher status hierarchy is rigid.
3. Power and communication flow downward, with a minimal upward flow.
4. Students must accept teacher decisions without question.
5. Student misbehavior is viewed (by the teacher or administrator) as a personal affront.
6. Students are seen as irresponsible and undisciplined persons of lower status and maturity level, who have to be controlled through punishment.[63]

They conclude that the custodial orientation alienated students significantly more than the humanistic orientation[64] and state that "custodial orientation makes it difficult for students to make a positive commitment to school and teachers."[65]

To the extent, then, that the custodial orientation toward pupil control is operative in the classroom, there would be a further concentration of power in the teacher, and a consequent increase in the teacher-student power discrepancy. Hence, it is apparent that the classroom as normally constituted operates with a significant power discrepancy (real and perceived) and that dominant, direct influence teaching and control strategies as well as custodialism increase that discrepancy.

There are a number of characteristics of today's adolescent students which would tend to increase the probability of conflict where there is a marked power discrepancy in the teacher-student relationship. Most of these characteristics relate to the willingness of students to "live with" the discrepancy. Keniston observes that today's high school and college students, compared with students in the 1920s: (1) achieve puberty one year

[63]Madeline Rafalides and Wayne K. Hoy, "Student Sense of Alienation and Pupil Control Orientation of High Schools," *The High School Journal* 55, no. 3 (December 1971), 102.
[64]*Ibid.*, p. 110.
[65]*Ibid.*

earlier, (2) have five more years of education, and (3) are about one standard deviation higher on standardized tests of intellectual performance.[66] He further observes that in spite of about a one-year advantage in physiological maturity and intellectual development over their parents at the same age, "they [the students] must defer adult responsibilities, rights, and prerogatives five years longer."[67]

The advanced stage of today's students' intellectual development should be contrasted with findings cited by Bay which indicate that education majors tend to be recruited from low achievers in college,[68] and tend to manifest conservative views[69] characterized by tendencies "to contain, to reject, and to take precautions against his fellow creatures."[70] Bay produces a composite description of bright students as tending toward militancy, liberality, and flexibility,[71] almost the opposite of the more conservative, inflexible education majors (the future teachers).

Commenting on the probable effects of the increased intelligence and intellectual development of today's students, Keniston concludes that "to oversimplify, today's students are more likely to challenge, to question, and to think for themselves than were students of earlier generations."[72] One could infer, then, that today's students would not be content to "live with" the power discrepancy which is so common in classrooms, hence, increasing the potential for conflict. They would tend to question the teacher's right to possess and exercise his disproportionate share of the power, and perhaps increasingly so as the intellectual and maturational levels of teachers and students approach equality.

[66]Kenneth Keniston, "What's Bugging the Students?" *Educational Record 51,* no. 2 (Spring 1970), 118.

[67]*Ibid.*

[68]Christian Bay, "Political and Apolitical Students: Facts in Search of a Theory," *Journal of Social Issues 23,* no. 3 (1967), 82–83.

[69]*Ibid.,* p. 83.

[70]*Ibid.,* p. 81.

[71]*Ibid.,* pp. 82–85.

[72]Keniston, *op. cit.,* p. 118.

This line of analysis would appear to be most applicable to power relationships between teachers and "high achievers." The high achievers and bright students would probably base their claim to shared power on grounds of approximate intellectual equality, and perhaps on nearly equivalent maturational levels. Among the less academically gifted, the claim might well be based on a claim to adult rights. Stinchcombe's analysis of rebellious students supports this assumption. The major focus of his study is the student who has rejected the academic achievement culture of the high school and who gives his allegiance to the subculture which attempts to achieve status by demanding adult rights which the school is unwilling to grant. He states:

> The rebellious peer group is oriented toward getting from legitimate institutions, rights that the institutions are not enthusiastic about giving . . . This claim of adult rights (and, less enthusiastically, adult duties) by people still subjected to the high school system of social control based on the doctrine of immaturity of adolescents creates severe conflicts.[73]

If we pull together the concepts that today's students are more mature and more prone to claim adult rights, more nearly the intellectual peers of teachers, and more liberal in their views than teachers, we get a composite picture of students demanding a greater share of the power which teachers exercise, supposedly for their benefit, and teachers generally resisting such demands. If these concepts are generally true, it appears unlikely that today's students will "live with" marked power discrepancies in the classroom.

That the student-teacher power discrepancy can lead to classroom conflict is pointed out by Chesler's discussion of the consequences of students' noninvolvement in school decisions about content of curriculum and curriculum sequencing, performance criteria, choice of teaching method, and organization of classes. He maintains that students who feel strongly about such nonin-

[73]Stinchcombe, *op. cit.*, p. 41.

volvement do "vote" by dropping out, sleeping in class, and avoiding courses and teachers.[74] But he notes:

> Others rebel and organize protests to seek redress and change. Still other students obediently move through the system, having learned that power is not shared and not worth arguing about. Yet they chafe, and yet they learn the lesson of impotence from their exclusion.[75]

A recent study by Branan indicates that students have many negative experiences in their relationships with teachers which frequently lead to conflict. Branan asked 150 college freshmen and sophomores to describe what they considered the two most negative experiences in their lives; 257 out of 300 responses pertained to interpersonal relations, and 84 of these involved teachers.[76] He notes that "individual situations of negative experiences with teachers involved humiliation in front of a class, unfairness in evaluation, destroying self-confidence, personality conflicts, and embarrassment."[77] He found that teachers were involved more often than any other persons in the most negative experiences reported and that the frequency of negative experiences with teachers was highest in the high school, followed by college, elementary school, and junior high school. He concludes:

> The current student unrest is primarily a reaction against being treated as a number or object rather than as a unique person who deserves to be treated with full consideration. Jourard (1964) believes that much student revolt is the result of the pain of one's "psychological bones being crushed."[78]

Several hypotheses and one conclusion concerning classroom conflict can be derived from the above discussion:

[74]Mark A. Chesler, "Shared Power and Student Decision Making," *Educational Leadership 28*, no. 1 (October 1970), 10.
[75]*Ibid.*
[76]John M. Branan, "Negative Human Interaction," *Journal of Counseling Psychology 19*, no. 1 (January 1972), 81–82.
[77]*Ibid.*, p. 82.
[78]*Ibid.*

CONCLUSION 1: The real and felt power discrepancy between students and teachers in the classroom is a source of teacher-student conflict.

HYPOTHESIS 3: As the teacher increases the frequency and intensity of dominating and direct influence teaching and control strategies, the probability of teacher-student conflict increases.

HYPOTHESIS 4: As the teacher moves more toward implementing the custodial orientation of pupil control, the probability of teacher-student conflict increases.

HYPOTHESIS 5: As teacher and student intellectual performance levels and maturational levels approach equality (real or as perceived by students), the probability of teacher-student conflict increases.

Although power discrepancies among student subgroups are minor, in comparison to those in the student-teacher relationship, they do exist in at least two areas: (1) students' occupational plans after graduation, and (2) access to school activities. Stinchcombe speaks of the symbolic, ritualistic status system which awards differing status levels to future occupations. At one point he observes that "the universal secondary school has a formal ritual structure which defines future manual workers as 'failures.' "[79] He emphasizes the differing status levels of future occupations when he writes:

> For those students who form an image of their future in the bureaucratic and professional labor market, the tests, grade averages, and respect of teachers are meaningful elements of a *curriculum vitae*. . . . Students destined for the working class are (inadvertently) defined negatively in the formal ritual idiom, as "those left over when the middle class is sorted out."[80]

It seems almost unnecessary to state that the status levels of "college prep students," "vocational education students," "general education students," "secretarial education students," etc. are perceived as "different." Even a cursory examination of course offerings in "comprehensive" high schools indicates that, generally, the college preparatory course dominates the curriculum. By the processes of emphasis and omission in curricula,

[79]Stinchcombe, *op. cit.*, p. 131.
[80]*Ibid.*, pp. 106–107.

the high school gives a non-verbal statement of what is most important, and hence, most valuable in terms of future occupational status. In any classroom with a mix of students in the various courses of study, all of which have "status gradings," a potential for perceived power discrepancy exists. Those students planning to enter high-status occupations would tend to be perceived as most powerful in that they command a disproportionate share of the school's resources, while those at the lower levels of the future occupational status hierarchy, who share least in these resources, could be perceived as least powerful. What results is a class system, complete with the privileged and underprivileged, and the concomitant potential for snobbery downward and resentment upward.

Stinchcombe views the different "courses of study" as containing differing definitions of future success, with the school "defining only middle-class choices positively."[81] Since rebellious students, according to his study, reject the achievement culture of the school, it is highly probable that they would also reject students who support this culture. Not having a prospect for future high-status occupations in sight, it is probable that students with poor future prospects would resent their more fortunate peers, who may well be "the conforming peer group [which] helps the institutions enforce the obligations laid down by authoritative people."[82]

Another potential power discrepancy among students concerns the allocation of participation in extracurricular activities. Such participation normally produces benefits like prestige and social acceptability which are normally highly valued by adolescents. Do certain groups of students get preferential treatment in the allocation process? Scales made a study of why students drop out of school and he found that: (1) Dropouts felt that other students did not want them in school group activities, and (2) some dropouts didn't even know of the activities.[83] Stinch-

[81]*Ibid.*, p. 135.

[82]*Ibid.*, p. 41.

[83]Harry H. Scales, "Another Look at the Drop Out Problem," *Journal of Educational Research* 62, no. 8 (April 1969), 343.

combe found that when high school students were asked "Do coaches and supervisors of extracurricular activities play favorites?" over 50 percent responded that the statement was either "certainly true" or "probably true."[84]

Another form of discrimination in allocating participation in school activities is the general practice of requiring a minimum grade average as an "entrance requirement." According to Glasser:

> Children with talent, however, have little opportunity to express it unless they get adequate grades. They are not even allowed in the door of certain activities, such as sports and drama, unless they show at least average grades.[85]

If participation in school activities is a scarce and valuable resource, then it seems to follow that unfairness (real or perceived) in allocating the resource would give rise to a felt power discrepancy between the "chosen" and "unchosen." A mix of "chosen" and "unchosen" students in a classroom, then, would bring the felt power discrepancy into the classroom.

HYPOTHESIS 6: Favoring some students over others when allocating school resources which promise present or future increments in students' status is a potential source of student-student conflict in classrooms made up of "favored" and "unfavored" students.

PROPOSITION 4: Value incompatability is, by definition, an element in conflict.[86]

Coser's definition of social conflict contains the element mentioned in proposition 4. His definition starts: "Social conflict is provisionally taken to mean a struggle over values. . . ."[87] Since incompatability of values is generally accepted as a source of social conflict, no attempt will be made to document this premise. Rather the existence of value incompatibility in the classroom will be explored.

The Committee on Adolescence notes the adolescent's "char-

[84]Stinchcombe, *op. cit.*, p. 30.
[85]Glasser, *op. cit.*, p. 63.
[86]Mack and Snyder, *op. cit.*, p. 61.
[87]Coser, *op. cit.*, p. 8.

acteristic questioning and challenging of adult values and cultural institutions,"[88] and goes on to state:

> [Due to support from the peer group] adolescents are able to subject the cultural values learned in earlier childhood to a careful and sometimes devastating scrutiny and criticism to determine their applicability to the world of today, as seen by adolescents. Some adolescents appear not to accept any adult values, even superficially; some pass through a phase of experimentation with many different value systems. . . .[89]

According to the Committee on Adolescence, the value system being challenged is normally that of the adolescent's parents. That this challenge is transferred into the classroom is evident from this observation by the Committee:

> So when other persons of authority come into a child's life, he perceives them more as extensions and copies of the parents than as new and different individuals, and cultural values and institutions also tend to be seen only as they were interpreted by the parents.[90]

Hence, whatever value conflicts an adolescent may be experiencing at home with his parents might well be transferred into the classroom by projecting the parents' values into the teacher who is perceived as "an extension of the parents." Brodbelt made a study of differences between the values of youth (those under 25) and those of the generation in power. He found that the older generation's value system stressed such values as materialism, patriotism, and the work ethic, while youth's value system stressed peace, social justice, and individual freedom.[91]

A survey conducted in all of the high schools in Ohio gives evidence of a generational conflict over materialism and patriotism. Reporting the results of this survey Della-Dora states:

> They [Ohio high school students] had some serious questions about basic aspects of living in this country. For example 48 percent *disa-*

[88]Committee on Adolescence, *op. cit.*, p. 39.

[89]*Ibid.*, pp. 39–40.

[90]*Ibid.*, p. 42.

[91]Samuel Brodbelt, "Values in Conflict: Youth Analyzes Theory and Practice," *The High School Journal 55*, no. 2 (November 1971), 66.

greed with the statement "The form of government in this country needs *no* major change." Only one in three agreed that "on the whole our economic system is just and wise."[92]

Assuming that the older generation's values are projected into teachers who are perceived as "extensions of parents" and representatives of the "generation in power," teacher-student conflict over these incompatible values seems probable. If we add to the situation the general tendency of teachers to stress citizenship and patriotism in teaching the social sciences, the stress on the work ethic which supposedly leads to high grades, and the frequently made promise that a good education leads to better jobs with a higher income, the probability of conflict over these general values increases.

In addition to these general areas of value conflict, there are several areas more specific to the classroom. One current issue that has produced considerable conflict is the question of relevance of education. Relevant education would tend to be perceived as valuable, while irrelevant education would tend to be perceived as worthless. That schools and teachers have different concepts of relevance than students is apparent from this statement by Frantz:

> According to Mallery (1962), school subjects are considered by students as unchallenging and unrelated to life, and contrived by teachers to keep them busy.[93]

Stinchcombe supports Frantz's observation when he writes:

> Except for pathological cases, any student can be motivated to conform if the school can realistically promise something valuable to them as a reward for working hard. But for a large part of the population, especially the adolescents who will enter the male working class or the female candidates for early marriage, the school has nothing to promise.[94]

Glasser notes that "while most high schools have good aca-

[92]Delmo Della-Dora, "What's Bothering Us?," *Educational Leadership 29*, no. 3 (December 1971), 225.

[93]Frantz, *op. cit.*, p. 139.

[94]Stinchcombe, *op. cit.*, p. 179.

demic programs for students who are college-bound"[95] and that "some central-city high schools have an adequate vocational program for those interested in a few specific vocations,"[96] "many students who are neither college-bound nor vocationally set find little of either academic or vocational significance to keep them in school. . . ."[97]

Speaking directly to the topic of irrelevant curricula in the classroom, Beck *et al.* state:

> There are many serious cases of irrelevance still with us today. They typically rest on one of two bases. Either the teacher does not recognize that the matter is now irrelevant, if it ever was relevant, or he is unwilling to change, discard, or restructure his materials and procedures as relevance demands. . . .
>
> Of the two bases upon which irrelevance seems to rest, it would appear that knowingly pursuing the inertia-bound or comfort-oriented courses of action is the most serious. However the consistent lack of knowledge of what is relevant to the lives of students can be just as devastating and just as unprofessional.[98]

Addressing himself to the topic of relevance in higher education, Warren concludes that "part of the current turmoil in higher education is due to the slowness of curricular change in relation to the demands students are placing on higher education."[99] In the same vein, Glasser reports the results of a survey taken at San Fernando Valley State College. He writes:

> The main dissatisfaction the students had with the curriculum was that it was not relevant to their lives. Almost 60 percent of the students said that they could see no relationship between what they were doing in school and what they expected to be doing later on. They were bitter and complaining about this lack of relevance.[100]

Glasser also suggests that a good part of college students' cur-

[95]Glasser, *op. cit.*, p. 215.

[96]*Ibid.*

[97]*Ibid.*

[98]Carlton E. Beck *et al.*, *Education for Relevance—The Schools and Social Change* (Boston: Houghton Mifflin, 1968), p. 238.

[99]Jonathan R. Warren, "Changing Students and Constant Curricula," *Educational Record 51*, no. 2 (Spring 1970), 182.

[100]Glasser, *op. cit.*, p. 54.

rent bitterness and anger may stem from "their sudden realization that all of their educational experiences from the first grade on have been irrelevant."[101]

The evidence presented suggests that two value systems are in conflict: The value system of the school and its agent, the teacher, define the curriculum as relevant and hence valuable, while the students' value system defines it as irrelevant and largely worthless. Hence, some type of conflict surrounding the issue of relevance appears highly probable. That such conflict does occur is evident from some of the results of Stinchcombe's study. He reports:

> The most rebellious, among both girls and boys, tend to perceive a poor connection between current academic activity and future status. This is indicated by the fact that those who express no curriculum interest are most rebellious and alienated, with other factors constant.[102]

Speaking to the same point, Glasser maintains that "fact-centered, non-thinking education is a prime cause of discipline problems and failure. . . ."[103]

CONCLUSION 2: Generalized generational value conflict is a potential source of student-teacher value conflict, when students perceive teachers as extensions of parents and/or representatives of the generation in power.

CONCLUSION 3: A classroom curriculum perceived as irrelevant by students and relevant by the teacher is a potential source of student-teacher value conflict.

HYPOTHESIS 7: As differences between students' and teachers' perceptions of the relevance of the classroom curricula increase, the probability of student-teacher value conflict increases.

The generational value conflict over "what is relevant education" extends into the related conflict over the value of the grades. Since grades are evaluations of achievement in the formal curriculum one would expect value conflicts over the worth of grades to closely parallel conflicts over the worth of the cur-

[101] *Ibid.*
[102] Stinchcombe, *op. cit.*, p. 80.
[103] Glasser, *op. cit.*, p. 80.

riculum. This seems to hold generally in that parents, schools, and teachers stress the value of the existing curricula and of high grades, while students alienated from school and the curriculum view grades as unimportant.

In the earlier discussion of power discrepancies, the almost overwhelming importance assigned to getting good grades by the school and teachers was documented. Nelson comments on parental pressure for good grades:

> Psychologists agree that parental pressure for academic achievement causes severe anxiety in at least 25 percent of school children. Many insist that the estimate should be higher.[104]

There is evidence that segments of the student population do judge grades to be of low value. Stinchcombe's rebellious students tend to reject the curriculum and the importance of grades. He states:

> The difference between the extreme rebels and the well-behaved is quite striking. Only half as many of the most rebellious boys answer that grades are important to themselves (36 percent), as answer that way among the well-behaved boys (80 percent).[105]

The well-behaved boys might either accept the curriculum as relevant, or they may perceive its irrelevance, and, as Glasser notes "take the bribe ("A" grade) and keep his mouth shut."[106] A recurrent theme in Stinchcombe's work is that boys who perceive themselves destined for the manual labor market and girls planning on early marriage see little value in grades and strive instead to achieve adult privileges which are more important and satisfying to them.

Glasser identifies the "thinking students" as another group which questions the value of grades. He contends that "grades are used to force irrelevant knowledge on students,"[107] and then sympathizes with the plight of thinking students as follows:

[104]Estelle Nelson, "Must We Pressure Our Children?" *Education 89*, no. 1 (September–October 1968), 72.

[105]Stinchcombe, *op. cit.*, p. 21.

[106]Glasser, *op. cit.*, p. 80.

[107]*Ibid.*, p. 65.

> . . . a student has two choices: concentrate on grades and give up thinking; or concentrate on thinking and give up grades. Unfortunately, if he gives up grades altogether, he can never get into the schools where important subjects are taught; but if he concentrates all his efforts on grades, he can graduate with little understanding of how to utilize the knowledge that he supposedly has learned.[108]

Glasser cites the results of a survey which was reported to the American Association of Medical Colleges in which it was found that "There is almost no relationship between the grades a student gets in medical school and his competence and success in medical practice."[109] He reports similar results for a survey encompassing professional persons in various fields who had won fellowships to Columbia University's Graduate School, and concludes that "Again, high grades were not a good indicator of high performance except in college."[110]

It is probable that students will become increasingly aware of the low or non-existent correlations between grades and future success. This is likely to happen because: (1) The evidence is multiplying; (2) it is being more widely publicized, and (3) today's students (as reported earlier) are brighter and more mature, and hence, are more likely to critically examine traditional values and practices than students of earlier generations.

Glasser and Stinchcombe both indicate in the substance of their works that there are in most schools: conformist students who embrace the grading system as a means of upward mobility, thinking students who inwardly reject the grading system but who outwardly conform to get the anticipated benefits, thinking students who reject the grading system, and alienated students who reject grades, the curriculum, the school, and ultimately, all of legitimate society. The conforming students and the outwardly conforming thinking students would be influenced the most by evidence of low correlations between grades and future success, for it is probable that the high value they attribute to good grades is based on perceived high, positive

[108]*Ibid.*, p. 62.
[109]*Ibid.*, p. 61.
[110]*Ibid.*, p. 62.

correlations. Knowledge of contradictory evidence would cause many of them to join the ranks of the disaffected and alienated. If, in spite of the evidence, schools, parents and teachers were to continue stressing the overwhelming importance of getting good grades in the face of mounting disaffection among students, it would appear that the intensity and frequency of value conflicts over grades would increase. In higher education, one result of student alienation from traditional grading systems has been student-faculty value conflicts which were often resolved through agreement on some form of the pass–fail grading system.

It would appear that under the present grading system, as generally constituted, there is potential for interpersonal conflict between students and teachers as well as among students who have varying degrees of allegiance to the grading system. As Burns states:

> Grading (and the tests on which grading is based) permits or causes vast areas of disharmony between teachers and students, schools and students, learning and students, and parents and their children.[111]

It should be noted that to the extent that students perceive teachers as "extensions of parents" the parent–student value conflict over grades will be carried into the classroom.

CONCLUSION 4: The grading system as normally constituted is a potential source of value conflict in the classroom.

HYPOTHESIS 8: As differences between students' and teachers' value judgments about grades increase, the probability of student–teacher value conflict increases.

HYPOTHESIS 9: As students' value judgments about grades become more divergent, the probability of student–student value conflict increases.

Norms governing social behavior may well be another potential source of value conflict. In earlier citations from Stinchcombe's study it was noted that rebellious high school students reject achievement-oriented behavioral norms and demand adult

[111]Burns, *op. cit.*, p. 13.

privileges which the school is unwilling to grant. Since the schools' pupil control system defines students as immature people who must be controlled by standards of behavior formulated by adults, a general climate conducive to value conflict is created. These school-determined standards tend to produce a definition of a model student which is pregnant with value judgments. Hansen discussed the effects of the "model student value system" on "students who had a higher need for assertive and intrusive kinds of behavior"[112]—a phrase which is quite similar to Stinchcombe's descriptions of rebellious students. After noting that these students reported a poorer mental adjustment to school than "model students," he concludes:

> These students would appear not to fit the role of the "model student" as set by the school and thus would find themselves in conflict with it.
>
> . . . Those who do not fall into the "model student" classification find themselves in conflict with the school.[113]

It appears then that students who value governing their behavior through adult norms of social behavior, and those who value assertive and intrusive behaviors, possess values which conflict with those imbedded in the rules-of-conduct definition of the model student. There appear to be different sets of values underlying these differing norms of social behavior.

HYPOTHESIS 10: When students and teachers have internalized contradictory norms for students' social behavior there is a potential for value conflict over which norms shall prevail.

The last two propositions to be explored seem to deal with variables that are operative in almost the total range of situations encompassed by the previous four propositions. In most of the situations discussed, elements of misperception or biased perception and competitive orientation appear to have been pervasive influences which contributed to the existence of sources of conflict as well as to conditions which increased the

[112]James C. Hansen, "Environmental Press, Student Needs and Academic Adjustment," *The Journal of Educational Research 63*, no. 9 (1970), 406.

[113]*Ibid.*

probability of overt social conflict. Perhaps these last two propositions really deal with "conditions of conflict" as discussed by Mack and Snyder. However, since both competition and misperception can also be viewed as source factors, they will be analyzed from this point of view. Where the two factors appear to be functioning as conditions, an appropriate comment will be made.

The discussion of misperception will conclude the analysis of interpersonal sources of conflict. Competitive orientation will be treated as a factor in the social context which pervades the entire school social environment and which permeates most classrooms.

PROPOSITION 5: Misperception and distorted perception of persons and events lead to interpersonal conflict.

Deutsch discusses the role of psychological factors in interpersonal conflict. He states:

> . . . The lack of conflict or the occurrence of conflict can be determined by misperception, misunderstanding, and misinformation concerning the objective state of affairs.[114]

Hence, psychological factors can produce conflict even when objective circumstances are favorable for nonconflict. He further explains how processes of misperception and biased perception can be a factor in escalating conflict[115] and how ambiguous or unclear contexts of social acts lead to assuming a context familiar to the person.[116] Three psychological factors can operate as sources of interpersonal conflict: (1) the subjectivity of perception, (2) the ambiguity or lack of clarity in social contexts, and (3) projection.

That subjectivity of perception is a potential source of conflict is apparent from the frequent use here of such terms as "perceived," "felt," and "viewed" when discussing potential sources of conflict. For example, power discrepancies were designated as "real" or "felt," some students were said to perceive favoritism

[114]Deutsch, *op. cit.*, p. 157.
[115]*Ibid.*, pp. 162–164.
[116]*Ibid.*

in the allocation of the school's resources, adolescents were said to view adults as hypocritical, and it was stated that some adolescents perceive their values and behavioral norms as differing from those of adults and other students. Since human beings tend to respond to situations in terms of *how they perceive them,* conflicts can be caused by a state of affairs that exists only, or mainly, in the subjective definitions of the situation furnished by the parties involved, even though the objective state of affairs calls for non-conflict.

Blair and Pendleton report an instance of misperception concerning the perceived existence of a "generation gap" between students and teachers. Responding to the statement, "The youth of today will agree that the generation gap is greater now than ever before in the history of our country," 63 percent of the students and 76 percent of the teachers agreed with the statement.[117] Having reported other data which demonstrated that teachers' and students' perceptions of youth's attitudes were quite similar, the authors concluded that "although there is no real gap between students and teachers in their perceptions of youth's attitudes, there is a perceived gap of considerable significance.[118]

The rebellious students in Stinchcombe's study report a series of perceptions, all of which could contain varying degrees of misperception and distortion. Among those reported are: "Future status is not clearly related to present performance;"[119] "the attendance office, student activities, and the informal student community are unfair;"[120] "you have to get in good with the teachers if you expect to get a fair grade in this school."[121] These possible misperceptions relate clearly to Proposition 3 (power discrepancy) and Proposition 4 (value incompatibility).

Rosenthal and Jacobson studied the effects of teacher ex-

[117]Glenn M. Blair and Charles W. Pendleton, "Attitudes of Youth Toward Current Issues as Perceived by Teachers and Adolescents," *Adolescence 6,* no. 24 (Winter 1971), 426.

[118]*Ibid.*

[119]Stinchcombe, *op. cit.,* p. 5.

[120]*Ibid.,* p. 47.

[121]*Ibid.,* p. 77.

pectations on pupils' intellectual development. According to some of their results, lower-track students are perceived by their teachers as having little potential for intellectual growth, and "when they showed greater gains in IQ, they were seen much more unfavorably than when they showed those more modest gains that were expected of them."[122]

Varying teacher expectations can be followed by a number of changes in students' intellectual development: (1) high expectation followed by marked development, (2) high expectation followed by little or no development, (3) low expectation followed by marked development. There are, of course, other options, but the last two appear to be misperceptions that could lead to student–teacher conflict. The marked development of the lower-ability student violates the teacher's perception of the student, and as Glasser observes, "Teachers may even resent the effort of a low-track student who tries to improve."[123] Although no direct evidence is available, one can speculate that high expectation followed by poor performance could lead to increased teacher pressure on the student to improve. Provided that the high expectation is a misperception, there is a potential for conflict.

Another type of misperception which can lead to conflict is the tendency to apply the wrong label to interpretations of events and to subsequent statements about these interpretations. According to Haney,[124] conflict occurs when persons perceive their "inferences" and "statements of inferences" as "facts" and "statements of fact." Since the latter are also usually perceived as "true" by the person making them, the parties involved in the interaction proceed on the false assumption that their subjectively derived inferences and statements of inference possess all the "truth" which they attribute to their "facts" and "statements of fact." When verbalizations about their inferences are challenged on the grounds that they are "only your opinion,"

[122]Rosenthal and Jacobson, *op. cit.*, p. 118.

[123]Glasser, *op. cit.*, p. 82.

[124]William V. Haney, *Communication: Patterns and Incidents* (Homewood, Ill.: Irwin, 1960).

conflict normally ensues, and each party may manifest hostility towards the other on the grounds that the other is so "stupid" or "blind" or "narrow-minded" that he cannot see a "fact" which is "as plain as the nose on his face." Generally, the more frequently and the more strenuously the challenge is made, the more the conflict is escalated.

HYPOTHESIS 11: Students' and teachers' misperceptions of each other and of events in the classroom are a source of interpersonal conflict.

HYPOTHESIS 12: As teachers and students increasingly misperceive their statements of inference as being statements of fact, and as the intensity and frequency of challenges to statements of inference increase, the probability for interpersonal conflict increases.

As was noted above, ambiguous or unclear contexts of social acts can cause a person to assume a context that is familiar to him. When a context or situation appears to be ambiguous, unclear or incomplete, the human organism experiences discomfort. The degree of discomfort experienced and the ability to withstand it, is a rough definition of tolerance for ambiguity. Although little direct evidence is available, one can speculate that a high degree of ambiguity or unclarity in the classroom situation combined with low tolerance for ambiguity among students could produce severe discomfort in students and strong student pressure on the teacher to clarify the situation. Since much of the discussion of "clarity" in educational settings pertains to stating objectives and testing, the ensuing discussion will be limited to these topics.

Gronlund maintains that "clearly defining the desired learning outcomes is the first step in good teaching" and then notes that although this "first step" is one of the most important, it is also one of the most neglected.[125] Gronlund is most critical of the "tendency to state educational objectives in such vague and general terms that they are difficult to translate into classroom practice."[126] Gilpin, writing in the foreword to Mager's book on instructional objectives states:

[125]Gronlund, *op. cit.*, p. 20.
[126]*Ibid.*, p. 25.

> The probable reason that objectives are usually stated poorly is that few people know how to proceed. . . . And with the all-important business of teaching occupying their capacities, it is easy for school teachers to feel that they have their objectives well "in mind," and that it is neither necessary nor possible to be more specific.[127]

Kibler, Barker, and Miles argue that it is not enough for the teacher to have his objectives "in mind," and for them to be stated clearly, but also that they should be shared with students.[128]

Walberg investigated some relationships between structuring a class for learning and certain affective variables. He found that clear learning goals were positively related to classroom satisfaction and that unclear goals were accompanied by increased alienation among students.[129] He also observes that groups working toward clear-cut goals were characterized by a general esprit de corps while more disorganized groups were hampered by the development of cliquey subsets.[130] Hence, unclear objectives can lead not only to increased pressure on the teacher to clarify, but also to alienation from the classroom society.

The argument here is that *if* objectives are unclear, and *if* they are not shared with students, then certain effects will result. The most probable effect is that students will clarify the situation by "psyching out the instructor." They end up producing their version of what they perceive the instructor's objectives to be, and if their version is inaccurate they pay the penalty on examination day.

It is probable that students with a low tolerance for ambiquity would be most likely to experience severe discomfort in a classroom operating with vaguely stated objectives, and would most

[127] John B. Gilpin, in preface to Robert F. Mager, *Preparing Instructional Objectives,* Palo Alto, Calif.: Fearon, 1962), p. v.

[128] Robert J. Kibler, Larry L. Barker, and David T. Miles, *Behavioral Objectives and Instruction* (Boston: Allyn & Bacon, 1970), p. 106.

[129] Herbert J. Walberg, "Structural and Affective Aspects of Classroom Climate," *Psychology in the Schools 5,* no. 3 (July 1968), 250.

[130] *Ibid.*

likely act immediately to clarify the situation. Clarification can be accomplished by demanding clarification from the teacher, by pooling perceptions with other students, or by "filling in the gaps" with information stored in the nervous system. The first can lead to direct conflict, particularly if the teacher is prone to ego-defensive behavior, and the last two can produce misperceptions which guide learning down the wrong track.

Glasser's discussion of the "certainty principle," supports the contention that the schools assiduously cultivate low tolerance for ambiguity in students. Glasser states:

> . . . almost all schools and colleges are dominated by the *certainty principle.* According to the certainty principle, there is a right and a wrong answer to every question; the function of education then is to ensure that each student knows the right answers to a series of questions that educators have decided are important.[131]

This illusion of certainty in the classroom is undoubtedly strengthened by the widespread use of multiple-choice, true-false, and other limited response types of tests which operationally define "truth" as lying within the range of alternatives presented in the test question. It does not take much imagination to interpret these practices in terms of their effects on tolerance for ambiguity. When students have been pressed throughout their schooling to give *the right answers* in class "discussions" and on tests, they undoubtedly develop a strong need for "certainty" in classroom settings. When presented with unclear, ambiguous objectives, they would tend to be distressed over the lack of certainty and fearful that not knowing what is expected of them they are ill-prepared to give the "right answers" on those all important examinations.

Kibler *et al.* comment on the relationship between anxiety level and statements of objectives as follows:

> One final value of giving behavioral objectives to students is intangible, yet very important. It is the sense of security a student experiences when he knows what specifically is expected from him in a course and the conditions under which he will be expected to exhibit

[131]Glasser, *op. cit.,* p. 36.

> his competencies. Psychologists suggest that generalized fears cause greater emotional anxiety than specific well-defined fears. Behavioral objectives can help students understand specific requirements of a course and also reduce the amount of generalized anxiety about course requirements.[132]

Hence, when students perceive instructional objectives as vague and unclear, they are likely to experience not only discomfort, but also anxiety.

> HYPOTHESIS 13: Ambiguous, unclear instructional objectives, combined with students' low tolerance for ambiguity produce misperceptions of the objectives which are a source of student-teacher conflict.

Most of what was said about unclear behavioral objectives applies as well to unclear test questions. The student may receive adequate clarification of the question from the teacher, but if not, he is likely to compose his own question and answer it. Such misperceptions usually lead to a lower score and to subsequent student-teacher conflicts over the clarity of the question and the "right answer," both of which are intensified by pressure for good grades. That ambiguous, vague questions can produce anxiety and discomfort in students is so widely discussed in the literature on "test anxiety" that it will simply be noted here.

Lack of content validity in a test may be a source of student-teacher conflict. In essence, a test with acceptable content validity will give emphasis to the various aspects of a course in proportion to the emphasis they received in the instructional process and in statements of instructional objectives. The most insidious type of test is one which emphasizes what students perceive as least important. Some teachers call this a "hard test," when in reality, it's a test almost devoid of content validity. It is not hard to envision the effects on a student of a test which violates all or most of his perceptions of what was emphasized in the course. He becomes the victim of a misperception that was almost impossible to avoid.

[132]Kibler, Barker, and Miles, *op. cit.*, p. 106.

Gronlund pursues the theme of content validity when he distinguishes between *stated* and *functional* objectives. Stated objectives are simply the ones prepared by the teacher for the course, while functional objectives are defined operationally through what is emphasized in the instructional process and on tests. He notes that "There is, frequently and unfortunately, a wide discrepancy between the objectives which are stated for the course and those which are implicit in the teaching-learning process."[133] He maintains that what is emphasized on the test probably has more influence on students' learning than formally stated course objectives.

The point is that if a student is encouraged to guide his learning by formally stated objectives and is later evaluated in terms of a different set of objectives which are implicit in the test, a misperception harmful to the student is produced. Mager states:

> Tests or examinations . . . are supposed to tell the teacher and the student the degree to which both have been successful in their achievement of the course objectives. But unless goals are clearly and firmly fixed in the minds of both parties [and utilized in testing], tests are at best misleading; at worst, they are irrelevant, unfair, or useless. To be useful they must measure *performance in terms of the goals.*[134]

Teacher emphases during classroom instruction, formally stated objectives, and emphases in examinations, then, are three variables which can influence students' perceptions of what is important in a course. When two or more of these variables are contradictory, a clear case of ambiguity results.

HYPOTHESIS 14: Unclear test items lead to student misperceptions which can produce student-teacher conflict.

HYPOTHESIS 15: Tests with low-content validity generate student hostility towards the teacher which can lead to student-teacher conflict.

Another psychological factor which contributes to distorted perceptions is projection. As is apparent from some of the earlier discussion of the adolescent's relationships to adults, students do

[133]Gronlund, *op. cit.*, p. 25.
[134]Mager, *op. cit.*, p. 4.

tend to project into teachers some of the traits of their parents and of adult authority figures in general. It was also shown that students projected into teachers, perceptions of the extent of the generation gap held by adults generally. In the reverse direction, Glasser observes that adults (teachers included) are much less likely to discuss, openly, personal and interpersonal relations problems noticed in a group situation than are children, and that children experience much less difficulty and anxiety in doing so. He then cautions adults not to "extend our adult anxieties and inadequacies to children and thereby teach them to be evasive as they grow into maturity,"[135] something which he views as happening all too often. Under these circumstances, for example, students might be ready and willing to discuss a conflict situation between two or more class members, while the teacher may well perceive that the students are too immature to handle the discussion or not interested in pursuing it. As a result, the conflict may well be suppressed rather than resolved.

Through the mechanism of projection, then, persons can be perceived as possessing characteristics which have the potential to provoke a conflict between the perceiver and the perceived. As is the case with all misperceptions, it is of no consequence whether or not the perceived persons possess the characteristics, because we tend to respond to our *perceptions* of events as though they *are* objective reality.

HYPOTHESIS 16: The mechanism of projection can result in misperceptions of students' and teachers' characteristics and these misperceptions are a potential source of conflict between the perceiver and the perceived.

Potential Sources of Conflict in the Social Context

The dominant variable in the school's social context appears to be students' competitive orientation toward each other, toward teachers, and toward the school as a whole. This variable is so pervasive and overriding in the schools that the social con-

[135] Glasser, *op. cit.*, p. 128.

text will be analyzed solely by examining competitive orientations.

PROPOSITION 6: Competition is an important source of interpersonal conflict.

Mack and Snyder note that "competition is not regarded as conflict or a form of conflict, though it may be an important source of the latter."[136] They define competition and distinguish it from conflict as follows:

> Competition involves striving for scarce objects (a prize or a resource usually "awarded" by a third party) according to established rules which strictly limit what the competitors can do to each other in the course of the striving; the chief object is the scarce object, not the injury or destruction of an opponent per se.[137]

Deutsch concurs with the premise that competition is a source of conflict when he states that "Although 'competition' produces conflict, not all instances of 'conflict' reflect competition."[138]

Some of the "scarce objects," "prizes," or "resources" that students compete for include good grades, scholarships, social popularity, prestige earned through successful competition in school activities, and affection. In a sense, the school is a miniature society which apes the competitive orientation of society as a whole. Leading in with the comment that "ours is a competitive, technological society,"[139] the Committee on Adolescence points out the consequent pervasiveness of competitive orientations in varying social contexts. They state:

> The adult world places emphasis upon winning the struggle for status and position, and since the outcome rather than the means is emphasized, ability is often subordinated to agility. . . . Children very early are initiated into this melee through the competitive sibling structure of our nuclear family unit, and are kept aware of this orientation throughout their school and playground activities. Grading systems also maintain this emphasis, and thoughtful teachers of adolescents complain that the real goal of many of their pupils is

[136]Mack and Snyder, *op. cit.*, p. 34.
[137]*Ibid.*
[138]Deutsch, *op. cit.*, p. 156.
[139]Committee on Adolescence, *op. cit.*, p. 46.

second-guessing the teacher and getting the grades, rather than learning for the sake of its lasting benefits.[140]

Our society as a whole is competitively oriented and the schools may simply be observing widely approved practices in passing out the scarce resources and valuable prizes to the victors in competitive struggles. The practice is observed in interscholastic athletics, choosing the homecoming queen, electing officers for school organizations, selecting participants in dramatic productions, selecting students for honor societies, honor rolls, and Dean's Lists, and most important of all, in awarding grades. All of these school-wide practices tend to strengthen and reinforce students' competitive orientations. When in the classroom, the students' competitive drives receive an immensely powerful booster shot from the dual needles of "grade book" and "examination."

It would be erroneous to maintain that competition in the classroom is invariably harmful and conducive to interpersonal conflict. Rather, it is the overemphasis on competition as a motivational force that tends to produce conflict. Mouly cites a study by Combs in which the latter argues against excessive use of competition in classrooms. Mouly writes:

> . . . as he [Combs] points out, the fact that competition exists in our society is no reason why we ought to have more competition in our schools, especially since certain teachers make their classrooms much more competitive—with the degree of success relative to that of others much more obvious and the freedom to withdraw much less—than is generally encountered out of school. Although the judicious use of competition can increase interest in schoolwork, it is essential that this competition not be of the dog-eat-dog variety and that everyone have a chance of winning.[141]

Mouly discusses a number of circumstances under which competition can have harmful effects. He cites two circumstances that are clear instances of overemphasis. They are:

1. When it [competition] is so intense that losing means loss

[140]*Ibid.*

[141]George J. Mouly, *Psychology For Effective Teaching*, second edition (New York: Holt, Rinehart, and Winston, 1968), p. 354.

of status, even in the case of individuals who did not wish to participate in the first place and whose fear of losing was a major factor in their defeat. Competition is harmful when everyone is so busy protecting himself from the threat of the achievements of others that no one can do his best.

2. When winning at all costs overshadows all other considerations; when children become obsessed with the need to surpass others; when values get lost in the pursuit of self-aggrandizement; when the success of others is a source of threat rather than happiness and good fellowship; when the need to win at all costs leads to dishonesty, rivalry, bitterness, and reprisals in the case of defeat.[142]

Undoubtedly the most important thing many students compete for in school is good grades. Good grades ("A's" and "B's") are scarce in most classrooms, or as Mouly observes "they are not available to all on an equitable basis."[143] Glasser points out how the use of the normal curve in grading practices further restricts the number of "good grades" available while increasing the number of "failures" ("C" and below).[144] When the teacher sets "high academic standards," this valued resource becomes even more scarce. Mouly comments on the "tough teacher" as follows:

> Students often get lower grades than they deserve because of undue difficulty in the examination or in the grading. Some teachers set standards in terms of what they could have done—or would have liked to have done—when they were in school. Some pride themselves in being tough and proceed to appoint themselves as watchdogs of academic standards.[145]

Good grades, scarce at the outset, are made even more scarce with the application of rigorous standards and the normal curve to the grade-dispensing process. That good grades are valuable has been shown in earlier discussions of the pressures on students to get good grades, the near-substitution of the grade

[142] *Ibid.*, p. 353.
[143] *Ibid.*, p. 350.
[144] Glasser, *op. cit.*, p. 71.
[145] Mouly, *op. cit.*, p. 439.

transcript for education, and the widely perceived positive correlations between grades and future success. Mouly observes that "Grades are so important to some students that accumulating a good scholastic record or surpassing others becomes *the* measure of academic and personal worth."[146] Since good grades are normally both scarce and valuable, it would seem that the generally observed procedures in awarding them would intensify competitive orientations in the classroom.

The intensity of competition for good grades in the classroom is revealed in what students will do in order to get them. Mouly contends that when competition for grades is overemphasized "grades simply serve to teach the child shortcuts such as cramming, cheating, apple-polishing, and other means of circumventing true learning."[147] With regard to cheating, Glasser cites a study in which it was found that 55 percent of college students in this country cheat to obtain better grades and that evidence of cheating was found in every one of the 99 schools involved in the survey.[148] He maintains that grades encourage cheating because "when grades become the currency of education, those who are greedy for riches cheat."[149] Glasser also discusses the phenomenon of negative cheating which he attributes to the intense competitiveness generated by grading on the normal curve. He explains that in negative cheating "students give each other wrong answers in the hope that these wrong answers will lower the places of others on the inflexible curve and thus raise the negative cheater to a higher spot."[150] Cheating and "brown-nosing," both the products of overemphasizing competition in grading, can lead to interpersonal conflicts among students: between "brown-nosers" and their accusers, between cheaters and non-cheaters, between cheaters who were caught and the informers. As Mouly observes, "Grades . . . tend to breed competitiveness and various anti-

[146]*Ibid.*, p. 344.
[147]*Ibid.*
[148]Glasser, *op. cit.*, pp. 64–65.
[149]*Ibid.*, p. 64.
[150]*Ibid.*, p. 71.

social attitudes and behaviors,"[151] and overemphasis on competition "tends to cause resentment, jealousy, and poor intragroup relations."[152]

Overly competitive grading systems can also produce student-teacher conflicts, since the teacher is the sole possessor of the scarce and valuable resource. The student's game is to wrest from his teachers as large a chunk as he can get, using whatever strategies that will work with each teacher. Glasser contends that "fact-and-answer-centered education," enforced by the grading system, "usually settles down to a struggle between teachers and pupils," and that it's an unequal struggle because the teacher has the "right answers" and the grades.[153] Mouly, at one point, characterizes grades as "weapons teachers hold over the heads of children,"[154] and later states:

> Teachers often find that giving the child a low grade destroys the pupil-teacher relationship they have been trying to cultivate. Many children, rather than blame themselves for a low grade, project the blame onto the teacher. . . .[155]

Simon contends that "Grades separate students and professors into two warring camps, both armed with dangerous weapons, none of which has anything to do with the notion of a community of scholars."[156]

It is probable, then, that competitive grading systems can produce conflicts between students and between students and teachers. Unfairness in grading and a strong competitive orientation accompanied by low academic ability are two factors that would tend to increase the probability of interpersonal conflict. With regard to unfairness Mouly cites evidence to show that while boys tend to score consistently higher than girls on standardized achievement tests, girls have a higher average grade point and are more frequently on the honor roll.[157] As was

[151]Mouly, *op. cit.*, p. 438.
[152]*Ibid.*, p. 355.
[153]Glasser, *op. cit.*, p. 79.
[154]Mouly, *op. cit.*, p. 350.
[155]*Ibid.*, pp. 438–439.
[156]Sidney B. Simon, "Grades Must Go," *School Review 78*, no. 3 (May 1970), 397.
[157]Mouly, *op. cit.*, p. 439.

reported earlier, Stinchcombe's rebellious students perceived the grading system as unfair, and Mouly when commenting on students who project blame for a low grade onto the teacher, observes that "there is enough invalidity and unreliability in the average test to make this entirely plausible."[158] Unfairness, then, can lead to student-teacher conflicts, and to conflicts between favored and non-favored students.

Mouly states that competition can have harmful effects "when success is over-restricted, when there are few winners and many losers to the point where losers, in self-defense, must decline further participation."[159] He goes on to observe that "Generally the weak ones are eliminated or withdraw for fear of coming up short so that competition denies participation to the very ones who need it most."[160] Mouly's "losers" and "weak ones" would include Stinchcombe's rebellious students. As was noted earlier, girl students destined for early marriage and boys destined for manual labor occupations are in a poor competitive position in the typical middle class, college-oriented high school. Since the emphases in curricula and grading favor the middle-class, college-bound student, Stinchcombe's rebels, who are still under pressure to compete for grades, find themselves at an unfair disadvantage. Stinchcombe maintains that "when a person is expected to accomplish more than he can possibly accomplish, he tends to reject either the goals or the rules which limit the means, or both."[161] Rejection of goals and rules often leads to student-teacher conflict.

Stinchcombe hypothesizes that "whenever the goals of success are strongly internalized but inaccessible, expressive alienation results."[162] He argues that pressure to compete for grades is strongest on middle class students, and stronger on boys than on girls. He indicates that the main burden of his analysis of "pressure to succeed and rebellion" falls on "those boys who are under great pressure to succeed . . . but who are intellec-

[158]*Ibid.*
[159]*Ibid.*, p. 353.
[160]*Ibid.*
[161]Stinchcombe, *op. cit.*, p. 7.
[162]*Ibid.*, p. 8.

tually ill-equipped for academic competition"[163] and predicts that "middle class students who are unsuccessful in school would be under exceptionally great strain."[164] His results support this prediction. He reports:

> Boys more than girls, and middle class boys more than working class boys, have internalized the standards of universalistic achievement as a standard of self-evaluation. Even when confronted with academic failure, boys, and particularly middle class boys, refuse to abandon the possibility of college, and among the academically unsuccessful, boys, particularly middle class boys, are the most rebellious.[165]

Hence, it would appear that a strong competitive orientation accompanied by low academic ability (especially in middle class boys) can precipitate teacher-student conflict when the student experiences a lack of academic success.

CONCLUSION 5: Excessive use of competition as a motivational force in classroom instructional settings is a source of interpersonal conflict.

CONCLUSION 6: Traditional grading systems, as generally utilized, intensify competitive orientations and, consequently, are a source of teacher-student and student-student interpersonal conflict.

HYPOTHESIS 17: As the number of available good grades ("A's" and "B's") become more scarce in a competitively oriented classroom, the probability of student-student and teacher-student interpersonal conflict increases.

HYPOTHESIS 18: Unfairness (real or perceived) in the classroom grading system increases the probability of interpersonal conflict.

HYPOTHESIS 19: As the number of students feeling strong pressure to compete academically and having low ability to do so increases, the probability of interpersonal conflict in the classroom increases.

CONCLUSIONS AND SUGGESTIONS FOR RESEARCH

There appears to be ample evidence to support the conclusion that there are a number of variables operative in the classroom which can precipitate interpersonal conflict. This conclusion

[163] *Ibid.*, p. 136.
[164] *Ibid.*
[165] *Ibid.*, p. 168.

should be weighed in terms of the tentativeness of any of the conclusions and hypotheses stated in the course of this analysis and in terms of the absence of any substantial discussion here of the conditions which influence the probability of existing sources leading to overt interpersonal conflict. Also missing here is any treatment of the effects of interpersonal conflict on the learning of students. Unless it can be shown that such factors as the suppression of conflict, the existence of conflict, and the effective management of conflict influence the learning processes, few educators could be expected to be interested in social conflict as it pertains to the classroom. The near absence of research evidence concerning the effects of interpersonal conflict on learning is a major obstacle to applying social conflict theory to the classroom.

A study done by Costin is suggestive of the type of research that can be instrumental in overcoming this obstacle. He found significant negative correlations between scores on a test of hostility toward the course and scores on tests of academic achievement in the course.[166] He also reports another study involving freshmen entering the University of Illinois under the special Educational Opportunity Program which yielded similar results. Although it would be erroneous to equate interpersonal conflict and hostility, the results of these studies do have strong implications for interpersonal conflict involving adolescents, since it was argued earlier that they are more likely than adults to have a strong affective investment in conflict.

However, until further research is conducted in this area, no defensible conclusions will be forthcoming concerning the relationships between learning and interpersonal conflict. Similarly, no direct evidence is available to suggest to teachers effective conflict management strategies. Although several general recommendations will be made shortly, specific recommendations must, again, await the results of relevant research in classroom conflict.

Looking at the evidence presented in this analysis, it appears

[166]Frank Costin, "Hostility and Learning in an Introductory Psychology Course," *Psychology in the Schools* 7, no. 4 (October 1970), pp. 370–74.

that several factors would tend to have a conflict-reducing effect on the classroom. Prior to listing them, however, it should be repeated that social conflict is not to be viewed as being necessarily socially dysfunctional: Some conflicts, properly managed, can have constructive effects on the classroom social system. With this precaution in mind, several general factors with probable conflict-reducing potential will be listed. They include:

1. Equal or proportional emphasis on the affective and cognitive outcomes of education
2. Teaching about social conflict and dealing with it effectively in the classroom
3. Including in teacher education programs strong emphases on interpersonal relations training and conflict management
4. Increasing the real and perceived relevance of the curricula at all levels and for *all* students
5. Developing classroom settings that approximate, as closely as possible, Miles's description of the T-Group
6. Maintaining affective support for adolescents experiencing disruption from intrapersonal conflicts and cognitive dissonance
7. Sharing, with students, the decision-making power related to choices of educational objectives, curricula, learning experiences, evaluation procedures, and norms governing classroom behavior
8. Teacher flexibility in moving along the direct-indirect influence continuum, with a preference for the indirect extreme
9. A preference for the humanistic over the custodial orientation toward pupil control in the entire school system as well as in the classroom
10. Avoidance of favoritism when allocating the school's resources to students, including curricula, good teaching, and participation in school activities
11. Direct study and discussion of the psychology of adolescence in the classroom focusing on potential sources of generational conflict
12. Abolition of traditional grading systems and substitution of an interactive student-teacher feedback system that is inter-

personally non-competitive and hence less prone to inducing harmful interpersonal conflict.

13. A substantial reduction of competitive pressure as a motivational force and an accompanying strengthening of cooperative orientations

14. Direct study and discussion of human perception, including person perception, as they relate to interpersonal behavior

15. Abolition of the "certainty principle" and the "right-answer syndrome" with an accompanying deliberate attempt to increase tolerance for ambiguity in students

16. A substantial increase in the validity and reliability of classroom tests

17. Clearly stated, instructional objectives which are nearly identical to the "functional objectives" defined in the total teaching-learning process

18. A substantial increase in the probability that all students will succeed academically in pursuit of educational goals important to them

19. Creating other conditions which favor non-conflict, as the results of additional research on the sources and conditions of conflict become available.

While the above list lacks the support of substantial research evidence it is suggestive of the kinds of steps educators can take while awaiting the results of additional research. It is apparent that implementation of any of these recommendations should be preceded by careful study of relevant writings in the area of conflict resolution and that special training in interpersonal relations may well be necessary. A half-informed, half-trained person can do immeasurably more harm than good when he proceeds to tamper with the immensely complicated web of interpersonal conflict. Evidence of this is found in some of the harmful effects of T-Groups and sensitivity sessions as conducted by ill-trained amateurs.

Birnbaum issues a warning concerning the probable harms that can result when sensitivity training sessions are conducted by untrained amateurs. He writes:

Two kinds of sensitivity training are particularly susceptible today to exploitation by the enthusiastic amateur or the enterprising entrepreneur: the area of non-verbal experience, and the confrontation session. Each requires a minimum of experience and knowledge to stimulate an initial response among participants, but in each case a maximum of expert knowledge and sophistication is required to extract a positive educational outcome. The most damning judgment that can be made about the non-verbal field is that a small bag of easily learned tricks, plus several 33⅓ rpm records, makes anyone a trainer. As for confrontation sessions, it is not difficult to evoke profound guilt feelings among participants by employing the tactics of staged aggression, but it requires great skill and understanding to follow through to a positive learning experience.[167]

Even the well-trained teacher with the best of intentions should not be overly optimistic over achieving a dramatic breakthrough in his relationships with adolescents. The Committee on Adolescence observes:

> Free communication between adolescent and adult is difficult, so much so that many professional observers doubt that the differences between the generations in a rapidly changing society can be bridged. They feel that perhaps the most that can be hoped for is mutual tolerance, sincere negotiation, and relatively peaceful coexistence.[168]

In spite of the obstacles to success in the form of the complexity of interpersonal conflict and the difficulty of bridging the generation gap, there are ample reasons why the educator should make the best effort possible to deal with interpersonal conflict in the classroom, unless, of course, he is satisfied with these two characterizations of the typical classroom:

1. Mouly states:

> The primary weakness of the teacher-centered approach stems directly from its orientation toward adult goals and reliance on adult direction, a situation which can easily run counter to the principle that experience is educative to the extent that it is brought into vital

[167]Max Birnbaum, "Sense and Nonsense About Sensitivity Training," *Sensitivity Training and Group Encounter—An Introduction*, eds. Robert W. Siroka, Ellen K. Siroka, and Gilbert A. Schloss (New York: Grosset and Dunlap, 1971), p. 187.

[168]Committee on Adolescence, *op. cit.*, p. 102.

relationship with the needs, goals, and purposes of the learner. It is based on a philosophical view of education as a preparation for life, a position which Snygg and Combs (1949) reject since the child cannot solve problems he does not—and cannot—have.[169]

2. Kapfer contends:

> To put it bluntly, we do not trust children, adolescents, young adults, or even mature adults *whenever they are placed in school-type situations.* For this reason, we do not permit them to make choices concerning what, when, how, and where they will learn. If they do not want to learn what *we* want them to learn, we make life so miserable for them that they have only three available choices. They can knuckle under and either lose their own identity or learn how to beat the system; they can become in-school dropouts; or they can become out-of-school dropouts.[170]

It would be a mistake to assume that a majority, or even a substantial minority, of educators are satisfied with classroom instruction as depicted above and elsewhere in this analysis. It is for this reason that what is foreseen is a marked increase in the emphasis given to affective education and to education in social conflict in the years ahead. Educators can make it happen by starting now to teach about social conflict in their classes and by learning effective strategies for conflict management both for their own use in the classroom and for use in developing a sequence in "conflict resolution through communication" as an integral part of the curriculum.

[169]Mouly, *op. cit.,* pp. 555–556.

[170]Philip G. Kapfer, "Behavioral Objectives and the Curriculum Processor," *Educational Technology 10,* no. 5 (May 1970), 14.

LEONARD W. DOOB
WILLIAM J. FOLTZ
ROBERT B. STEVENS

The Fermeda Workshop: A Different Approach to Border Conflicts in Eastern Africa

A. INTRODUCTION

The Fermeda Workshop in August, 1969, was an attempt to determine whether sensitivity training could be employed effectively in an international setting. The Workshop focused upon two difficult border problems and sought to discover whether the use of such methods in detached surroundings could produce positive solutions which might strengthen peace and security in the Horn of Africa. Sensitivity training involves a prolonged series of small-group sessions which are unstructured so far as procedure is concerned and which enable the participants gradually to gain greater insight into themselves and to communicate their feelings and ideas more effectively than is the case in most formal meetings.[1]

From Leonard W. Doob, William J. Foltz, and Robert B. Stevens, "The Fermeda Workshop: A Different Approach to Border Conflicts in Eastern Africa," *The Journal of Psychology 73*, 1969, 249–266.

[1]In an enterprise of this kind the list of those to whom we would express gratitude and thanks should be very long. Some, especially those connected with governments, must alas remain nameless as, here at least, must the African participants. But in particular we must thank the Academy for Educational Development, the Honorable W. Averill Harriman, and above all the Concilium on International Studies of Yale University

The disputes with which the Workshop concerned itself are between Somalia and Kenya and also between Somalia and Ethiopia. One fact in these situations is uncontested: The majority of the inhabitants of the Ogaden which is part of Ethiopia and of the North Eastern Province which is part of Kenya are ethnically and linguistically Somalis, who, being largely nomads, use the land as grazing grounds for their herds of camels and cattle. The conflict between the nomadic tradition and the fixed boundaries based on the colonial tradition have kept that part of Eastern Africa in a state of war or near conflict for almost a generation, and have caused the inevitable economic drain which follows from war and military preparedness.

For over three years, the three of us—as members of the Yale faculty—sought to find English-speaking African scholars from the three countries who would be qualified and interested in participating in such a workshop, to obtain the informal permission of the three African governments for them to attend, and of course to raise the necessary financial support. As participants, we looked for persons with an interest in the problems caused by the disputes and who also had sufficient emotional stability to submit to the vicissitudes of a T-group. We particularly did not want government officials who would be obliged to defend their nation's articulated point of view. Governmental permission was needed because our African colleagues and we did not wish to run the risk of jeopardizing their careers at home. The major foundations in America turned down our

---

for financial support and encouragement. Edward W. Barrett, in charge of the Academy's International Mediation Study, devoted some of his prodigious energy and enthusiasm to helping us raise funds. Oscar Schachter of UNITAR provided us with moral and institutional support which was absolutely invaluable. E. A. Bayne of the American Universities Field Staff originally directed our attention to the problems of the Horn and provided generous advice and logistical support. Miss Sonya Haddad functioned efficiently and warmly as secretary and house sister during the Workshop. Otherwise we are tempted to heap scorn and abuse on various villains who either prevented the Workshop from taking place sooner or hindered our efforts when they might have been helpful. We forgive them and render thanks to Dame Fortune and our own constitutions for enabling the Wild Idea to be realized.

requests for funding for reasons which did not always reflect favorably upon their courage or their desire to innovate. One of us has already described our preliminary misery at least up to the spring of 1967 and we can thus spare our readers and ourselves a recataloging of these early misfortunes (1), but some sense of the approach can be gleaned from the fact that we ourselves have constantly referred to the project as the Wild Idea, so unrealistic did the chance of its ever taking place appear to us. Yet whenever we contemplated abandoning it, some friend was persuasive enough to encourage us to carry on.

During 1967, prospects began to look bright. The one government which refused to come to a decision eventually expressed its *nihil obstat*, perhaps because we had received the backing of the United Nations Institute for Training and Research. In 1968, funds began to appear from two American sources and, with UNITAR's help, from a British trust. Two of us revisited Ethiopia, Kenya, and Somalia to reactivate the interest of the African participants and to find substitutes for those who were no longer available. Through UNITAR we obtained the use of a neutral site for the Workshop, a school on the island of Malta; but then, three months before the event was scheduled to be held in the summer of 1968, the leader of one of the three countries withdrew his consent, for reasons associated with his own political career. The funds had to be returned, the invitations to the participants withdrawn. We felt discouraged.

The Wild Idea, however, seemed too good to drop, perhaps because any attempt to develop new techniques to lessen international tensions would have implications far beyond these particular disputes. In 1969 we adopted a strategy which involved one final attempt to bring off the Workshop, at the shortest possible notice. On June 21 one of us again visited the country whose leader had caused us to cancel the Malta meeting, and this time obtained from him an enthusiastic "green light" (his expression). Both here, and in the other two capitals, the weary task of rounding up potential participants for the Workshop was made all the more difficult by the previous cancellation. A half dozen "intellectuals" in each country, nevertheless, agreed to attend; in Kenya and Ethiopia they all had appointments in the national universities; in Somalia (whose university is only beginning to be developed) they were academically trained persons holding government, educational, or professional positions. None of them officially represented his government.

When we had acquired the 18 best participants available, other staggering administrative problems remained. The Workshop had to be held during the first two weeks of August, since that was the only period when all of the participants could be detached from their institutions, but it was not easy to produce four skillful, experienced, adventurous T-group trainers at such short notice. We were most fortunate, therefore, finally to obtain the services of William J. Crockett,[2] Charles K. Ferguson,[3] Richard E. Walton,[4] and Thomas A. Wickes.[5] These men were intrigued enough by the challenge to reorganize their busy schedules at the shortest possible notice and join in a project which at that stage they had heard described only over the telephone by persons they had never met. Finally, we discovered that Malta and most of the sites we had been considering were not available in the midst of the tourist season. Other sites were politically unacceptable to some of the participants. Eventually we located a comfortable ski hotel (named the Fermeda) three-quarters of the way up a mountain in the South Tyrol of northern Italy. There, in the midst of woods and mountain streams and against a backdrop of the Dolomites, we met from August 2 to August 14, 1969.

B. METHOD

The entire group consisted of 26 persons: the 18 Africans, the four trainers, a secretary who concentrated upon the numerous housekeeping details of the enterprise, and the three of us. Most of us assembled at the airport in Rome and then immediately

[2]Saga Administrative Division.
[3]University of California at Los Angeles.
[4]Harvard Business School.
[5]T.R.W. Inc.

established a common bond by journeying together on a bus for 12 hours to Fermeda. At the hotel, each African, with two exceptions, had a room of his own. Seating at meals was optional so that individuals from at least two of the African nations almost always sat down together; the Americans generally scattered themselves at different tables among the participants.

The participants had been told beforehand that the first part of the exercise would be unrelated to the border disputes, but instead would concentrate upon training them in the development of communication skills. The trainers, therefore, were in charge and for the first five days consulted with the three of us very little concerning procedural matters; we, in fact, readily agreed to be not merely observers but also participants in the training. After the first session which was attended by everybody—thereafter a session of the entire group became known as the General Assembly—most of the interaction and the exercises were carried on in two T-groups. These groups were initially selected in such a way that they contained three participants from each of the three countries whose professional interests were more or less balanced; two of us, the lawyer and the psychologist, were in one group, and the third, the political scientist, was in the other. These T-groups, therefore, were formed to increase the possibility of building cross-national ties and overall interest.

Some of the exercises, especially at the outset, could have occurred elsewhere in any kind of sensitivity training workshop. Participants complained about the deliberately unstructured character of the early meetings; they yearned for a chairman, parliamentary procedure, and agenda. They often became furious, however, when any of the American or, later on, African participants made a procedural proposal. Some of the aggression against the trainers, us, and one another was fierce. Conflict occurred between individuals belonging to the same or different nations. Mostly, however, the participants wanted the training to begin when, in fact, they were right in the midst of it.

Sessions usually ended by self-evaluation of what the group had accomplished, although resistance to this was never entirely broken. Games in small groups were played in more or less traditional T-group fashion. The initial lecture established the distinction between content (what you say) and process (what you really mean, what your motivations are); a later one outlined the factors which make for group cohesion.

This preliminary training, however, differed markedly from the ordinary sensitivity training in a number of significant respects. First, the participants did not come, as it were, from a single organization. Across nations they were in effect complete strangers, although a few had heard of some of the others. Within a country they belonged to the same university, or in the case of the Somalis from the same rather tightly knit educated community, but few of them were in the same clique. A member of a law faculty, for example, may have known an engineer, but he might well not have participated with him in university or social affairs. Then again the aim of the training was not individual therapy, nor improvement of relations within a particular group, but a more nebulous goal: possible solutions for these border disputes.

Overshadowing the training, at almost all times, was the knowledge that despite the idyllic surroundings, we had assembled to discuss these serious disputes. Some of the participants voiced complaints against us or asserted they would reveal nothing personal about themselves because, they claimed, we were delaying the progress of the Workshop; "get on with the show," they said, "come to grips with the problem at hand"; but others sought to learn as much as they could about sensitivity training because they believed such knowledge would help them professionally at home. The trainers understood this dilemma and handled it excellently. Time and again, they provided the appropriate training. Thus, one of the most successful games, we think, involved competition between small groups in waging war or disarming (The Disarmament Game). Topics, such as the nature of conflict, the Organization of African Unity, and university-student disturbances were discussed in the early T-groups because their processes seemed to relate to the border disputes.

From our standpoint, however, we were in a somewhat strange predicament. As participants, although participating to differing degrees, we experienced some of the *Sturm und Drang* of any workshop. Then the real participants, the Africans, kept reminding us that we were not ordinary participants, for we had organized the enterprise, we held the purse strings, and at least one of us was looked up to somewhat as a father figure with all the ambivalence the role entails. In addition, we were observers interested in eliciting information about attitudes and values in a manner ordinarily not accessible to conventional research techniques; and our African friends, looking upon us as three Americans, kept observing our reactions to personal stress and their political problems. We tried to avoid injecting our own conceptualizations of political problems into the discussion, although we achieved that goal with differing degrees of success.

Toward the end of the first week, the trainers and we decided to shift gradually from sensitivity training to the substantive issues of the border disputes. We had planned a break of two days—most of the Africans and the Americans went to Venice which offered as sharp a contrast to Fermeda as anyone could imagine—and so before then we encouraged the participants, in the language of the trainers, to "ventilate" and to a lesser degree to "diagnose" the border disputes. This they did, or tried to do, by working in national groups with the instruction to list their own grievances against the other country or countries and to anticipate what their opponents' grievances would be.

After Venice, we all concentrated upon the border disputes, more often than not in the two T-groups. Possible solutions were first listed after small-group "brainstorming sessions." Overall plans were drawn up in the T-groups, with the intention of being presented ultimately to the General Assembly. Each day's or session's program was then no longer proposed by the trainers or by them in conjunction with us, but by a Planning Group composed of two persons from each country but from different T-groups, two trainers, and one of us.

C. RESULTS AND DISCUSSION

1. Expectations and Behavior

As social scientists will, we approached the Workshop with partially defined expectations about the way the Workshop would proceed and about possible outcomes. Our expectations were based on our own previous research, assertions made in the established literature, and our individual or joint "feel" of the situation.

Perhaps our firmest expectation was that nationality would provide the most salient principle of association, trust, and like-mindedness among the African participants. We further expected that this principle would become less salient as the Workshop proceeded, and indeed, encouraged the trainers in their plan to design things so as to "lace these people together a half-dozen different ways," and thereby encourage association on other bases. These expectations proved more nearly false than true. After the first day, in which fairly standard, although eager, "get-acquainted" procedures were evident, observable informal groups of both a substantive and recreational nature almost always included more than one nationality. Since all three national groups, with varying ease, could communicate among themselves in an indigenous language incomprehensible to nonnationals, and furthermore might be expected to enjoy the relaxation and distinctiveness such communication would afford, the multinational character of the groups was particularly noteworthy. In addition to whatever links the intangibles of interpersonal sympathies might have created, we observed international links were created on the bases of both political ideology and attitude toward the training experience. The most obvious ideological links were forged across national boundaries as a result of intellectual or emotional proclivities for some radical solution as opposed to more incremental change. In addition, at least one person from each national group was consistently interested in the Workshop technique for its own sake and strongly supportive of its technical operation, and at least one was for much of the time reserved or hostile. Like ideology, these orientations carried over to create cross-cutting linkages which persisted within and outside the formal sessions.

Indeed our strongest surprise came toward the end of the first week when for the first time participants were asked formally to caucus in national groups to accomplish a substantive task jointly with their fellow countrymen. Reluctance was widespread, affecting to some degree members of all three national groups, and two of the three groups insisted on redefining the task in a less sensitive direction once they had finally agreed to meet. Several factors, including perhaps the way the task was presented (some participants clearly resented the authoritarian nature of the directive to produce complaints) and of course the effects of the preceding "lacing" may have contributed to the reluctance. In individual conversations with us, however, participants suggested that a lack of complete trust in their fellow countrymen was a motivating factor in at least two of the national groups. When dealing with sensitive issues, many of the participants preferred to associate with persons with whom they could reasonably expect to have only exceptional contact once the Workshop ended, even though such persons involved might objectively be classed as enemies on the issue in question.

The avoidance of one's own national group was most evident in the case of the Kenyans, perhaps because of the high level of political tensions in Kenya following Mboya's then recent assassination, perhaps because of their background which inclined them to behave in a less cohesive manner under most circumstances, or perhaps simply because of traits idiosyncratic to that particular group. This, too, caught us by surprise, since on the basis of the existing literature we had expected intragroup trust to be clearly lowest among the Ethiopians. As expected, the Somalis' individualism permitted them to work together easily and openly.

Rather than decreasing in strength, however, nationality became more salient at the end than at the beginning of the Workshop. Two factors appeared to be at work here. First, as the discussion focused increasingly on the substantive issue and as easy compromise solutions proved inadequate, national positions became more solid and more salient in determining overall patterns of interaction. Second, something of a "re-entry" phenomenon occurred during the last two days when several individuals retreated from previously established conciliatory positions in a manner to suggest either, consciously or unconsciously, that they were preparing a safe record of suitably nationalistic statements with which to protect themselves from attack once they had returned home or, possibly, as they realized that they were about to resume their normal lives, they were reminded of the importance of nationalistic symbols.

Other expectations related to mechanisms through which the African participants might build interpersonal solidarity among themselves or avoid direct confrontation with the substantive issues dividing them. One such mechanism likely to be particularly useful in a stressful context in which non-Africans were exercising at least limited authority would be the building of solidarity on the basis of antiwhite sentiments. Contrary to our expectations, at no point was such sentiment mobilized. Other participants greeted the only such attempt with embarrassment and hostility. A few individuals, particularly in the early days, did make punishing remarks about whites generally, but these were made in passing and were not picked up by the group. Specific condemnations of acts or policies of specific groups of whites were frequent, but were usually not misplaced nor did they betray any latent purpose.

A second expected mechanism, evident in many formal inter-African meetings particularly of major political leaders, was the avoidance of conflictual substance in favor of utopian appeals to eventual political unity of all Africa. This was much in evidence. In each of the two T-groups, and even more so in the General Assembly, participants would attempt to avoid or soften points of stress by emphasizing that all would be worked out "in the framework of the unity which we all seek." Alternatively, the positions were phrased in terms of some blind adherence to a slogan of "federation now." The mechanism served two distinct purposes: to avoid current concrete problems whose discussion might lead to disharmony within the group, and, perhaps more subtly, to soften conflictual assertions by reassuring one's opponent that opposition was only temporary and that nothing personal was implied, since the speaker would be happy to share citizenship with his opponent and all his relatives.

One further (and unexpected) mechanism of cross-national solidarity was a willingness to criticize one's own government. This openness created solidarity by putting many participants in a similar stance and so removing the speaker from direct responsibility for any of his nation's hurtful actions toward other participants' fellow citizens. As with the attitudes toward African unity, we cannot assess the sincerity or depth of these feelings by those who expressed them—much less their legitimacy—nor can we draw any conclusions about connections between overt statements, internalized attitudes, and any concrete action which might be taken on the basis of these attitudes. At this point we merely note the functions they performed in the Workshop context.

2. Formal Workshop Group Processes and Problems

Each of the two matched T-groups which became the basic working units of the Workshop developed strong group loyalties and pride at moving faster and more productively than the other. Occasional visitors from the other group were treated as interlopers. In classic style, the T-groups began in confusion, proceeded to frustration, and on the third day suddenly coalesced to conduct an impressive and profitable discussion without benefit of formal leadership or agenda. Succeeding sessions were even better, though both groups eventually returned to some semblance of the initial frustration during the first sessions in which the border dispute was discussed directly. After that, one T-group made notably greater progress than the other: Brainstorming sessions were more serious and productive; the disputes were examined more carefully and with less avoidance behavior; the solutions proposed were more specific; and the group stood more solidly behind its own recommendations. The difference is most simply, and perhaps sufficiently, explained by the presence in the laggard group of an individual whose aggressive, uncontrolled behavior, often exacerbated by drink, seemed most probably to be ideosyncratically, not culturally, determined. That group never developed a means of reducing or neutralizing his erratic and sometimes calculatedly disruptive behavior, which seemed to manifest itself most when some progress or agreement was close to hand.

The more effective T-group contained two persons who never became constructively involved, but their deviance took the form of nonparticipation. One of these men was a last-minute recruit and was possibly inadequately briefed about what to expect. He attended sessions regularly, but passively, and was made obviously uncomfortable by any attempts to bring him into discussions. Such attempts eventually ceased. The second of these misfits arrived five days late and then spent more time sleeping and playing cards with guests at the inn than participating in the Workshop. His occasional contributions, while valuable in content, had limited impact because of his failure to participate in the early sessions. Although at times distressing to the organizers, and some of the Africans, the silent deviants in that T-group proved nondisruptive, and the group learned to function effectively without their contributions.

In contrast to the T-groups' general success was the weakness of the General Assembly. Only rarely were these larger discussions productive. Avoidance behavior, intransigence, and various forms of posturing and undercutting, which had earlier been overcome in the T-groups, reappeared in the General Assembly. One procedural sign of difficulty was the General Assembly's stifling reliance on formal parliamentary procedure which reasserted its grip despite repeated and seemingly unanimous efforts to follow freer styles of discussion. Somehow the pompous parliamentary atmosphere—analogous to that which many of the participants derided in their own national parliaments—became so compelling that even the organizers found themselves rising deferentially before Mr. Chairman to a point of order, personal privilege, or the like.

Rather than a cause of the General Assembly's difficulties, the exacerbated parliamentarism seems more a reaction to them, a largely ineffective way to cope with real procedural problems. Among the problems, again, was the disruptive figure mentioned earlier, who in the General Assembly had new and broader fields to disrupt. Certainly his presence in the General Assembly was a major reason why most of the members of the more productive T-group sought to avoid plenary sessions. Also, of course, conducting a chairmanless nondirected meeting of 21 people is more difficult than conducting one with ten persons. The trainers felt, in retrospect, that a different design which would have placed more emphasis on sensitivity training in the plenary session, rather than the T-groups, could have overcome the difficulty. While this cannot be proved by our experience, this view is given some credence by the remarkable similarity of speech patterns in the final General Assembly sessions to those present in the T-groups a week earlier before the effect of training had been felt. Even so, the creation of effective communication and interpersonal trust in the larger group might well have required more time than the Workshop allowed.

The Workshop, in sum, confirmed the old dictum that the expression of attitude depends in part upon the situation at hand. Again and again, we witnessed instances of the same person inconsistently expressing, for example, conciliatory views in his T-group and then being silent or defending a more rigid position in the General Assembly. National groups caucused without Americans present, but our informal reports suggest that this context also influenced expression, as well as content. Perhaps the T-groups succeeded too well and thereby prevented the participants from transferring their emotional attachments either to the General Assembly or the national groups.

3. Attitudes and Opinions

We have obtained some sense of the attitudes and opinions of the participants on the two disputes in question from the documents which the nationals of each country composed in response to the request to list their grievances and to anticipate the grievances of their opponents, as well as from our observations of views expressed in the T-groups, the General Assembly, and informal conversations.

One point is clearer than all the rest: The Somalis were well acquainted beforehand with the arguments and values of the Kenyans and Ethiopians, and vice versa. For example, the Somalis anticipated that the Ethiopians would claim that "Ethiopia is a heterogeneous state and cannot admit ethnic separatist movements"; while the Ethiopians in fact noted a "failure to appreciate the far-reaching consequences of redrawing African boundary lines (a) through the advancement of linguistic and ethnic ties as a basis of nationhood, and (b) through the rejection of existing borders." At the same time some of the issues were probably more salient than others, or else the participants may have been reluctant to express them. Thus, the Somalis, in their written document, did not perceive that the Kenyans might describe Somalia as "being looked at by Russia as a stepping-stone to Eastern Africa and therefore being substantially armed."

The three of us also submitted a document to the General Assembly in which we tried to anticipate, on the basis of our knowledge of the countries, the grievances which each side would express. One noteworthy fact about our lists was that virtually every item was independently mentioned by the participants. This we take to be further evidence of the common knowledge concerning the border disputes which educated and informed persons, whether Africans or non-Africans, share. In addition we, unlike the Africans, did not hesitate to describe the stereotypes frequently held by the nationals of each of these countries about the inhabitants of the other two. Significantly, there was no disagreement with our characterization.

Both in the documents and in the discussions there were few disputes over facts. Obviously, there could be no argument about the role of the European powers in dividing and governing the Horn in accordance with the treaties they had enforced upon themselves and the African peoples there. That the majority of the persons in the disputed areas are Somalis, ethnically and linguistically, was not subject to debate. More surprising, however, was assent to facts which in other international conflicts are likely to produce charges and countercharges, such as the offensive quality of the propaganda broadcast from the

Somali radio stations or the brutal treatment of some Somalis by the Ethiopian and Kenyan army and police. The facts could be accepted, but then the evaluation differed markedly.

The most critical difference in evaluation involved the issues of self-determination and sovereignty. The Somalis never retreated from their view that "the inhabitants of these areas [have the right] to determine their own fate," nor the Kenyans and the Ethiopians from their position that each of them is a nation defined, in the words of the former, as "a people [having] a defined territorial border [and] a recognized political structure [with] legal authority, internationally recognized political boundaries, [and] territorial integrity." These were the most intensely held attitudes and, almost always whenever affect was expressed, the clash was between the two irreconcilable positions.

The Workshop and informal conversations could not probe more deeply to uncover the reasons for the strength of these values. If we asked a Somali why he felt so strongly about the people of the Ogaden, he would either consider the question slightly insane or else he would mention relatives of his who reside there or shrines and waterholes needed by his people. The Kenyans and the Ethiopians were likewise surprised when asked why it mattered whether or not the territories were retained: they could supply economic reasons, they could mention treaty rights, they could stress the possibility of other ethnic groups also wanting to leave their multiracial states, but most of all they expressed incredulity that anyone would even wonder why a government would be unwilling to relinquish its sovereign rights. "What is in it for us?" the Kenyans and Ethiopians asked again and again when confronted with proposals that buffer zones be created within or outside the disputed areas. In a sense the overriding symbol which had reality for these men was land: land for grazing, land belonging to the tribe or the nation, tangible land. Although they may have used the fashionable jargon of the times, especially the phrase "national identity," they really attached deep emotional significance to the concepts and extrapolated very easily from personal or tribal concepts of land and property to attribute such concepts to the modern African state.

All of us experienced the intensity of feeling which was expressed especially toward the end of the Workshop. But cracks also appeared in the national armor. Anecdotes were slipped in which had a less absolutistic tone; it is such a nuisance, one man remarked, to have to stop driving when the national flag is being raised or lowered. It may be, some of the participants said, that we have to sacrifice some of our sovereignty to attain peace; or perhaps some of the history is not relevant to the present problem; or we must also consider the circumstances under which plebiscites or other forms of self-determination should be encouraged.

A set of values which did not change was the willingness to criticize one's own government. One man in a T-group stated that he would be critical at home but not abroad, yet he was soon joined by the other participants in pointing out the abuses to which he and others are subjected. Sometimes it was even suggested that the governments had a vested interest in continuing the border disputes in order to distract people's attention from domestic problems; at other times it was stated openly that no solution for the disputes could possibly be achieved under the present regimes. It is doubtful whether such views would be expressed if the participants had been questioned directly, for we had sought out men whose opinions might be listened to by government. We now know that the government connections do exist but that any group of intellectuals in these countries is likely to express attitudes some of which are critical of the *status quo* without, however, being unpatriotic or disloyal. One participant in fact arose and accused the others of "betraying" their countries because in his view they were making no greater progress toward solving the disputes than the governments whose views they were criticizing. Obviously, each side learned something about this critical stance inside the other countries.

We hold the tentative opinion, therefore, that no fundamental changes were wrought directly by the Workshop, but that new political, economic, and social facts may well have been learned. The participants certainly had the opportunity to discover that their antagonists, with the exception of very few, were men of good will who subscribed to opposing viewpoints with an intensity and conviction as strong as their own. It is this insight which may possibly have repercussions and produce change—eventually.

4. Proposing Solutions

Even more central to the Workshop's purpose than changing participants' attitudes was the joint exploration and prescription of solutions for the border disputes. Each of the T-groups argued through and eventually proposed a detailed solution to the disputes, and each of the two proposals received the general assent of the members of the T-group responsible. The emotional and intellectual involvement of T-group members with their joint product was strikingly intense; even the disruptive individual subscribed to his group's proposals. At this short remove from the event it is yet impossible to know how much of that involvement represented calculated appreciation of the worth of one's labors, how much represented pride in and support for one's T-group, and how much just the exhilaration of having finally gotten something down on paper. Although national-interest bargaining was sharp within the T-groups, support for the proposals as they finally emerged was apparently genuinely international.

Subsequent publications will deal with the substance of these and other proposals, but here it is worth mentioning the main similarities and differences. One group, largely at the insistence of one of its strongest and most useful members (a non-Somali), began with the affirmation of the right to self-determination of the peoples in the area under dispute, though this was somewhat attenuated by the affirmation that "it is a right to be exercised only under specified circumstances." The other group had repeatedly reached an impasse on the self-determination issue (it was seen as a subtle Somali device for dismembering Ethiopia and Kenya), and had carefully avoided any statement of general principles of the sort. Both proposals provided for some form of joint administration of the "disputed areas" for an interim period, with the question of sovereignty over the areas held, nonprejudicially, in abeyance. Various alternate definitions of the "disputed areas" and of the means and time for terminating the neutralization arrangements were advanced. Each proposal insisted on demilitarization of the disputed areas, with law and order being made the responsibility of a local police independent of direct control by any of the three nations. Both proposals foresaw some role for an expanded East African Community or other formal political arrangements among the three parties as part of a permanent solution.

Under extreme time pressure, the joint Planning Group, which in the second week had taken over the planning of the sessions, amalgamated the two proposals into one for presentation on the last day to the General Assembly. This shotgun wedding of what had been the products of subtly different group processes did not, alas, produce a well-integrated child. One example of the difficulties of the compromise was the reappearance of a *deus ex machina* role for political unity of the three nations as the sole way of effecting a permanent solution for the border dispute. In retrospect, it is easy to see that the amalgamation of the two documents was a major tactical mistake. When the combined document was presented to the General Assembly, it seemed to satisfy no one, and the whole group reached a frustrating and infuriating stalemate. The principal reasons included disappointment at seeing one's original ideas, product of so much arduous thought and negotiation in the T-group, modified or omitted in the compromise document: "What I see here is that my group's document has been adulterated!" The re-entry phenomenon also played its part: "As time goes by here, I am becoming more reluctant to agree that part of our country should be given up." The difficulty of communication in the General Assembly was very much in evidence. The disrupter was his usual unhelpful self—he reversed his usual revolutionary and anti-European stance to quote, approvingly, Churchill in favor of absolute defense of territorial integrity of one's possessions—but even had he been absent in these final meetings the other problems would have remained.

The sticking point was reached over the definition of the areas to be neutralized in the interim period, particularly over whether or not the Somali Republic would have to include some of its own territory in the "neutralized zone." On the one hand, Somalis could claim with perfect accuracy that there was no dispute over any territory now part of the Somali Republic and that it would be senseless to introduce dispute where none existed. On the other hand, Kenyans and Ethiopians could claim perfectly reasonably that all parties to the dispute would have to give up something in any reasonable compromise and that the Somalis just seemed to be looking for something for nothing. "What is it that the Somalis really want?" one participant kept repeating. The various elaborate proposals for resolving or avoiding the issue which had been worked out in the T-groups were rejected in the General Assembly. Yet if some of the national stereotypes were again conjured up, even at the most heated moments, it was clear that national lines did not hold entirely firm. T-group loyalty, ideological proclivity, and new-found intellectual conviction cut across national boundaries to produce smaller groupings of like-minded men on specific issues.

The Fermeda Workshop, thus, did not end with a final communique proposing a single peace formula and signed happily by all, but it did produce general agreement on a two-stage approach involving neutralization of disputed areas during the initial period. This approach was embodied in two detailed proposals, not widely different one from the other, with each commanding the assent of some influential citizens of all three countries involved in the dispute. As we all knew from the outset, the important steps would have to be taken by the politicians of the three countries. We are now in a position to investigate whether these incremental gains of the Workshop are communicated effectively back to the men whose actions could make a difference.

D. SUMMARY

The reader must share some of our ambivalence about the Fermeda Workshop—and possibly some of our exhilaration and some of our frustrations.

One success cannot be questioned except by those who did not have to endure our travail: the Workshop took place, all the African participants arrived, the governments voiced no objection, competent trainers were obtained, and we were able to keep our promise of providing a permissive atmosphere in which any view could be expressed. We had no authority, and until the very end no funds to compel these people to gamble their time and come to Fermeda. Private initiative through university connections was sufficient. In addition, the participants certainly became acquainted with one another and in many instances, we surmise, formed strong friendships across national lines. They expressed to themselves and to us the basic grievances of the countries regarding the border disputes and in this manner revealed their attitudes and values.

From a research point of view, we believe the technique revealed attitudes and complex cognitive processes not obtainable through more standard questioning techniques; but the Workshop inevitably involved only a small sample of persons, and data have been derived in a form that makes coding extremely difficult. The lack of a control group was unavoidable. Finally, the fact that the sample's composition is sure to be known to the governments concerned poses confidentiality problems of a very high order. Against such difficulties in using the technique as a research tool, one clear-cut advantage stands out, particularly when dealing with a group like ours. In contrast to the usual relation between researcher and subject—which is increasingly resented in the developing nations as a subtle form of "academic imperialism"—no information was available to us which was not equally available to the African participants and, should they so choose, to their governments as well. More so than anything we may write, it will be through the African participants' public and private communications that the Fermeda Workshop will have its greatest impact.

On the other hand, the main objective of the Workshop, at least on the surface, was certainly not achieved. No original solution to the disputes was evolved which won the instant acclaim of all the participants. Therefore for the moment we remain skeptical whether the two schemes evolved by the T-groups will be diffused to one or more of the governments and so serve as the basis for any form of agreement among the nations of the Horn.

We equally have no way of knowing definitely whether the successes and the failures of the Workshop, whatever they were, can be attributed to the use of sensitivity training and the various techniques which our valued trainers employed. As we have already noted, there was no control group—and perforce there could be none—to ascertain whether the mere congregating of three groups of sincere African scholars atop a Tyrolean mountain would have produced the same, better, or worse results, if they had begun discussing the substantive issues immediately without the delay which such training entailed. Lectures and games were infrequently referred to in subsequent sessions, but this does not mean that a residue therefrom had no affect upon the men's behavior.

We venture the opinion, the guess, the clinical judgment that the training did contribute appreciably to the breaking-down of reserve and to the enhancing of communication between participants from different nations. It is possible that, in the absence of the disrupter and of the tension resulting from the assassination of Tom Mboya, the more laggard of the T-groups and the General Assembly itself might have made greater progress. We cannot, we repeat, prove these statements of faith, we can only express confidence in them. On the other hand, the genial atmosphere created by the scenery around Fermeda, by the drinking, by the card-playing, and perhaps by the T-groups may have encouraged the participants to be polite to one another, and in this way to avoid rather than face head-on the complicated issues. Our presence—scholars from the West with white skins—may have been inhibiting, although several participants told us they appreciated non-African auspices.

In the future, if the Fermeda technique is to prove useful in other conflicts, we would hazard the opinion that the participants must make a firmer commitment than we were able to procure to support and carry through with the procedural requirements a workshop imposes. No hard sell should be applied by enthusiastic organizers. Participants must want to come, and must want to get the dispute settled badly enough to sacrifice some personal dignity and to make substantive concessions. Were we to do this again, we are uncertain whether we should insist on a stiffer or milder dose of initial sensitivity training despite any objections the participants might raise. We might also favor a more authoritarian regimen for the entire enterprise, including the right to eject participants.

Aside from the obvious point that, as of this writing, the dispute has not been solved even to the satisfaction of three groups of influential intellectuals, other limitations on the future use of the technique must be spelled out. First, such a workshop is not an inexpensive undertaking. The Fermeda costs ran about $40,000, not including many hidden expenses including salaries and overheads absorbed by Yale over an extended period. Secondly, a workshop is very time-consuming, and it is difficult to find men of the caliber required who can give up a particular two weeks of their lives. The time involved for the organizers, before, during, and after the workshop, at least equals that spent on any major research effort. Should the organizers be so foolish as to start such a venture from scratch and take on the responsibility of arousing interest on the part of participants, governments, and foundations, they may find the effort involved disproportionate to any conceivable results.

But against all these points, one must restate the obvious: the travail, the time, and the expense are all of little importance, if a Fermeda-type workshop contributes even marginally to the settlement of a major international dispute.

REFERENCE

1. Doob, L. W. Facilitating Rapid Social Change in Africa. In A. Rivkin, *Nations by Design*. Garden City, N.Y.: Doubleday, 1967. Pp. 332–386.

CLAGETT G. SMITH

A Comparative Analysis of Some Conditions and Consequences of Intra-Organizational Conflict

With the recognition that intergroup conflict is a characteristic phenomenon of organizations and not simply a manifestation of irrationality negating the harmonious functioning of bureaucratic organizations, increasing attention is being devoted to the conditions generating intra-organizational conflict and their management. Despite the growing concern with conflict and its resolution on the international level, little systematic research on this problem has been undertaken in complex organizations. This paper attempts to complement other studies by reporting the results of a comparative analysis of some of the conditions generating intra-organizational conflict in complex organizations and their consequences.

APPROACH

Three limited aspects of the problem of intra-organizational conflict are considered:

1. What are the interpersonal processes underlying, or result-

From Clagett G. Smith, "A Comparative Analysis of Some Conditions and Consequences of Intra-Organizational Conflict," *Administrative Science Quarterly 10*, 1966, 504–529.

ing in conflict between members occupying different levels in the organizational hierarchy?

2. What are the social-structural determinants of such interpersonal processes?

3. What are some of the organizational mechanisms that influence the consequences of interlevel conflict for the effectiveness of an organization?

Thus conceived, a basic premise of the problem is that intra-organizational conflict has its source in the nature of the organization as a social system, in the way it is structured and in the manner in which the component subsystems are interrelated. It is further proposed that the effects of structural variables in generating interlevel conflict are mediated by interpersonal processes. The final premise is that the effect of intra-organizational conflict on organizational functioning will depend partly upon the mechanisms used by the organization to manage or control the conflict.

For formulating specific hypotheses, some interpersonal processes underlying conflict suggested in the literature are reviewed, together with their accompanying structural determinants; then some of the factors conditioning the effects of intergroup conflict are considered. The specific focus will be limited to interlevel conflict; i.e., conflict involving lower participants (the rank and file) and those higher in the organizational hierarchy.

Determinants of Intra-Organizational Conflict

Intergroup conflict in organizations has been attributed to (1) problems of communication between the parties involved, (2) differences in basic interests and goals, and (3) a lack of shared perceptions and attitudes among members at different echelons.

Communication Hypothesis. The first approach concentrates upon the barriers to adequate communication between echelons. If the information given is sufficient quantitatively and qualitatively, effective and acceptable decisions can be made, and the required coordination can be achieved through the development of common programs and feed-back processes. Such decisions and concerted action would mitigate against the development of any high degree of conflict.[1]

According to this familiar hypothesis, achieving adequate interlevel communication is a problem inherent in large complex organizations.[2] Organizational size inevitably gives rise to specialization and a proliferation of organizational roles. Because of this, increasing reliance is placed upon supervisory roles and the supporting staff functions to achieve the necessary coordination.[3] Achieving coordination in this manner has the effect of placing further impediments to the flow of information in the organization.

Conflict of Interest Hypothesis. This explanation views conflict as stemming essentially from basic differences of interests between participants occupying different positions in the organizational hierarchy. Katz emphasizes that conflict arises not simply from "misunderstandings," but from differences among subgroups who are in functional competition with one another, rationally pursuing different goals and struggling for limited organizational rewards.[4] Such differences are viewed as inherent in a hierarchical organization. The increase in supervisory or leadership roles, together with the accompanying differentiation of authority, lead to increased centralized control. As a consequence of the disproportionate representation of the interests of

[1]For a review of the communications approach employed in the study of complex organizations, see summaries by Clagett G. Smith and Michael A. Brown, Communication Structure and Control Structure in a Voluntary Association, *Sociometry*, 27 (1964 A), 449–468; and Jay M. Jackson, "The Organization and Its Communication Problems" (Paper presented at the seventh annual meeting of the Society of Public Health Educators, Atlantic City, N.J., Nov., 1956).

[2]For an examination of the effects of size on communication processes, see Bernard P. Indik, Some Effects of Organizational Size on Member Attitudes and Behavior, *Human Relations*, 16 (1963), 369–384.

[3]See for example Victor A. Thompson, Hierarchy, Specialization, and Organizational Conflict, *Administrative Science Quarterly*, 5 (1961), 485–521.

[4]Daniel Katz, "Approaches to Managing Conflict," in Robert L. Kahn and Elsie Boulding (eds.), *Power and Conflict in Organizations* (New York: Basic Books, 1964), ch. vii, pp. 105–114.

the leaders, such centralized control has the effect of displacing organizational goals, so that they are even less of a reflection of the interest of those lower in the hierarchy. Moreover, as Thompson observes,[5] hierarchical organization increases the disparity between authority, technical competence, and share in the rewards of the organization. As a result, most of the participants become less committed to the organization and fail to accept the goals of the organization.

CONSENSUS HYPOTHESIS. This approach interprets intra-organizational conflict as stemming essentially from a lack of shared perceptions and attitudes among members at different echelons.[6] In this view, member consensus arises primarily through processes of cohesiveness and participation in the group or organization. Participation, particularly when communication channels are adequate, permits members to ascertain the norms of the organization or other echelons, as well as facilitating their enforcement. Under conditions of high cohesiveness, members would be motivated to accept influence attempts and adhere to normative prescriptions. A variant of this view also would highlight the importance of shared perceptions and attitudes in the prevention of conflict, but would stress the importance of "pre-programming" of consensus through selection for organizational roles, career perspectives, or other latent roles.[7]

Although there is some empirical and conceptual support for each of these approaches, no attempt has been made to assess their tenability by comparative analysis of different types of organizations. As Smith and Brown note, different types of organizations face different system problems, whether these

[5]Thompson, *op. cit.*

[6]For a more complete discussion of this viewpoint with particular reference to organizational control, see Clagett G. Smith and Oguz Ari, Organizational Control Structure and Member Consensus, *American Journal of Sociology*, 69 (1964), 623–638.

[7]James D. Thompson has presented a discussion of some of the mechanisms used in different organizations to build in consensus through selection procedures; cf., Organizational Management of Conflict, *Administrative Science Quarterly*, 4 (1960), 389–409.

involve pursuing objectives efficiently, achieving member involvement in the organization, integrating the organization into the institutions of the larger social system, or achieving coordination with the environment.[8] Consequently, the relationships to be expected in different organizations may not be simple or invariant. Furthermore, identification, consensus, and interlevel communication may not interact in a simple additive fashion in the generation of organizational conflict. For example, Thompson and Tuden observe that the type and degree of consensus in organizations will dictate different optimal strategies of decision making, such as a reliance on facts or compromise. In turn such strategies will condition the level of cooperation or conflict.[9] Then whether such decision processes actually occur will depend upon existing practices for communication in the organization. Moreover, in the light of Newcomb's discussion of balance theory,[10] the effect of consensus in the prevention of interlevel conflict may be expected to vary depending upon the nature and level of commitment of organization members.

Consequences of Intra-Organizational Conflict

Two aspects of this phase of the problem are considered: (1) the consequences of intra-organizational conflict for achieving organizational objectives; (2) the processes alleviating or intensifying such consequences. Intra-organizational conflict is not considered as invariably having dysfunctional consequences for the performance of an organization. Although conflict may in some instances be so intense as to destroy the organization, in other instances, it may stimulate creative problem-solving and innova-

[8]Clagett G. Smith and Michael A. Brown, "A Comparative Analysis of Factors in Organizational Control" (Unpublished report, Institute for Social Research, The University of Michigan, 1964 B).

[9]James D. Thompson and Arthur Tuden, "Strategies and Processes in Organizational Decision," in *Comparative Studies of Administration* (Pittsburgh, Pa.: University of Pittsburgh Administrative Science Center, 1959).

[10]Theodore M. Newcomb, "Individual Systems of Orientation," in S. Koch (ed.), *A Study of Systematic Resources* (Washington, D.C.: American Psychological Association and National Science Foundation, 1961).

tion.[11] This view is consistent with that of Litwak, who states that the traditional bureaucratic organization can tolerate very little conflict, the human-relations organization somewhat more, whereas the professional organizations are structured to permit a great deal of conflict.[12] The organizations included in the present analysis represent a range along this continuum.

Equally important, it is assumed that the consequences of intraorganizational conflict for the functioning of an organization will depend to a large extent upon the processes employed to control or manage the conflict. As Katz observes,[13] the strategies utilized in organizations for dealing with various types of conflict range from those which simply attempt to make the system work, to those which introduce additional machinery for conflict adjudication, to those involving restructuring the organization to reduce built-in conflict. A few of these strategies are examined in the present analysis: (1) the reliance upon general bureaucratic rules, as a means of "making the system work"; (2) leadership practices of planning, coordinating, and providing supportive functions as a way of either preventing conflict or adjudicating it once it has arisen; (3) the effects of a system of high mutual influence cross-cutting specialities and hierarchical levels as a means of restructuring an organization to reduce built-in conflict. The relative efficacy of these three processes is assessed in different types of organizations, which, in

[11]The findings of Donald Marquis and his associates on the prediction of scientific performance suggest that when conflict consists of differences in ideas and approaches, in contrast to differences in values and basic motivations, it may have a constructive and stimulating effect; cf. W. M. Evan, R. R. Blain, and G. R. Mackethan, "Four Types of Conflict in Research and Development Performance," in Donald G. Marquis, *Organizational Research Program* (Cambridge, Mass.: Massachusetts Institute of Technology, Dec. 9, 1963). L. Richard Hoffman has recently attempted to specify conceptually the conditions under which such differences will lead to problem solving and creative solutions; cf. Conditions for Creative Problem Solving, *Journal of Psychology*, 52 (1961), 429–444.

[12]Eugene Litwak, Models of Bureaucracy Which Permit Conflict, *American Journal of Sociology*, 67 (1961), 177–184.

[13]Katz, *op. cit.*

view of their different system problems, might be expected to stress different mechanisms of conflict resolution.

PROCEDURE

Sample of Organizations and Source of Data

In a test of the alternative hypotheses of the determinants and consequences of intra-organizational conflict, a comparative analysis was made in approximately 250 separate organizational units from six organizations.[14] The six organizations include the following:

1. Four locals of an international trade union
2. A sample of 112 local leagues of the League of Women Voters
3. Thirty geographically separate stations within a nationally organized delivery company
4. Thirty-three geographically separate dealerships of an automotive sales organization
5. Forty geographically separate agencies of a nationally organized insurance company
6. Thirty-six branch offices of a national brokerage firm

Several aspects of these organizations lend themselves to a comparative analysis: (1) Each organization has component units with identical purposes, similar technologies, and comparable formal structures. (2) The component units generally operate within similar environments and are located in or near large metropolitan areas. (3) Each organization exhibits significant variation with respect to the general level of intra-organizational conflict. (4) Comparable measures of social structure, interpersonal processes, and organizational performance are available, particularly with respect to the conceptual definitions of these variables.

[14]This comparative analysis complements that of Smith and Brown, *op. cit.*, (1964 B), which is devoted to an assessment of factors underlying organizational control and its effects, and which gives a more extensive description of the general approach utilized, the organizations studied, and the specific operationalization of the measures common to both analyses.

Equally important, the six organizations differ greatly in organizational structure, purposes, and the participants who benefit from the output of the organization. This makes it possible to ascertain the general or limited applicability of the explanations being assessed. For example, the unions and the voluntary associations, with their member orientation, contrast sharply with the business organizations, with their emphasis on the efficient pursuit of objectives established by the owners. Consequently, the potential for intra-organizational conflict, as well as the mechanisms employed for managing conflict, can be expected to differ markedly in these two clusters of organizations.

The information about each of these organizations came originally from the organizations and their members as a product of collaborative research with the Survey Research Center of the University of Michigan. The data are taken from the research archives of this research center. The data on organizational performance, as well as on most of the measures of social structure, are based on official organizational records or reports of individual organization members. The data on interpersonal processes are derived from questionnaires administered by Survey Research Center personnel to members of these organizations.

Intra-Organizational Conflict

Conflict was defined as a situation in which the conditions, practices, or goals for the different participants are inherently incompatible. Responses of members of each organization to similar questions ascertained on a five-point scale the amount of conflict and tension between all possible combinations of hierarchical groups within the organizational unit. The amount of conflict between two hierarchical levels in an organizational unit was computed by averaging judgments of respondents about the two levels in question. An index of the general level of intra-organizational conflict was derived by computing for each organizational unit, the sum of the averaged judgments of all possible combinations of hierarchical groups. In the interests of comparability and of limiting the index to a measure of *intra*-organizational conflict alone, a measure of direct conflict between the company and the union was excluded from this computation.

Two reservations must be made. Although the questions were similarly phrased in all organizations, one cannot be entirely sure that respondents in different organizational contexts attributed precisely the same meaning to the question. The data obtained, however, indicate that this is not a serious problem. Moreover, the present preliminary investigation is limited to a concern with conflict as a general phenomenon and does not deal with different varieties of conflict in all their complexity.

Social Structure

Five measures of social structure were developed which were thought to bear either on the generation of interlevel conflict or on its resolution. These included organizational size, complexity or specialization, differentiation, and two measures of organizational control structure. Size was operationalized in terms of the total number of members in each organizational unit. For all organizations, complexity was defined simply as the number of formal positions in the organizational unit. It was determined by summing the total number of formal positions specified in the organizational chart at both the rank-and-file and officer level, thus indicating the degree of specialization or complexity of the role system. Differentiation refers to the development of the officer or supervisory level, and was operationalized in terms of the ratio of actual supervisory or officer personnel (including staff or advisory personnel) to the size of the organizational unit.

Control refers to "any process in which a person (or group, or organization) determines or affects what another person (or group, or organization) will do."[15] Measures of control were based on responses of members in each organization to similar

[15]This definition follows that of Arnold S. Tannenbaum, Control in Organizations: Individual Adjustment and Organizational Performance, *Administrative Science Quarterly*, 7 (1962), 236–257. For a further discussion of this concept, see that of Smith and Ari, *op. cit.*

questions ascertaining (on a five-point scale) the amount of influence that each of several hierarchical groups or persons had upon activity within the organization. The amount of control exercised by each of the hierarchical levels in a given organizational unit was computed by averaging judgments of respondents about each of the levels. Indices defining the pattern of control included the relative distribution of control among hierarchical levels—whether centralized or decentralized—and the total amount of control exercised by all hierarchical levels. Measures of the relative distribution of control were derived by computing for each organizational unit the average of the algebraic differences between the amount of influence reported to be exercised by successive hierarchical levels. A high score would represent high rank-and-file control relative to upper echelons, a low score the converse. The total amount of control was computed for each organizational unit simply by summing the amount of control reported to be exercised by all the various hierarchical levels. Previous research suggests that these indices provide reasonably valid measures of control structure, even though they are subject to some unreliability.[16]

It was expected that conflict between lower participants and those higher in the organizational hierarchy would be most directly related to how closely the goals or subgoals of the organization were oriented toward the rank-and-file members; i.e., represented their interests. For the six organizations, this was measured as shown in Table 1.

Interpersonal Processes

Member attitudes toward the organization, participation in the organization, consensus of organizational members, and in-

[16]See for example, Arnold S. Tannenbaum and Clagett G. Smith, The Effects of Member Influence in an Organization: Phenomenology versus Organizational Structure, *Journal of Abnormal and Social Psychology*, 69 (1964), 401–410; and Jerald Bachman, Clagett G. Smith, and Jonathan A. Slesinger, Control, Performance, and Satisfaction: An Analysis of Structural and Individual Effects, *Journal of Abnormal and Social Psychology* (in press).

TABLE 1 Measures of Member-Oriented Goals

Organization	Measure
Brokerage Firm	Whether policies were oriented toward the account executives or the firm
Insurance Company	Economic gain of the agents relative to the volume of sales
Automotive Sales	Personal gain on the part of the salesmen if the dealership was successful
Delivery Company	Extent to which the company was interested in its employees
Voluntary Association	Extent to which sociability among members was emphasized
Union Locals	Degree to which specific utilitarian goals existed

terlevel communication were thought to have a strong effect on interlevel conflict. These measures of members' attitudes toward their organization were taken as representing identification with or commitment to the organization and its goals and are described in Table 2.

The participation of members in the organization was taken as the degree of time and energy they devoted to organizational activities (Table 2). Consensus was defined as agreement in attitude among organizational members toward the job, the policies and goals of the organization, its manner of operation (including its pattern of control), or other organizationally relevant attitudes. In each organization, questionnaire items were selected which pertained to areas in which differences might be expected to generate friction or conflict among members and ultimately impede concerted activity. After items were selected in terms of this criterion, as well as a statistical one which would rule out the possibility of any ceiling effect, inverse of variances were computed from member responses for each organizational unit in each of the six organizations. The data on the separate items were then averaged to provide measures of general consensus for each organizational unit. The specific items utilized in each organization have been previously described by Smith and Brown.[17]

Measures of interlevel communication considered the amount or adequacy of communication between lower participants and those higher in the organizational hierarchy, and are described in Table 2.[18]

Measures of organizational mechanisms which were thought to have implications for the resolution of interlevel conflict, or for preventing it, included the existence of general rules and types of leadership practices. The other hypothesized mechanism of conflict resolution is the total amount of control resulting from the mutual influence occurring across specialities and hierarchical levels.

In each organization, indices were developed to indicate the degree to which formal rules and procedures were available for carrying out the objectives of the organization, and are described in Table 2. For the present analysis two major leadership functions were developed: an "initiation of structure" function and a "supportive" function. The first was defined as the degree to which the leaders in each organizational unit performed a planning, administrative, or coordinative function. This function was thought to be of primary importance in developing a setting that would encourage cooperative, consistent, interrelated activity. The supportive function pertains to the material or social rewards in response to the followers' needs for achievement or affiliative experiences, needs which might be expected to be substantially frustrated by an overbureaucratized or hierarchical

[17]Smith and Brown, *op. cit.* (1964 B).

[18]The measures of communication thus employed are not strictly comparable in the six organizations, particularly the measure employed in the voluntary association as compared to those used in the business organizations. Such differences should be borne in mind in the ensuing analyses. Under conditions of free and open communication in the voluntary association, however, it was thought that the measure of the amount of communication employed would be highly correlated with its adequacy, if such a measure were available.

TABLE 2 Measures of Interpersonal Processes

Organization	Commitment	Participation
Brokerage Firm	Indices of general satisfaction derived from items which included policies and goals of firm	Member's reports on average number of hours per week
Insurance Company	As in brokerage firm	As in brokerage firm
Automotive Sales	Preference of salesmen to remain in their particular dealerships given the possibility of moving to another	As in brokerage firm
Delivery Company	Level of morale which members judged to exist in their respective stations	This index not available since length of work week constant
Voluntary Association	Index of member loyalty; i.e., the willingness of members to expend additional effort if existence of organization was threatened either by external or by internal circumstances	Number of meetings of various kinds attended and involvement of members in various committees
Union Locals	As in voluntary association	As in voluntary association

form of organization. In each organization, similar indices were derived which reflected the basic aspects of these two functions. The specific operations employed in each organization to define these functions have been described previously.[19]

[19] Smith and Brown, *op. cit.* (1964 B).

TABLE 2 (continued)

Interlevel Communication	Formal Rules and Procedures
Adequacy of knowledge about the officc	Two questions about the importance of rules and regulations and willingness of members to set aside rules in interest of production
Ease of obtaining technical information	The degree to which work procedures are programmed
Adequacy of knowledge about dealerships	Extent to which general rules govern relations among salesmen
Adequacy of knowledge about the job	Inversely indicated by percent of respondents who answered that there were no work standards
Total amount of communication between members and board members	Degree of understanding by members of formal procedures and objectives of the League
Measure of communication not available	Degree of observance of formal democratic procedures

Effectiveness

Following Georgopoulos and Tannenbaum,[20] organizational effectiveness was defined as the extent to which an organization,

[20]Basil Georgopoulos and Arnold S. Tannenbaum, A Study of Organizational Effectiveness, *American Sociological Review, 67* (1961), 177–184.

TABLE 3 Measures of Effectiveness

Organization	Measure
Brokerage Firm	Average standardized performance of office salesmen measured in dollar productivity with the effects of differential individual experience eliminated
Insurance Company	Productivity records provided by company officials indicating their annual volume of business
Automotive Sales	Extent to which actual sales met assigned sales quotas in each dealership
Delivery Company	Objective productivity measures provided by the company
Voluntary Association	Ratings of 29 officers of the national headquarters of the League who evaluated the local leagues they were familiar with in terms of formal objectives established for the local leagues by the national organization
Union Locals	Judgments by original researchers of the union's power vis-à-vis their respective managements

given certain resources and means, achieves its objectives without incapacitating its means and resources, and without placing undue strain on its members. The actual measures of effectiveness employed (see Table 3) while consistent with this definition, varied in the different organizations studied.

ANALYSIS AND RESULTS

The hypotheses to be tested in this paper involve essentially hypothesizing relationships among an independent variable, one or more intervening or mediating variables or processes, and a dependent variable, the latter in turn serving as an independent variable in another set of processes. In order to test the hypotheses in this manner, a correlational procedure was adopted, which was originally suggested by Simon,[21] and is illustrated in

[21]Herbert A. Simon, *Models of Man* (New York: Wiley, 1957).

the work of Indik.[22] The procedure is illustrated in the figures below Tables 4 through 7. The explanation is taken as valid if all the variables are significantly related in the manner specified in the figures. The assumption of mediating variables is particularly critical for the validity of the hypotheses. A variable which is related both to the measures of the independent variable and the dependent variable is taken as representing a mediating or intervening variable. A variable which is related to the independent variable but not to the dependent variable is taken as representing one which conditions the effects of the independent variable. Strictly speaking, this technique does not by itself permit conclusions about causality with respect to the place of a variable in a given chain of events. If the relationship obtained is consistent with the *a priori* conceptual explanation, it affords us partial confidence in the type of relationship obtained, but the conclusion must be buttressed by additional (longitudinal) analyses and strong theory.

Determinants of Intra-Organizational Conflict

Table 4 presents the basic results bearing on the tenability of the relationships expected in terms of the three hypotheses. The relationships obtained in terms of Explanation 1, the communication hypothesis, are presented in Table 5. Table 6 summarizes the relationships obtained in terms of Explanation 2, the conflict of interests hypothesis. Table 7 summarizes the relationships obtained in terms of Explanation 3, the consensus hypothesis. Table 4 summarizes the intercorrelations among identification, consensus, and interlevel communication. This allows us to compare their respective contribution to the level of intra-organizational conflict in the organizations studied.

COMMUNICATION HYPOTHESIS. This hypothesis on the importance of adequate interlevel communication in the prevention of conflict seems more appropriate to the business organizations than to the union or the voluntary association. In Table 4 it can be seen that especially in the delivery organization ($r_6 = -0.72$)

[22]Indik, *op. cit.*

TABLE 4 Determinants of Intra-Organizational Conflict: Comparison of Hypotheses

Variables Correlated	Hypothesis	Union Locals	Voluntary Association	Delivery Company	Automotive Sales	Insurance Company	Brokerage Firm
r_1 identification; member consensus	+	1.00**	0.53**	0.42**	0.53**	0.29**	0.43*
r_2 identification; interlevel communication	+	NA	0.38**	0.63**	0.38**	0.29**	0.36*
r_3 identification; organizational conflict	–	0.80*	0.07	–0.76**	–0.22	–0.20	–0.29*
r_4 member consensus; interlevel communication	+	NA	0.31**	0.63**	0.38**	0.20	0.16
r_5 member consensus; organizational conflict	–	0.80*	–0.03	–0.57**	–0.20	–0.49**	–0.18
r_6 interlevel communication; organizational conflict	–	NA	–0.09	–0.72**	0.09	–0.44**	–0.10

NA missing data
*significant at the 0.10 level of confidence
**significant at the 0.05 level of confidence or greater

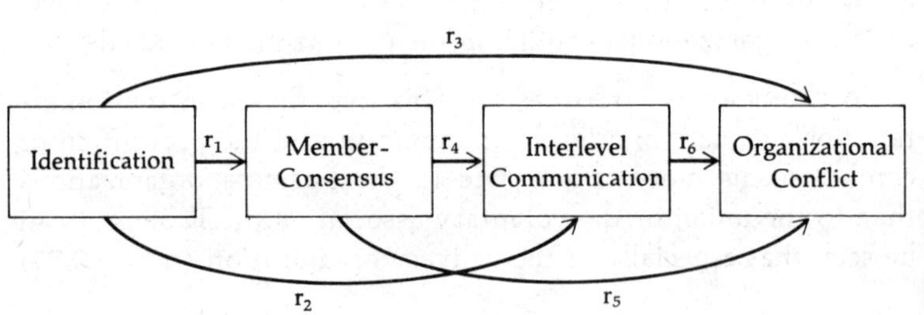

TABLE 5 Determinants of Intra-Organizational Conflict: Communication Hypothesis

Variables Correlated	Hypothesis	Union Locals	Voluntary Association	Delivery Company	Automotive Sales	Insurance Company	Brokerage Firm
r_1 size; interlevel communication	–	NA	–0.51**	–0.26*	–0.26*	0.30**	–0.07
r_2 size; complexity	+	1.00**	NA	0.84**	0.66**	0.62**	NA
r_3 size; differentiation	+	–0.15	0.13	0.39**	–0.36**	–0.30**	0.31**
r_4 complexity; differentiation	+	–0.15	NA	0.57**	0.13	0.39**	NA
r_5 complexity; interlevel communication	–	NA	NA	–0.19	–0.05	0.51**	NA
r_6 differentiation; interlevel communication	–	NA	0.07	–0.23**	0.43**	0.35**	–0.06

NA missing data
*significant at the 0.10 level of confidence
**significant at the 0.05 level of confidence or greater

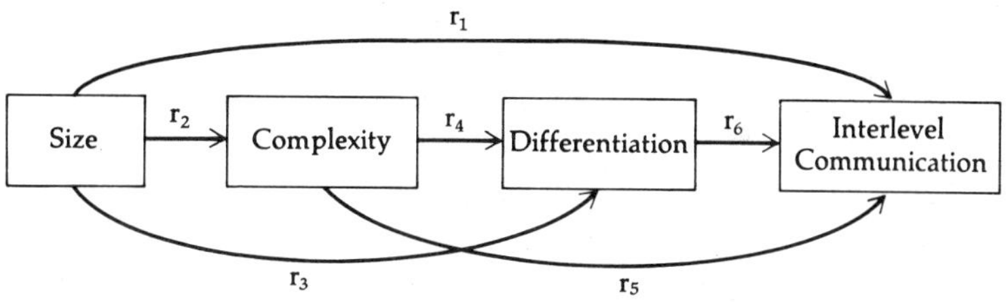

and in the insurance company ($r_6 = -0.44$), the predicted correlations between the measures of interlevel communication and intraorganizational conflict are significantly substantiated. The small number of significant relationships, however, temper any general conclusion, and indicate that, for the organizations in general, poor communication and lack of understanding between members occupying different positions in the hierarchy are not in themselves inevitably a major source of interlevel conflict.

TABLE 6 Determinants of Intra-Organizational Conflict: Conflict of Interest Hypothesi

Variables Correlated	Hypoth-esis	Union Locals	Volun-tary Asso-ciation	Deliv-ery Com-pany	Auto-motive Sales	Insur-ance Com-pany	Bro-kerag Firm
r_1 differentiation; identification	–	0.15	0.03	–0.42**	0.14	0.38**	–0.05
r_2 differentiation; hierachical control	+	0.95**	–0.23**	–0.11	–0.15	0.45**	–0.12
r_3 differentiation; member-oriented goals	–	0.35	0.08	–0.33**	0.05	–0.05	0.37
r_4 hierarchical control; member-oriented goals	–	0.25	–0.28**	–0.35**	–0.31**	0.06	–0.3[illegible]
r_5 hierarchical control; identification	–	–0.40	–0.25**	–0.05	0.25	0.06	0.0[illegible]
r_6 member-oriented goals; identification	+	0.65	0.36**	0.63**	0.37**	0.34**	0.1[illegible]

NA missing data
*significant at the 0.10 level of confidence
**significant at the 0.05 level of confidence or greater

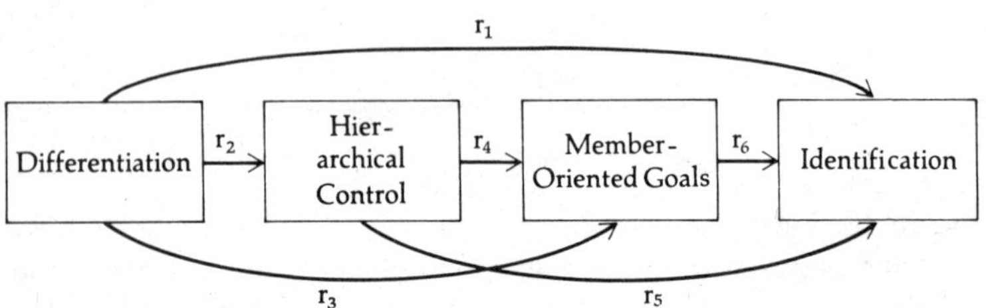

These results seem partially explainable in terms of the relationships found with respect to the structural factors associated with the adequacy of communications, as summarized in Table 5. Although size is accompanied by an increased complexity of roles, in most cases complexity does not lead to an increased differentiation of the leadership or to poor interlevel communication. Furthermore, a relatively high ratio of leadership roles, as indicated by differentiation, does not generally lower the adequacy of communication between rank-and-file members and officers; in fact in the automotive sales organization and the insurance company it facilitates interlevel communication. Although large size does have some of the effects predicted by this hypothesis, size does not appear to affect communications to the degree that would by itself lead to serious conflict between echelons.

CONFLICT OF INTEREST HYPOTHESIS. This hypothesis also receives partial confirmation, as indicated by the correlations between the measures of identification and intra-organizational conflict (see Table 4). Again, this hypothesis seems more appropriate to the business organizations than to the union or the voluntary association. It is particularly in the brokerage firm ($r_3 = -0.29$) and in the delivery organization ($r_3 = -0.76$) that significant correlations emerge. By contrast, the predicted relationships are not obtained in the voluntary association or in the union; in fact, in the union, high loyalty among the members is accompanied by heightened conflict between members and officers ($r_3 = 0.80$). It is also evident in Table 6 that although differentiated structure does not necessarily lead to hierarchical or centralized control, centralized control is generally accompanied by organizational goals which do not reflect the interests of the rank and file. In all six of the organizations, this is associated with lower identification with the organization, but as the results above indicate, lack of identification is related to organizational conflict only in the business organizations.

CONSENSUS HYPOTHESIS. This hypothesis also seems tenable, as indicated by the correlations between the measures of consensus and interlevel conflict summarized in Table 4. Here too, the hypothesis seems particularly appropriate to the business organizations and receives significant support in the delivery organization ($r_5 = -0.57$) and in the insurance company ($r_5 = -0.49$). From the structural correlations of consensus in

TABLE 7 Determinants of Intra-Organizational Conflict: Consensus Hypothesis

	Variables Correlated	Hypothesis	Union Locals	Voluntary Association	Delivery Company	Automotive Sales	Insurance Company	Brokerage Firm
r_4	identification; participation	+	0.80*	0.56**	NA	0.27	0.13	0.12
r_5	identification; member consensus	+	1.00**	0.53**	0.42**	0.53**	0.29**	0.43*
r_6	participation; member consensus	+	0.80*	0.35**	NA	0.23	0.19	0.33

NA missing data

*significant at the 0.10 level of confidence.

**significant at the 0.05 level of confidence or greater.

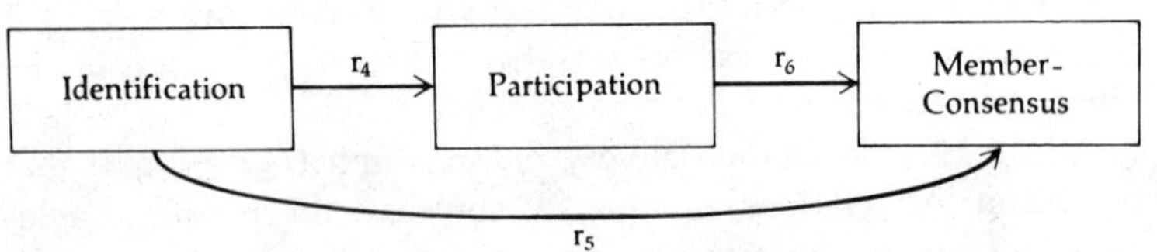

Table 7, it is evident that identification with the organization is strongly associated with a high level of member consensus in all six of the organizations. Frequency of participation in the activities of the organization does not, however, appear to be an important condition mediating this relationship. Rather, consensus appears to have a motivational basis as indicated by the significant correlations between the measures of identification and member consensus obtained in all six organizations. Although lack of shared perception and attitudes may have the general effect of impeding coordination, it does not seem sufficient to bring about actual conflict in the union or the voluntary association. In fact, member consensus operates to increase the degree of interlevel conflict in the union ($r_5 = 0.80$).

Discussion of Results

Taken together, the general pattern of results indicates that each hypothesis is more appropriate to the business organizations than to the union or the voluntary association. These findings are not unexpected. As Litwak notes,[23] the potential for conflict tends to be greater in centralized, bureaucratic organizations. Furthermore, as a consequence of the limited material or "utilitarian" type of compliance in these organizations,[24] any condition which further decreases the commitment of members (or increases their alienation), or makes for disagreements in perceptions and attitudes (both reflecting unfavorable rewards or returns) is more likely to result in conflict in these organizations.

It is not entirely clear why the generally positive findings are stronger in the delivery company and insurance company than in the brokerage firm, and are very slight in the automobile dealerships. Perhaps goals are more operational or the tasks are more highly interdependent and require more concerted activity in the delivery and insurance companies; this seems to be particularly the case in the delivery organization. If the hypothesis of March and Simon[25] is valid, there should be a greater need for joint decision making; and organizational strains arising from a complex, differentiated role structure and centralized control are more likely to give rise to problems in interpersonal relations. In short, under conditions of a heavily structured organization where there is need for joint decision making, the possibility of conflict is greater. Another possibility is that competition may be less exclusively regulated by bureaucratic mechanisms in the brokerage firm and even less regulated in the automobile dealerships. In the dealerships, competition may be controlled or regulated by informal means, so that it does not develop into actual conflict. In effect, there may be more flexible means for dealing with problems of communications, and differences in perceptions, attitudes, and interests. But it should be emphasized that in all the business organizations the relation-

[23]Litwak, *op. cit.*

[24]This follows the postulate presented by Amitai Etzioni, *A Comparative Analysis of Complex Organizations* (New York: The Free Press, 1961).

[25]James G. March and Herbert A. Simon, *Organizations* (New York: Wiley, 1958), ch. v.

ships are generally in the expected direction. The variations in the strength of the relationships for the different business organizations may simply reflect statistical "noise" or lack of strict comparability of the measures.

There is a notable lack of support for the three hypotheses in the voluntary association and the union; in fact, the evidence is negative for the union. These findings are also not unexpected. These member-oriented organizations are designed to promote the shared values and goals of the members; consequently there are no basic differences of interests between the rank-and-file members and the officers, even though this condition may develop in other types of trade unions or voluntary associations. Furthermore, the union and voluntary association examined are structured to facilitate majority rule, freedom of discussion and dissent, and joint decision making; consequently, interpersonal problems generated by an over-structured, bureaucratic organization are less apt to arise. If anything, high identification with the organization and consensus among members tends to increase intra-organizational conflict in the union (r_3, $r_5 = 0.80$). In contrast to the voluntary association, these union locals have predominantly bread-and-butter goals and the rank and file have a utilitarian orientation. It is not surprising then that, under conditions of high identification and basic consensus, members' actions should result in conflict that may reflect disagreements as to the *means* of actualizing their interests, or dissension that is encouraged by the officers and the executive committee. Such disagreements and dissension of a self-interested nature are likely to be minimized or more formally regulated in the voluntary association.

Consequences of Intra-Organizational Conflict

Table 8 presents some findings on the consequences and management of intra-organizational conflict. This table summarizes the correlations between general rules, initiation of structure, supportiveness, and the total amount of control and organizational conflict and organizational effectiveness. The relationships between the independent variable of intra-organizational conflict and these four mediating variables are assumed to operate in both directions; that is, these variables are assumed to operate either to prevent conflict or to reduce its consequences for the effectiveness of the organization. The findings are striking in indicating that intra-organizational conflict does not inevitably have negative consequences for the effectiveness of an organization. As expected, the measure of interlevel conflict is negatively related to performance in three of the four business organizations: $r_1 = -0.55$ in the delivery company; $r_1 = -0.16$ in the sales organization; $r_1 = -0.25$ in the insurance company. This finding is again consistent with the contention of Litwak,[26] that if conflict arises in the traditional bureaucratic organization, it is likely to impede the coordinated pursuit of objectives. And it is particularly the organizations that have a complex, differentiated structure with control centralized in the upper echelons (the delivery company and the insurance company) that conflict has the most significant consequences. As was also seen in Table 4, conflict in these organizations is accompanied by low identification on the part of members and lack of shared perceptions and attitudes. Under these conditions, conflict between echelons has its most detrimental effects.

By contrast, intra-organizational conflict is positively associated with effectiveness in the union ($r_1 = 0.80$) and in the voluntary association ($r_1 = 0.22$). With the basic agreement in interests and attitudes, and high loyalty in these member-oriented organizations, interlevel conflict has constructive consequences for organizational performance. Instead of a bitter struggle for limited rewards by interest groups pursuing different goals, conflict in these organizations probably reflects discussion, dissent, and a conflict over means rather than ends. This is the type of conflict that the formal machinery of these organizations strives to promote, and that increases the effectiveness of these organizations.

It was further proposed that the consequences of intra-organizational conflict for the functioning of an organization would

[26]Litwak, *op. cit.*

TABLE 8 Consequences of Intra-Organizational Conflict

Variables Correlated	Hypothesis	Union Locals	Voluntary Association	Delivery Company	Automotive Sales	Insurance Company	Brokerage Film
r_1 intra-organizational conflict; organizational effectiveness	–	0.80*	0.22**	–0.55**	–0.16	–0.25**	0.19
r_2 intra-organizational conflict; general rules	–	0.00	0.15	–0.12	0.06	–0.14	–0.28**
r_3 intra-organizational conflict; initiation of structure	–	0.00	–0.09	–0.61**	0.02	–0.37**	–0.17
r_4 intra-organizational conflict; supportiveness	–	0.00	–0.15**	–0.64**	0.12	–0.70**	–0.32**
r_5 intra-organizational conflict; total amount of control	–	0.80*	0.03	–0.68**	–0.29**	–0.46**	–0.22
r_6 general rules; organizational effectiveness	+	0.40	0.10	–0.10	–0.03	0.02	–0.14
r_7 initiation of structure; organizational effectiveness	+	0.40	0.15**	0.34**	–0.29**	0.59**	0.34**

r_8 supportiveness; organizational effectiveness	+	0.40	0.12	0.44**	0.10	0.43**	0.28**
r_9 total amount of control; organizational effectiveness	+	1.00**	0.18**	0.46**	0.11	0.49**	0.30**

*significant at the 0.10 level of confidence
**significant at the 0.05 level of confidence or greater

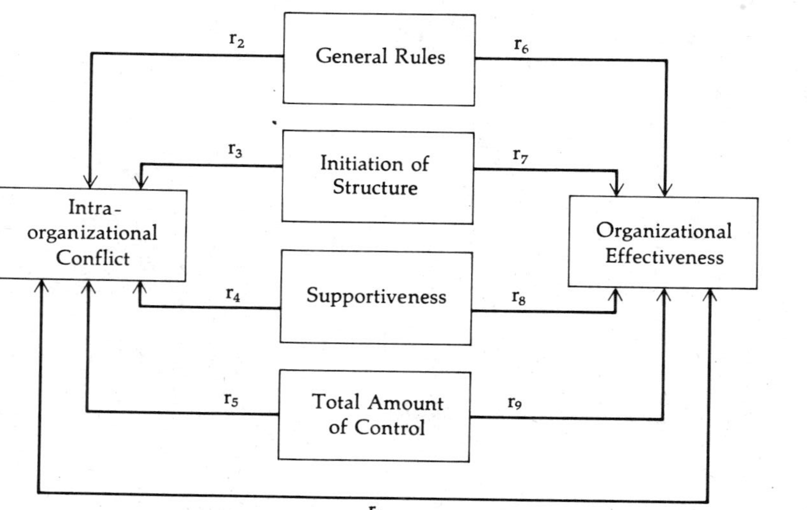

depend upon the techniques for managing the conflict. As seen from the data in Table 8, general bureaucratic rules alone have little relevance in either preventing or managing interlevel conflict (with the exception of the brokerage firm). This may mean that simply applying general rules to resolve conflict; i.e., attempting to make the system work better, has little effect in solving basic problems of communication, consensus, or conflicting interests, particularly when the rules are imposed by groups at the top of the hierarchy.

On the other hand, effective leadership seems to be an important variable in the prevention or resolution of conflict. Advanced planning and coordination, as indicated by the index of initiation of structure, appear to be important in some of the organizations, specifically, in the delivery organization ($r_3 = -0.61$) and the insurance company ($r_3 = -0.37$), in managing conflict generated by an over-bureaucratized form of organization. In these organizations, this leadership practice probably introduces flexibility and direction, so that interlevel conflict is either controlled in advance or mediated once it has arisen.

More important, supportiveness on the part of the leaders appears to have a more general applicability in managing conflict; significant negative relationships between the measures of this function and intra-organizational conflict occur in four of the six organizations examined. By providing practical or social support, the leadership may operate as a compensatory mechanism to offset problems of communication, organizational commitment, or differences of interests generated by a hierarchical form of organization. In effect, there are actually fewer differences in status, the technical competence of members of lower echelons is utilized more, and the gap between the unequal rewards accruing to the members and the leaders is bridged to some extent This interpretation is particularly tenable in three of the four hierarchically organized business organizations, where the relationships are most definitive.

If the results suggest factors generating intra-organizational conflict that are ultimately inherent in large, hierarchical organization, they also indicate a way of restructuring the organization to reduce built-in conflicts. A pattern of high mutual influence among organizational members that crosses hierarchical levels and specialities may prevent destructive conflict, or it may help manage it once it has arisen—as indicated in three of the four business organizations—or stimulate constructive conflict—as in the union. This pattern of control may be effective partly because of better communications and interpersonal relationships, allowing a more flexible way of resolving conflicts. From earlier research,[27] this pattern of reciprocal influence is also likely to facilitate the development of a broader range of shared perceptions and attitudes among organizational members. Probably of most significance, the expansion in the control exercised by those lower in the hierarchy tends to counteract the consequences of hierarchical organization and serves to equalize, to some extent, the differences in status, authority, and organizational rewards which appear to be significant in the development of conflict in organizations.

The efficacy of this pattern of control in the prevention or management of conflict also obtains under conditions where such mutual influence complements the hierarchical form of organization. If carried to the extreme where there is no centralized direction, it might create new problems of communications, decision making, and coordination. As Zald's study suggests,[28] a system of shared influence among the parties can operate to intensify the level of conflict, particularly where there is a lack of agreement over ultimate goals and values to be pursued, or when the "game" is actually "zero-sum" in nature.

SUMMARY AND CONCLUSIONS

This study has presented a comparative analysis of some determinants and consequences of intra-organizational conflict in

[27]See Arnold S. Tannenbaum, Control Structure and Union Functions, *American Journal of Sociology*, 61 (1956), 536–545; Smith and Ari, *op. cit.*; and Smith and Brown, *op. cit.* (1964 B).

[28]Mayer N. Zald, Power Balance and Staff Conflict in Correctional Institutions, *Administrative Science Quarterly*, 7 (1962), 22–49.

complex organizations. A test of three hypotheses about the structural and interpersonal processes generating intra-organizational conflict indicates that each is valid to some extent, but none completely represents the complexities of the relationships. Instead, the factors or combination of factors significant in the development of serious interlevel conflict depends upon the type of organization examined; some organizations, such as the business organizations, are more conflict-prone than others. Furthermore intra-organizational conflict does not inevitably have negative consequences for the performance of an organization. In certain types of organizations, as in the union and voluntary association, intra-organizational conflict may have constructive effects. Also, the consequences of intra-organizational conflict for the functioning of an organization seem to be contingent upon the techniques employed to manage the conflict. The findings suggest that two such techniques may be important: certain techniques of supportive leadership, and a system of high mutual influence cross-cutting specialities and organizational echelons. They seem to provide counter-balances to the strains induced by hierarchical organization. Although this study has been limited to certain aspects of the problem of intra-organizational conflict, and consequently has underemphasized other aspects, it is hoped that the findings will provide hypotheses for more extensive comparative analyses.

PART V
Societal Conflict

No topic has generated more popular concern than conflict on the societal level. Since December 1, 1955, when Mrs. Rosa Parks refused to give up her seat on a Montgomery, Alabama bus, "Middle America" has been made aware of minorities' revolt and the peace movement.[1] Blacks, Chicanos, women, and the peace movement have all employed conflict tactics to force change on society.

Daniel Katz in "Group Process and Social Integration: A System Analysis of Two Movements of Social Protest" (1966 Kurt Lewin Memorial Award Address), examines the civil rights movement, as extending preexisting trends and the protests against the war in Vietnam, as opposing preexisting trends. Other views of change in our social system have been presented by Raymond Mack,[2] Kenneth Boulding,[3] and Amitai Etzioni.[4]

The two remaining selections deal with other aspects of social up-

[1]See Louis E. Lomax, *The Negro Revolt*, New York, New American Library, 1963.

[2]Raymond W. Mack, "The Components of Social Conflict," *Social Problems 12*, 1965, 388–397.

[3]Kenneth E. Boulding, "Towards a Theory of Protest," *Etc.: A Review of General Semantics 24*, 1967, 49–58, reprinted from the October, 1965 issue of *Bulletin of the Atomic Scientists*.

[4]Amitai Etzioni, "Toward a Theory of Guided Societal Change," *Social Casework 49*, 1968, 335–338.

heaval. Joseph S. Himes in his essay "The Functions of Racial Conflict" asserts that racial strife has facilitated the group and individual identity of the black American. In his essay, "Ghetto Riots and Others: The Faces of Civil Disorder in 1967," Louis C. Goldberg provides an analysis of 23 civil disturbances in the summer of 1967, giving particular attention to those in Newark and Detroit.[5]

These selections were written in the 1960s, and it is interesting to compare the rapid evolution of language and events over this period of time: use of the word "Negro" rather than "black"; reference to Martin Luther King in the present tense; the "escalation" phase of the Vietnam conflict as the focus of liberal attack. The speed and intensity of change is reinforced in reading these selections.

[5]For additional information on the Newark and Detroit riots see Thomas A. Johnson, "Newark's Summer, 1967," *Crisis* 74, 1967, 371–380, Sheldon J. Lachman and Thomas F. Waters, "Psychosocial Profile of Riot Arrestees," *Psychological Reports* 24, 1969, 171–181, and Donald I. Warren, "Suburban Isolation and Race Tension: The Detroit Case," *Social Problems* 17, 1969–1970, 324–339.

DANIEL KATZ

Group Process and Social Integration: A System Analysis of Two Movements of Social Protest

Social psychology as the area which lies between individual psychology and the social sciences has in the past been polarized toward psychology. The focus has been upon an understanding of the individual as he functions in social settings with limited investigation of those social settings. The study of small groups has pushed beyond this framework but not very far. Group process is generally examined as personal interaction divorced from social context. In fact, the major advances in social psychology since its gradual emergence as a discipline of its own in the late twenties and early thirties have been the growth of an experimental or laboratory social psychology and the accumulation of findings about the nature of small groups. Both types of contributions have been of such substantial character that social psychologists are no longer marginal men in departments of psychology. Indeed the introductory text in psychology which does not utilize fairly heavily the findings of social psychological research is the exception. And the success of these approaches will reinforce continued work along similar lines with potentially valuable outcomes. Nonetheless, it is my thesis that the

From Daniel Katz, "Group Process and Social Integration: A System Analysis of Two Movements of Social Protest" (Kurt Lewin Memorial Award Address—1966), *The Journal of Social Issues 23*, 1967, 3–22.

significant area for the social psychology of the future lies not in a continuation of these main streams of research directed at the individual and small group isolated from social context. Rather, it lies in a social psychological analysis of social structure and the study of societal process. This is the area which led to the creation of SPSSI [the Society for the Psychological Study of Social Issues, Box 1248, Ann Arbor, Mich. 48106] when psychologists became concerned with economic justice, industrial conflict, social cleavages based upon economic and racial differentials and war and peace. And it was to these problems which Kenneth Clark (1965) addressed himself in a discussion of social power just a year ago in his Lewin Memorial talk.

The overriding concern of social psychology with the individual and the small group can be seen in the conventional accounts of its historical development. These accounts trace its origins in the United States to the work of McDougall representing the individual approach of the biological evolutionists and to the work of E. A. Ross reflecting the social interaction doctrines of French sociologists. This is correct but it ignores a persisting though minor stream of influence, namely the theorists concerned with social structure and social change, such as Durkheim, Marx, and Weber. The French sociological contributions of Tarde and LeBon which were the basis of Ross's approach were not as much sociological as applications of concepts of French abnormal psychology to social problems. The true societal doctrines coming from Durkheim and Weber were much slower in affecting social psychology and even today are fragmented in their impact. Thus, we have seen the utilization of such concepts as norms and roles, social stratification, anomie, legitimacy, power, norms of reciprocity, and interdependence—but generally as fairly isolated concepts.

SOCIETAL PROCESS

The social psychology of the future, moreover, can well devote itself to the problems of societal process as well as group process, to the patterning of individuals which make up social structure, as well as to the cognitive structures of the individual. In the larger sense we have won the fight at the small group level. We know a great deal about how individuals are tied into the small group through processes of participation, of sociometric attraction, of mutual social reinforcement, of shared objectives. This has been the thrust of the group dynamics movement for the past twenty-five years. The work of the Tavistock researchers has demonstrated, moreover, that some of the individual processes of participation in a meaningful work cycle hold for the small group as well as for the personality under given conditions (Rice, 1958; Trist, 1963), a finding foreshadowed by the earlier work of Lewis and Franklin (1944) and Horwitz (1954) on the group Zeigarnik and more recently extended to the level of aspiration concept by Zander and Medow (1963). Much of course remains to be done in mopping up operations at the small group level and even more in applying these findings in many appropriate group settings. But there has been little major advance in the work on group process in recent years save for the move toward its use in therapeutic fashion for working through problems of defensive reactions of group members toward one another.

The major problems we face, however, need new approaches, new concepts, and new research. We have too long neglected the nature of social systems and the dynamics of their functioning. We have made little progress in studying the role relationships which constitute social systems and with the relationships of subgroups to the larger societal framework. We have been remiss in applying ourselves to an understanding of social movements and conflicts between organized groups. The general reason given is that these problems belong to the other social sciences. But since social systems exist only as patterns of human behavior, they are an appropriate field of study for social psychologists. Artifacts or products of a society can be studied at a superorganic level, but the actual production of such artifacts in the complex actions of people can be studied at the social psychological level. Our constructs for such a study need to be social system concepts so that we are directed toward the relevant aspects of collective and reciprocal behaviors. The variables to be observed and measured are still psychological. The conceptualizations we use, however, should be such as to guide us to the appropriate interdependent behavior. Otherwise we are likely to employ a direct and misleading equivalent of a group outcome in searching for individual patterns of belief and action. Wars are made in the minds of men but this statement can be deceptive if it equates the declaration or prosecution of a war with the aggressive impulses of the members of the warring nation. The nation is not an aggregate of similarly minded aggressive individuals acting in parallel, but a complex organization of many criss-crossing cycles of social behavior (Allport, 1962).

TWO MOVEMENTS OF SOCIAL PROTEST

Let us look at two movements of social protest in our society as examples of the relevance of social structure and system forces for an understanding of social phenomena—the civil rights movement and the protests against the war in Vietnam. From the conventional approach of individual psychology, they seem very similar. They have both been led by much the same type of people, largely those outside the basic power structure of the society: small groups of student activists, part of the academic and intellectual world, some Church groups, and some members of the Negro community. The power groups of industry and business, organized labor, and organizations representing the professions of law, medicine, and education have not been conspicuously arrayed in support of either of these movements. In addition to the overlapping personnel and overlapping group membership behind the two trends, there has been a similarity in their dedication to values of egalitarianism, humanitarianism, democracy, and nonviolence. They are alike in their appeals to the American public and in their tactics for achieving their objectives.

They have one other major similarity which is more at the

system than at the individual level. They both have the advantage that the values which justify their thrust are part of the value system of the larger society. In other words, they have legitimacy in the broader sense of the term in that they are sanctioned by the accepted ideology of society. The opposition in contrast has had great difficulty in finding a rationale to justify its position. The doctrine of racism furnishes little support for the opposition to civil rights in a political democracy of a multiethnic character recently involved in an all out war against Nazi Germany. Such a racist ideology appeals only to very limited sectors of the society. The legal doctrine of interposition in its absurd legalism was merely a delaying tactic. The plea for nongovernment intervention on issues of civil rights makes little sense in a bureaucratic society committed to legislation as a means of solving problems. In brief, the discriminatory practices of our society had going for them some local laws, much internalized prejudice, and specific economic advantage to certain subgroups, but no ideological legitimacy. In passing, it might be mentioned that there are those who see some danger in the slogan of black power in that it opens an ideological door to the rightists which had been slammed shut in their faces.

In similar fashion the protestors against the Vietnam war had the legitimizing values of the society on their side. Democracy demands the right of self-determination of small as well as large nations. It does not justify the intervention of large powers in small nations merely because of their power. Our societal values are not consistent with the support of a military junta whose leaders fought on the side of the French rather than their own people in expelling colonial rule. Nor do they countenance the killing and wounding of women and children in an undeclared war. The United States, as Kenneth Boulding has commented, has all the advantages in the conflict in economic might, technological strength, military weapons, and fire power—everything in short but legitimacy. This is one reason why American intervention in Vietnam has been so unpopular abroad even among our allies and so unenthusiastically received at home. There is, of course, the ideological justification of combatting communism, but why communism has to be combatted in this particular way has not been clear either to American or to world opinion. The legitimacy for the conflict that does exist is more at the pragmatic level growing out of the dynamics of the conflict itself.

I have distinguished between legitimizing values at the societal level as a system force as against the individual values of the members of a protest movement. Individual values are internalized in the personality. System ideology is the set of values accepted as appropriate general guides for the behavior of members of the system. These values may or may not be internalized by a majority of system members and certainly are not internalized in their entirety. When a social system collapses, its ideology often collapses which would not be true if there were a one-to-one correspondence between personal and system values.

SYSTEM LEVEL DIFFERENCES

Though the civil rights movement and the antiwar cause resemble one another in personnel, in individual motivation, in group tactics, and in the system values utilized, the similarities of the two movements pretty well ends there. Their differences at the system level are great. The civil rights movement is basically consistent with the forces in our societal structure and is moving in the same direction as these forces. The antiwar movement opposes some of the dominant trends in the national system. Though the same individual motivations and sometimes the same individuals are found in the two movements, their progress and their effectiveness are radically different. It is necessary, then, to consider the nature of the social system which affect these outcomes.

American society is basically an organizational, or bureaucratic, technological society in which role systems based upon rules and functional requirements have replaced traditional authority and absolutistic standards. Three characteristics of bureaucratic structure are relevant to our discussion: its growth or maximization dynamic, its conflict-reducing mechanisms to achieve an integrated system and the functional nature of its legitimizing values.

The dynamic of a bureaucratic system, once it is established, is to maximize its input-output ratio of energy to place it in a more powerful position with respect to other systems and to its environment (Yuchtman, 1966). It will ingest resources outside its boundaries, it will seek to control its external environment, it will grow until checked by outside forces (Katz and Kahn, 1966). With all our attempts to control monopolistic growth, our industrial enterprises have grown bigger and bigger. With all out talk about curbing the size of the federal government, its payroll, and its activities, it continues to grow in size and in function. It is much more difficult in a bureaucratic structure to eliminate a subsystem once established than to add two new ones.

The dynamic of maximization is related to the second characteristic of bureaucratic systems, the development of mechanisms for reducing internal conflict. Cleavages within the system impair its effectiveness in competition with other systems. Conflicts about interests, privileges, and ideas are met basically by compromises and mutual concessions, and by not permitting all of the dissident voices representation in decision making. The general pattern for conflict reduction is the narrowing of channels for their expression so that many divergent views are reconciled or silenced at lower levels in the structure. A small unit has to resolve differences among members so that it speaks with one voice in its own subsystem and not with a multitude of opinions. Within the subsystem the unit differences have to be compromised so that the subsystem represents but one position to the higher levels in the structure. This pattern means that many conflicts are handled at lower levels. Though the final position of a large subsystem has the power of the entire subsystem behind it, this position is already a compromise of generalities which has blunted the sharpness of the conflicting interests and factions. The example par excellence of this pattern is the two-party system. By the time the wishes of the many interest and factional groups have been filtered up through the hierarchical structure, the party line is not far from dead center. The many competing groups are not represented directly and formally in the Congress, the top decision-making political body. Many conflicts have thus been compromised and Congress has an easier task of reaching decisions. A multi-party system with proportional representation, on the other hand, gives more adequate representation to divergent interest and ideological factions, but it has the disadvantage of making it more difficult to achieve national unity (Valen and Katz, 1964). The general trend in bureaucratic structures is toward the pattern achieved by the two-party system in getting agreement at various levels so that many sharp conflicts are absorbed along the line.

RESTRICTED COMMUNICATION—A NECESSITY

Ashby (1952) in his brilliant system analysis gives some of the reasons why this is so. Stability of the system would take infinitely long to achieve if all the elements in the system were in full contact and communication. All the variables of all the subsystems would have to be satisfied at once—a highly unlikely event. If, however, communication is restricted among subsystems, or they are temporarily isolated, then each subsystem can achieve its own stability. With restricted communication, success can accumulate from successive trials whereas in the single suprasystem success is all-or-none. An overall system can move toward equilibrium through sufficient connectedness of its subsystems so that the operation of one can activate another and enough separation so that each can reach agreement within itself. Equilibrium can be approached in the system as a whole, but no complex suprasystem would ever have equilibrium in all its subsystems at the same time.

To the general Ashby description of subsystem and suprasystem we should add the concept of hierarchical levels. The need to reach some agreement at each succeeding level further structures and restricts the full interplay of communication and conflicting forces.

One reason why group process is inadequate for the study of

social systems is that it deals with genuine group consensus through group discussion and decision-making. This can only be realistically applied at the very lowest level in social structures, for the moment the decision of the local group is carried by its representatives to a higher level, we are dealing with a political process of compromise and majority rule. At the next higher level, the representatives are no longer free to work through to a full agreement as individuals. They are role representatives of their local groups as well as members of the higher group in the structure. They must take back something to their constituents and hence they bargain and trade and finally reach some compromise rather than the integrated solution of group process. The dynamics differ from small group process and the outcomes differ.

BUREAUCRATIC SYSTEM— A PROCESS OF PROGRESSIVE AGREEMENT

In brief, the bureaucratic system handles conflict by a process of progressive agreement among subunits at each level of the structure. Many dissident voices are lost long before the final decision-making circles are reached. The structure is built to accommodate conflict, to mute its expression and to redefine clashing positions on clear-cut issues as moderate stands on ambiguous generalities.

There are also more direct mechanisms of repression as in the denial of the franchise to certain groups or the use of complex machinery to make difficult the participation of many people even at the local level.

Another device for slowing down change within a bureaucratic system comes from the character of the managerial and administrative roles. These roles are built around procedures for getting things done and not around the analysis of substantive issues. The administrator's major task is to keep things moving, to seek enough compromise to prevent the machinery from breaking down, in short to be an expert on procedure not on content. Thus the head of the poverty program was selected because of his administrative skills not because of his understanding of the poverty problem. In his administrative role the official takes his cues about general policy from those above him in the structure. Basic changes in the system, however, require issue-oriented rather than procedure-oriented managers, i.e. men with genuine knowledge and understanding of the change objectives.

A third characteristic of bureaucratic structures is the functional nature of their legitimizing values. The system is unified not only through devices for handling internal conflict but also through the values which reflect the functional interdependence of the people in the system. These values, moreover, do not represent transcendental principles based upon divine revelation or an absolutistic morality. They have to relate to the functioning of the system to supply both cognitive structure and ideological justification for its activities. The essential justification for the assumption of roles is not that the role itself is morally correct, but that it is necessary for the operation of the system.

The process of building a social structure begins in early socialization and it takes on specification with adult socialization into given social systems. Individuals begin early to learn that family, school and social groupings all have expectations, rewards, and sanctions for many specific roles in which the justification of the required behavior is not necessarily carried by the nature of the activity itself. There is a divorce from the meaning of the activities as desirable in and of themselves, and the goals which they are expected to accomplish. To be a good group member means that the individual accepts his role assignments as part of the rules of the game.

The justification for the assumption of roles lies in the rewards to the individual for being a member of the system. The system values then must be capable of translation into pragmatic programs. This is further emphasized by the technological character of our organizational society in which the criterion is constantly employed: Does it work? Finally, this system has the congruent property of a democratic ideology. Since people are required to assume many roles, since they are to be interchangeable for many purposes save where there is a high degree of specificity for an important role, their essential equality with respect to system demands and opportunities for participation becomes important. To utilize manpower resources effectively implies that surplus meanings of such characteristics as ethnic group membership, sex or hair color are irrelevant. And, as we move away from transcendental and traditional principles as the source of morality, an egalitarian democratic philosophy geared to the privileges and rights of all individuals becomes the common ground for the commitment of all citizens to their society.

THE CIVIL RIGHTS MOVEMENT—EXTENDING PREEXISTING TRENDS

To return, then, to a consideration of the two liberal movements, I would call attention to some of the system forces which have been working to accord a different reception to the civil rights issue than to the antiwar cause. The racial cleavage in our society, deepened by economic stratification, has been under attack by liberals for more than a century. But it was not until World War II that the problem of racial integration was seriously considered in the perspective of national unity. Negroes were needed in defense industry, in governmental services and in the armed forces. It was no accident that some of the first moves toward integration were made in the armed forces and, moreover, in combat units at the front. And at home wartime agencies were directed to give employment to all qualified personnel. Shortly after the war President Truman issued the order authorizing integration throughout the armed forces. The realization grew, moreover, that in a world where the majority of the people were nonwhite and where millions of people in the areas uncommitted in the conflict between the United States and Russia were nonwhite, assigning third-class citizenship to American Negroes was not a wise policy. Nor was it a wise policy in an economy with little need for unskilled labor to deprive citizens of education and training for the economic needs of the nation.

Against this background, the civil rights movement utilized

two other system forces to achieve some of its initial successes. It obtained legitimacy in the narrow sense of legal sanctions by pushing for new interpretations and enforcement of existing laws of the land. The discriminatory practices of generations were clearly inconsistent with the legal basis of our political system. The precedent had been set by President Truman in his executive order making discrimination in the armed services illegal. Mention already has been made of the larger legitimacy of the movement in gearing into the values of a democratic society. The economics of the system in effectively using its manpower was thus not the sole cause of the changes brought about, but when economics, law, and ideology were all on the same side, something was going to give.

Why, then, has the Negro revolution been so slow in achieving its objectives if the changes involved are so consistent with the general trends in the national system? The reason is that in addition forces for change pushing the system to maximizing its character there are also built-in maintenance forces representative of the older equilibrium. There are defenses in depth which slow down the change process. Subsystems with some power of their own operate in any large structure and can be resistant for limited periods to changes initiated in other parts of the system. We had an interesting example of the problem of change and the steady state of a system last semester when Selective Service put into effect the old device of draft deferment based upon standing in college or in national tests. This policy hit those groups with poorest academic preparation the hardest and can nullify the moves to open up channels for the training of Negroes for professional positions.

In other words, the overall system is not a single homogeneous structure. Subsystems exist such that political democracy does not have a corresponding parallel in economic structures with full equality of opportunity. The political system has been more open to change with the greatest advances occurring in this domain with the enfranchisement of Negroes and growing acquisition of equal legal rights. In the economic and social sectors, however, the built-in defenses in depth have been much more resistant to change.

MECHANISMS FOR DEALING WITH INTERNAL CONFLICT

More specifically, however, we need to take account of the mechanisms of a bureaucratic society for dealing with internal conflict. The most common devices are those of compromise and of indirect ways of meeting the conflict. Compromise has been conspicuous as in the gradualism doctrine, in the concessions made by nationwide employers, and in the agreements reached at the community level. The difficulty with the compromise technique is that its outcome is partially dependent upon the power of the bargaining group. This method places a premium upon the mobilization of threat of economic and political sanctions. As the integration movement has mobilized power to exact concessions, it has had considerable success, but progress has not been great. The majority group still has the power of superior numbers, superior resources, and an entrenched position in the social hierarchy. Moreover, if the struggle is confined to mobilization of black power rather than generalized to embrace broad values, it produces repercussions in certain sectors of the white population. Nevertheless, such power mobilization is an important if not the most important means for continuing progress with respect to civil rights.

The common mechanism for reducing conflict is the attenuation of its representation in decision-making centers. In a two-party system the Negroes are limited in their influence to the old AFL technique of rewarding friends and punishing enemies, and generally this has to be done within a single-party structure. The attempt to secure direct representation through a party of their own in Mississippi achieved some purposes but not the avowed objective. The system is so set up as to accommodate minority groups without integrating them. There were no institutional channels through which the civil rights movement could directly affect decision-making circles, apart from the judicial system.

Thus they have taken to the streets and to demonstrations as well as to the use of economic boycotts and voter registration drives. The effectiveness of these tactics has been in part a matter of the power mobilized and in part a matter of making visible to important sectors of the American public the unjustified practices of discrimination.

Another way of damping the fire of an underprivileged group is through the many established blocks to their rise in the various power and prestige structures. Negroes have been successful in law and medicine but more within their own community than within the larger society. They have achieved some breakthroughs in the political system. In the world of finance and industry, however, there has been less progress. They have lacked the training, the resources for commiting themselves to such careers, the social background, and the personal associations necessary to move into the economic sector in leadership roles.

Integration has been achieved at the political level so that great advances have been made in the citizenship rights of voting and equality before the law. Opportunities for schooling have been opened up in law though not always in practice. One would predict in terms of system forces that the greatest progress will continue to be in the political domain with full enfranchisement of all Negro citizens, with equal legal rights, with equal access to public institutions and with increasing numbers of Negroes achieving positions of importance in the political structure. Where discrimination is reinforced by economic stratification, change will be much slower. Relative to past economic standards there will be improvement but relative to the rising standards of the white population, the improvement will not seem significant. The general economic upgrading of the national population has been proceeding rapidly and the person just entering the race may have great difficulty catching up to the accelerated pace.

In brief, then, the civil rights movement has achieved much as it has interacted with other system forces, received their support and helped to give them more adequate definition. It has not revolutionized the social system but has pushed it toward greater consistency. The threatened revolution has been contained within the system.

THE PROTEST MOVEMENT—OPPOSING PREEXISTING TRENDS

The protest movement against the Vietnam war and the peace movement in general have the major difficulty of opposing some of the dynamic trends in the national system. The maximization dynamic is expressed in the extension of national interests and national power. There is the push to utilize our influence and power, for as we are now reminded, we have to assume our responsibilities in the world. Moreover, the major forces which challenge our international position come from the expansion of communism. And the assumption is that it is better to meet this challenge at distant points from our own shores which means protecting weaker nations less capable of resisting than the U.S.

Secretary of State Dean Rusk, has acknowledged our military commitments to 40 nations around the globe. He denied that this represented a policy of *pax Americana* but there are those who interpreted this as diplomatic language. Such language needs to be understood in the context in which it appears. Since World War II we have been engaged in a continuing process of extending our psychological boundaries beyond our geographical borders. Conflict with other expanding systems are bound to occur. These conflicts do not inevitably mean war but the immediate past suggests that we need to do more to take advantage of the degrees of freedom, to seek counter forces in the social situation for the maintenance of world peace.

The facts are that Vietnam is only one instance of the collisions between the U.S. and other nations in Asia. Before Vietnam there was Laos; before Laos, Korea. After South Vietnam, there may be North Vietnam, Laos, Cambodia, Korea, and even China. In addition to our fighting forces in Vietnam, we have military bases in other parts of east Asia. The other day the press reported that we now have 27,000 troops in Thailand and are presently expanding our four military bases there by a new complex costing almost $100,000,000. [Katz was writing in 1966.] Nor does the present conflict seem to be a function of the warlike personalities of our national leaders. Recall that in 1964 the American people chose between two slates of candidates, the trigger-happy Goldwater and his equally belligerent running-mate, Miller, and the consensus-seeking Johnson and the liberal Humphrey. Remember, too, it was supposed to be a choice not an echo. I am contending, then, that the decisions in national leadership roles are in good measure determined by system forces and that the conventional interpretation of these requirements in the Asian situation was an escalation of warlike measures. I am also arguing that such decisions were not inevitable and that there was enough range of interpretation of the situation and of appropriate national policy, for an *unusual* national leadership to have followed a different course. National interests, national prestige, national honor as well as the struggle against communism could have been defined in other ways. Though the dice were loaded, the players could have discarded them.

NATIONAL LEADERS—WHAT DEGREE OF FREEDOM?

The degree of freedom of movement for national leaders is greater at an early stage in international relations. Once, however, the decisions are made to utilize the military power of the nation, then it is extremely difficult at later stages to reverse the policy. At the early stage the problem is one of progressive commitment, i.e., what look like small steps in the beginning become binding decisions for more complete involvement. The decision to furnish aid to an anti-Communist government, the use of American military as advisers rather than as participants, the partial involvement of limited forces, and then greater and greater escalation were not necessarily thought through in advance as the desirable policy. One step led to another. To break out of this pattern of progressive commitment requires unusual qualities of statesmanship at the national level. The present and the preceding three administrations were all involved in this pattern though there are indications that the Kennedy administration, if it had continued, might have been more resourceful in arresting the trend. A statesmanlike leadership would have to rise above some of the relevant central subsystems in the national structure specifically the Department of State, the CIA, the Defense Department, the National Security Council, and the Joint Chiefs of Staff. These subgroupings concerned with problems of national interest, prestige, and power develop narrow conceptions of their goals and the means for achieving them. There are doves as well as hawks in these groups but the system tends to select more hawks than doves and to damp dovelike voices. Moreover, these agencies are already locked into a limited set of strategy alternatives dictated in part by their own responses to the moves of the international opponent and the subsequent reactions of the opposition.

The protest movement against our involvement in Vietnam was not effective in influencing the policy of the Administration as it moved from one critical decision to another. The protestors lacked organized power. The academic community did not speak with a single voice. Moreover, the voices were those of individuals not of organized groups of strength. There were no easily identifiable blocks of voters like Negroes or labor union members to support the movement. The pacifist organizations were courageous but tiny. The members of Congress who furnished the one source of leverage and who gave additional legitimacy to the movement received little support from the mass media. They were not able to contend with the strong executive-legislative combination of forces arrayed against them. Nor was there a peace lobby in Washington to compete with the lobbies representing business and industry interested in defense expenditures.

Once embarked upon the policy of military intervention and limited escalation, the system forces are even stronger in resisting a change toward peaceful alternatives. Even without a formal declaration of war, the use of American armed forces and the resulting casualty lists produce a situation in which the national membership character of the people becomes salient. The nation state becomes more than ever the dominant social structure. The state is the formal organized system to which all other structures are legally subservient. It functions as the final arbiter of decisions within the society when conflicts cannot be resolved at other levels. It has a monopoly on physical force for implementing these decisions.

THE AROUSAL OF NATIONAL ROLES

This is the formal description at the level of political science. What does it mean psychologically? It means that when national roles are aroused they take precedence over any other social role the individual can play as a member of his family, his church, his profession, his work organization, etc. National sovereignty also means that every organized group in the society must function as an arm of the state in times of national emergency if so ordered. This is most obvious when industries are nationalized in wartime but there are less thorough manifestations as when organizations cooperate with the government in not employing citizens whose loyalty is under suspicion. In times of peace, national roles are latent roles so that the average citizen spends most of his time in activities of making a living, being a member of his family, engaging in leisure time activities, etc. Apart from observing laws and voting, he gives little time or thought to his citizenship rights and obligations. The national state and his membership as an American citizen are remote considerations. But when the emergency of possible war or actual international conflict arises, national roles take priority over other roles. The basic institutional pattern that has been built into the members of the society through the socialization process and which has indirectly mediated the relationship of their activities to need satisfaction, now takes over. As a member of the national system the individual must either assume his national roles or leave the system. And there are no places to go save prison or exile.

Even an undeclared war provides the conditions for the arousal of national roles. One aspect of such arousal is the restriction of freedom of movement at all levels in the structure.

Other roles are no longer open choices. And the definition of the national role assumes clearer structure with the decisions of national leaders. These leaders themselves lose freedom of movement. Not only are they committed by their previous decisions in their own eyes, but these decisions have activated expectations throughout the structure which further lock them into a given pattern of behavior. And, as leaders guiding the nation in an international conflict, they are more vulnerable to criticism from their political opponents if they do not play their roles in a militant manner ostensibly supportive of national interest. Freedom of movement is also reduced for groups and individuals with respect to actions and words opposing national policy. People not happy about the war and its escalation now take the position that we should get it over with in some fashion rather than complete withdrawal. The function of public opinion in affecting national policy becomes weak and negligible.

The solution to the war in Asia of a complete withdrawal of our armed forces, though logical, is unrealistic. It neglects not only the dynamics of the arousal of national roles but also the expansionist push of the American power system in Asia. We have established military bases in Asian countries other than Vietnam and have committed ourselves to fighting the spread of communism on the Asian continent. The pattern of commitment is not the same, however, for the administration and for the American people. The objectives of the administration go beyond the successful prosecution of the undeclared war. If it were to be won, or if some favorable peace could be negotiated, the conflict could readily flare up again either in Thailand, Laos, or Cambodia. The American people, however, at the present time would be satisfied with the settlement of the Vietnam war.

Discouraging as the prospects are for a peaceful settlement in Vietnam and for a permanent peace in Asia, there are factors which conceivably can work toward international stability in this part of the world. For one thing, the American people after Korea and after Vietnam may be more reluctant to support further military intervention so far from our shores. Consistent with the interpretation is the fact that the motivational basis for national involvement has seen some change in the development of our bureaucratic society during the past forty years.

SYMBOLIC, NORMATIVE, OR INSTRUMENTAL INVOLVEMENT

Individuals can be tied into a bureaucratic system in one of three ways or some combination of them: symbolic, normative, or instrumental involvement (Katz, 1965). *Symbolic* attachment refers to emotionally held attitudes in which the symbols represent absolute values and have a life of their own. They are not the means to an end but are ends in themselves. Emotional conditioning in childhood to symbols of the nation such as the flag, the national anthem, or national heroes is one basis for symbolic commitment. *Normative* involvement on the other hand does not imply internationalization of the sanctity of given symbols but rather the acceptance of specific legitimate requirements of the system necessary for system membership. Thus one meets the demands of one's role because one wants to stay in the system not because one is emotionally attached to signs representing its abstract values. Finally, *functional* involvement has to do with commitment to the system because its demands are *instrumental* to his needs. The union member may be committed to his union because it is a group means for dealing with his needs. Such a functional attachment is not limited to bread-and-butter matters. It can also be related to his own values which find meaningful realization in group action which advance his beliefs and attitudes. I am thus trying to differentiate between an ideological commitment of a functional character where values get translated into specific programs of action as against symbolic attachment to nonoperational goals. In the Vietnam war the man who enlists because his heart quickens at the sight of the flag shows symbolic commitment. The man who accepts his call to the service primarily because this is the requirement for the American male of certain ages is demonstrating normative commitment. The underprivileged youth who sees in armed service a way of getting an education and technical training is an example of functional commitment. So, too, would be the man who enters the service because he feels that democratic values are threatened by communism in Asia and armed intervention is necessary to prevent a communist takeover.

With the development of a bureaucratic society there has been a relative decline in symbolic commitment to national roles and a rise in normative and functional commitment. The great majority of the men in our armed forces are there not so much because of the considerations of national honor as because they received the notice from their draft boards. Bureaucratic society, emphasizing as it does the authority of rules rather than of tradition, is carried much more by role readiness and functional interdependence than by the internalization of emotional symbols. This is a relative matter, moreover, and suggests a different emphasis in the mix of motivational patterns in the history of our nation (Katz, Kelman, and Flacks, 1963).

AN IMPLICATION: MORE FREEDOM OF ACTION

What are the implications of this analysis if we still find ourselves in war? What difference does it make if men carry out their military obligations on a different motivational basis than in World War I, as long as the end result is the same? I believe it does make a difference for these reasons: With greater functional and normative involvement there is more freedom of action than with symbolic commitment. Functional and normative nationalism can lead to other than military paths to objectives. It can lead to international negotiation and cooperation in situations in which symbolic patriotism would demand war.

National leaders often operate as if symbolic commitment were still the dominant way in which people were tied to the nation. Thus they sometimes perceive less freedom for action than they really have. They may assume that a conciliatory series of moves will mean political suicide because people will feel that national honor and interests are imperiled. The political opposition can be depended upon to try to arouse patriotic sentiments to discredit such soft policies. Though there are people who still are readily moved by slogan appeals of a superpatriotic character, they are not as numerous or as powerful as is often assumed. Both public opinion polls and election returns show that flag waving by those out of office does not necessarily defeat the incumbent.

EIGHTY-EIGHT PERCENT OF POPULATION FOR NEGOTIATION

In late February and early March of this year Sidney Verba and a group of social scientists at Stanford University in cooperation with the National Opinion Research Center conducted a nation-wide survey on opinions toward the war in Vietnam (1966). This survey differed from the Gallup Poll in that it dug more deeply into the complex of attitudes toward the war. Its major findings indicated that people have very mixed feelings about the war and that there is more of a potential in American public opinion for *deescalation* than for *escalation*. In the first place, there are very few real hawks or doves. Only six percent of the national sample take consistent positions in favor of escalation and opposed to deescalation. Fourteen percent are consistent doves. In the second place, the great majority (some 88%) are willing to negotiate with the Vietcong and would support (some 70%) a UN-negotiated truce in Vietnam. "A 52 percent majority would be willing to see the Vietcong assume a role in a South Vietnam coalition government and a 54 percent majority favor holding free elections in South Vietnam, even if the Vietcong might win." In the third place, "the majority of American citizens have reservations about containing the war when faced with its possible costs. The study asked whether people wanted to continue fighting in Vietnam if it meant cutting back various Great Society programs (such as aid to education and medicare), increasing taxes, and imposing economic controls. On every count majorities were registered in opposition."

Though 60 percent would continue the war if it required calling up the National Guard, only 40 percent would want to continue if it meant full-scale mobilization. And only 38 percent would be in favor of a continuation of the conflict if it meant that several hundred American soldiers would be killed each week. Though the people are evenly divided about having a half a million troops in South Vietnam, a majority oppose steps of escalation such as bombing the cities of North Vietnam, fighting a ground war in China, or the use of atomic weapons. Finally, in spite of press reports, it is not true that the opposition to President Johnson on the war comes mainly from those who are in favor of a more vigorous prosecution of the conflict. The opposition is 2 to 1 from the other side; those who favor deescalation.

It is true, however, that 81 percent of the people would disapprove of an immediate withdrawal of American troops if the Communists were to take over.

VIETNAM—A FUNCTIONAL COMMITMENT

I have cited these findings at some length because they come from the most thorough study we have had of American public reaction to the war. Moreover, they indicate that there is more freedom for our political leaders to follow other alternatives than escalation of the conflict than political leaders themselves seem to assume. People are concerned about winning the war in Vietnam but they are against continuing the war if it means genuine sacrifice. Thus their commitment is more functional than symbolic, in that a symbolic commitment calls for pursuance of policy no matter what the cost. Symbolic commitment in its absolutistic character emphasizes national sovereignty and opposes internationalism. Functional involvement finds no difficulty in accepting an international arrangement consistent with broadly defined national goals. In a recent Michigan study we found that the functionally committed person wanted to strengthen the UN, the symbolically wanted to withdraw from it; the functionally committed were willing to abide by decisions of the World Court, the symbolically committed were not, and in general the symbolically committed favored a more aggressive stance toward communist countries than did the functionally involved.

The European community was achieved not because nations gave up their identity but because they had a functional basis to their nationalism (Haas, 1958). DeGaulle with his symbolic attachment has set back the clock with respect to furthering European integration.

Clear recognition by national leaders of the functional involvement of the American in the national structure and an application of the same logic would call for a realistic assessment of the gains and costs for alternative strategies in southeast Asia. The U.S. has the weapons and the manpower to conquer South Vietnam and for that matter, North Vietnam. The costs, however, would be huge in the death and devastation visited upon the civilians in those countries, in American lives, in the diversion of funds from the building of the Great Society at home. The extension of the war to North Vietnam and the destruction of that country, moreover, brings us perilously close to the next step, the use of atomic weapons. Even if all of Vietnam were conquered, the price of holding it would be high. It would require economic rehabilitation of both countries and a continuing large force of American troops to resist communist infiltration from the surrounding areas. Moreover, the objective of defeating communism would not necessarily be achieved. To many of the uncommitted people in Asian countries, the escalation of the war would seem to them to validate the communist claims about the nature of American imperialistic might. We are judged not by our final objectives but by means we use to achieve them. The means are the visible proof in the opinion of other countries of what we are trying to do, rather than some idealized statement of what we assert is our objective. Finally, the basic answer to the spread of communism lies only partially in superior fire power. It also lies in superior ideology as that ideology can be implemented in securing a better way of life for the masses of people.

TO REVERSE THE SPIRAL OF ESCALATION

Alternatives to our present policy in Vietnam must be considered in terms of a realistic step which would move toward deescalation of the war. The spiral of escalation is difficult but not impossible to reverse. In international conflict it receives two positive types of feedback: one from the counter-moves of the opponent, the other the internal feedback from the aroused nationalism of the people. Both cycles of feedback interact. But the aroused nationalism of the American people about the Vietnam war has not reached the proportions of intensity which means we have passed the point of no return. The majority of people would welcome a cessation or reduction of the war even if it did not mean the unconditional surrender of the Vietcong and the North Vietnamese. The external cycle is more difficult to predict but since the limited period of the cessation of bombing we have not experimented with specific moves of deescalation. We have increasingly seen the conflict in purely military terms.

I have given considerable emphasis to the role of national leadership and some of the factors affecting decision making at high levels. Another structural aspect of this concerns the information and ideas which the system furnishes for decision making. Here the nation suffers from the lack of an adaptive subsystem concerning foreign policy which would have the functions of research and intelligence to provide an accurate assessment of the world situation, an analysis of the effects of our policies, and a thoughtful consideration of alternative strategies. For the internal economy we have moved in the direction of such a subsystem with the President's Council of Economic Advisers. In the international field, however, we rely upon the State Department and the CIA which are action rather than intelligence agencies. From the point of view of furnishing information and ideas, these agencies are redundant systems. They operate to filter out new information and new ideas. They are closed information loops which receive and process the answers predetermined by their limited questions and their restricted coding sets. They operate in such fashion as to maintain rather than break out of the locked-in patterns of past strategy (Schlesinger, 1965). Exceptional presidents in the past have been able to by-pass these conventional structures in the determination of foreign policy. What is required as a reliable basis for system functioning in international relations is some governmental restructuring to provide an adequate adaptive subsystem available to national leadership. National decision making, then, would not be imprisoned by its own closed information circuits, would not have to repeat past errors, and could consider alternatives to atomic destruction. The apparent success of brinksmanship in the past is a poor guide for the future. Time has a way of running out on us as individuals. It can also run out for social systems.

REFERENCES

Allport, F. H. A structuronomic conception of behavior: individual and collective. *Journal of Abnormal and Social Psychology*, 1962, 64, 3–30.

Ashby, W. R. *Design for a brain*. New York: Wiley, 1952.

Clark, K. Problems of social power and social change. *Journal of Social Issues*, 1965, 21, 4–20.

Haas, E. B. *The uniting of Europe*. Stanford: Stanford University Press, 1958.

Horwitz, M. The recall of interrupted group tasks. *Human Relations*, 1954, 7, 3–38.

Katz, D. Nationalism and strategies of international conflict resolution. In H. C. Kelman (Ed.), *International Behavior*. New York: Holt, Rinehart and Winston, 1965, 354–390.

Katz, D., Kelman, H., and Flacks, R. The national role: some hypotheses about the relation of individuals to nation in America today. Peace Research Society, *Papers I*, Chicago Conference, 1963.

Katz, D. and Kahn, R. L. *The social psychology of organizations*. New York: Wiley, 1966.

Lewis, H. B. and Franklin, M. An experimental study of the ego in work. *Journal of Experimental Psychology*, 1944, 34, 195–215.

Rice, A. K. *Productivity and social organization*. London: Tavistock Publications, 1958.

Schlesinger, A. M., Jr. *A thousand days*. Boston: Houghton, Mifflin, 1965.

Trist, E. L., Higgin, C. W., Murray, H., and Pollock, A. B. *Organizational choice*. London: Tavistock Publications, 1963.

Valen, H. and Katz, D. *Political Parties in Norway*. London: Tavistock Publications, 1964.

Verba, S. et al. Public opinion and the war in Vietnam. 1966. (mimeo)

Yuchtman, E. The study of organizational effectiveness. Unpublished doctoral dissertation, University of Michigan, 1966.

Zander, A. and Medow, H. Individual and group levels of aspiration. *Human Relations*, 1963, 16, 89–105.

JOSEPH S. HIMES

The Functions of Racial Conflict

When one contemplates the contemporary American scene, he may be appalled by the picture of internal conflict portrayed in the daily news. The nation is pictured as torn by dissension over Vietnam policy. The people are reported being split by racial strife that periodically erupts into open violence. Organized labor and management are locked in a perennial struggle that occasionally threatens the well-being of the society. The reapportionment issue has forced the ancient rural–urban conflict into public view. Religious denominations and faiths strive against ancient conflicts of theology and doctrine toward unification and ecumenism. Big government is joined in a continuing struggle against big industry, big business, big finance, and big labor on behalf of the "public interest."

The image created by such reports is that of a society "rocked," "split" or "torn" by its internal conflicts. The repetition of such phrases and the spotlighting of conflict suggest that the integration, if not the very existence of the society is threat-

From Joseph S. Himes, "The Functions of Racial Conflict," *Social Forces* 45, 1966, 1–10. Presidential address delivered at the annual meeting of the Southern Sociological Society, New Orleans, April 8, 1966. I am indebted to Professors Ernst Borinski, Lewis A. Coser, Hylan G. Lewis, and Robin M. Williams, Jr., for their critical reading of this manuscript.

ened. It is thus implied, and indeed often stated that the elimination of internal conflict is the central problem for policy and action in the society.

These preliminary remarks tend to indicate that there is widespread popular disapproval of social conflict. In some quarters the absence of conflict is thought to signify the existence of social harmony and stability. According to the human relations theme, conflict, aggression, hostility, antagonism, and such divisive motives and behaviors are regarded as social heresies and therefore to be avoided. Often the word conflict is associated with images of violence and destruction.

At the same time, in contemporary sociology the problem of social conflict has been largely neglected. As Coser, Dahrendorf, and others have pointed out, this tendency issues from preoccupation with models of social structure and theories of equilibrium.[1] Conflicts are treated as strains, tensions, or stresses of social structures and regarded as pathological. Little attention is devoted to the investigation of conflict as a functional social process.

However, some of the earlier sociologists employed social conflict as one central element of their conceptual systems. Theory and analysis were cast in terms of a process model. Conflict was viewed as natural and as functioning as an integrative force in society.

To Ludwig Gumplowicz and Gustav Ratzenhofer conflict was the basic social process, while for Lester F. Ward and Albion W. Small it was one of the basic processes. Sumner, Ross, and Cooley envisaged conflict as one of the major forces operating to lace human society together.[2] Park and Burgess employed social conflict as one of the processual pillars of their sociological system.[3]

[1]Lewis A. Coser, *The Functions of Social Conflict* (New York: The Free Press, 1956), p. 20; Ralf Dahrendorf, *Class and Class Conflict in Industrial Society* (Stanford: Stanford University Press, 1959), chap. 5.

[2]William Graham Sumner, *Folkways* (Boston: Ginn, 1906); Edward Alsworth Ross, *The Principles of Sociology* (New York: Century, 1920); Charles Horton Cooley, *Social Process* (New York: Scribner's, 1918), and *Social Organization* (New York: Scribner's, 1909).

[3]Robert E. Park and Ernest W. Burgess, *Introduction to the Science of Sociology* (Chicago: University of Chicago Press, 1924).

At bottom, however, the two analytic models of social organization are really not inconsistent. Dahrendorf argues that consensus-structure and conflict-process are "the two faces of society."[4] That is, social integration results simultaneously from both consensus of values and coercion to compliance. Indeed, in the present study it is observed that the two sources of social integration are complementary and mutually supporting.

Coser has led the revival of sociological attention to the study of social conflict. In this task he has injected the very considerable contributions of the German sociologist Georg Simmel into the stream of American sociological thought. Ralf Dahrendorf, among others, has made further substantial contributions to the sociology of social conflict. One latent consequence of this development has been to sensitize some sociologists to conflict as a perspective from which to investigate race relations. Thus race relations have been called "power relations" and it has been proposed that research should be cast in terms of a "conflict model."[5] This approach is consistent with Blumer's thesis that race prejudice is "a sense of group position" and that empirical study involves "a concern with the relationship of racial groups."[6]

In the present discussion the term racial conflict is used in a restricted and specific sense.[7] By racial conflict is meant rational

[4]Dahrendorf, *op. cit.*, pp. 157–165. Arthur I. Wastow makes the same point in his concepts of "church," "state," and "government" as models of social integration. See *From Race Riot to Sit-In, 1919 and the 1960s: A Study in the Connections Between Conflict and Violence* (Garden City, N.Y.: Doubleday, 1966).

[5]Lewis M. Killian and Charles M. Grigg, *Racial Crisis in America* (Englewood Cliffs, New Jersey: Prentice-Hall, 1964), p. 18 ff.; H. M. Blalock, Jr., "A Power Analysis of Racial Discrimination," *Social Forces*, 39 (October 1960), pp. 53–59; Ernst Borinski, "The Sociology of Coexistence–Conflict in Social and Political Power Systems," unpublished, pp. 6–7; Wilson Record, *Race and Radicalism* (Ithaca: Cornell University Press, 1964); Ernst Borinski, "The Litigation Curve and the Litigation Filibuster in Civil Rights Cases," *Social Forces*, 37 (December 1958), pp. 142–147.

[6]Herbert Blumer, "Race Prejudice as a Sense of Group Position," in J. Masuoka and Preston Valien (eds.), *Race Relations* (Chapel Hill: The University of North Carolina Press, 1961), p. 217.

[7]In much authoritative literature the concept conflict in racial relations is used in various other ways. See for example, George Simpson and J. Milton Yinger, *Racial and Cultural Minorities* (New York: Harper & Row,

organized overt action by Negroes, initiating demands for specific social goals, and utilizing collective sanctions to enforce these demands. By definition, the following alternative forms of conflict behavior are excluded from the field of analysis.

1. The aggressive or exploitative actions of dominant groups and individuals toward minority groups or individuals.
2. Covert individual antagonisms or affective compensatory or reflexive aggressions, and
3. Spontaneous outbursts or nonrationalized violent behavior.

As here treated, racial conflict involves some rational assessment of both means and ends, and therefore is an instance of what Lewis Coser has called "realistic conflict."[8] Because of the calculating of means and ends, racial conflict is initiating action. It is a deliberate collective enterprise to achieve predetermined social goals. Of necessity, conflict includes a conscious attack upon an overtly defined social abuse.

Merton has pointed out that groups sometimes resort to culturally tabooed means to achieve culturally prescribed ends.[9] Under such circumstances one might assume that if legitimate means were available, they would be employed. But, Vander Zanden has observed "Non-violent resistance is a tactic well suited to struggles in which a minority lacks access to major sources of power within a society and to the instruments of violent coercion."[10] He goes on to add that, "within the larger American society the Negro's tactic of non-violent resistance has gained a considerable degree of legitimacy."[11] Three principal manifestations of Negro behavior fit this definition of racial conflict.

1965), chap. 4; Killian and Grigg, *op. cit.*; Leonard Broom and Norval D. Glenn, *Transformation of the Negro American* (New York: Harper & Row, 1965), esp. chaps. 3 and 4.

[8]Coser, *op. cit.*, pp. 48–55.

[9]Robert K. Merton, *Social Theory and Social Structure* (New York: Free Press, 1957), pp. 123–149.

[10]James W. Vander Zanden, "The Non-Violent Resistance Movement Against Segregation," *American Journal of Sociology*, 68 (March 1963), p. 544.

[11]*Ibid.*, p. 544.

1. Legal redress, or the calculated use of court action to achieve and sanction specific group goals. Legal redress has been used most often and successfully in the achievement of voting rights, educational opportunities and public accommodations.

2. Political action, or the use of voting, bloc voting, and lobby techniques to achieve legislative and administrative changes and law enforcement.

3. Non-violent mass action, or organized collective participation in overt activity involving pressure and public relations techniques to enforce specific demands.

This paper examines some of the social functions of conflict as here defined. It is asked: Does realistic conflict by Negroes have any system-maintaining and system-enhancing consequences for the larger American society? To this question at least four affirmative answers can be given. Realistic racial conflict (1) alters the social structure, (2) enhances social communication, (3) extends social solidarity and (4) facilitates personal identity. Because of space and time limitations, considerations of societal dysfunctions and goal achievements are omitted.

STRUCTURAL FUNCTIONS

H. M. Blalock has noted that within the American social structure race relations are power relations.[12] Thus, realistic social conflict is an enterprise in the calculated mobilization and application of social power to sanction collective demands for specific structural changes. Yet, because of minority status, Negroes have only limited access to the sources of social power. Robert Bierstedt has identified numbers, resources and organization as leading sources of power.[13] Of these categories, resources which Bierstedt specifies as including money, prestige, property and natural and supernatural phenomena, are least accessible to Negroes.

[12]Blalock, *op. cit.*, pp. 53–59.

[13]Robert Bierstedt, "An Analysis of Social Power," *American Sociological Review*, 15 (December 1950), pp. 730–738. Bierstedt argues that numbers and organization as sources of social power are ineffectual without access to resources.

Perforce then, realistic racial conflict specializes in the mobilization of numbers and organization as accessible sources of power. Thus a boycott mobilizes and organizes numbers of individuals to withhold purchasing power. A demonstration organizes and mobilizes numbers of individuals to tap residual moral sentiments and to generate public opinion. Voter registration and bloc voting mobilize and organize numbers of citizens to influence legislative and administrative processes. Legal redress and lobby techniques mobilize organization to activate legal sanctions or the legislative process.

The application of mobilized social power in realistic racial conflict tends to reduce the power differential between actors, to restrict existing status differences, and to alter the directionality of social interaction. First, in conflict situations, race relations are defined unequivocally in power terms. Sentimentality and circumlocution are brushed aside. The power dimension is brought into central position in the structure of interaction. The differential between conflict partners along this dimension is thus reduced. The power advantage of the dominant group is significantly limited. In this connection and perhaps only in this connection, it may be correct to liken embattled Negroes and resisting whites to "armed camps."

Second, alteration of the power dimension of interracial structure tends to modify status arrangements. In the traditional racial structure, discrimination and segregation cast whites and Negroes in rigid and separate orders of superiority and inferiority. The limited and stylized intergroup contacts are confined to a rigid and sterile etiquette. However, in realistic conflict initiating actors assume, for they must, a status coordinate with that of the opposition.[14]

Status coordination is one evident consequence of power equalization. Moreover, it is patently impossible to make demands and to sanction them while acting from the position of a suppliant. That is, the very process of realistic conflict functions to define adversaries in terms of self-conception as status

[14]Thomas F. Pettigrew, *A Profile of the Negro American* (Princeton: D. Van Nostrand Co., 1964), p. 167.

equals. Martin Luther King perceives this function of realistic conflict in the following comment on the use of non-violent action and deliberately induced tension.[15]

> Non-violent direct action seeks to create such a crisis and foster such a tension that a community which has constantly refused to negotiate is forced to confront the issue. It seeks so to dramatize the issue that it can no longer be ignored.

That is, social power is used to bring interactors into status relations where issues can be discussed, examined and compromised. There are no suppliants or petitioners and no condescending controllers in a negotiation relationship. By the very nature of the case, interactors occupy equal or approximately equal positions of both status and strength.

Third, power equalization and status coordination affect the interactional dimension of social structure. The up and down flow of interaction between super- and subordinates tends to level out in relations between positional equals. That is, rational demands enforced by calculated sanctions cannot be forced into the molds of supplication and condescension.

The leveling out of social interaction is inherent in such realistic conflict mechanisms as sit-ins, freedom rides, bloc voting, voter registration campaigns, and boycotts. Thus, for example, the interruption of social interaction in a boycott implies an assumption of status equality and the leveling of interaction. The relationship that is interrupted is the up and down pattern inherent in the status structure of inequality. No relationship is revealed as preferable to the pattern of supplication and condescension. Whether such structural functions of realistic conflict become institutionalized in the larger social system will depend on the extent of goal achievement of the total Negro revolution. That is, structural consequences of conflict may be institutionalized through the desegregation and nondiscrimination of education, employment, housing, recreation, and the like. Changes in these directions will provide system-relevant roles

[15]Martin Luther King, *Why We Can't Wait* (New York: Harper & Row, 1963), p. 81.

under terms of relatively coordinate status and power not only for the conflict participants, but also for many other individuals. Developments in these directions will also be influenced by many factors and trends apart from the process of realistic racial conflict.

We may now summarize the argument regarding the structural functions of realistic racial conflict in a series of propositions. Realistic conflict postulates race relations as power relations and undertakes to mobilize and apply the social power that is accessible to Negroes as a minority group.

In conflict, the traditional interracial structure is modified along three dimensions. The power differential between interactors is reduced; status differentials are restricted; and social interaction tends to level out in directionality. Whether these structural consequences of realistic conflict become institutionalized in the general social system will depend on the extent and duration of goal achievement in the larger social structure.

COMMUNICATIONAL FUNCTIONS

It is widely claimed that Negro aggression interrupts or reduces interracial communication. Whites and Negroes are thought to withdraw in suspicion and hostility from established practices of communication. The so-called "normal" agencies and bridges of intergroup contact and communication are believed to become inoperative. Such a view of conflict envisages Negroes and whites as hostile camps eyeing each other across a "no man's land" of antagonism and separation.

It is true that racial conflict tends to interrupt and reduce traditional communication between whites and Negroes. But traditional interracial communication assumes that communicators occupy fixed positions of superiority and inferiority, precludes the consideration of certain significant issues, and confines permitted interchanges to a rigid and sterile etiquette. "The Negro," write Killian and Grigg, "has always been able to stay in communication with the white man and gain many favors from him, so long as he approached him as a suppliant and as an inferior, and not as a conflict partner."[16]

It will be evident that intergroup communication under such structural conditions is both restricted in content and asymmetrical in form. However, our analysis indicates that realistic conflict functions to correct these distortions of content and form and to extend the communication process at the secondary mass media level.

First, realistic racial conflict heightens the individual level and extends the social range of attention to racial matters. Individuals who have by long custom learned to see Negroes only incidentally as part of the standard social landscape, are brought up sharply and forced to look at them in a new light. Persons who have been oblivious to Negroes are abruptly and insistently confronted by people and issues which they can neither avoid nor brush aside. Many individuals for the first time perceive Negroes as having problems, characteristics, and aspirations that were never before recognized, nor at least so clearly recognized. Racial conflict thus rudely destroys what Gunnar Myrdal aptly called the "convenience of ignorance."[17]

In *Freedom Summer,* Sally Belfrage gives a graphic personal illustration of the attention-arresting function of realistic racial conflict.[18] In the most crowded and hottest part of an afternoon the daughter of one of Greenwood's (Mississippi) leading families walked into the civil rights headquarters. In a lilting southern voice she asked to everybody in general: "I jus' wanted to know what y'all are up to over here."

At the same time the "race problem" is brought into the focus of collective attention by realistic conflict. Negroes as well as their problems and claims insist upon having both intensive and extensive consideration. To support this contention one has only

[16]Killian and Grigg, *op. cit.,* p. 7.

[17]Gunnar Myrdal, *An American Dilemma* (New York: Harper & Row, 1944), pp. 40–42.

[18]Sally Belfrage, *Freedom Summer* (New York: The Viking Press, 1965), p. 48.

to consider the volume of scientific, quasi-scientific and popular literature, the heavy racial loading of the mass media, and the vast number of organizations and meetings that are devoted to the racial issue.

Further, realistic racial conflict tends to modify both the cognitive and affective content of interracial communication. Under terms of conflict whites and Negroes can no longer engage in the exchange of standardized social amenities regarding safe topics within the protection of the status structure and the social etiquette. Communication is made to flow around substantive issues and the calculated demands of Negroes. Communication is about something that has real meaning for the communicators. It makes a difference that they communicate. In fact, under terms of realistic conflict it is no longer possible to avoid communicating. Thus Martin Luther King argued that non-violent mass action is employed to create such crisis and tension that a community which has refused to negotiate is forced to confront the issue.[19]

In conflict the affective character of communication becomes realistic. The communicators infuse their exchanges of cognitive meanings with the feelings that, within the traditional structure, were required to be suppressed and avoided. That Negroes are permitted, indeed often expected to reveal the hurt and humiliation and anger that they formerly were required to bottle up inside. Many white people thus were shocked to discover that the "happy" Negroes whom they "knew" so well were in fact discontented and angry people.

Thus the cognitive-affective distortion of traditional interracial communication is in some measure at least corrected. The flow of understanding and affection that was permitted and encouraged is balanced by normal loading of dissension and hostility. The relationship thus reveals a more symmetrical character of content and form.

Finally, attrition of primary contacts between unequals within the traditional structure and etiquette is succeeded, in part at

[19]King, *op. cit.*, p. 81.

least, by an inclusive dialogue at the secondary communication level. The drama of conflict and the challenges of leaders tend to elevate the racial issue in the public opinion arena. The mass media respond by reporting and commenting on racial events in great detail. Thus millions of otherwise uninformed or indifferent individuals are drawn into the public opinion process which Ralph H. Turner and Lewis M. Killian have analyzed as defining and redefining the issue and specifying and solving the problem.[20]

Much obvious evidence reveals the secondary communication dialogue. Since 1954 a voluminous scientific, quasi-scientific and popular literature on the race issue has appeared. Further evidence is found in the heavy racial loading of newspapers, magazines, television and radio broadcasting, and the motion pictures. The race problem has been the theme of numerous organizations and meetings at all levels of power and status. From such evidence it would seem reasonable to conclude that few if any Americans have escaped some degree of involvement in the dialogue over the race issue.

We may now summarize the argument briefly. Realistic racial conflict tends to reduce customary interracial communication between status unequals regarding trivial matters within the established communication etiquette. On the other hand, conflict tends to extend communication regarding significant issues with genuine feelings and within noncustomary structures and situations. At the secondary level both the volume of communication and the number of communicators are greatly increased by realistic conflict. These observations would seem to warrant the conclusion that communication within the general social system is extended by realistic racial conflict.

SOLIDARITY FUNCTIONS

A corollary of the claim that racial conflict interrupts communication is the assertion that conflict also is seriously, perhaps

[20]Ralph H. Turner and Lewis M. Killian, *Collective Behavior* (Englewood Cliffs, New Jersey: Prentice-Hall, 1957), chaps. 11 and 12.

even radically disunifying. Struggles between Negroes and whites are thought to split the society and destroy social solidarity. It is at once evident that such a claim implies the prior existence of a unified or relatively unified biracial system. Notwithstanding difference of status and condition, the racial sectors are envisaged as joined in the consensus and structure of the society.

A judicious examination of the facts suggests that the claim that racial conflict is seriously, perhaps even radically disunifying is not altogether correct. On the one hand, the image of biracial solidarity tends to be exaggerated. On the other, realistic racial conflict serves some important unifying functions within the social system.

As Logan Wilson and William Kolb have observed, the consensus of the society is organized around a core of "ultimate values."[21] "In our own society," they assert, "we have developed such ultimate values as the dignity of the individual, equality of opportunity, the right to life, liberty, and the pursuit of happiness, and the growth of the free personality."

Far from rejecting or challenging these ultimate values, the ideological thrust of realistic racial conflict affirms them.[22] That is, the ultimate values of the society constitute starting points of ideology and action in racial conflict. As Wilson Record and others have observed, Negro protest and improvement movements are thoroughly American in assumption and objectives.[23]

This fact creates an interesting strategic dilemma for the White Citizens Councils, the resurgent Ku Klux Klan and similar manifestations of the so-called "white backlash." The ideology of racial conflict has preempted the traditional high ground of the core values and ultimate morality. The reactionary groups are thus left no defensible position within the national ethos from which to mount their attacks.

One consequence of realistic racial conflict, then, is to bring the core values of the society into sharp focus and national at-

[21]Logan Wilson and William L. Kolb, *Sociological Analysis* (New York: Harcourt, Brace Jovanovich, 1949), p. 513.

[22]Pettigrew, *op. cit.*, p. 193.

[23]Record, *op. cit.*; Pettigrew, *op. cit.*; Broom and Glenn, *op. cit.*

tention. People are exhorted, even forced to think about the basic societal tenets and to consider their meaning and applications. A dynamic force is thus joined to latent dedication in support of the unifying values of the society. Thus, as Coser has observed, far from being altogether disunifying, realistic conflict functions to reaffirm the core and unifying values of the society.[24] In other words the "two faces of society" are seen to be complementary and mutually supporting.

The primacy of core values in realistic racial conflict is revealed in many ways. Martin Luther King places the ultimate values of the society at the center of his theoretic system of non-violent mass action.[25] In his "Letter from Birmingham Jail" he refers to "justice," "freedom," "understanding," "brotherhood," "constitutional rights," "promise of democracy" and "truth." See how he identifies the goal of racial freedom with the basic societal value of freedom. "We will reach the goal of freedom in Birmingham and all over the nation, because the goal of America is freedom."[26]

One impact of realistic racial conflict is upon interpretation of core values and the means of their achievement. Thus, the issue is not whether or not men shall be free and equal, but whether these values are reserved to white men or are applicable to Negroes as well. Or again, the phrases "gradualism" and "direct action" depict an important point of disagreement over means to universally affirmed ends. But, it may be observed that when men agree on the ends of life, their quarrels are not in themselves disunifying.

Further, the very process of realistic racial conflict is intrinsically functional. Participants in the conflict are united by the process of struggle itself. The controversy is a unique and shared social possession. It fills an interactional vacuum maintained in the traditional structure by limited social contacts and alienation.

At the same time, as Coser has argued, a relationship estab-

[24]Coser, *op. cit.*, pp. 127–128.
[25]King, *op. cit.*, pp. 77–100.
[26]*Ibid.*, p. 97.

lished by conflict may lead in time to other forms of interaction.[27] It is conceivable that Negroes and whites who today struggle over freedom and justice and equality may tomorrow be joined in cooperation in the quest of these values.

Conflict is also unifying because the object of struggle is some social value that both parties to the conflict wish to possess or enjoy. The struggle tends to enhance the value and to reveal its importance to both actors. A new area of consensus is thus defined or a prior area of agreement is enlarged. For example, that Negroes and whites struggle through realistic conflict for justice or freedom or equality tends to clarify these values for both and join them in the consensus regarding their importance.

"Simultaneously," as Vander Zanden observes, "within the larger American society the Negro's tactic of non-violent resistance has gained a considerable degree of legitimacy."[28] That is, conflict itself has been defined as coming within the arena of morally justifiable social action. The means as well as the ends, then, are enveloped within the national ethos and serve to enhance societal solidarity. In this respect realistic racial conflict, like labor-management conflict, tends to enter the "American way of life" and constitutes another point of social integration.

Many years ago Edward Alsworth Ross pointed out that nonradical conflicts may function to "sew" the society together.[29]

> Every species of conflicts interferes with every other species in society . . . save only when lines of cleavage coincide; in which case they reinforce one another. . . . A society, therefore, which is ridden

[27]Coser, *op. cit.*, pp. 121–122.

[28]Vander Zanden, *op. cit.*, p. 544.

[29]Ross, *op. cit.*, pp. 164–165. Dahrendorf, *op. cit.*, pp. 213–215, argues that conflicts tend to become "superimposed," thus threatening intensification. "Empirical evidence shows," he writes, "that different conflicts may be, and often are, superimposed in given historical societies, so that the multitude of possible conflict fronts is reduced to a few dominant conflicts. . . . If this is the case, (class) conflicts of different associations appear superimposed; i.e., the opponents of one association meet again—with different titles, perhaps, but in identical relations—in another association." (Pp. 213–214.) Such an argument, however, fails to recognize that conflicts may superimpose along religious, regional, ethnic or other fronts and thus mitigate the strength of the class superimposition.

by a dozen oppositions along lines running in every direction may actually be in less danger of being torn with violence or falling to pieces than one split just along one line. For each new cleavage contributes to narrow the cross-clefts, so that one might say that society is sewn together by its inner conflicts.

In this sewing function, realistic racial conflict is interwoven with political, religious, regional, rural–urban, labor–management, class and the other persistent threads of struggle that characterize the American social fabric. What is decisive is the fact that variously struggling factions are united in the consensus of the ultimate societal values. The conflicts are therefore nonradical, crisscrossing and tend to mitigate each other.

The proposition on the solidarity function of realistic racial conflict can now be formulated briefly. The claims that racial conflict is disruptive of social solidarity, though partially true, tends to obscure other important consequences. Conflict not only projects the combatants into the social consensus; it also acts to reaffirm the ultimate values around which the consensus is organized. Moreover, conflict joins opposing actors in meaningful interaction for ends, whose importance is a matter of further agreement. From this perspective and within a context of multifarious crisscrossing threads of opposition, realistic racial conflict is revealed as helping to "sew" the society together around its underlying societal consensus. We now turn to a consideration of certain social-psychological consequences of realistic racial conflict.

IDENTITY FUNCTIONS

The fact is often overlooked that realistic racial conflict permits many Negroes to achieve a substantial measure of identity within the American social system. This function of racial conflict is implied in the foregoing analyses of communication and solidarity. However, the analysis of the identity function of racial conflict begins with a consideration of the alienation of the American Negro people. Huddled into urban and rural slums and concentrated in menial and marginal positions in the work force, Negroes are relegated to inferior and collateral statuses in the social structure. Within this structural situation, discrimination prevents their sharing in the valued possessions of the society. Legal and customary norms of segregation exclude them from many meaningful contacts and interactions with members of the dominant group.

Isolated and inferior, Negro people searched for the keys to identity and belonging. The social forces that exclude them from significant participation in the general society also keep them disorganized. Thus identity, the feeling of belonging and the sense of social purpose, could be found neither in membership in the larger society nor in participation in a cohesive racial group. Generation after generation of Negroes live out their lives in fruitless detachment and personal emptiness. In another place the alienation of Negro teenagers has been described as follows.[30]

> The quality of Negro teenage culture is conditioned by four decisive factors: race, inferiority, deprivation and youthfulness. Virtually every experience of the Negro teenager is filtered through this complex qualifying medium; every act is a response to a distorted perception of the world. His world is a kind of nightmare, the creation of a carnival reflection chamber. The Negro teenager's culture, his customary modes of behavior, constitute his response to the distorted, frightening, and cruel world that he perceives with the guileless realism of youth.

Yet the search for identity goes on. It takes many forms. In the Negro press and voluntary organizations it is reflected in campaigns for race pride and race loyalty. One sector of the Negro intelligentsia invented the "Negro history movement" as a device to create a significant past for a "historyless" people. For the unlettered and unwashed masses the church is the prime agent of group cohesion and identity. The National Association for the Advancement of Colored People and other militant organizations provide an ego-enhancing rallying point for the emancipated and the aggressive. The cult of Negro business,

[30]Joseph S. Himes, "Negro Teen Age Culture," *Annals*, 338 (November 1961), pp. 92–93.

escapist movements like Father Divine's Heaven, and nationalist movements like Marcus Garvey's Universal Negro Improvement Association, and the Black Muslims provide still other arenas for the Negro's search for identity.

Despite this variegated panorama of effort and search, the overriding experience of Negroes remains isolation, inferiority and the ineluctable sense of alienation. Whether involved in the search or not, or perhaps just because of such involvement, individuals see themselves as existing outside the basic American social system. Vander Zanden puts it this way: "By virtue of his membership in the Negro group, the Negro suffers considerably in terms of self-esteem and has every incentive for self-hatred."[31] Thus self-conception reflects and in turn supports social experience in a repetition of the familiar self-fulfilling prophecy.

In this situation, collective conflict had an almost magical although unanticipated effect upon group cohesion and sense of identity among Negroes. Group struggle, as Coser and others have pointed out, functions to enhance group solidarity and to clarify group boundaries.[32] The separations among collective units are sharpened and the identity of groups within a social system is established. In the course of conflict collective aims are specified, defined and communicated. Cadres of leaders emerge in a division of labor that grows clearer and more definite. Individuals tend to find niches and become polarized around the collective enterprise. All participants are drawn closer together, both for prosecution of the struggle and for common defense.

As the racial conflict groups become more cohesive and organized, the boundaries with other groups within the American social system become clearer. The distinction between member and nonmember is sharpened. Individuals who stood indecisively between groups or outside the fray are induced or forced to take sides. The zones of intergroup ambiguity diminish. Internally, the conflict groups become more tightly unified and the positions of members are clarified and defined more precisely.

Further, conflict facilitates linkage between the individual

[31]Vander Zanden, *op. cit.*, p. 546.
[32]Coser, *op. cit.*, p. 34.

and his local reference group as the agent of conflict. The individual thus achieves both a "commitment"[33] and a "role" as a quasi-official group representative in the collective struggle. Pettigrew writes:[34]

> Consider the Student Non-Violent Coordinating Committee (SNICK), . . . The group is cohesive, highly regarded by Negro youth, and dedicated entirely to achieving both personal and societal racial change. Recruits willingly and eagerly devote themselves to the group's goals. And they find themselves systematically rewarded by SNICK for violating the "Negro" role in every particular. They are expected to evince strong racial pride, to assert their full rights as citizens, to face jail and police brutality unhesitatingly for the cause. . . . Note, . . . that these expected and rewarded actions all publicly commit the member to the group and its aims.

In the general racial conflict system individuals may act as leaders, organizers and specialists. Some others function as sit-inners, picketers, boycotters, demonstrators, voter registration solicitors, etc. Many others, removed from the areas of overt conflict, participate secondarily or vicariously as financial contributors, audience members, mass media respondents, verbal applauders, etc.

In the interactive process of organized group conflict self-involvement is the opposite side of the coin of overt action. Actors become absorbed by ego and emotion into the group and the group is projected through their actions. This linkage of individual and group in ego and action is the substance of identity.

Paradoxically, the personal rewards of participation in conflict groups tend to support and facilitate the larger conflict organization and process. Edward Shils and Morris Janowitz have noted this fact in the functions of primary groups in the German Army in World War II.[35] That is, for the individual actor the

[33] Amitai Etzioni employs the concept "commitment" to designate one dimension of cohesiveness and operational effectiveness in complex organizations. See his *Complex Organizations: A Sociological Reader* (New York: Holt, Rinehart and Winston, 1961), p. 187; and *A Comparative Study of Complex Organization* (New York: Free Press, 1961), pp. 8–22.

[34] Pettigrew, *op. cit.*, pp. 165–166.

[35] Edward A. Shils and Morris Janowitz, "Cohesion and Disintegration in the Wehrmacht in World War II," *Public Opinion Quarterly*, 12 (Summer 1948), p. 281.

sense of identity is grounded and sustained by gratification of important personal needs.

In the case of realistic racial conflict, groupbased identity functions to facilitate sociopsychic linkage between the individual and the inclusive social system. It was shown above that racial conflict is socially unifying in at least two ways. First, the conflict ideology identifies parties to the conflict with the core values of the social heritage. Thus sit-inners, and demonstrators and boycotters and all the others in the drama of racial conflict conceive themselves as the latter-day warriors for the freedom, justice and equality and the other moral values that are historically and essentially American. For many Negroes the sense of alienation is dispelled by a new sense of significance and purpose. The self-image of these embattled Negroes is consequently significantly enhanced.

Second, the conflict process draws organized Negroes into significant social interaction within the inclusive social system. Some of the crucial issues and part of the principal business of the society engage Negroes of all localities and stations in life. Though often only vicariously and by projection, life acquires a new meaning and quality for even the poorest ghetto dweller and meanest sharecropper. The sense of alienation is diminished and the feeling of membership in the inclusive society is enhanced.

We may now formulate the argument as follows. Intense alienation kept alive the Negro's quest for identity and meaning. Miraculously almost, realistic racial conflict with its ideological apparatus and action system functions to alleviate alienation and to facilitate identity. Conflict enhances group solidarity, clarifies group boundaries and strengthens the individual-group linkage through ego-emotion commitment and overt action. In-group identity is extended to the larger social system through the extension of communication, the enlargement of the network of social interactions and ideological devotion to national core values. It may be said, then, that through realistic racial conflict America gains some new Americans.

LOUIS C. GOLDBERG

Ghetto Riots and Others: The Faces of Civil Disorder in 1967

1. INTRODUCTION

Civil disorders in American cities in 1967 were not all of the same kind. The term *riot* has been too loosely applied to denote

From Louis C. Goldberg, "Ghetto Riots and Others: The Faces of Civil Disorder in 1967," *Journal of Peace Research* 2, 1968, 116–132. This paper is based primarily on data published in *The Report of The National Advisory Commission on Civil Disorders* (New York: Bantam Books, 1968). The ideas for this particular analysis were formulated while I worked as a member of the social science research group of the commission. The group was directed by Dr. Robert Shellow and included David Boesel and myself as full-time analysts; Dr. Elliot Liebow, Dr. Gary Marx, and Dr. Derek Roemer as part-time analysts; and Drs. Neil Smelser, Nathan Kaplan, Ralph Turner, Kurt Lang, and David Sears as consultants. Nothing included here should be construed as the official view of either the social science group or the entire commission.

I should, however, like to express my debt to the entire staff of the commission, particularly the field teams who collected the data. Further, I should particularly like to thank my friend and partner David Boesel, who in certain respects must share equal responsibility for the ideas in this paper, for his encouragement and criticism. I also owe an idea to Professor Ralph Turner, and another to Betsy Jameson of Antioch College. Professor James S. Coleman of Johns Hopkins University was kind enough to express ambivalence toward an earlier version of this paper. While I would argue that objective evidence compels a harsher attitude toward civil and police authority stupidities in describing events than he would, I want to thank him for encouraging me to moderate the tone of the analysis.

disturbances, often quite varied, which occurred last summer and in the previous three years. It has been used to refer to anything from a group of excited teenagers breaking windows after a dance, to a general social upheaval. All were civil disturbances; but only a few warranted the label *riot*.

It is misleading also to think of the civil disturbances simply as "Negro riots." To do so suggests that the immediate responsibility for the course of the disturbances and the extent of damage lies solely with the Negro participants. It is necessary, of course, to underscore the reality of violent and aggressive mass actions involving looting, burning, and defiance of local authority within Negro areas; and the initiative of Negro rioters in events. But the threats to civil order and innocent life and property did not come only from the Negro side. In some cities, the behavior of various official control agents—police, national guardsmen, and the courts—in fact constituted official lawlessness: abuses of power in the name of law and order. For the largest disorders especially, the concept of a *tandem riot*—a riot by Negroes against public authorities, followed by a riot of control agents against Negroes—is appropriate.

In other cities, Negro riots were more imagined than real. For such disorders, we must distinguish between *actual* collective violence by Negroes, and the *perception* of a riot by white authorities. There is much evidence that in several cities white anticipation of Negro violence led to heavy-handed uses of official force that provoked violence which might not have otherwise occurred.

The news media, for their part, sometimes contributed to building expectations of community violence by over-dramatizing disturbances and helping to create an emotional climate in which even minor incidents were seen as major riots.

2. PROMINENT FEATURES OF DISORDERS: CLASSIFYING THE RIOTS

A sample of 23 disturbances which occurred last summer shows clearly that the particular combination of circumstances in each city was to some extent unique. But at the same time certain characteristics of different disturbances were so similar that we may *group the disorders, particularly the largest ones, on the basis of their most prominent features.*

2.1. GENERAL UPHEAVALS

Over a period of time a disturbance may develop into an upheaval which draws in thousands or tens of thousands of participants from a Negro ghetto, exhausts the resources of local police, severely taxes the capacities of city institutions, and involves an extraordinarily wide range of lawless activities on the part of both Negroes and control authorities. After the disorder has ended, an area often looks as if it has been through a state of civil warfare. Such was the case in Detroit and Newark, 1967, and in Los Angeles, 1965. These disorders were so massive, events so much beyond the control of either civil authorities or Negro community leadership, the points of street confrontation between police and Negroes so numerous and widespread, that it is difficult to characterize the whole complex of actions over the course of a disturbance in simple terms.

In all three cases, however, a similar pattern of development stands out: the violence in each went through two distinct phases. *In the first, widespread and aggressive action by ghetto Negroes overwhelmed local police forces, leaving them virtually powerless to enforce order in the streets. In the second, reinforced control authorities engaged in harsh retaliatory actions to reassert dominance.*

Phase 1: Negro Rebellion

In this phase *collective* violence was initiated by Negroes. In Detroit and Newark, as well as in Watts, aggressive action by Negroes escalated spontaneously from an initial confrontation with police into a highly generalized rebellion against white authority and white-owned property in the ghetto. In the face of an expanding rebellion, local police lacked the resources to act with the even-handed decisiveness necessary to bring the violence under control; their efforts inflamed rather than quieted Negro participants.

As the ability of police to enforce control of the streets diminished, more and more segments of the Negro community—older people, women, children—joined the young men who had been in the forefront. At the peak of this phase there was a euphoric realization among Negro rioters that they had nullified police control over their territory. Overwhelmed, the police floundered helpless and frustrated.

Phase 2: Control Force Retaliation

Under the strain of widespread rioting, police order had begun to dissolve; many officers became subject to the same principles of crowd behavior that motivated Negro rioters. Deep-rooted racial prejudices surfaced. The desire to vent hostility, to re-establish dominance, and to avenge police honor became compelling motives. Rumors and racist attitudes fed into each other as determinants of police behavior with the breakdown of routine arrest procedure, police communication systems, and police leadership control of their men on the street.

Once reinforcements arrived in the form of state police and National Guard units, the second phase of disorder was inaugurated. With police discipline severely weakened, many lawless acts initiated by lower-echelon police officers coincided with the reassertion of police dominance over Negro rioters. Many National Guardsmen, ill-disciplined and afraid, showed little restraint in using weapons in areas in which they were strangers. This period was characterized by a marked tendency among control authorities to treat all Negroes categorically as enemies. The presence of massive official force, or its withdrawal, or the exhaustion of Negro rioters and control authorities alike, would finally bring the violence to an end.

Patterns of Escalation

DETROIT: PHASE 1. These two phases of disorder in Los Angeles, Detroit, and Newark—in part the product of a high level of community polarization prior to the upheaval—directly emerged as a result of reciprocating hostile actions by police and Negro activists.

In Detroit, the first phase had 5 escalation points, each occurring within 12 hours from the start of the disturbance.[1] The initial event was a police raid on a blind pig[2] that mobilized a crowd. The second escalation point occurred shortly after the police left the scene, looting beginning as an agitator, emerging from the crowd which had grown angry, broke the first window. This was followed by several hours in which the police, returning to the area undermanned, made no visible effort to stop the looting going on under their eyes. Police inaction encouraged a massive expansion in community participation. Then, a sudden and ineffective crackdown—a sweep of the streets by a tough elite riot squad armed with bayonets—outraged the community while simultaneously demonstrating police impotence as the dispersal tactic failed. Shortly thereafter, firebombing, with Negro youths at the forefront, greatly accelerated. The riot had become totally out of control.

NEWARK: PHASE 1. The steps in the development of the Newark rebellion—which preceded and gave impetus to the one in Detroit—differed somewhat from the first phase of the Detroit upheaval but paralleled it in basic process. As in Detroit, a police incident initiated the chain of events. Here, the first step was the arrest and beating of a Negro cab driver which initially mobilized a large and angry crowd of Negroes in front of the police station. While the police in Detroit were permissive in the face of the initial stage of looting, those in Newark were both indecisive and punitive toward the increasingly hostile and aggressive crowd that literally began to lay siege to the police station. A cycle occurred in which the bombardment of the station with bricks, bottles, and Molotov cocktails by some members

[1]This brief analytical summary is not designed to capture the richness and concrete details of the events. The reader is encouraged to refer to the excellent narrative of the Detroit, Newark, and other disorders provided in *The Report of the National Advisory Commission on Civil Disorders*, pp. 35–108.

[2]A "blind pig" is a slang term for private social clubs that serve as after-hours drinking and gambling spots.

of the crowd would be followed by a rush of the police toward the crowd, a backoff of the crowd, a police withdrawal to the station, and a reassembly of the crowd to begin the process again. Each time this occurred the crowd's contempt for the police and its own sense of power grew.

As the police sweep in Detroit was followed by firebombing, so in Newark a period of minor looting followed a police charge which nullified efforts by civil rights leaders to organize a march away from the station. Police action subsequently alienated a major source of grapevine information in the ghetto. Twenty-five cabdrivers who had transported some people down to city hall to conduct a non-violent protest and picket became extremely indignant to find their double-parked cars being ticketed and towed away.

The difference between Newark and Detroit at this point, however, was that the possibility existed to save the situation through a political solution between the Italian city administration and Negro militant leaders. Such a solution did not materialize.

Then on the second evening, escalation began again. Events moved almost directly into a period in which rioting was out of control, completing the process that was truncated the evening before. The stopping of a picket line in front of the police station to announce a concession considered trivial by the crowd catalyzed Negro youth into stone throwing at the station. The police in turn charged the crowd. Discipline cracked. Even Negro newspaper reporters, and in one instance a Negro policeman, were beaten by white policemen caught up in an anti-black frenzy. While police in Detroit were permissive toward looters in the first stage, those in Newark had already lost control on the second evening when the looting started in earnest. The absence of police in many areas and the widespread looting in turn produced pressures for participation that proved irresistible for many ordinarily law-abiding people.

DETROIT: PHASE 2. With the introduction of state police and National Guard, and removal of constraints on use of weapons, the character of the riots began to change.

In Detroit the removal of restraint on the use of weapons by control authorities caused violence to escalate on both sides. For the control forces frequent gunfire, and some firing of weapons by some Negroes led to pervasive rumors of massive Negro sniping activity. Fear combined with motives for revenge led many troopers to see themselves as embattled soldiers in a war situation against an enemy people, and they acted accordingly. Lack of command discipline in the general confusion led to situations in which guardsmen became lost, made mistakes, or violated standing orders (e.g., even after federal troops arrived and the commanding general instructed guardsmen to unload their weapons, 90% of the guardsmen did not).

A similar situation occurred for the police. With the top leadership of the police department having lost control over lower echelon officers by midweek, the latter being fatigued from over-work and the arrest procedure system having fallen apart, many policemen engaged in vengeful action. It was not until regular army troops arrived, official violence brought under control, and all parties reduced to a state of exhaustion that the disorders finally ceased.

NEWARK: PHASE 2. In Newark, the statements of the governor telling Negroes they were forced to choose between "the jungle" and "law and order" became interpreted by some policemen as a license for summary justice. Police retaliation was further spurred by the killing of one officer: Acts of ritual revenge were even carried out in his name. As in Detroit, rumors of snipers, lack of coordination between police and guard forces, and motives of retaliation produced massive onslaughts of gunfire directed at Negro occupied or owned buildings. With a growing retaliatory mood among Negro youth, violence did not end until the governor ordered the guard units withdrawn from the Negro areas.

2.2. RIOTS AS POLITICAL CONFRONTATIONS

Newark and Detroit are extreme examples of massive disorder in the summer of 1967. A few disturbances showed many of the characteristics of these general upheavals but developed over time in a distinctly political direction. As in the general upheaval, the level of disorder in the streets was quite large. *But in these disorders explicit political confrontation*[3] *between Negro leadership and civil authorities was at least as important a feature of the riot as violent street confrontation between Negro masses and the police.* This was true in such cities as Cincinnati and Plainfield.

On the first night of disorder in Plainfield, for example, a local Negro politician tried to steer the youth toward a meeting with the mayor to talk about their grievances. The meeting was held, but was unsatisfactory, the youth leadership representatives walking out twice, a minor riot occurring after the second walkout. On the next day, a meeting they were having in a park to formulate grievances and reduce them to writing was broken up by the police. Shortly thereafter violence rapidly escalated as a policeman was killed by a mob after he shot a youth, and the youths, fearing retaliation from the police, stole 46 carbines from a gun factory. Later, one of their representatives—a young man who has since become an important political figure in the community—attempted to use the possession of the guns as a bargaining tool, offering to exchange them in return for a sign of good faith from the authorities. An agreement was reached and Negro-initiated violence ceased, although the guns were not in fact returned. During a two-day period when police were

[3]The use of the term "political" here is not meant to imply either (1) conspiracy, (2) prior organization to achieve specific political objectives through the use of violence (e.g., intimidating election opponents or forcing a city administration to grant a specific concession), or (3) a precipitant which was markedly "political." Nor is calling some disturbances "political riots" meant to imply that the general upheavals in Newark and Detroit lacked a powerful political component. A high level of political grievance on the part of Negroes, and the lack of significant responses by civil authorities contributed greatly to events in Newark and Detroit. But it would not do justice to the many non-political aspects of generalized chaos in those cities to refer to their disorders as simply political riots. However, in cities like Plainfield and Cincinnati, the actions of Negro participants became directly focused at civil authorities. In turn, the responses of civil authorities to demands—particularly the demand for recognition—dramatically affected the level of aggressive action by Negro rioters.

kept out of the area of disturbance, the youths in effect took responsibility for keeping order. In the aftermath, the activities of the youth militants have involved the use of pressure group tactics in council meetings, their first victory being the defeat of an anti-loitering amendment.

Unlike the general upheaval, events in Plainfield, although violent, were not entirely out of the control of community leaders. In Detroit, where there may have been tens or hundreds of bands of rioters at work, any kind of coherence or control over events was impossible. In Newark, the possibility for a political solution was quickly foreclosed by the severe political polarization between the mayor and the middle-class Negro militants, and the lack of control of the latter over the young. But in Plainfield, the existence of a leadership group among the youth who were rioting, and their willingness to negotiate, made possible a political compromise of sorts.

Indeed, a politicized focus and coherence to events occurred wherever rioters were sufficiently organized to "select" their own leadership for negotiation, or where there were leaders within the general community who would act and be accepted as "spokesmen." In such cases, militancy around the conference table would match, and often substitute for, militancy in the streets.

2.3. THE RIOT AS EXPRESSIVE RAMPAGE

While many of the larger disorders had pronounced instrumental and political components, there is also a type in which a quality of expressive rampaging on the part of the Negro participants was predominant. All of the ghetto riots involved the spontaneous gathering of an angry crowd in the first phase. But in this third type, the behavior of rioters gained little focus or direction over time. The clearest image is a wandering street mob, angry, drunken, milling about, lacking leadership or direction, engaged in breaking windows, or random acts of vandalism.

The riot in Dayton in 1966, which preceded two smaller disturbances during the summer of 1967, was of this type. From the start those engaged in the disturbance were a "bar crowd" of petty hustlers and drunks, marginal elements in the community. Efforts by the mayor to reach a "political solution" to the riot by negotiating with a militant civil rights leader on the scene was ineffective, because the rioting crowd was organized around drinking and chaotic emotional expression. Efforts to organize the crowd into a meeting to express grievance and negotiate failed totally. The disorder was finally suppressed by heavy arrests once local police were buttressed with National Guard forces.

2.4. THE RIOT AS FULFILLMENT OF ANTICIPATIONS

While the largest disorders generally began with an aggressive ghetto riot followed by a tough police response, there is another category of disturbance in which the flow of events proceeded in the opposite direction. *The first acts of collective aggression came not from Negroes but from control forces—subsequent Negro responses tending to be defensive, protective, or retaliatory.* In such cities as Cambridge, Maryland; Jersey City and Elizabeth, New Jersey, anticipations of Negro lawlessness, rather than actual lawlessness itself, led to periods of disturbance.

These were initiated by precipitous "riot control tactics" or "shows of force" by white authorities. Compared with cities that did have massive ghetto rioting, such disturbances remained fairly minor, although their actual proportions were often greatly exaggerated at the time they occurred.

In Cambridge, Maryland, the presence and speech of H. Rap Brown had a great effect in stimulating local authorities to acts of disorder against the Negro community. His mere presence evoked images in the minds of white leadership that there was an organized conspiracy afoot to lead Cambridge's Negroes in a rampaging pillage of the town's white business district. His inflammatory speech, although failing to galvanize Negro youth to start breaking things up, did produce a wave of hysteria in the Negro police officers who heard it. These reported that a riot was underway—thus confirming the worst fears of local white officials. At one point, after an injury to an officer, the local police chief wanted to go shooting into the area, and only restraints by state authorities prevented bloodshed. Later on, the white volunteer fire department refused to go into the Negro area to put out a small fire that finally spread into a blaze consuming a block of Negro businesses. This non-action stemmed in part from a fear of a preplanned plot to "trap" fire department equipment in the Negro area, thus leaving the downtown area to be burned and plundered.

In a few disorders, white anticipatory action overlapped with an expressive rampage by Negro youth. In Milwaukee, the first evening of disorder began with window breaking and looting by youths on a "hell-raising" spree after a dance. But the authorities had been waiting for some time in anticipation for a try at containing a riot. The response of officials was to call for the mobilization of 4800 Guardsmen, 200 state police, and 800 policemen.

In a few cities *joint expectations* held by *both* Negroes and whites that a "riot was coming" had something of a self-fulfilling character. However, in the absence of truly intense community polarization, the disturbances possessed a staged or simulated quality. The participants seemed to be going through the motions of a riot more than carrying out serious conflict. Lacking was the quality of vengeance and retribution which pervades so much of the behavior on all sides during a riot out of control.

Staged conflict in this sense occurred in New Brunswick, where youths put on a riot in the main street. An effective political response by the lady mayor brought a quick end to the disorder. The second night of rioting in Tucson was "staged" in another sense. Following queries by a newspaper reporter as to where and when they were going to riot that evening, youths put on a minor riot for the benefit of the press.

2.5. THE RIOTS THAT DIDN'T HAPPEN: "MINI-RIOTS" AND OTHERS

In most of the events in which anticipations of violence played an important role, the level of disorder on the Negro side was so minimal as to suggest calling these disturbances "Negro riots that didn't happen." There were also some low-level disturbances—"mini-riots" is an apt term—that reflected in germinal or aborted form dimensions more fully developed in the largest disorders.

The Atlanta and Tampa disturbances showed many characteristics in common with certain northern disorders. In Atlanta, as in Newark and Detroit, a crowd formed in a community gathering place in a high density area. The scene in this instance was a neighborhood shopping center where police-related incidents had occurred the two previous nights. Stokely Carmichael, present to urge the crowd to take to the streets, found an audience willing to take matters into its own hands. But (1) the police immediately moved in with major force and were extremely effective; (2) the mayor quickly responded to the political aspect of the event by beginning visible construction the next day on long-delayed projects demanded by area residents; and (3) a newly-formed Negro Youth Corps helped keep the rest of the summer cool.

In a northern city like Dayton, there was a significant potential in its two 1967 disturbances for a major Negro riot. The first disturbance followed a meeting protesting the cut of a grassroots poverty program. H. Rap Brown was the featured out-of-town visitor at the meeting. He excited youth who were already looking for an excuse to riot.

The second followed a bitter meeting protesting the release of a vice squad officer after a controversial killing of a middle-class Negro professional. An initially decisive police response and the "cooling effect" of the Dayton White Hats in both cases rapidly attenuated the escalation potential in the disturbance.

Finally, in the category of "riots which did not occur" is the traditional race riot which has often marked American history. The potential nevertheless was there. In Cincinnati, New Haven, Newark, and Cambridge, whites were attracted to the scene, ready to take up the banner against Negroes and to defend white property. In such cities, effective police practice prevented white outsiders from coming into Negro areas, thus aborting the race riot process. In Cambridge, where there has been a continuing danger of racial confrontation for several years, the state National Guard acted in its customary role as a buffer against violence.

3. PROCESSES IN DEVELOPING DISORDERS

3.1. URBAN UPHEAVALS AND SATELLITE RIOTS: THE PROPAGATION OF VIOLENCE

As a nationwide phenomenon, the propagation of violence across the land follows the close link between major ghetto upheavals, or reports thereof, and "satellite" disorders in which authority over-reaction occurs. The former has clearly acted as a trigger to the latter. In the wake of a disturbance the size of Newark or Detroit, rumors of small incidents in a local area become magnified as the beginning of a riot. On the white side, a climate of anxiety is produced by stories of planned violence, and fears of outside agitators and conspirators.

After the Detroit upheaval, eight other Michigan cities reported disorders. After the Newark riot, fourteen cities in the surrounding area had some sort of disturbance. *In at least two-thirds of fifteen cities studied in which disorders occurred shortly after major riots, the immediate precipitant of disorder seems to have been a police action prompted by ghetto violence elsewhere.*

The Propagation of Disorder in the New Jersey Chain

To illustrate the propagation effect, let us examine some of the cities in the chain of disturbances that occurred in New Jersey in the aftermath of the Newark riot. In Englewood, police outnumbered participants three to one. In Jersey City, 400 armed police occupied the Negro area several days before the disorder occurred. In most cases, relations became strained as the appearance of armed police patrols increased the likelihood of confrontation with Negro residents. The most frequent citizen demands were for police withdrawal and/or a less visible show of arms. In six of the seven New Jersey "satellite" cities, removal of police from the ghetto signalled an end to violence. Rumors of violence often become self-fulfilling prophecies when credited and responded to with a visible show of force and fear.

Errors in judgment produced by a climate of fear in the white community were typified in many New Jersey cities. One prominent example was officials reacting to rumors that Stokely Carmichael was bringing carloads of Negro militants into the community, although Carmichael was in London at the time. Planning for disorder by New Jersey police departments, even before the Newark upheaval occurred, showed similar elements of irrationality in the face of uncertainty.

On June 5, 1967, the police chiefs of at least 75 New Jersey communities met in Jersey City. They discussed rumors of planned violence by various militant groups who reportedly intended to kill Jersey City police officers in their homes and foment disorder in other New Jersey communities. Jersey City, Newark, and Elizabeth were said to have "Triple A" ratings for violence over the summer. Plans to coordinate control efforts were established, and the chiefs were informed of the procedures for calling in the state police and National Guard.

Thus, a month and a half before Newark erupted, there were rumors of planned violence, and counter-plans were designed. Riot control training was held in a number of communities. In one instance, Negro residents became alarmed when tear gas used in a practice exercise drifted into the Negro section of town. Whether the rumors of planned violence were solid or merely a product of the preconceptions of city officials is difficult to say. But these rumors existing prior to the Newark riot were confirmed in the minds of officials in other New Jersey cities when Newark erupted, subsequently becoming the basis for "riot control" responses.

Another force in the proliferation of disturbances in the vicinity of the big city riots is the network of kinship and friendship relations between Negroes in major cities and outlying areas. For some it was literally true that "the brothers" in Newark or Detroit were "getting some of the action." Many people in Grand Rapids, for example, have relatives in Detroit. Reports that some of these relatives were killed in the Detroit riot increased tension and the potential for violence in that city.

The intensity of the flow of personal information from the Newark and Detroit ghettos to outlying areas at the peaks of the riots is indicated by the high number of out-of-town phone calls from the areas of greatest disturbance. These equalled top loads for a Mother's Day weekend, one of the periods in the year when telephone lines across the country become overloaded.

3.2. THE MEDIA AND THE PROPAGATION OF DISORDER

The majority of people in outlying areas and across the country do not, of course, learn about a riot through immediate personal information. TV can bring people hundreds or thousands of miles distant directly to the scene of a major disorder. *The effect can often be that of the crowd acting at long distance.* This was a typical feature of the non-violent demonstrations of the civil rights movement at its peak. TV pictures of mob violence in the South would spark spontaneous sympathy demonstrations all across the North. And, in many instances, local civil rights movements would indigenously evolve from there.

In the case of the recent disorders, the "crowd at long distance" generated the impression that there was in fact a conspiracy some place for New Jersey to go up all at once. Actually, outbreaks of civil violence were quite spontaneous and unplanned—information from the media lowering the threshold for disorder all across an area.

One definite effect of the media seems to be the determination in time and place that latent tensions will surface into disorder. The potential for major riots in Plainfield and Detroit led by militant Negro youth had been there for some time. It was the Newark riot that dramatically changed "the mood" in Detroit and helped galvanize Negro youths to aggressive action in Plainfield. They might have "blown" anyway—if not at that time, then perhaps at a later date. On the other hand, these cities went through crisis periods before, in which a major disorder could have exploded but did not. Perhaps if Newark had not occurred or if information about it had been totally suppressed, other cities might have weathered the storm—at least temporarily. Progress through institutional channels might have kept one step ahead of the chaos breathing on its heels.

3.3. "OUTSIDE AGITATORS" AND THE SPREAD OF DISORDER

A discussion of the mass media effects in propagating disorder naturally leads into an examination of the actual influence over events of such nationally known, "headline-making" Negro radical "leaders" as Stokely Carmichael and H. Rap Brown. Their role in spreading disorder is by no means simple.

A cursory overview of the points where the distribution of disorder around the country crosses the distribution of appearances of Stokely Carmichael or H. Rap Brown would indicate that most disturbances occurred without their presence to help things along. Of 23 disturbances in our sample, in only 6 were either Carmichael or Brown around the scene at the time. And in only three of these were their appearance and rhetoric immediately linked with the immediate precipitants of disorder. In the other cities they arrived at the scene after action was already underway. In Cincinnati, for example, Brown's major role was presenting a list of some 20 demands from a nationalist group to a representative from the Human Relations Commission on the fourth day of the disturbance.

Thus the number of specific situations with which the presence of a national firebrand could be associated with disorder were very few. *And considering the large number of communities where Brown and Carmichael appeared which did not have riots, their "riot batting-average," if indeed their purpose was to provoke a disorder on the spot, was extremely low.* Nevertheless, Carmichael and Brown do have influence over some events, which stems from the particular way they "lead" people. Their leadership is symbolic rather than organizational. They cannot "command" others to riot—at least at this time—by coming in from out of town and passing down "orders" from the top. But as a symbolic focus for hopes and fears they can generate the emotional predisposition which might encourage disorder.

In this respect, a good deal depends on the mood of their audience when they arrive on the scene. In Atlanta, Carmichael's speech to a crowd suggesting that they force the police to work until they "drop in their tracks" brought a tumultuous response. In Dayton the youth were "looking for an excuse to riot" before Brown arrived. However, in Jersey City, Negro youth quickly fled a meeting at which Brown was speaking when a rumor spread that the police were coming. Brown reportedly left town muttering "the people here aren't ready."

White authorities, as the Cambridge and New Jersey cases illustrate, have often been emotional "followers" of the "leadership" of Brown and Carmichael, in the sense that fears of the influence or presence of the latter generated precipitous actions.

It should be stressed too that the influence process between audience and agitators is a two-way street. In Detroit it was an unknown local man who took upon himself the role of the agitator. But in so doing, he was responding as well to the mood of the crowd and a situation which "commanded" agitation. And while Brown and Carmichael have a utilitarian interest in seeing violence directed against white society's control of Negroes until equality is produced, most of the evidence indicates that crowds use them as much as they use crowds.

Like headliners and public men everywhere, they become tools of community groups in developing motivation and commitment in followers, creating resources, and getting actions going. Thus far, they have been the focal point for a great deal of emotional energies on the part of both Negroes and whites. It is easier, for example, for whites to see riots as caused by H. Rap Brown and Stokely Carmichael, with whom they are familiar, than by the conditions of local Negro communities, with which they are not. Negroes, for their part—especially the young—experience great jubilation in hearing a speaker "tell it like it is" and frighten whites in the process.

Whatever their role at a specific local disorder, however, the major source of influence of leaders like Brown and Carmichael over events is that the media provides them with a national audience. Brown and Carmichael have argued that violence is necessary—violence is occurring around the country—both are reported side by side on TV and in the press. Such a recurrent linking of spokesmen for disorder and actual violence produces cause and effect associations difficult to dispel. Brown and Carmichael become seen as having the extraordinary and dangerous power to spell-bind Negroes into rioting.

While such a conclusion greatly exaggerates their power, we must not underestimate the real importance of their posturing as revolutionaries in the creation of an emotional climate around the country which is conducive to violence. But here too they are not alone. The news media, the political authorities, the reports of the occurrence of actual riots are also central elements in creating a "riot climate."

It would, perhaps, be more appropriate to consider the development of a major ghetto riot, and the appearance of symbolic leaders arguing that violence is legitimate, as but different reflections of the processes of polarization going on throughout the society. It is the role of "spokesmen for rebellion" created by the fact that ghetto rebellions are occurring which is significant, and not Brown or Carmichael specifically. Previously that role was singularly filled by Malcolm X; now new men are moving to fill the gap, rushing to keep up with events more than they are guiding them.

The real source of Brown and Carmichael's influence thus far has been the failure of the white community to make their role irrelevant. Lacking recognition from the white community in other respects, without a place in society for themselves, young Negroes learn quickly that whites are afraid of Brown and Carmichael. *When whites fear your power to cause riots they take you seriously: that is the lesson of events. In this respect whites "load the dice." The role of the militant demagogue and activist is rewarded again and again.*

3.4. INITIAL CONDITIONS IN THE SPREAD OF DISORDER

"Loading the dice" occurs within disturbances. At any phase, the events that have gone before shape the events that follow. This begins before actual violence erupts. If aspirations have been raised but community issues and conflicts continually find ghetto Negroes on the losing end, if a high degree of community polarization has developed, if racial solidarity and militancy within the ghetto has been growing, if there is a large pool of aggressive and ambitious youth available for confrontation, it may be as difficult to contain a disturbance in its first phase as to contain an atomic chain reaction once the critical point has been reached.

This was the case in Detroit where events happened extremely fast, telescoping in a matter of hours community involvement processes that took three days to develop in Watts. In other cities where a truly explosive potential did not exist, it was very likely that a disorder would have died out of its own accord through normal processes of communal restraint without formal authority controls (e.g., mothers scold sons for rampaging, the youth not being serious about rioting, etc.).

Initial features of a disorder, where it was located, the time of day, who was involved, the weather, etc., also were important in determining the direction an incipient disturbance was to move. Rain stopped some incipient riots. Whether the people who initially became riotous were marginal elements of the Negro community or whether they were stable residents was an important consideration. Disorders that pulled in ambitious, achievement-oriented people were more violent.[4] Disorders that began near housing developments, shopping centers, or other places where ordinary people in the community gathered always had an extremely dangerous potential.

Grievances in the Riot Process

Like the question concerning the role of Negro leadership in events, the question of the role of grievances, or the grievance process in disorders, is complicated. A popular model of riot causes sees a high level of unacted grievances, producing community tensions, which in turn produce riots. This theory is popularly held by people with programs or ideas they would like to sell that would ameliorate tensions by reducing grievances.

But there were cities in which the grievance level, in an

[4]As in other areas of community life, the quality of a riot is affected by the level of energy and competency people bring with them. Those who participate in riots (see pp. 174–178 in *The Report of the National Advisory Commission on Civil Disorders*), as compared with those who do not, tend to be younger, better educated, more politically aware, more achievement oriented, more acculturated to the values of an industrialized urban society, and more dissatisfied with their place within it. Across cities, there is some evidence that the quality and character of Negro mass actions (political focus, degree of organization, volatility) is affected by differences in the level of unincorporated youthful talent.

absolute sense, was very high during the summer of 1967 which did not experience aggressive Negro riots. There were others in which the grievance level was much lower which did have aggressive ghetto rioting.

The importance of grievances in an event seems to be determined less by the *level of grievance* than the *kind* of grievance involved. People do not riot *for* better schools, but they will riot *against the police* and government as outside oppressors. Concerns for territory, domination, and hate of "double standards" (social injustice) run like a common thread through most of the largest disorders.

ITEM: In Plainfield, the "double-standard" issue of a policeman failing to make an arrest Negro youth thought he should have was the immediate precipitant.

ITEM: In Cincinnati, the issue of "double-standards" in the courts generated a sense of rage as a Negro was sentenced for murder and a white man for manslaughter within the same month. The first act of direct action was the stopping of delivery trucks by youths objecting to whites getting most of the jobs in Negro areas.

ITEM: In Detroit, the failure of a white newspaper to carry news of a Negro Vietnam veteran's murder at the hands of a white mob created bitterness as the local Negro newspaper reported the incident, including the miscarriage of the murdered man's pregnant wife, in full detail. A few weeks later and a short distance from where the murdered man lived a police raid in an after-hours club where a party for some Negro servicemen was in progress found an agitator haranguing an angry crowd that the police wouldn't do what they were doing in a white area.

ITEM: In Los Angeles in 1965, plaintive appeals of a Negro youth that he was not going to let the police take him to jail, aroused a tug-of-war between local community residents and white police which was the first incident in the Los Angeles riot.

ITEM: In Newark, a massive urban renewal project which would displace thousands of Negroes became the source of a bitter political struggle between the Italian political leadership and Negro militants, and was considered an important "cause" of the riot. Later, the belief of neighborhood residents that the police had not only beaten a taxicab driver but had beaten him before they got him to the police station catalyzed a mood of rebellion and community solidarity.

Grievances of one Negro group against another can also be considered as having a role in precipitating and shaping several disorders.

ITEM: Leadership competition between the Negro militants opposed to the mayor of Newark and the group of conservative Negro leaders who supported him in part prevented an effective counter-riot response to the developing Newark crisis.

ITEM: In Cincinnati, the first outbreak of violence followed a speech by a Negro conservative at a protest rally which supported an anti-loitering law and angered Negro youths.

ITEM: In Dayton's June 1967 disturbance, an intense controversy between militants and conservatives over the funding of an anti-poverty program found a militant leader threatening a riot which shortly occurred.

ITEM: In Cambridge, white fear began to mount as two newly forming Negro groups, one conservative, one militant, began to compete for the leadership role left vacant since Gloria Richardson had left town.

ITEM: In Grand Rapids, entrenched vice elements in the Negro community, who where being threatened by the rising influence of poverty workers in the community, attempted to use the disorder to buttress their declining domination.

ITEM: In Detroit, a developing indigenous community organization leadership of a very militant character was threatening established middle-class leaders who were well-incorporated into the Detroit political system. The latter were willing to go along with a policy of extreme repression the first day of the disturbance. Since the riot, they have been outraged at the willingness of city leadership to meet directly with lower-class representatives, and have fought increases in power for the militant groups.

Finally, the *grievance process*—the effectiveness of the response of authorities to Negro grievances whatever these are—can be a crucial source of grievance itself. The substantive grievances (police practices, neighborhood services, schools, housing, etc.) serve as indicators for measuring exactly how much and in what manner white authorities care about Negroes. They become tests of commitment.

In this respect, "liberal" or "moderate" cities are far more vulnerable to incidence of disorders than racially "conservative" ones. Examination of the 23 disorders in our sample indicates that those cities characterized by a general liberalizing, more "humanitarian" trend in elite attitudes—i.e. public recognition of the legitimacy of Negro complaints—are more likely to have the largest and most violent disorders. This is not surprising.

Prolonged aggressive action by Negroes in racially conservative cities is less likely, because whites promise little, and what they do promise is immediate and extreme use of violent force to quell any disturbance at the outset, regardless of the merits of Negro complaints. In these cities, Negroes are continually reminded of "their place," and if some do not accept this definition they may be persuaded to refrain from violent protest anyhow.

The "tokenistic" pattern of race relations in more moderate or racially liberalizing cities encourages Negro demands for equalities, lifts the fear of extreme force (policemen increasingly attack the civil libertarian and community-relations emphasis of liberal government on the grounds that "law-enforcement is being handcuffed"), yet generally fails to work great immediate changes in the conditions of ghetto life. Individual members of the group have greater mobility and opportunity than ever before, but many still lag behind, their increased desires for advancement unfulfilled. The dilemma of liberalizing governments is that lifting the more overt forms of repression and promises of equalities encourages a more rapid rate of change in the psychology of Negroes than anything else. In such circumstances where old dominance relations are being undermined or are uncertain, grievances can be expected to escalate as Negroes test out white commitments in more and more areas. Growing "black consciousness" and sense of community increases the desire for action against obstacles that cramp ghetto Negroes in daily life, at the same time that white reaction to Negro "pushiness" invokes a sense of betrayal.

This seems extremely crucial for developing a mood of rebellion. Prior to the disorder there, Newark would have been considered a city undergoing racial liberalization. A Negro-Italian political coalition had put the mayor into office, and there had been many promises to the Negro community. Compared with other Northern cities, the level of political access of Negroes in Newark might have been considered fairly high. But a split had developed in the coalition with the Italian political leadership, and Negro community elites engaged in bitter, emotionally charged disputes over police practices, a plan to tear down Negro-occupied areas to construct a medical complex, appointments to the board of education, and other issues. The Negroes saw broken promises, and an attempt by the Italians to establish their political hegemony at Negro expense. By the second evening of disorder in Newark, people were far beyond the stage where they would be willing to accept a token concession at the price of mitigating their righteous vengeance which had been so long in developing. Once that mood was there, a sudden concession itself triggered disorder as Negroes so to speak threw the concession of a Negro police captain back into the faces of the authorities with the attitude "keep it, you can't buy us that cheaply *now*."

3.5. THE COMPETITIVE PROCESS IN DEVELOPING DISORDER

Negotiations at such points fail because many people want combat more than peace. During a disorder itself, a competitive sense among Negro youths may become a powerful impetus to keeping the violence going. In Newark, some youths did not want to stop the riot because the score in deaths stood "25–2" with the police and guardsmen leading.

The Game of Riot: Emasculating the Police

Within various groups on the street, people were quite conscious of the heroism and daring exhibited by young men. For Negro youth, challenging the police with taunts and dares involved a dangerous and dramatic competition. Their goal was to disrupt police order, to make the police "lose their cool," to produce situations in which police worked until they "dropped in their tracks." Much of the behavior of the youth during a riot can be accounted for by this motivation: *They are interested not in killing policemen, but in humiliating them.* As Negroes have been rendered powerless for so long, as the police have continually disrupted the activities of the ghetto, the disorder becomes the grand opportunity to turn the tables.

In this respect, the riots also serve the functions of "ritual ceremonies" in which manhood is demonstrated. Many acts of confrontation (e.g., laying bear the chest and taunting police to shoot), which have a great intensity and seriousness about them are also dramatic posturing—open and public proof to both oneself and the police that things have changed. The test has dangers, but afterwards one can never go back to what he was before.

This form of street confrontation with the police, it should be noted, is not new. If we include the Southern non-violent movement, it has been going on for 6 years. In the South during 1962–1965 militant civil rights activists, many of whom were of Northern background, became experts in the technique of disorganizing Southern police through non-violent demonstrations.

Negro youth in the North are now the aggressors. Instead of "non-violent" demonstrations, breaking white property, setting fires, and racial taunting have become major aspects of the techniques of breaking up the police.

Much Negro youth "crime" has always had this quality of testing by "street games" with authorities. Confronting police and courts in efforts to construct a self-definition in which one does have some kind of place in society—if only a criminal one—does have a functional basis. Those who have served time return to their old associations with a new status as someone who is really tough and knows the ropes.

What is distinctive now is that this same process feeds into community confrontation. Traditional street testing behavior by Negro youth is channeling into the disruption of city institutions. The massiveness of the disruption in a riot stems from the fact that a great number of youth are getting their badges of manhood all at once. Previously this occurred through the orderly and recurrent process of one-by-one confrontation which white institutions easily handled in the past.

Cross-City Competition

Evidence in our data indicate that cross-city competition among youth: "who holds the record, now?" becomes a salient force once control by police is lost. Cities that have already had major upheavals acquire symbolic value and become standards for comparison in other disturbances. For some participants there is a quite explicit desire to outdo New York, or Watts, etc. A Negro girl in Newark asked a reporter, "Was the Harlem riot worse than this?" and assured that it was not, she cried, "that's good, that's great!"

Distinctive features of several major disturbances during the summer of 1967 can in part be attributed to the excitement generated among young Negroes that they were either doing something in a riot that had not been done before, or that they were doing it better than ever. Negro youths in Newark were quite proud that they were the "first" to ever lay siege to a police station. As the governor passed by in a National Guard tank, there were heated street side discussions on "How do you get into a tank with a Molotov cocktail?"

There is no reason to preclude the possibility of disruptive acts more consequential than any that have yet occurred. The "first" tank to be fire bombed, the "first" power station to be blown up, are but logical extension of the present pattern of disorder. "We're number one!" after all is an old American tradition.

4. THE MEANING OF THE DISORDERS FOR AMERICAN SOCIETY

Jubilant Negro youths trying to set a "record," however, are not always to be cheered as they go about their work. Nor are the absurdities of white social beliefs concerning "planned, organized conspiracies" or the existence of armies of "snipers" to be laughed at when these contribute to chaos and the loss of life. Yet both are very much a part of the American social scene today. And if we consider the disorders in terms of their meaning for the future of American society, the future looks even more troublesome than the present.

There is, for example, no reason to believe that aggressive ghetto rioting will cease of its own accord, or that new violent tendencies on the side of Negroes—such as terrorism—will not develop out of the present pattern of disorder. There is also the possibility of race riots—white and Negro confronting each other directly in violent struggle—in the future. So far these tendencies have been checked by the confinement of black uprisings to attacks on white authority and property within the ghetto. But this does not rule out the possibility of punitive forays across the boundaries of the ghetto by either whites or blacks in the future. It could also happen that the white majority in the society—preferring order at any cost—will encourage the adoption of repressive police policies which would greatly restrict liberty and undermine liberal institutions.

These are possibilities, not predictions. In any event, it is clear that the disorders as we have attempted to picture them were not momentary collective aberrations but reflected the workings of powerful forces in American society. The energies of Negro youth are one of these forces. With those under 21 years of age comprising 50% of the Negro population of the country, and a considerably higher percentage of those at the forefront of the disturbances, Negro youth have been the most prominent actors in the drama of ghetto disorders. Acculturated in the values of an industrial, urban society, increasingly finding a solution to the problem of identity in "Black Awareness," more and more confident, yet living in a country that denies them the structures to realize their aspirations,[5] Negro youth can be expected to continue to take matters into their own hands —one way or another.

The major obstacle to their desires for power is the racial basis of political culture in the United States—a tendency to view the workings of democracy and institutional power in white-only terms. It would not exaggerate present reality to say that democratic America is effectively ruled by a racist majority. "This is not a riot but a rebellion against white man's rules

[5]An interesting case in point is the rapid rise in Negro youth unemployment in recent years. The explanation for this is not that jobs are unavailable, but that Negro youth refuse to take jobs traditionally available to them. The desire is for occupational employment which provides status, good income, and responsibility: in short, their aspirations are typical American aspirations.

against constitutional authority: We're fighting a war. This is war!" declared a high-ranking official in the New Jersey fraternal order of police at the time of the Newark upheaval. His statement reflected the popular attitude of many whites which fuses the concepts of law and order, with white rule. Such an attitude is fundamentally antagonistic to Negro demands for greater control over the conditions of their existence. White racism, in this respect, is a cause for violence.

This is not to deny, however, that society has not become more racially liberal in recent years. In fact the values of the American Dream—of a nation of nations and opportunity for all individuals of talent—is more highly institutionalized than ever before. But it is this very liberalism with its civil rights laws, poverty programs, and constraints on arbitrary police practices which has provided the context within which the present clashes have become inevitable. In undermining the basis of legitimacy of the more overt forms of racial domination, American liberalism has brought into question inequalities between Negroes and whites in all areas of life. In the present circumstances nobody is happy. While the mood of Negro youth is that "We're a Winner,"[6] the barriers of the ghetto, which they hate so much, have yet to be fully broken down. The police, on the other hand, hate the constraints which they feel are inhibiting them in dealing effectively with the rising tide of Negro "law violators." Thus, the backdrop to the conflicts on the streets is the mortal combat between American racism and American liberalism. So far, the latter has failed to find the strategies and resources for moving society through change so quickly that neither the police nor Negro youth have the inclination or energy to fight each other.

Given the present impasse, the effective choice open to those in public authority does not seem to be peace vs. violent disorder, but the character and type of violent disorder that occurs.

[6]The reader is encouraged to listen carefully to the lyrics of a song entitled: "We're a Winner," presently very popular among Negro youth. One recording is by The Impressions, "We're a Winner," (ABC Records, S–635.).

The present need is to find ways of limiting the intensity of physical confrontations in the short-run, at the same time using their occurrence as a tool to encourage rapid cultural and institutional changes in the direction of racial democracy. In this respect, disorders which are political confrontations, in which leaders exercise effective control over events, in which violence is focused rather than random, are probably to be preferred to anarchic mass rioting or terrorism, lack of co-ordinated leadership control, and indiscriminate attacks on persons and property in which race alone is a sufficient designator of friend or foe.

While the role of civil authority and police control tactics in the development of disorders is too large to be handled in this paper, it is clear that programs aimed at changing law enforcement practices such that the police are simultaneously effective in maintaining public order and respected within Negro areas are to be encouraged. Congruently, there would seem to be a need for programs aimed at developing stable and effective leadership within Negro communities—albeit militant, nationalist, and occasionally violent—that will enable the incorporation of Negro youth into the American Dream.

SUMMARY

Civil disorders in American cities in 1967 popularly referred to as "Negro riots" varied in many critical respects. Some can more appropriately be described as *social upheavals* characterized by a two-phase flow of lawless activities. Others had the character of *political confrontations*, disorder being used as a political tool by emerging Negro groups to encourage civil authorities to bargain and negotiate with them. Few disorders can be viewed simply as *expressive rampages:* riots by the anarchic and criminal elements in the community whose binge of antisocial destruction can only be stopped by "get tough" police practices. "Get tough" police policies were also the cause of some notable disturbances where the *fulfillment of anticipations* of Negro initiated disorder rather than its reality. Across the nation, ghetto upheavals would trigger "satellite" disorders in which authority over-reaction occurred. The spread of news about disorders was an important factor in the propagation of violence, considerably more so than actions of Negro radical leaders to foment such events.

The initial conditions out of which a disorder emerged affected its course. Pre-existing grievances have a role, but the *kind of grievance* rather than the *number* of grievances seems more important. Negro youths have grievances against the police, and a ghetto uprising may take on the character of a competitive game in which youth attempt to humiliate the police.

The contradictions between American liberalism and American racism make the future seem troublesome. Short-run strategies of conflict amelioration might profitably be concerned not with eliminating violence but with limiting it such that it promotes rather than hinders the movement toward racial democracy.

PART VI
Research

Part VI concludes the presentation of conflict in this book by returning to the focus of Part II which was general theories of social conflict. In "Research Models and Designs for the Study of Conflict," Delmer M. Hilyard establishes a perspective for the study of conflict and cooperation as a process which is *not* limited to any particular setting and which can account for individual differences. Hilyard's research perspective can be used to integrate the diverse general theories of conflict.

DELMER M. HILYARD

Research Models and Designs for the Study of Conflict

"Hey, ugly old woman, carry that lumber over here to this pile!"

That statement, which I once heard a 65-year-old husband caustically shout to his wife of more than 40 years in their backyard, has long stood for me as an example of the difficulties in research on conflict. In my view, the woman *was* old, she *was* ugly, and her husband was tactlessly, even ruthlessly, demanding that she perform an unwomanly, inappropriate task. Those words, which would have been considered "fighting words" where I come from, were clearly not considered negatively in this backyard. Her reaction as I perceived it was accepting and responsive—but not unduly submissive and without apparent loss of self-integrity. If the statement were to represent conflict, it had to be conflict at another time and at another place. In this context, the statement that could be considered a hostile provocation, assumed the characteristics of endearment.

Fight behaviors or acts of physical violence may similarly be construed as supportive actions. When the dazed movie hero responds to a slap in the face with a "Thanks, I needed that," we are quick to recognize cooperative intent and cooperative response. The marital pair, who energetically trade blows and demand that arbitrators remain out of "our quarrel," tends to leave us rather bewildered but accepting the idea that they represent a cooperative pairing. The sadist-masochist encounter, regardless of how bloody it may be, is by definition designated as a cooperative event. In contrast, sit-ins, lie-ins, and picket lines are examples of non-violent, physical actions from which a condition of conflict is inferred.

A major difficulty for behavioral scientists who may wish to study conflict is suggested by such examples. Actions, even sets of reciprocal actions, do not necessarily provide a sufficient identification of conflict or of cooperation. Conflict, it seems, like beauty is in "the eye of the beholder."

Despite the difficulties that idiosyncracy imposes on classification, conflict behavior is "real" enough. Just as almost all observers can agree at times that a given object is beautiful, so too can they agree that an observed *X* is incompatible and in conflict with an observed *Y*. Agreement, however among observers about a specific *X–Y* incompatibility does not eliminate other difficulties involved in the study of conflict. Decisions must still be made about which conflict events are the most likely to increase our understanding of conflict and which research methods are the most efficiently adaptive to the events of interest.

The labyrinth of perspectives, definitions, and procedures identified with the study of conflict (e.g., through inclusion as content or as bibliographic items within this volume) suggests, on the one hand, the open alternatives to study and, on the other hand, the degree of "conflict" that the development of conflict theory is likely to induce among behavioral scientists.

A faculty colleague has stated to me on past occasions that he took particular positions on issues of the moment "not because I believed that extremely, but because I wanted to hear what it sounded like." Analogously, the research models and strategies presented in the remaining sections of this chapter are not intended as rejections of other perspectives, but as a testing of some alternatives in the hope that clarification might be gained in the process.

BASIC RESEARCH ASSUMPTIONS

Fictional writings have traditionally been classified according to the dominant conflicts that serve as central themes. Such conflict themes are (1) life–death, (2) man–his physical environment, (3) man–other men, and (4) man–his society. This scheme, developed from a study of literature, has a useful correspondence to the organizational pattern incorporated into observational studies of conflict behavior. Biological, psychological, sociological, and anthropological data have all been considered as relevant inclusions into perspectives regarding conflict.

Although the central concern here is social-psychological conflict, other conflict themes also support a clarification of perspective. The biological theme (life–death) is a particularly valuable example if life processes (growth) are contrasted with death processes (decay). Three factors regarding growth and decay are presented as explanatory analogies for important assumptions that underlie the development of model and research orientations for the study of social-psychological conflict.

The *first* factor is our awareness as humans that growth and decay are *simultaneous* processes. Life as a condition is definable only in terms of growth as the prevailing, dominant process at a specific point in time. Decay as the countering process (and regardless of the value or probability attached to it) is also "on the scene." By analogy, the first two assumptions are (1) that conflict (or competition) and cooperation (or collaboration) are also simultaneous processes, and (2) that the evaluation of a specified behavior as competitive or cooperative is a relative judgment about which process is dominant.

Second, life generally has high psychological and social value but death does not. Within this dichotomous value system, doctors, for example, work diligently to maintain life (i.e., growth or regeneration) as the dominant process. However, once it has been confirmed that life is no longer a sustainable alternative, the decay process is accepted and its social value is regarded as more positive. That is, we expect bodies including human bodies to decay and can appreciate the fact that they do.

From this analogy an additional pair of assumptions is derived. The first is that social-psychological processes (e.g., behavioral interaction) are predominantly conflict processes only during those time periods that alternatives are being reduced and new values are being assigned to the remaining alternatives. The corollary assumption is that cooperation processes are dominant during those times that alternatives are increasing and that valuations are being redistributed to accommodate the additions to the set of choices.

These assumptions are, of course, based on the notion of process, change, or non-constancy. So-called "steady-state" conditions, such as "continued cooperation" or "continued fighting" are assumed to be changing in one direction or another, even though such change is imperceptible or ignored. Peace, for example, becomes an alternative undergoing reevaluation as soon as war has been declared.

A *third* factor is the recognition that biological and psychological (plus sociological and cultural) processes are interrelated. Psychological factors affect and are affected by growth and decay. An increase (gain) in physical growth may be accompanied by a decrease (cost) in psychological well-being. Psychological comforts (e.g., drugs) may be countered by a cost in physical health. A third set of assumptions is (1) that conflict–cooperation is accompanied by a change in the relationships among other counter-processes, and (2) that a change in another set of counter-processes affects the conflict/cooperation process. For example, the price for maintaining interpersonal cooperation may be an ulcer; an ulcer may be an antecedent of hostile reactions to messages of cooperative intent.

A GENERAL CONFLICT–COOPERATION MODEL

The earlier example, that doctors work to sustain life, also points to the interrelatedness of conflict themes. Biological counter-processes are also in a sense intra-cultural even cross-cultural counter-processes; oppositely, cultural compatibilities–incompatibilities are in a sense biological. As "cultural agents" doctors add their efforts to the regenerative processes of the individual in order to keep life dominant. Life is a cultural concern.

This interrelatedness has more specific application to the study of interpersonal competition and cooperation. Competition between two individuals or two groups most frequently occurs within a context which includes a third individual or third group. At times, the third party is viewed as the "cultural agent" or the "keeper of the rules." The third party's task is to monitor, manage, and control the behavioral progression of the cooperative/competing parties. Monitor-control tasks, for example, provide definition for such socio-cultural roles as marriage counselors, court justices, and referees for sports events.

Dispute frequently shifts away from the "competitive" relationship and shifts toward the "cooperative" relationship between the "competitors" and the "judge." Sports umpires, for example, appear to lead as dangerous (conflict-filled) lives as the sportsmen.

The frequency with which conflict appears to shift away from a presumed focal relationship (at a specified time and place) to involve other relationships (at other times or other places) suggests that study must include more than the behaviors and/or attitudes identifying the focal conflict. For example, it does not appear sufficient to study only the reciprocal grievances in labor/management relations. It seems also necessary to study labor and management's relationships with mediators, or more broadly, with socio-cultural "rules" or contexts. Similarly, it does not seem likely that an understanding of marital conflict and divorce (as one example of dyadic conflict) can be based only on the answers to the question of "How often do you beat your wife?" Understanding must necessarily include information about "How often do you beat the judge?" and "How often does the judge beat you?" The study of interpersonal conflict obviously is a multifaceted, multirelational undertaking.

This perspective regarding the concept of conflict to this point is certainly general enough to incorporate virtually all social science into the domain of interpersonal conflict theory and research. There is little doubt that the most useful research regarding these processes requires interdisciplinary approaches. I do not intend to be facetious in asserting that "cooperation" specialists are essential to "conflict" research, just as it is essential that some researchers collect data regarding the focal relationships while others observe and classify the contexts. Despite such all-inclusiveness, however, the definitions (assumptions) which have been presented do suggest some theory and research orientations as being more centrally important than others.

MODELS OF INFORMATION PROCESSING

In his 1951 book *Language and Communication,* George A. Miller stated that if people did not have some degree of similarity, communication would not be possible, and if they did not have some degree of difference (incompatibility), communication would not be necessary.[1] A similar insight is indicated in Jandt's statement that "only through communication can we engage in social conflict and the resolution of that conflict."[2] Also, Blake and Mouton's wish is that people "work out their differences face-to-face," that people talk or "communicate" with one another.[3] Clearly, communication models are conflict–cooperation models.

If research models and designs are kept in correspondence with the assumptions regarding the conflict–cooperation processes, then some communication models are more useful than others and some models are useful only if modified. For example, Lasswell's early model "Who says what to whom and with what effect?" must necessarily have modification to include such additional phrases as "And at what cost to the source

[1]George A. Miller, *Language and Communication,* New York: McGraw-Hill, 1951.

[2]Fred E. Jandt, *Conflict Resolution Through Communication,* Preface.

[3]Robert R. Blake and Jane Srygley Mouton, "The Fifth Achievement," *Journal of Applied Behavioral Science 6,* 1970, 413–426.

(who)?"[4] Even with that modification, however, the Lasswell model does not sufficiently correspond to the assumptions regarding conflict–cooperation.

To meet the basic assumptions about conflict, an appropriate model must be a *process* model. That is, it must accommodate, or account for, a progression of changes through time. In addition, since the progression of changes is assumed to be directional (increasing or decreasing numbers of alternatives), a useful conflict–cooperation model must also be able to accommodate a sufficient number of differences, alternatives, or "incompatibilities" to warrant a judgment that it adequately fits "real world" processes.

Such models are evolving and are being used in communication research. For example, "information-processing" models are being developed as concept models with application to intrapersonal and interpersonal processes. As such models evolve they are accompanied by developments in statistical, analytical models and procedures which promote their feasibility as research-relevant conceptual frames. Multivariate statistical procedures are now a visible component of communication study.[5]

Three examples of "information-processing" models that are applicable to conflict–cooperation research are Neisser's cognitive-processing model based on perception research problems and data,[6] Bieri's cognitive complexity–simplicity model of personality structure,[7] and Fisher's decision modification model of small-group processes.[8]

The applicability of these and other information-processing models is their general accommodation to assumptions regarding

[4]Harold D. Lasswell, "The Structure and Function of Communication in Society," in *The Communication of Ideas,* ed. Lyman Bryson, New York: Harper & Row, 1948, p. 37.

[5]Philip Emmert and William D. Brooks, eds., *Methods of Research in Communication,* Boston: Houghton Mifflin, 1970.

[6]Ulric Neisser, *Cognitive Psychology,* New York: Appleton, 1967.

[7]J. Bieri, "Cognitive Complexity-Simplicity and Predictive Behavior." *Journal of Abnormal and Social Psychology 51,* 1955, 263–268.

[8]B. Aubrey Fisher, "Decision Emergence: Phases in Group Decision-Making," *Speech Monographs 37,* 1970, 53–66.

patterned changes (increases and decreases) in number of alternatives or items of information. Research related to such model development has provided useful insights regarding structural and time dimensional limits of intrapersonal and interpersonal "coping" with alternatives.

TRANSACTIONAL OR EXCHANGE MODELS

Coser has defined social (interpersonal) conflict as "a struggle over values or claims to status, power, and scarce resources in which the aims of the conflicting parties are not only to gain the desired values but also to neutralize, injure, or eliminate their rivals."[9] Much conflict research has tended to operationalize from a perspective similar to the premises underlying Coser's definition. Although Coser's concerns and his vocabulary are sociological rather than *logical* only, the definition is roughly equivalent to the defining conditions of the "constant-sum game" of rational-game theory.[10]

In each case conflict is established as a condition on the basis of defined goals. Game-theory, based on assumptions of rational decision-making processes, assumes well-defined *interests* of the conflicting parties as well as the existence of alternative courses of action.[11] Coser similarly assumes status, power and scarce resources to be goals defining conflict and/or motivating conflict behavior.

Other conflict theorists support the notion that incompatibility with respect to means or subgoals is also a conflict situation.[12] The inadequacy of goal-definitions of conflict appears to be the emphasis on gains, i.e., goals, with restricted or neglected

[9] Lewis A. Coser, "Conflict: Social Aspect," in *International Encyclopedia of the Social Sciences*, ed. David L. Sills, New York: Free Press, 1968.

[10] Anatol Rapoport, "Conflict Resolution in the Light of Game Theory and Beyond," in *The Structure of Conflict*, ed. Paul Swingle, New York: Academic, 1970, pp. 1–43.

[11] *Ibid.*

[12] Bertram H. Raven and Arie W. Kruglanski, "Conflict and Power," in *The Structure of Conflict*, ed. Paul Swingle, New York: Academic, 1970, pp. 69–109.

attention to costs. (Although costs may be defined as outcomes or products, costs for the moment are considered as *means* relative to gains as *goals*.) Game theory, which has been a major component of conflict theory and research, restricts costs to the resources within the game. The winner of a zero-sum game by definition has no cost.

Transactional models of communication incorporate both costs and gains as factors or variables of the communication process. Homans' exchange theory[13] and Thibault and Kelley's conceptualization of social power[14] are two well-known transactional models. Bauer has considered communication at the societal, mass media level as a transactional process in discussion of "The Obstinate Audience."[15] As far as I am aware, however, no model considers costs and gains in terms of the interrelated counter-processes assumed to define conflict at all levels of man's transactions.

If conflict management is the goal of research efforts, then the needed communication models are ones that take gain–cost changes into account. Conflict management, if the assumptions regarding conflict and cooperation are accepted, becomes primarily the control and distribution of gains and costs in such a way that they occur as relatively small, and therefore, relatively frequent adjustments, adaptations, or changes in relations at intrapersonal and interpersonal levels. An adequate communication model thus incorporates the relational elements where gains might be expected, but most importantly, *also* incorporates relational elements where costs might be simultaneously expected.

Triadic-relation models appear to be the minimal representations of this cost–gain perspective. For example, role-conflict models that attempt to account for the changes in A–B, A–C, and B–C relationships are relevant to the transactional perspec-

[13]George Homans, *Social Behavior: Its Elementary Forms*, New York: Harcourt Brace Jovanovich, 1961.

[14]J. W. Thibault and H. H. Kelley, *The Social Psychology of Groups*, New York: Wiley, 1959.

[15]Raymond Bauer, "The Obstinate Audience," *American Psychologist 19*, 1964, 319–328.

tive. In illustration of the example, the employee's wife, as well as the employer, has a cost–gain stake in the employee's decision to accept or reject a request to work late. In turn, the wife's satisfaction with the decision is a cost–gain factor for both the employer and the employee.

Although not stated in cost–gain language, Newcomb's analysis of interpersonal balance includes a comparable statement that

> . . . problems of consistency that involve both one's own and another person's cognitions of some common object are psychologically different from those involving one's own cognitions of two objects. The former set of cognitions typically includes the other person as a source of attitudes, and this introduces the possibility of his agreement or disagreement with oneself.[16]

Newcomb's balance studies and related research such as Aronson and Cope's study of "My Enemy's Enemy Is My Friend" involve triadic relations that serve as beginning points for conflict and cooperation studies in interpersonal affairs.[17]

NEEDED RESEARCH EFFORTS: FIELD AND LABORATORY

Gamson, in his analysis of laboratory studies of coalition formation, advised experimenters of ways to provide empirical support for each of four alternative theories of coalition. His guidelines suggest that variation of communication networks, that is, experimentally controlled differences in interaction relationships, can account for differences in the explanatory relevance of minimum resource, minimum power, anticompetition and "utter confusion" theories.[18] It is the study of communication network patterns, in terms of cost–gain relationships and of ongoing processes, that represents an appropriate focal point for

[16]Theodore M. Newcomb, "Interpersonal Balance," in *Theories of Cognitive Consistency*, R. P. Abelson, ed., Chicago: Rand McNally, 1968, pp. 28–51.

[17]Elliot Aronson and Vernon Cope, "My Enemy's Enemy Is My Friend," *Journal of Personality and Social Psychology 8*, 1968, 8–12.

[18]William A. Gamson, "Experimental Studies of Coalition Formation," in *Advances in Experimental Social Psychology*, Leonard Berkowitz, ed., Vol. I (New York: Academic, 1964, pp. 81–110).

conflict research and theory development. Most importantly, the perspective presented here, that conflicts are identifiable as conditions of alternative, or choice, reduction, requires that conflict research include the study of communication under more conditions than only those situations within which hostility is presumed to dominate relationships.

I am quite ready to admit that we live in an imperfect, oftentimes threatening world, but also to assert that there is much "real-world" evidence that conflict is managed successfully, with apparently well-distributed gains and costs in many interpersonal relationships. Such successful management occurs at cross-cultural as well as provincial levels. In order for an adequate theory of conflict to be developed it is undoubtedly necessary that field-research efforts include the collection of cost–gain data regarding cooperative relationships. Successful marriages, including those of "ugly old women," can provide information about cost–gain distribution and patterns of increasing and decreasing alternatives, just as marital conflict–divorce relations can provide information about unsatisfactory management. Similarly, continued study of group and organizational patterns of information-processing and decision-making can furnish insights into conflict and cooperation management.

Laboratory studies appear to be most relevant if they attend to individual or group development and identification of alternatives, and/or if they attend to information-processing, alternative-reducing, problem-solving processes. For example, brainstorming groups, whose research task is to develop as many problem solutions as possible, can provide data as relevant for a theory of conflict as the data from groups which have a limited set of alternatives fixed by the experimenter. As Gerald Miller has suggested elsewhere, an understanding of conflict is likely to require more than studies of persuasion hypotheses regarding pro–con, either–or alternatives.[19] Miller's suggestion may be more generally applied to most social-psychological experimentation: laboratory studies appropriate to conflict theory necessarily have to account for and test hypotheses regarding multi-alternative conditions.

[19]Gerald R. Miller, Foreword.

One of the most potentially useful means for study of multi-alternative conditions is in the use of social simulation and role-playing activities in the extended laboratory situation.[20] The utility of these procedures is based on their relative correspondence to "real-world" conditions while there is some retention of control by the experimenters through specification of the role and/or simulation "rules of the game." Such approaches, while possibly sacrificing some the "physical-science model" rigor of laboratory experimentation, provide more suitable opportunity for observation of interpersonal communication processes.

Simulation procedures appear particularly appropriate for studying variations in communication networks. For example, there is recognition that communication can lead to a similarity of perspective (i.e., an ethnocentric, singular alternative) and that differences can arise because communication channels are unavailable or unused. Simulations for the purpose of studying various uses and non-uses of communication channels could provide highly relevant information about conflict and cooperation management. Questions appropriate for study through simulation procedures include: (1) How does conflict intensity vary as groups are kept apart, given different perspectives within the groups, before intergroup channels are made available or are used? (2) What communication behaviors can provide the cues for "opening" or "closing" communication channels at times that are best suited for minimal-conflict distribution of gains and costs? (3) What are the intergroup costs (perhaps defined as negative attitudes) of intragroup gains (positive attitudes, supportive behaviors, etc.)?

CONCLUSION

These suggestions for research are merely indicative of the broad efforts that appear necessary for developing an adequate

[20]Fred E. Jandt, "The Simulation of Social Conflict," paper presented at Speech Communication Associated sponsored conference, March 2–4, 1972, at Sugar Loaf, Temple University, Philadelphia.

theory of conflict. Prior research, as the representative articles of this volume attest, has contributed significantly to a more discriminatory awareness of interpersonal conflict behavior. Continued research efforts within the communication framework that have been suggested can add to that knowledge base.

The major defining condition presented here—namely, that conflict is a process of reducing alternatives—shows to both the writer and the reader the paradox of interpersonal communication. As a writer it has been necessary for me to structure my message, to make choices, to reduce alternatives to a singular perspective. In short, it has been necessary that I accept some psychological conflict in order to fulfill a goal of writer–reader cooperation.

As seems to be the case with conflict in general, the psychological conflict shifts from the writer to you as the reader. That is, your task has been to consider your own as well as the alternative view presented here and to reduce those alternative views to a singular one. Hopefully, you have managed successfully (i.e., with a reasonable diffusion of frustration and hostility). The knowledge that I have intentionally introduced conflict makes it seem appropriate to use a phrase of our times—"sorry about that"—and to assure us both that we are ready once again to consider alternatives regarding the scope and focus of conflict behaviors.

Bibliography

Albee, Edward. *Who's Afraid of Virginia Woolf?* (New York: Atheneum, 1962).

Alger, Ian. "The Superego in Time of Social Conflict." *Journal of Contemporary Psychotherapy 3*, 1970, 51–56.

Alinsky, Saul D. *Reveille for Radicals* (New York: Random House, 1969).

Alinsky, Saul D. *Rules for Radicals: A Practical Primer for Realistic Radicals* (New York: Random House, 1971).

Arnold, William R. "Criminality, Conflict and Adolescent Ambivalence." *Social Science Quarterly 49*, 1968, 360–367.

Assael, Henry. "Constructive Role of Interorganizational Conflict." *Administrative Science Quarterly 14*, 1969, 573–582.

Atthone, John M., Jr. "Types of Conflict and Their Resolution: A Reinterpretation." *Journal of Experimental Psychology 59*, 1960, 1–9.

Aubert, Vilhelm. "Competition and Dissensus: Two Types of Conflict and Conflict Resolution." *Journal of Conflict Resolution 7*, 1963, 26–42.

Ayoub, Victor F. "Conflict Resolution and Social Reorganization in a Lebanese Village." *Human Organization 24*, 1965, 11–17.

Bailey, Norman A. "Toward a Praxeological Theory of Conflict." *Orbis 11*, 1968, 1081–1112.

Barbu, Zeuedi. "Social Conflict and National Myth." *Listener 78*, 1967, 116–117.

Bard, Morton. "A Community Psychology Program in Police Family Crisis Intervention: Preliminary Impressions." *International Journal of Social Psychiatry 15*, 1969, 209–215.

Bard, Morton, and Joseph Zacker. "Design for Conflict Resolution." *American Psychology Association Proceedings 5*, 1970, 803–804.

Barkun, Michael. "Conflict Resolution Through Implicit Mediation." *Journal of Conflict Resolution 8*, 1964, 121–130.

Barry, William A. "Marriage Research and Conflict: An Integrative Review." Psychological Bulletin 73, 1970, 41–54.

Bass, Bernard M., and George Dunteman. "Biases in the Evaluation of One's Own Group, Its Allies and Opponents," *Journal of Conflict Resolution 7*, 1963, 16–20.

Bateman, Mildred M., and Joseph S. Jensen. "The Effects of Religious Background on Modes of Handling Anger," *Journal of Social Psychology 47*, 1958, 133–141.

Bay, Christian. "Political and Apolitical Students: Facts in Search of Theory," *Journal of Social Issues 23*, 1967, 76–91.

Beck, Dorothy Fahs. "Marital Conflict: Its Course and Treatment as Seen By Caseworkers," *Social Casework 47*, 1966, 211–221.

Becker, Joseph, and Eileen Iwakami. "Conflict and Dominance Within Families of Disturbed Children," *Journal of Abnormal Psychology 74*, 1969, 330–335.

Beer, Stafford. "Operational Research Approach to the Nature of Conflict," *Political Studies 14*, 1966, 117–132.

Bennett, Lerone, Jr. *Confrontation: Black and White* (Chicago: Johnson, 1965).

Bennett, Lerone, Jr. "Confrontation on the Campus," *Ebony 23*, 1968, 27–34.

Bennett, William. "Conflict Rhetoric and Game Theory: An Extrapolation and Example," *Southern Speech Communication Journal 37*, 1971, 34–46.

Berger, Stephen E., and James T. Tedeschi. "Aggressive Behavior of Delinquent, Dependent, and Normal White and Black Boys in Social Conflict," *Journal of Experimental Social Psychology 5*, 1969, 352–370.

Berkowitz, Leonard. "The Expression and Reduction of Hostility," *Psychological Bulletin 55*, 1958, 257–283.

Bernard, Jessie. "Where is the Modern Sociology of Conflict?" *American Journal of Sociology 56*, 1950, 11–16.

Bernard, Jessie. "Parties and Issues in Conflict," *Journal of Conflict Resolution 1*, 1957, 111–121.

Bernard, Jessie. "The Sociological Study of Conflict," *The Nature of Conflict: Studies on the Sociological Aspects of International Tensions.* UNESCO, Tensions and Technology Series (Paris: UNESCO, 1957).

Bings, Donald A., and E. G. Williamson. "Conflict Resolution on the Campus: A Case Study," *Journal of College Student Personnel 11*, 1970, 97–102.

Blake, Robert R., and Jane Srygley Mouton. "The Fifth Achievement," *Journal of Applied Behavioral Science 6*, 1970, 413–426.

Blood, Robert O., Jr. "Resolving Family Conflicts," *Journal of Conflict Resolution 4*, 1960, 209–219.

Boskin, Joseph. "The Revolt in the Urban Ghetto 1964–1967," *Annals of the American Academy of Political and Social Sciences 382*, 1969, 1–14.

Boulding, Elise. *Conflict Management in Organizations* (Ann Arbor, Michigan: Foundation for Research on Human Behavior, 1961).

Boulding, Kenneth E. "Organization and Conflict," *Journal of Conflict Resolution 1*, 1957, 122–134.

Boulding, Kenneth E. *Conflict and Defense: A General Theory* (New York: Harper & Row, 1962).

Boulding, Kenneth E. "Where Are We Going If Anywhere?" *Liberation 7*, 1962, 17–21.

Boulding, Kenneth E. "Towards a Theory of Protest," *ETC: A Review of General Semantics 24*, 1967, 49–58.

Bowers, John Waite, and Donovan J. Ochs. *The Rhetoric of Agitation and Control* (Reading, Mass.: Addison-Wesley, 1971).

Brager, George. "Commitment and Conflict in a Normative Organization," *American Sociological Review 34*, 1969, 482–491.

Bridey, Warren M., and Majorie Hazden. "Intrateam Reactions: Their Relations to the Conflicts of the Family in Treatment," *American Journal of Orthopsychiatry 27*, 1957, 349–355.

Brody, Eugene A. "Social Conflict and Schizophrenic Behavior in Young Adult Negro Males," *Psychiatry 24*, 1961, 337–346.

Broyles, J. Allan. "John Birch Society: A Movement of Social Protest of the Radical Right," *Journal of Social Issues 19*, 1963, 51–62.

Brunswick, Ann F. "What Generation Gap?: A Comparison of Some Generational Differences Among Blacks and Whites," *Social Problems 17*, 1970, 358–371.

Burke, Ronald J. "Methods of Managing Superior-Subordinate Conflict: Their Effectiveness and Consequences," *Canadian Journal of Behavioral Science 2*, 1970, 124–135.

Burke, Ronald J. "Methods of Resolving Superior-Subordinate Conflict: The Constructive Use of Subordinate Differences and Disagreements," *Organizational Behavior and Human Performance 5*, 1970, 393–411.

Burton, John Wear. *Conflict and Communication: The Use of Controlled Communication in International Relations* (New York: Free Press, 1969).

Bwy, D. "Dimensions of Social Conflict in Latin America," *American Behavioral Scientist 11*, 1968, 39–50.

Carter, Barbara. "Fight Against Kodak," *Reporter 36*, 1967, 28–31.

Carver, T. N. "The Basis of Social Conflict," *American Journal of Sociology 13*, 1968, 628–637.

Cavan, Ruth S. "Family Tensions Between the Old and Middle Aged," *Marriage and Family Living 18*, 1956, 323–327.

Cenkner, William. "Gandhi and Creative Conflict," *Thought 45*, 1970, 421–432.

Chapman, A. W. "Group Approach to the Reduction of Tensions and Conflict," *Journal of Human Relations 1*, 1952, 39–47.

Cohen, Bernard P. *Conflict and Conformity: A Probability Model and Its Application* (Cambridge, Mass.: M.I.T. Press, 1963).

Cohnstaedt, Martin L. "Process and Role of Conflict in the Community," *American Journal of Economics and Sociology 25*, 1966, 5–10.

Colburn, Donald L. "Conflict and Conflict Resolution," in *Contemporary Studies in Social Psychology and Behavior Change*, Joseph L. Philbrick, ed. (New York: Selected Academic Readings, 1966), pp. 71–86.

Coleman, James Samuel. *Community Conflict* (New York: Free Press, 1957).

Converse, Elizabeth. "The War of All Against All: A Review of the Journal of Conflict Resolution," *Journal of Conflict Resolution 12*, 1968, 471–532.

Corwin, Ronald G. "Patterns of Organizational Conflict," *Administrative Science Quarterly 14*, 1969, 507–520.

Coser, Lewis A. *The Functions of Social Conflict* (New York: Free Press, 1956).

Coser, Lewis A. "Social Conflict and Theory of Social Change," *British Journal of Sociology 8*, 1957, 197–207.

Coser, Lewis A. "The Sociology of Poverty—To the Memory of Georg Simmel," *Social Problems 13*, 1965, 140–148.

Coser, Lewis A. *Continuities in the Study of Social Conflict* (New York: Free Press, 1967).

Cox, Bruce A. "Conflict in the Conflict Theories: Ethological and Social Arguments," *Anthropologica 10*, 1968, 179–191.

Dahrendorf, Ralf. "Toward a Theory of Social Conflict," *Journal of Conflict Resolution 11*, 1958, 170–183.

Dahrendorf, Ralf. *Class and Class Conflict in Industrial Societies* (Palo Alto, Calif.: Stanford University Press, 1959).

Dahrendorf, Ralf. "Conflict and Liberty: Some Remarks on the Social

Structure of German Politics," *British Journal of Sociology 14*, 1963, 197–211.

Danzger, Herbert. "A Quantified Description of Community Conflict," *American Behavioral Scientist 12*, 1968, 9–14.

Darbonn, A. "Crisis: A Review of Theory," *International Journal of Psychiatry 6*, 1968, 377–379.

de Berker, Paul. "Staff Strain in Institutions," *British Journal on Delinquency 6*, 1956, 278–284.

de Kadt, Emanuel J. "Conflict and Power in Society," *International Social Science Journal 17*, 1965, 454–471.

Delhees, Karl H. "Conceptions of Group Decision and Group Conflict Applied to Vector Space: A Research Model," *ACTA Psychologica Amsterdam 34*, 1970, 440–450.

Deutsch, Morton. "Trust and Suspicion," *Journal of Conflict Resolution 2*, 1958, 265–279.

Deutsch, Morton. "Conflicts: Productive and Destructive," *Journal of Social Issues 25*, 1969, 7–41.

Deutsch, Morton, and Robert M. Krauss. "The Effect of Threat Upon International Bargaining," *Journal of Abnormal and Social Psychology 61*, 1960, 181–189.

Deutsch, Morton, and Robert M. Krauss. "Studies of Interpersonal Bargaining," *Journal of Conflict Resolution 6*, 1962, 52–76.

Dillman, Everett. "A Source of Personal Conflict in Police Organizations," *Public Personnel Review 28*, 1967, 222–227.

Dodson, Dan W. "The Creative Role of Conflict Reexamined," *Journal of Intergroup Relations 1*, 1959–1960, 5–12.

Doob, Leonard William. *Resolving Conflict in Africa: The Fermeda Workshop* (New Haven: Yale University Press, 1970).

Doob, Leonard W., William J. Foltz, and Robert B. Stevens. "The Fermeda Workshop: A Different Approach to Border Conflicts in Eastern Africa," *Journal of Psychology 73*, 1969, 249–266.

Driver, Peter M. "Towards An Ethology Of Human Conflict: A Review," *Journal of Conflict Resolution 11*, 1967, 361–374.

Druckman, Daniel. "Dogmatism, Prenegotiation Experience, and Simulated Group Representation as Determinants of Dyadic Behavior in a Bargaining Situation," *Journal of Personality and Social Psychology 6*, 1967, 279–290.

Druckman, Daniel. "Prenegotiation Experience and Dyadic Conflict Resolution in a Bargaining Situation," *Journal of Experimental Social Psychology 4*, 1968, 367–383.

Dubin, Robert. "Theory of Conflict and Power in Union Management Relations," *Industrial and Labor Relations Review 13,* 1960, 501–518.

Eckhardt, William. "Prejudice: Fear, Hate or Mythology," *Journal of Human Relations 16,* 1968, 32–41.

Eckhardt, William. "Psychology of War and Peace," *Journal of Human Relations 16,* 1968, 239–249.

Edelman, Murray. "Escalation and Ritualization of Political Conflict," *American Behavioral Scientist 13,* 1969, 231–246.

Eisenstein, Morris L. "Project Summary: Reducing Delinquency Through Integrating Delinquents and Non-Delinquents in Conflict Resolution," *Crime and Delinquency Abstracts 6,* 1969 supplement, 33.

Emshaff, James R., and Russel L. Ackoff. "Prediction, Explanation and Control of Conflict," *Papers of the Peace Research Society 12,* 1969, 109–115.

Ephron, Lawrence. "Group Conflict in Organizations: A Critical Appraisal of Recent Theories," *Berkeley Journal of Sociology 6,* 1961, 53–72.

Etzioni, Amitai. "Toward a Theory of Guided Societal Change," *Social Casework 49,* 1968, 335–338.

Exline, Ralph V., and Robert C. Ziller. "Status Congruency and Interpersonal Conflict in Decision-Making Groups," *Human Relations 12,* 1959, 147–162.

Farber, Seymour M. *Man and Civilization: Conflict and Creativity; A Symposium* (New York: McGraw-Hill, 1963).

Feirerabend, Ivo K., and Rosalind L. Feierabend. "Aggressive Behaviors Within Polities, 1948–1962: A Cross-National Study," *Journal of Conflict Resolution 10,* 1966, 249–271.

Fellner, Carl H. "Provocation of Suicidal Attempts," *Journal of Nervous and Mental Disorders 133,* 1961, 55–58.

Ference, Thomas P. "Feedback and Conflict as Determinants of Influence," *Journal of Experimental Social Psychology 7,* 1971, 1–16.

Feuer, Lewis Samuel. *The Conflict of Generations: The Character and Significance of Student Movements* (New York: Basic Books, 1969).

Finer, S. E. "Reflections on Violence," *New Society 14,* 1967, 792–793.

Fink, Clinton F. "Some Conceptual Difficulties in the Theory of Social Conflict," *Journal of Conflict Resolution 12,* 1968, 412–460.

Fish, Kenneth L. *Conflict and Dissent in the High Schools* (New York: Bruce, 1970).

Fisher, B. Aubrey. "Decision Emergence: Phases in Group Decision-Making," *Speech Monographs 37,* 1970, 53–66.

Fisher, B. Aubrey. "Process of Decision Modification in Small Discussion Groups," *Journal of Communication 20*, 1970, 51–64.

Foa, Uriel G. "Cross-cultural Similarity and Difference in Interpersonal Behavior," *Journal of Abnormal and Social Psychology 68*, 1964, 517–522.

Foss, B. M. "The Variety of Human Conflict and Frustration and Their Consequences," *British Journal of Animal Behavior 4*, 1956, 39.

Friedenberg, Edgar Z. "Current Patterns of Generational Conflict," *Journal of Social Issues 25*, 1969, 21–28.

Frisch, Morton J. "Democracy and the Class Struggle," *Ethics 74*, 1963, 44–52.

Frohlich, Werner D. "Age Differences in Ways of Resolving Interpersonal Conflicts: A Pilot Study," *Interdisciplinary Topics Gerontology 4*, 1969, 158–166.

Galtung, Johan. "Institutionalized Conflict Resolution: A Theoretical Paradigm," *Journal of Peace Research 4*, 1965, 348–397.

Galtung, Johan. "Conflict as a Way of Life," *New Society 16*, 1969, 590–592.

Gangrade, K. D. "Intergenerational Conflict: A Sociological Study of Indian Youth," *Asian Survey 10*, 1970, 924–936.

Gans, Herbert J. "Ghetto Rebellions and Urban Class Conflict," *Academy of Political Science Proceedings 29*, 1968, 42–51.

Garnett, J. C. "Conflict and Strategy," *Political Studies 14*, 1966, 174–185.

Gassner, Suzanne, and Edward J. Murray. "Dominance and Conflict in the Interactions Between Parents of Normal and Neurotic Children," *Journal of Abnormal Psychology 74*, 1969, 33–41.

Geschwender, James A. "Social Structure and the Negro Revolt: An Examination of Some Hypotheses," *Social Forces 43*, 1964–1965, 248–256.

Geschwender, James A. "Civil Rights Protest and Riots: A Disappearing Distinction," *Social Science Quarterly 49*, 1968, 474–484.

Gluckman, Max. *Custom and Conflict in Africa* (New York: Free Press, 1955).

Golavine, Michael N. *Conflict in Space: A Pattern of War in a New Dimension* (London: Temple Press, 1962).

Goldberg, Louis C. "Ghetto Riots and Others: The Face of Civil Disorder in 1967," *Journal of Peace Research 2*, 1968, 116–132.

Goldman, Ralph M. "A Theory of Conflict Processes and Organizational Offices," *Journal of Conflict Resolution 10*, 1966, 328–343.

Goldman, Ralph M. "Confrontation at San Francisco State," *Dissent 16*, 1969, 167–179.

Goodwin, Glenn A. "Toward a Theory of Social Change," *Mosaic 1*, 1966, 13–26.

Grant, Joanne. *Black Protest: History, Documents and Analysis, 1619 to the Present* (New York: Fawcett, 1968).

Green, R. T., and G. Santori. "A Cross-Cultural Study of Hostility and Aggression," *Journal of Peace Research 6*, 1969, 13–22.

Grimshaw, Allan D. "Lawlessness and Violence in America and Their Special Manifestation in Changing Negro–White Relationships," *Journal of Negro History 44*, 1959, 52–72.

Grimshaw, Allan D. "Violence: A Sociological Perspective," *The George Washington Law Review 37*, 1969, 816.

Grinspoon, L. "Private Conflict With Public Consequences," *American Journal of Psychiatry 25*, 1969, 1074.

Guetzkow, Harold, and John Gyr. "An Analysis of Conflict in Decision-Making Groups," *Human Relations 7*, 1954, 367–382.

Gutter, Henry C. "Conflict Models, Games and Drinking Patterns," *Journal of Psychology 58*, 1964, 361–368.

Hacon, Richard J. *Conflict and Human Relations Training* (Elmsford, N.Y.: Pergamon, 1965).

Hahn, Harlan. "Ghetto Sentiments on Violence," *Science and Society 33*, 1969, 197–208.

Hamblin, Robert L., David A. Bridger, Robert C. Day, and William L. Yancey. "The Interference-Aggression Law?" *Sociometry 26*, 1963, 190–216.

Hammond, Kenneth R. "New Directions in Research on Conflict Resolution," *British Psychological Society Bulletin 19*, 1966, 1–20.

Hammond, Kenneth R., Frederick J. Todd, Marilyn Wilkins, and Thomas O. Mitchell. "Cognitive Conflict between Persons: Application of the 'Lens Model' Paradigm," *Journal of Experimental Social Psychology* 2, 1966, 343–360.

Hanson, David Jay. "The Idea of Conflict in Western Thought," *International Review of History and Political Science 5*, 1968, 90–105.

Hasswell, Harold D. and Richard Arens. "Role of Sanction in Conflict Resolution," *Journal of Conflict Resolution 11*, 1967, 27–39.

Havens, A. Eugene, and Harry R. Potter. "Organizational and Societal Variables in Conflict Resolution: An International Comparison," *Human Organizations 26*, 1967, 126–131.

Hawkins, James L., and Kathryn Johnsen. "Perception of Behavioral Conformity, Imputation of Consensus and Marital Satisfaction," *Journal of Marriage and the Family 31*, 1969, 507–511.

Heilizer, Fred. "Conflict Models, Alcohol and Drinking Patterns," *Journal of Psychology 57*, 1964, 457–473.

Heirich, Max. *The Spiral of Conflict: Berkeley, 1964* (New York: Columbia University Press, 1971).

Henderson, Donald. "Minority Response and the Conflict Model," *Phylon 25*, 1964, 18–26.

Himes, Joseph S. "The Functions of Racial Conflict," *Social Forces 45*, 1966, 1–10.

Hobart, Charles W. "Commitment, Value, Conflict and the Future of the American Family," *Marriage and Family Living 25*, 1963, 405–414.

Hoedemaker, Edward D. "Distrust and Aggression: An Interpersonal-International Analogy," *Journal of Conflict Resolution 12*, 1968, 69–81.

Horowitz, Irving Louis. "Consensus, Conflict and Cooperation: A Sociological Inventory," *Social Forces 41*, 1962, 177–188.

Howard, J. Woodford, Jr. "Adjudication Considered as a Process of Conflict Resolution: A Variation on Separation of Powers," *Journal of Public Law 18*, 1969, 339–370.

Indik, Bernard P., and Georgina M. Smith. "Resolution of Social Conflict Through Collective Bargaining: An Alternative to Violence," *The George Washington Law Review 37*, 1969, 848–861.

Isard, Walter. "Toward a More Adequate General Regional Theory and Approach to Conflict Resolution," *Papers of the Peace Research Society 11*, 1969, 1–21.

Jackman, Norman R. "Collective Protest in Relocation Centers," *American Journal of Sociology 63*, 1957, 264–272.

Jackson, H. Merrill. "Social Progress and Mental Health," *Journal of Conflict Resolution 14*, 1970, 265–275.

Jacobs, Martin A., Aron Spilken, and Martin Norman. "Relationship of Life Change, Maladaptive Aggression, and Upper Respiratory Infection in Male College Students," *Psychosomatic Medicine 31*, 1969, 31–44.

Jasinski, Frank J. "Technological Delimitation of Reciprocal Relationships: A Study of Interaction Patterns in Industry," *Human Organization 15*, 1956, 24–28.

Jayawardena, Chandra. "Ideology and Conflict in Lower Class Communities," *Comparative Studies in Society and History 10*, 1968, 413–446.

Johnson, David W., and Richard Dustin. "The Initiation of Cooperation Through Role Reversal," *Journal of Social Psychology 82*, 1970, 193–203.

Johnson, David W., and Ray J. Lewicki. "The Invitation of Superordinate Goals," *Journal of Applied Behavioral Science 5*, 1969, 9–24.

Johnson, Thomas A. "Newark's Summer, 1967," *Crisis 74*, 1967, 371–380.

Joseph, Edward D. "Memory and Conflict," *Psychoanalysis Quarterly 35*, 1966, 1–17.

Kading, Daniel. "Role of the Social Scientist Regarding Social Conflicts," *Southwestern Social Science Quarterly* 32, 1952, 271–276.

Kadt, Emanuel J. "Conflict and Power in Society," *International Social Science Journal* 17, 1965, 454–471.

Kahn, Robert L., and Elise Boulding (eds.). *Power and Conflict in Organizations* (New York: Basic Books, 1964).

Kahn, Si. *How People Get Power* (New York: McGraw-Hill, 1970).

Kahn-Freund, O. "Intergroup Conflicts and Their Settlement," *British Journal of Sociology* 5, 1954, 193–227.

Kamano, Dennis K. "Relationship of Ego Disjunction and Manifest Anxiety to Conflict Resolution," *Journal of Abnormal and Social Psychology* 66, 1963, 281–284.

Katz, Daniel. "Group Process and Social Integration: A System Analysis of Two Movements of Social Protest," *Journal of Social Issues* 23, 1967, 3–22.

Kaufman, Charles. "Some Ethological Studies of Social Relationships and Conflict Situations," *Journal of the American Psychoanalytic Association* 8, 1960, 671–685.

Killian, Lewis M., and Charles Grigg. *Racial Crisis in America* (Englewood Cliffs, N.J.: Prentice-Hall, 1964).

Kinloch, Graham C. "Parent-Youth Conflict at Home: An Investigation Among University Freshmen," *American Journal of Orthopsychiatry* 40, 1970, 658–664.

Krauss, Robert M. "Structural and Attitudinal Factors in Interpersonal Bargaining," *Journal of Experimental Social Psychology* 2, 1966, 42–55.

Lachman, Sheldon J., and Thomas F. Waters. "Psychosocial Profile of Riot Arrestees," *Psychological Reports* 24, 1969, 171–181.

Lammers, Cornelis J. "Strikes and Mutinies: Nine Comparative Studies of Organizational Conflicts Between Rulers and Ruled," *Administrative Science Quarterly* 14, 1969, 558–572.

Lapreato, Joseph. "Class Conflict and Image of Society," *Journal of Conflict Resolution* 11, 1967, 281–293.

Lapreato, Joseph. "Authority Relations and Class Conflict," *Social Forces* 47, 1968, 70–79.

Larson, Allan. "Politics, Social Change and the Conflict of Generations," *Midwest Quarterly* 11, 1970, 123–137.

Lent, Richard H. "Binocular Resolution and Perception of Race in the United States," *British Journal of Psychology* 61, 1970, 521–533.

Levin, Gilbert, and David D. Stein. "System Intervention in a School-Community Conflict," *Journal of Applied Behavioral Science* 6, 1970, 337–352.

LeVine, Robert A. "Anthropology and the Study of Conflict: An Introduction," *Journal of Conflict Resolution* 5, 1961, 3–15.

Levinger, George. "Kurt Lewin's Approach to Conflict and Its Resolution: A Review With Some Extensions," *Journal of Conflict Resolution 1,* 1957, 329–339.

Lewin, Kurt. *Resolving Social Conflicts* (New York: Harper & Row, 1948).

Liff, Zawel A. "Impasse: Interpersonal, Intergroup, and International," *Group Process 3,* 1970, 7–30.

Lindskold, Svenn and James T. Tedeschi. "Self-Confidence, Prior Success, and the Use of Power in Social Conflicts," *Proceedings of the Annual Convention of the American Psychological Association 5,* 1970, 425–26.

Litvak, I. A. and C. J. Maule. "Conflict Resolution and Extra-territoriality," *Journal of Conflict Resolution 13,* 1969, 305–319.

Litwak, Eugene. "Models of Bureaucracy Which Permit Conflict," *American Journal of Sociology 67,* 1961–1962, 177–184.

Lloyd, Kent. "Urban Race Riots vs. Effective Anti-Discrimination Agencies," *Public Administration 45,* 1967, 43–53.

Loomis, Charles P. "In Praise of Conflict and Its Resolution," *American Sociological Review 32,* 1967, 875–890.

Lowie, Robert H. "Compromise in Primitive Society," *International Social Science Journal 15,* 1963, 182–229.

Lungerg, George. "How To Live With People Who Are Wrong," *Humanist 20,* 1960, 74–84.

McGinn, Noel F., Ernest Harburg, and Gerald P. Ginsburg. "Responses to Interpersonal Conflict by Middle Class Males in Guadalajara and Michigan," *American Anthropologist 67,* 1965, 1483–1494.

Mack, Raymond W. "The Components of Social Conflict," *Social Problems 12,* 1965, 388–397.

Mack, Raymond W. and Richard C. Snyder. "The Analysis of Social Conflict—Toward an Overview and Synthesis," *Journal of Conflict Resolution 1,* 1957, 212–248.

McNeil, Elton. *The Nature of Human Conflict* (Englewood Cliffs, N.J.: Prentice-Hall, 1965).

Majak, R. Roger. "Political Integration Revisited: A Review of Three Contributions to Theory Building," *Journal of Conflict Resolution 11,* 1967, 117–126.

Manas (Editors of). "The Psychology of Social Morality," *Liberation 11,* no. 7, 1966, 33–34.

Martin, J. G. "Intergroup Tolerance: Prejudice," *Journal of Human Relations 10,* 1962, 197–204.

Marwell, Gerald. "Conflict Over Proposed Group Actions: A Typology of Cleavage," *Journal of Conflict Resolution 10,* 1966, 427–435.

Marx, Karl. *Das Kapital,* various editions.

Mason, H. L. *Mass Demonstrations Against Foreign Regimes: A Study of Fine Crisis* (New Orleans: Tulane University Press, 1966).

Mazur, Allan. "A Nonrational Approach to Theories of Conflict and Coalitions," *Journal of Conflict Resolution 12*, 1968, 196–205.

Mead, Margaret. *Culture and Commitment: A Study of the Generation Gap* (New York: Natural History Press), 1970.

Meier, August, and Elliot Rudwick. "Negro Protest and Urban Unrest," *Social Science Quarterly 49*, 1968, 438–443.

Meltzer, Jack. "The Urban Conflict," *Urban Affairs Quarterly 3*, 1968, 3–20.

Minuchin, Salvador. "Conflict-Resolution Family Therapy," *Psychiatry 8*, 1965, 278–286.

Misner, Gordon. "The Response of Police Agencies," *Annals of the American Academy of Political and Social Sciences 38*, 1969, 109–119.

Mitchell, Howard E., James W. Bullard, and Emily M. Mudd. "Areas of Marital Conflict in Successfully and Unsuccessfully Functioning Families," *Journal of Health and Social Behavior 3*, 1962, 88–93.

Moon, Henry Lee. "Of Negroes, Jews and Other Americans," *Crisis 74*, 1967, 146–150.

Moore, R. B. "Century of Color Conflict," *Negro Digest 17*, 1967, 4–7.

Moraze, Charles. "The Settlement of Conflicts in Western Culture," *International Social Science Journal 15*, 1963, 230–256.

Morley, Ian E., and Geoffrey M. Stephenson. "Interpersonal and Inter-Party Exchange: A Laboratory Simulation of an Industrial Negotiation at the Plant Level," *British Journal of Psychology 60*, 1969, 543–545.

Mosher, D. L., R. L. Mortimer, and M. Grebel. "Verbal Aggressive Behavior in Delinquent Boys," *Journal of Abnormal Psychology 73*, 1968, 454–460.

Mudd, Stuart (ed.). *Conflict Resolution and World Education* (The Hague: Dr. W. Junk, Publishers, 1966).

Mueller, William J., and Harry A. Grater. "A Stability Study of the Aggression Conflict Scale," *Journal of Consulting Psychology 30*, 1966, 357–359.

Murphy, Robert F. "Intergroup Hostility and Social Cohesion," *American Anthropologist 59*, 1959, 1018–1035.

Murray, Edward J., and Mitchell M. Burkun. "Displacement as a Function of Conflict," *Journal of Abnormal Psychology 51*, 1955, 47–56.

Murray, Henry A. "Studies of Stressful Interpersonal Disputations," *American Psychologist 18*, 1963, 28–39.

Nader, Laura, and Duane Metzger. "Conflict Resolution in Two Mexican Communities," *American Anthropologist 65*, 1963, 584–592.

Nakamyra, Charles Y. "Relations Between Children's Expression of Hostility and Discipline by Dominant Overprotective Parents," *Child Development 30*, 1959, 109–117.

Nehru, J. "Racism: That Other Face of Nationalism," *Journal of Human Relations 14*, 1966, 2–16.

Nelson, Linden, and Millard C. Madsen. "Cooperation and Competition in Four Year Olds as a Function of Reward Contingency and Subculture," *Developmental Psychology 1*, 1969, 340–344.

Neuringer, Charles, and Lowell W. Wandke. "Interpersonal Conflicts in Persons of High Self-Concept and Low Self-Concept," *Journal of Social Psychology 68*, 1966, 313–322.

Norbeck, Edward. "African Rituals of Conflict," *American Anthropologist 65*, 1963, 1254–1279.

North, Robert C., Howard E. Koch, Jr., and Dina A. Zinnes. "The Integrative Functions of Conflict," *Journal of Conflict Resolution 4*, 1960, 355–374.

Oppenheimer, Martin. "Directions of Peace Research: Conflict or Consensus?" *Journal of Human Relations 13*, 1965, 314–319.

Oppenheimer, Martin. "Southern Student Sit-Ins: Intra-Group Relations and Community-Conflict," *Phylon 27*, 1966, 20–26.

Palley, Howard A. "Community in Conflict: Family Planning in Metroville," *Social Service Review 41*, 1967, 55–65.

Parsons, Talcott. "Social Classes and Class Conflict in the Light of Recent Sociological Theory," *American Economic Review 39*, 1949, 16–26.

Patchen, Martin. "Models of Cooperation and Conflict: A Critical Review," *Journal of Conflict Resolution 14*, 1970, 389–407.

Plaitner, Paul. *Conflict and Understanding in Marriage* (Richmond, Va.: Knox, 1970).

Plastrik, Stanley. "Backlash, Violence and Politics," *Dissent 16*, 1969, 373–375.

Ploss, Sidney L. *Conflict and Decision-Making in Soviet Russia: A Case Study of Agricultural Policy, 1953–1963* (Princeton University Press, 1965).

Podair, S. "How Bigotry Builds Through Language," *Negro Digest 16*, 1967, 38–43.

Pollay, Richard W. "Intrafamily Communication and Consensus," *Journal of Communication 19*, 1969, 181–201.

Pondy, Louis R. "Organizational Conflict: Concepts and Models," *Administrative Science Quarterly 12*, 1967, 296–320.

Pondy, Louis R. "Varieties of Organizational Conflict," *Administrative Science Quarterly 14*, 1969, 499–505.

Popplestone, G. "Conflict and Mediating Roles in Expanded Settlements," *Sociological Review 15*, 1967, 339–355.

Porsholt, Lars. "On Methods of Conflict Prevention," *Journal of Peace Research 2*, 1966, 178–193.

Preston, Malcolm G., *et al.* "Impressions of Personality as a Function of Marital Conflict," *Journal of Abnormal and Social Psychology 47*, 1952, 326–336.

Pruitt, Dean G. "Stability and Sudden Change in Interpersonal and International Affairs," *Journal of Conflict Resolution 13*, 1969, 18–38.

Rapoport, Anatol. "Is Warmaking a Characteristic of Human Beings or of Cultures," *Scientific American 213*, no. 4, 1965, 115–118.

Rapoport, Anatol. "Experiments in Dyadic Conflict and Cooperation," *Bulletin of the Menninger Clinic 30*, 1966, 84–91.

Rapoport, Anatol. "Violence in American Fantasy," *Liberation 11*, 1966, 18–22.

Reich, Charles A. *The Greening of America: How the Youth Revolution is Trying to Make America Livable* (New York: Random House, 1970).

Rex, John. "The Plural Society in Sociological Theory," *British Journal of Sociology 10*, 1959, 114–124.

Rex, John, and Robert Moore. *Race, Community, and Conflict: A Study of Sparkbrook* (New York: Oxford University Press, 1967).

Reynolds, M. B., and P. A. Nicholson. "General Systems, the International System and the Eastonian Analysis," *Political Studies 15*, 1967, 12–31.

Richmond, Anthony H. "Conflict And Authority In Industry," *Occupational Psychology 8*, 1954, 24–33.

Rinder, Irwin D. "Identification Reaction and Intergroup Conflict," *Phylon 15*, 1954, 365–370.

Rinquiette, Eugene L. "Mode of Conflict Resolution: A Replication and Extension," *California Mental Health Research Digest 3*, 1965, 17–18.

Rinquiette, Eugene L. "Selected Personality Correlates of Mode of Conflict Resolution," *Journal of Personality and Social Psychology 2*, 1965, 506–512.

Rose, Arnold M. "Voluntary Associations Under Conditions of Competition and Conflict," *Social Forces 34*, 1955, 159–163.

Rose, Arnold M. "The Comparative Study of Intergroup Conflict," *Social Quarterly 1*, 1960, 57–66.

Rose, Arnold M., and Caroline B. Rose. "Intergroup Conflict and Its Mediation," *International Social Science Bulletin 6*, 1954, 25–43.

Rosenau, James N. "Intervention as a Scientific Concept," *Journal of Conflict Resolution 13*, 1969, 149–171.

Rothchild, Donald. "Ethnicity and Conflict Resolution," *World Politics* 2, 1970, 597–616.

Roy, Donald F. "Role of the Researcher in the Study of Social Conflict: A Theory of Protective Distortion of Response," *Human Organization* 4, 1965, 62–71.

Rubenstein, Amnon. "Struggle Between Founders and Sons," *Encounter* 31, 1968, 64–68.

Sampson, Edward E. "Achievement in Conflict," *Journal of Personality* 31, 1963, 510–516.

Sappenfield, Bert R. "Repression and the Dynamics of Conflict," *Journal of Consulting Psychology* 9, 1965, 266–270.

Scanzoni, John. "A Social System Analysis of Dissolved and Existing Marriages," *Journal of Marriage and the Family* 30, 1968, 452–461.

Schachter, Stanley, and others. "Cross-Cultural Experiments on Threat and Rejection: A Study of the Organization for Comparative Social Research," *Human Relations* 7, 1954, 403–439.

Scheffier, H. W. "Genesis and Repression of Conflict: Choiseul Island," *American Anthropologist* 66, 1964, 789–804.

Schelling, Thomas C. *The Strategy of Conflict* (Cambridge: Harvard University Press, 1960).

Schermerhorn, R. A. "Polarity in the Approach to Comparative Research in Ethnic Relations," *Sociological and Social Research* 51, 1967, 35–40.

Schiamberg, Lawrence. "Some Socio-Cultural Factors in Adolescent-Parent Conflict: A Cross-Cultural Comparison of Selected Cultures," *Adolescence* 4, 1969, 333–360.

Schroeder, Carolyn, and Stephen R. Schroeder. "Decision Conflict in Children in a Risk Situation," *Psychological Record* 20, 1970, 457–463.

Schroeder, Pearl. "Relationship of Kuder's Conflict Avoidance and Dominance to Academic Accomplishment," *Journal of Counseling Psychology* 12, 1965, 395–399.

Schwartz, Emmanuel K. "The Interpreter in Group Therapy: Conflict Resolution Through Negotiation," *Archives of General Psychiatry* 18, 1968, 186–193.

Schwartz, Norman B. "Conflict Resolution and Impropriety in a Guatemalan Town," *Social Forces* 48, 1969, 98–106.

Schwartz, Shalom H., Kenneth A. Feldman, Michael E. Brown, and Alex Heingartner. "Some Personality Correlates of Conduct in Two Situations of Moral Conflict," *Journal of Personality* 37, 1969, 41–57.

Sears, David. "Riot Ideology in Los Angeles: A Study of Negro Attitudes," *Social Science Quarterly* 49, 1968, 485–503.

Segal, Ronald. *The Race War: The World Wide Clash of White and Non-White* (New York: Viking, 1966).

Sereno, Kenneth, and C. David Mortensen. "The Effects of Ego-Involved Attitudes on Conflict Negotiation in Dyads," *Speech Monographs 36*, 1969, 8–12.

Sharmann, Franz. "On Revolutionary Conflict," *Journal of International Affairs 23*, 1969, 36–53.

Sherif, Muzafer. "Superordinate Goals in the Reduction of Intergroup Conflict," *American Journal of Sociology 63*, 1958, 349–356.

Sherif, Muzafer. *Intergroup Conflict and Cooperation: The Robber's Cave Experiment* (Institute of Group Relations, University of Oklahoma, 1961).

Shoham, Shlomo. "Conflict Situations and Delinquent Solutions," *Journal of Social Psychology 64*, 1964, 185–215.

Shore, Richard P. "Conceptions of the Arbitrator's Role," *Journal of Applied Psychology 50*, 1966, 172–178.

Siegel, Bernard J. "Conflict, Parochialism and Social Differentiation in Portuguese Society," *Journal of Conflict Resolution 5*, 1961, 35–42.

Silvert, Kalman. *The Conflict Society: Reaction and Revolution in Latin America* (New York: American University and Field Staff, 1966).

Simmel, Georg. *Conflict and the Web of Group Affiliations* (New York: Free Press, 1964).

Simmel, Georg. "The Poor," *Social Problems 13*, 1965, 118–140.

Singer, J. David, and Paul Ray. "Decision-making in Conflict: From Inter-personal to Inter-national Relations," *Bulletin of the Menninger Clinic 30*, 1966, 300–312.

Singer, J. David. "Man and World Politics: The Psycho-Cultural Interface," *Journal of Social Issues 24*, 1968, 127–156.

Singer, Susan. "Factors Related to Participants' Memory of a Conversation," *Journal of Personality 37*, 1969, 93–110.

Skolnick, Jerome H. "Social Control in the Adversary System," *Journal of Conflict Resolution 11*, 1967, 52–70.

Smith, Clagett G. "A Comparative Analysis of Some Conditions and Consequences of Intra-Organizational Conflict," *Administrative Science Quarterly 10*, 1965–1966, 504–529.

Smith, David H. "Communication and Negotiation Outcome," *Journal of Communication 19*, 1969, 248–256.

Smith, Ewart E. "Individual vs. Group Goal Conflict," *Journal of Abnormal and Social Psychology 58*, 1959, 134–137.

Smith, Noel. "On the Origin of Conflict Types," *Psychological Record 18*, 1968, 229–232.

Smock, Charles. "An Inferred Relationship Between Early Childhood Conflicts and Anxiety Responses in Adult Life," *Journal of Personality 23*, 1954, 88–98.

Sorenson, Robert C. "The Concept of Conflict in Industrial Sociology," *Social Forces 29*, 1951, 263–267.

Spector, Samuel. "Teacher Reaction to Conflict Situations," *Journal of Educational Psychology 46*, 1955, 437–445.

Stager, Paul. "Conceptual Level as a Composition Variable in Small-Group Decision Making," *Journal of Personality and Social Psychology 5*, 1967, 152–161.

Stagner, Ross. "Personality Dynamics and Social Conflict," *Journal of Social Issues 17*, 1961, 28–44.

Stanley, Gordon, and Donald S. Martin. "Eye-Contact and the Recall of Material Involving Competitive and Noncompetitive Associations," *Psychomonic Science 13*, 1968, 337–338.

Steiner, Jürg. "Conflict Resolution and Democratic Stability in Subculturally Segmented Political Systems," *Res Publica 11*, 1969, 775–798.

Steiner, Jürg. "Nonviolent Conflict Resolution in Democratic Systems: Switzerland," *Journal of Conflict Resolution 13*, 1969, 295–304.

Stevens, Carl M. "A Note on Conflict Choice in Economics and Psychology," *Journal of Conflict Resolution 4*, 1960, 220–224.

Stoll, Clarice S., and Paul T. McFarlane. "Player Characteristics and Interaction in a Parent-Child Simulation Game," *Sociometry 32*, 1969, 259–272.

Sugarman, Barry. "Tension Management Deviance and Social Change," *Sociological Quarterly 10*, 1969, 62–71.

Summers, David A. "Conflict, Compromise, and Belief Change in a Decision-Making Task," *Journal of Conflict Resolution 12*, 1968, 215–221.

Suttinger, Gunter. "Conflict Situations and Socially Aberrant Behavior of Juveniles," *Monatsschrift fur Kriminologie und Strafrechtsre form* (Berlin) *51*, 1968, 241–254 (Refer *Crime and Delinquency Abstracts 6*, 1969, 195).

Swingle, Paul G. *The Structure of Conflict* (New York: Academic, 1970).

Sykes, A. J. M., and James Bates. "Study of Conflict Between Formal Company Policy and the Interests of Informal Groups," *Sociological Review 10*, 1962, 313–317.

Tanner, R. E. S. "Conflict Within Small European Communities in Tanganyika," *Human Organization 23*, 1964, 319–327.

Tanter, Raymond. "Dimensions of Conflict Behavior Within and Between Nations," *Journal of Conflict Resolution 10*, 1966, 41–64.

Taylor, Richard W. "Logic of Research in Group and International Conflict," *Bulletin of the Research Exchange on the Prevention of War 1*, 1953, 1–5.

Theodorson, George A. "The Function of Hostility in Small Groups," *Journal of Social Psychology 56*, 1962, 57–66.

Thompson, John D. "Notes on Aggression," *Commentary 47*, 1969, 63–65.

Tillman, James A., Jr. "The Nature and Function of Racism: A General Hypothesis," *Journal of Human Relations 12*, 1964, 50–59.

Todd, Frederick J., Kenneth R. Hammond, and Marilyn M. Wilkins. "Differential Effects of Ambiguous and Exact Feedback on Two-Person Conflict and Compromise," *Journal of Conflict Resolution 10*, 1966, 88–97.

Tripodi, Tony. "Cognitive Complexity and the Perception of Conflict: A Partial Replication," *Perceptual and Motor Skills 25*, 1967, 543–544.

Truitt, W. H. "Human Nature and the Cooperative Impulse," *Journal of Human Relations 14*, 1966, 580–594.

Turk, Austin. "Conflict and Criminality," *American Sociological Review 31*, 1966, 338–352.

Varela, Jacobo A. *Psychological Solutions to Social Problems: An Introduction to Social Technology* (New York: Academic, 1971).

Waelder, Robert. "Conflict and Violence," *Bulletin of the Menninger Clinic 30*, 1966, 267–274.

Walton, Richard E. "Interpersonal Confrontation and Basic Third Party Functions: A Case Study," *Journal of Applied Behavioral Science 4*, 1968, 327–344.

Walton, Richard E. *Interpersonal Peacemaking: Confrontations and Third Party Consultation* (Reading, Mass.: Addison-Wesley, 1969).

Walton, Richard E. "A Problem-Solving Workshop on Border Conflicts in Eastern Africa," *Journal of Applied Behavioral Science 6*, 1970, 453–489.

Walton, Richard E., and John M. Dutton. "The Management of Interdepartmental Conflict: A Model and Review," *Administrative Science Quarterly 14*, 1969, 73–84.

Walton, Richard E., John M. Dutton, and Thomas P. Cafferty. "Organizational Context and Interdepartmental Conflict," *Administrative Science Quarterly 14*, 1969, 522–542.

Wanderer, Julius J. "An Index of Riot Severity and Some Correlates," *American Journal of Sociology 74*, 1969, 500–505.

Warren, Donald I. "Conflict Intersystem and the Change Agent," *Journal of Human Relations 13*, 1965, 339–355.

Warren, Donald I. "The Effects of Power Bases and Peer Groups on Conformity in Formal Organizations," *Administrative Science Quarterly 14*, 1969, 544–546.

Warren, Donald I. "Suburban Isolation and Race Tension: The Detroit Case," *Social Problems 17*, 1969–1970, 324–339.

Wastow, Arthur I. *From Race Riot to Sit-In; 1919 and the 1960's: A Study in the Connections Between Conflict and Violence* (Garden City, N.Y.: Doubleday, 1966).

Wedge, Bryant. "The Case Study of Student Political Violence: Brazil, 1964, and Dominican Republic, 1965," *World Politics 21*, 1968–1969, 183–206.

Weingart, Peter. "Beyond Parsons? A Critique at Ralf Dahrendorf's Conflict Theory," *Social Forces 48*, 1969, 151–195.

Weller, Leonard. "The Effects of Anxiety on Cohesiveness and Rejection," *Human Relations 16*, 1963, 189–197.

White, Harrison. "Management Conflict and Sociometric Struggle," *American Journal of Sociology 67*, 1961, 185–199.

Whiting, Beatrice B. "Sex Identity and Physical Violence: A Comparative Study," *American Anthropologist 67, 1965* (special issue), 123–140.

Williams, J. "Race, War, and Politics," *Negro Digest 16*, 1967, 4-9.

Williams, R. "Social Change and Social Conflict: Race Relations in the United States, 1944–1964," *Social Inquiry 35*, 1965, 8–25.

Wolfe, John, and Paul Horn. "Racial Friction in the Deep South," *Journal of Psychology 54*, 1962, 139–152.

Woodmansey, A. C. "The Internalization of External Conflict," *International Journal of Psycho-Analysis 47*, 1966, 349–355.

Worell, Leonard. "The Preference For Conflict: Some Paradoxical Reinforcement Effects," *Journal of Personality 32*, 1964, 32–44.

Yates, Aubrey J. *Frustration and Conflict* (New York: Wiley, 1962).

Zand, Dale E., and William E. Steckman. "Resolving Industrial Conflict—An Experimental Study of the Effects of Attitudes and Precedent," *Industrial Relations Research Association: Proceedings of the 1st Annual Winter Meeting*, 348–359.

Zawondy, Janusz Kazimenerz. *Man and International Relations; Contributions of the Social Sciences to the Study of Conflict and Integration* (San Francisco: Chandler, 1966).

Zeigler, Harmon, and Robert C. Ziller. "The Neutral in a Communication Network Under Conditions of Conflict," *American Behavioral Scientist 13*, 1969, 265–281.

Zinnes, Dina A. "Comparison of Hostile Behavior of Decision Makers in Simulation and Historical Data," *World Politics 18*, 1966, 474–502.

Zinnes, Dina A. "Introduction to the Behavioral Approach: A Review," *Journal of Conflict Resolution 12*, 1968, 258–267.

Zurcher, S. Louis, Jr., Arnold Meadow, and Susan Lee Zurcher. "Value Orientation, Conflict and Alienation From Work; A Cross-Cultural Study," *American Sociological Review 30*, 1965, 539–548.

Index

73 74 75 76 9 8 7 6 5 4 3 2 1